TENNESSEANS
AT WAR, 1812–1815

T0288318

TENNESSEANS
AT WAR, 1812–1815
ANDREW JACKSON, THE CREEK WAR,
AND THE BATTLE OF NEW ORLEANS

TOM KANON

THE UNIVERSITY OF ALABAMA PRESS
Tuscaloosa

The University of Alabama Press
Tuscaloosa, Alabama 35487-0380
uapress.ua.edu

Hardcover edition published 2014.
Paperback edition published 2015.
eBook edition published 2014.

Inquiries about reproducing material from this work should be addressed
to the University of Alabama Press.

Typeface: Caslon

Manufactured in the United States of America
Cover illustration: *Battle of New Orleans, January 8th, 1815* (nineteenth-
century engraving); courtesy of the Tennessee State Library and Archives
Cover design: Erin Kirk New

∞
The paper on which this book is printed meets the minimum
requirements of American National Standard for Information Science–
Permanence of Paper for Printed Library Materials, ANSI Z39.48-1984.

Paperback ISBN: 978-0-8173-5849-5

A previous edition of this book has been catalogued by the Library of
Congress as follows:

Library of Congress Cataloging-in-Publication Data
    Kanon, Tom, 1951–
    Tennesseans at war, 1812–1815 : Andrew Jackson, the Creek War, and
the Battle of New Orleans / Tom Kanon.
    pages   cm
    Includes bibliographical references and index.
    ISBN 978-0-8173-1829-1 (trade cloth : alk. paper) — ISBN 978-0-8173-
8752-5 (e-book) 1. Tennessee—History—War of 1812. 2. United States—
History—War of 1812. 3. Soldiers—Tennessee—History—19th century.
4. Tennessee—Militia—History—19th century. 5. New Orleans, Battle
of, New Orleans, La., 1815. 6. Jackson, Andrew, 1767–1845. 7. Creek War,
1813–1814. I. Title.

E359.5.T4K36   2014
973.5'2—dc23

                                                    2013049815

For Sandra

Contents

Illustrations follow page   110

Introduction

In May 1846, over thirty years after the conclusion of the War of 1812, veteran Thomas Bradley, now elderly and ill, had an opportunity to once more exhibit patriotic ardor when the United States declared war on the Republic of Mexico. Shortly after the declaration, volunteers began assembling throughout the various counties of Tennessee. In Wilson County, the volunteer spirit received an additional spark when ex-governor James C. Jones vowed to lead one of the organized companies "to the fields of glory or of death." At that time, Bradley supposedly stepped up to the ex-governor and remarked: "I understand, Governor, you are raising volunteers. I am now very old, and of late have been much afflicted with pains . . . I have, however, two sons, and though I am too old to work, and they are all my dependence to sustain me in my old age, yet I wish you to put them both down on your list—they must go with you." According to the newspaper covering this event, Bradley participated in the 1813 battle at Tallushatchee against the Creek Indians, "when the messengers of death flew thick and fast in all directions." "Looking along the line of his regiment, and seeing no field officer left to lead on the charge, [Bradley] daringly rushed forward—bawling aloud to the line—'Come on boys! and don't wait for officers!!'"[1]

The components of this anecdote defined the public memory of the War of 1812 to most nineteenth-century Tennesseans: patriotic self-sacrifice, inspired heroism, a slight dig at authoritarianism, and, most importantly, the volunteer spirit that pervaded the state's early history. Indeed, Tennessee's epithet as the Volunteer State still evokes pride among the state's inhabitants—a moniker first thought to have been publicized during the Mexican War, but with roots extending back to the War of 1812.[2] As a result of this connection, the War of 1812 holds a special status in Tennessee's history, despite the war's otherwise precarious position in the foggy memory of the United States. The War of 1812 occurred three decades before the clash with Mexico and three decades after the American Revolution. Although the War of 1812 rests chronologically between those two conflicts, the events of 1812–15 hearken much more to the Revolutionary War. Significantly, proponents of the War of 1812 often referred to it as the "second war for independence." The so-called War Hawks filled their rhetoric with numerous references to the Revolutionary War, drawing on that epoch period of American history as a yardstick for the 1812 generation to measure up. Thomas Bradley represented the second-generation revolutionaries, those too young to have participated in the American Revolution but old enough to fight in the War of 1812. Bradley's generation had the unenviable task of living up to the legacy carved out by their celebrated fathers. The fact that those who fought in the Mexican War often alluded to their 1812 "fathers" reveals the success (at least partial) of Bradley's generation in establishing a continuum of republican principles and ideals. Furthermore, it is telling that America's first war fought purely for reasons of territorial expansion—the Mexican War—should have as its commander in chief (and Jackson disciple), Tennessee's James K. Polk.

Mired in a morass of causation issues, the War of 1812 has been labeled the "forgotten conflict" by historian Don Hickey.[3] At the time, the war created deep divisions in the nation as to its legitimacy. The war was marked, militarily, by some stunning defeats punctuated with a few face-saving victories. Moreover, its conclusion gave the appearance that not much had been accomplished. One unforgiving historian referred to the war as a "political, administrative, legislative, and military nightmare." Even those committed to the remembrance of the War of 1812 admit it is "not a Hollywood kind of war."[4] Yet for Tennessee at least, the period between 1812 and 1815 proved to be a watershed moment in its young development. Personalities such as Andrew Jackson and William Carroll (as well as iconic figures Sam Houston and David Crockett) proved their mettle on the battlefields and advanced their subsequent political careers by way of the popularity their martial activities generated. Politicians such as Felix Grundy and George Washington Campbell left their mark on the congressional battlegrounds of the day, steering the nation toward a war stamped with unpopularity and ill preparedness. And while the expansionist tendencies of the United States provided an outlet to extend southern slavery, the War of 1812 (via the Creek War of 1813–14) also set the pattern for the eventual removal of the Indians east of the Mississippi River. In the wake, Tennessee began its slow march from a nascent frontier community to a "civilized" center of commerce and culture.

This book offers mostly a military and political history of the Old Southwest—in particular, the state of Tennessee—during the War of 1812. (The author plans on a separate volume dealing with the social and cultural history of Tennessee during the War of 1812.) It also treats the Creek War, often referred to as a subconflict of the War of 1812. To be sure, both "wars" overlap and intertwine; yet for most Tennesseans who served between 1812 and 1815, the Creek War *was* the War of 1812. The conflict with the Creek Indians provided the backdrop for most of Tennessee's military activity in the War of 1812, notwithstanding the state's limited participation in the northern campaigns; the takeover of Pensacola in 1814; and, more famously, the stunning victory at New Orleans.

One issue of this book is to explain *why* so many Tennesseans volunteered in the War of 1812, although one can only provide conjectures based on available evidence. Like wars before and after it, the War of 1812 attracted recruits for the adventure it offered, the sting of battle, and the glory of victory. Some volunteered out of genuine patriotism, some from purely personal reasons never explained, some because of peer pressure, and some out of sheer boredom. This book approaches the motivation question by analyzing the factors that caused the war—for by looking at the overall causation, we can better ascertain specific inducements. In addition, we must try to "see" the world as Tennesseans in 1812 saw it. This is no mean task, as it immerses us in a society where one could legally purchase and sell another human being; where women were relegated to a rather submissive (albeit critical) support role; where a verbal slight could lead to a deadly duel; where death and violence were all too commonplace; where imagined Indians "lurked" in the dark recesses of the forests waiting for human prey; and where foreign enemies, bent on subterfuge, huddled on the nation's borders.

Some reoccurring themes in this book include the legacy of Indian warfare in the backcountry, western expansionism, and the influence of the American Revolution on the War-of-1812 generation. Irrevocably tied to these subject matters are the subtopics of Indian hating (and Indian removal) in the early republic, foreign entanglements along the borderlands, and a quest for worthiness in the shadow of a larger-than-life past that seemed to overwhelm the aspirations of a generation seeking to establish its own identity. All of these threads weave together the fabric of the story of Tennessee in the War of 1812—a saga marked by conflict, loss, transformation, and, ultimately, victory at a price others had to pay.

The "others" included, of course, the Southeast Indians, especially the Creek and Cherokee Nations. The Creeks, in particular, suffered from the devastation of the war with an estimated 1,600 deaths on the battlefield (as opposed to an estimated 2,260–3,700 Americans killed in action during the entire War of 1812). Equally damaging was the destruction of at least sixty Creek towns and villages, as well as fields of crops, by the burning torches of American militiamen that displaced up to eight thousand famished Creeks.[5]

The Cherokees, allies of the Tennessee forces, fared somewhat better than the Creeks, but in the long run they had to submit to the indignity of repeated attempts by whites to acquire Cherokee lands, despite the sacrifices of Cherokee warriors to the American cause. Weaned on a steady diet of Indian-depredation stories, the War-of-1812 generation viewed most Indians, at best, with suspicion and, at worst, with an antagonism bordering on blind hatred. The history of Tennessee in the War of 1812 cannot be narrated without careful consideration of Indian/settler relations on the frontier in the early nineteenth century.

Interestingly, despite all the animosity that existed between Indians and white Americans, it was symptomatic of the frontier mentality to blame much of the enmity on foreign intrigue and influence. Settlers pointed to British or Spanish interference whenever Indians lashed back at white incursions. Americans put most of the responsibility for Indian participation in the War of 1812 squarely on the British. One author of an 1815 history of the war professed that Indian depredations were "applauded by the British orders." The writer went on to accuse the British of inciting the Creeks to war against the Americans and supplying the Creeks with arms—allegations based more on supposition than fact.[6] These assumptions exemplify the global aspects of the War of 1812, and attention must be paid to the international consequences of Americans who overstepped their authority by "invading" foreign soil, as Andrew Jackson's army did in Spanish-held Florida. In the north, military campaigns along the Canadian border brought cries of protest not only from British Canadians, but also from Federalists concerned about the United States' true reason for going to war. It is wise to remember that foreign machination of western Indians—whether real or supposed—lay at the core of the early stages of manifest destiny.

The United States, as a newcomer within the international community, ranked low in high culture and technological production. Despite its unique brand of exceptionalism, the young nation no doubt chafed under the yoke of an inferiority complex. Part of the predicament lay in the fact that the United States, comparatively speaking, had no "history" and, hence, no national identity. Obviously, the generation of the American Revolution represented the creators or parents (Founding Fathers) of the new republic, but it would be their progeny who would define that republic. "With the passing of the Revolutionary generation that had heard the voices at Sinai," historian Fred Somkin wrote, "it remained for a generation of Americans born free to discover for themselves in a shifting environment what it meant to be an American and what the destiny of America was."[7] Elevating the status of the Founders had one major drawback: it was a tough act to follow. The patriotic expressions of the War-of-1812 generation are rife with doubts of the deservedness of the "sons" regarding their inheritance of the sacred goals of their "fathers." Fighting the same enemy as their fathers fought—Great Britain—must have lent credence to the cause of the second-generation revolutionaries.

In the West (states and territories west of the Appalachians), the lionization of revolutionary heroes took on a slightly different scope. With little or no Revolutionary War battlegrounds to speak of, westerners had difficulty claiming a share of the patriotic pride of which eastern states easily boasted—a source of envy westerners felt keenly. Backcountry hostilities during the American Revolution largely took the form of clashes with Indian populations who, for the most part, sided with Great Britain. Thus the "history" westerners wrote for themselves consisted largely of eulogistic narratives portraying besieged settlers (mostly women and children) cowering in fear of the tomahawk and scalping knife, being rescued by brave and hardy Indian fighters. In return, these Indian killers were accorded the respect and deference reserved for the nation's founders. These "Frontier Fathers" (as I have coined them) were the men who fought Indians, surveyed the conquered land, established commercial links with the East, and wielded political power in the freshly carved settlements of the backcountry. In Tennessee, Frontier Fathers such as John Sevier and James Robertson sealed their lofty reputations with the blood of the Indians killed from the raids they commanded. Ironically, as their fighting years declined, the Frontier Fathers often served as agents treating with Indian nations they tried, in prior decades, to decimate. There is little doubt the vicious warfare between Indians and white settlers in the early phase of Tennessee's history left a bitter impression (on both sides), causing a knee-jerk reaction when any sign of Indian hostility broke out in the period just prior to the War of 1812.[8]

As a frontier state, Tennessee, much like her sister states of Kentucky and Ohio, faced the same cast of stereotyping the United States endured on the global stage. Eastern demagogues eagerly pointed to the backwoods mentality of the West as evidence of their own superiority—a state of affairs that irked the sensitivities of frontiersmen determined to create commercial and cultural strongholds in the wilderness. Westerners, not content to adopt defensive measures in repelling the slings of ridicule, convinced themselves their world was not only on par with their eastern counterparts, it was, in many ways, superior. The frontier represented an opportunity to start anew, a second chance at redemption. Nature aided in promoting this scheme. Inviting river systems watered an abundance of untilled land, and land, after all, was the ultimate lure of any enterprising American in the early nineteenth century. As emigrants flocked to the West, sheer numbers demanded that easterners take notice of the new Promised Land. The eagerness of the newly arrived incomers, coupled with the openness of opportunistic vistas, charged the atmosphere with activity and drive. "Take the mass of the people in the western Country," one excited emigrant wrote in 1807, "and they are much more keen and enterprising than in the Eastern."[9] In a reversal of roles, then, westerners became convinced that envious eyes belonged to easterners resentful of losing their favored sons. Note this Fourth of July toast offered by Andrew Jackson at a Nashville celebration in 1805: "The rising greatness of the West—may it never be impeded by the jealousy of the East."[10] The War of 1812 gave western states an opportunity to further enhance their rising-star status through military exploits. In a stroke of fortune, the war legitimized the West's efforts to oust the one major impediment to its continuing growth: the Indians who occupied the coveted lands Anglo-Americans sought.

An East-versus-West mindset was also apparent within the state of Tennessee. As the reins of political power shifted from East Tennessee to West Tennessee—Nashville replacing Knoxville as the state capital in 1812—a growing animosity festered within the influential spheres of both regions. "Nashville has always been considered the opponent of Knoxville," stated a Nashville newspaper in 1814, "and for a number of years past the West Ten[nessee] members have acted in hostility to the East; and vice versa."[11] This rivalry, replete with personality clashes, proved to be a frustrating deterrent in efficiently conducting the war. (The region then known as "West Tennessee" is now referred to as "Middle Tennessee," the area west of the Cumberland Plateau to the Tennessee River. What is now West Tennessee [the region between the Tennessee and Mississippi Rivers] was Indian territory. This book will consistently use the designation "West Tennessee" when referring to what is now "Middle Tennessee.")

The campaign on the southern frontier during the War of 1812 involved the fighting forces of Georgia, the Mississippi Territory (present-day Alabama and Mississippi), and Tennessee. In the case of the latter, East and West Tennessee often worked in opposition to each other so that, in effect, there were two separate expeditionary armies from the state. The Georgia militia, though late in its efforts, achieved some success in the Creek War, as did the volunteers and militia from the Mississippi Territory. Added to this mix were various elements of the US Regular Army and US Rangers. In each case the lack of sufficient supplies, cooperation, and overall leadership plagued the armies that conducted operations in the South. Tennessee has been chosen as *the* pivotal entity for the study of this book, based on the knowledge that the state participated in more southern battles than any other state in the region. Also, its adopted son, Andrew Jackson, is arguably the most associated figure of the War of 1812 and, in particular, the Creek War. As one historian of the Creek conflict has admitted: "Of all the American generals facing the Redsticks, Andrew Jackson proved to be the most tenacious and most effective."[12]

Tennessee's pride in their role of the War of 1812 rests mostly on Jackson's laurels and his victories in the Creek War and, of course, at New Orleans. But the story of *Tennesseans at War* reveals a much more complicated version of the war than has been presented in the past, particularly in terms of the tensions that existed between the different participating factions. Contentiousness showed itself most prominently during the war in contests between the rank and file of the militia and their military authorities. Enlistment disputes, mutinies, and riots marred the much-flaunted volunteer spirit of Tennessee. The lack of uniform militia laws in the early republic, coupled with an array of volunteer army acts, contributed to this dilemma. The enlistment discord also reveals a glimpse of the decline of the deference that subordinates accorded to superiors. True, thousands of Tennesseans willingly flocked to the standard, but, once convinced they had done their duty, were equally eager to return home. The reality of the situation is that Tennesseans who participated in the War of 1812 were not exactly the iconic, stalwart protectors of freedom as they sometimes have been portrayed, nor were they Indian-killing, self-serving individuals who cared nothing for nation and honor. They were, in fact, human beings possessing all the foibles and aspirations akin to any mortals who preceded or followed them. The goal of telling their "story" is not to tear down any vaunted statues; it is to reconstruct a reality as genuine as the human saga. As much as possible, this book attempts to reconstruct the southern campaign of the War of 1812 through the words and actions of those Tennesseans (and others) who lived through that period.

1

"America is the fortunate Country, and the State of Tennessee is the fortunate spot in America," wrote David Campbell in 1809 from Knoxville. "No part of the Earth exceeds us in Soil, climate, and fine Streams of Water. . . . I rejoice I have settled here, where my family can enjoy plenty, and ease." Campbell, formerly a judge on the Tennessee Superior Court of Law and Equity, penned these lines to his old Virginia acquaintance, Thomas Jefferson. Campbell noted with enthusiasm the rising population of the frontier state as well as the prospect that the Cherokee Indians might soon be leaving the state to resettle west of the Mississippi River. Ultimately, Tennessee's story in the late eighteenth and early nineteenth century is tied to land and its capacity for profit, whether in speculation or productivity. During the same time, Indian removal became an inseparable element to white autonomy in the region. By the War of 1812, Tennessee consisted of two grand divisions—East and West—separated by the Cumberland Plateau. East Tennessee, stretching from the western border of North Carolina to the plateau, comprised well-watered valleys, thick forests of deciduous trees, and generally fertile soil. West Tennessee (also known as the Nashville or Cumberland Basin), extending from the Cumberland Plateau to the Tennessee River, offered gently rolling hills and plains with an abundance of springs, streams, timber, and natural grasslands. Contemporaries referred to the barren region separating the two divisions as the "Wilderness"—an area about one hundred miles long and fifty miles wide. This geographic barrier became a physical reminder of the "distance" between the two rival divisions.[1]

Census figures for Tennessee in 1810 reveal a total population of 262,000—a nearly 150 percent increase from 1800. Forty percent were under the age of ten, a reflection that the West was a land of youth. (The United States was literally a young nation—the median age of population in 1800 being sixteen—with a third of its entire population under ten years of age.) The 1810 census also disclosed that the majority of Tennesseans now lived, for the first time, in West Tennessee. In fact, the population of that section increased 500 percent during the decade of 1800–1810—a far cry from 1790, when East Tennessee commanded over four times the population of its western counterpart. The census also divulged a more ominous statistic: 79 percent of the state's 44,300 slaves resided in the western part of the state, particularly in the middle counties of Davidson, Wilson, Maury, Williamson, and Bedford. The population growth of West Tennessee, coupled with its huge slave base, reflected the development of a complex market economy based on cotton, tobacco, land speculation, and slavery.[2]

The rise of the Tennessee frontier came as no surprise to those who experienced it. Daniel Smith, a surveyor and secretary of the Southwest Territory, prophetically wrote in 1793: "The progress of population in that country is no more to be prevented or restrained than the flowing of the rivers. It cannot be retarded by laws, nor by treaties, nor by a stronger curb—the fear of death." Smith cited the progress made by Kentucky, where migration thrived "in the face of numerous and hostile savages." He correctly predicted a similar pattern for Tennesseans, then in the midst of a bloody and gruesome war with the aboriginal inhabitants of the territory—a conflict that left lasting psychological scars on both Indians and Anglo-Americans. James Winchester, as colonel in the West Tennessee militia, experienced firsthand the devastation of Indian raids in the early 1790s. His brother was ambushed and slain in July 1794, along with two young cousins killed and scalped, and a Cumberland man "shot with nine balls, and a tomahawk left sticking in his skull." William Hall, another Cumberland settler, vividly remembered an Indian attack in 1793 on a small party of whites, including a seventeen-year-old girl whose father was executed and scalped. She then fell to the same fate. Hall arrived with a rescue party and found the girl "lying on the ground, terribly, mortally wounded, scalped and bleeding." "She was faintly moaning when I came up, and was lying on her face," he somberly recalled. Hall was no stranger to such grisly sights. In June 1787 he witnessed his brother's death; two members of a group of ambushing Indians sunk their tomahawks into each side of his brain. Two months later, Hall and his family were waylaid again. This time another brother and Hall's father were shot to death ("he fell pierced by thirteen bullets"). In the eastern section of the state, in the Holston settlements, Tennesseans shared similar stories. The *Knoxville Gazette* reported seventy-one deaths by Indian depredations in less than a seven-month period in 1793.[3]

Anglo-American settlers responded to Indian depredations with a savagery equaling (and, at times, surpassing) that of their enemies. In May 1793 Indians committed a series of raids near Knoxville, where one small party killed a white man and his son. Territorial governor William Blount ordered Captain John Beard, with fifty mounted infantry, to pursue the perpetrators. Beard later claimed the trail led to the town of Hanging Maw (friendly to the United States), where envoys from Chickamauga (or lower Cherokees) towns had gathered. Although Beard's orders specified he not cross the Tennessee River in his pursuit, he attacked the town in a spirit of vengeance, killing about a dozen individuals, including a white man with his Indian wife and family. The attackers severely wounded Chief Hanging Maw, his wife, and daughter. Fearing the outbreak of a general war, Secretary Daniel Smith pleaded with Hanging Maw and other Cherokee leaders not to react violently. Beard was tried before a court-martial but acquitted due to strong public sentiment in his favor. Beard's raid and its consequences typified the powder-keg situation in the southern backcountry in the early 1790s. On one hand, besieged settlers endured swift, brutal attacks designed to spread fear throughout the white communities encroaching on land Indians declared as their own. The federal government, on the other hand, aware of the expense involved in subduing warring Indians (nearly five-sixths of federal operating expenditures went to support the Indian wars between 1790 and 1796), made efforts to deflect the growing tension on the frontier. For instance, in its attempt to pacify the warring southern Indians, the federal government quietly increased the Cherokee annuities by 50 percent.[4]

Although the War Department sympathized with the Tennesseans, the agency did not condone any invasions of Indian territory. Instead it authorized militiamen to assume defensive positions and dispatched ammunition when it could. Combined forces of Cherokee, Creek, and Shawnee Indians, bent on creating havoc in both East and West Tennessee, pressured the settlers' endurance to the limit. Tennesseans, not satisfied with a defensive posture, took matters into their own hands, as exemplified by the September 1794 expedition to the Nickajack towns where Major James Ore (under orders from James Robertson) attacked and destroyed the Chickamauga villages of Nickajack and Running Water. Territorial governor William Blount, on the surface, condemned the act, but he certainly knew of it ahead of time and may have even helped plan it. Thus the situation in Tennessee in the early 1790s comprised a double-edged imbroglio for territorial officials: frustration over Indian depredations and white settlers killing innocent Indians—and a federal government reluctant to make a military commitment. As a result, Tennesseans set a pattern for learning how to deal with the Indian "problem" on their own.[5]

The Indian warfare of the 1790s produced at least three key lessons for future Tennesseans: *all* Indians were to be held in suspicion, whites intruding on Indian land only acerbated the situation, and violence represented the ultimate solution against Indian hostility. In the midst of the frontier fighting in 1792, Governor Blount received a letter from a constituent who admitted that many Cherokees desired peace, but there were those who killed settlers and stole horses. The writer of the letter preferred an open war with the Cherokees because, as he put it, "a man would then know when he saw an Indian he saw an Enemy & be prepared & act accordingly."[6] Because backcountry settlers justified their own hatred and cruelty toward Indians by labeling them as hostile, savage, and inferior beings, depredations were seldom blamed on individual Indians or even tribes, but on Indians as a whole. The literature of the day, the narratives handed down from generation to generation, and visual depictions (such as paintings and museum displays) consciously promoted this slanted view.

The distrust of the Southeast Indians as promulgated by Anglo-Americans is epitomized in the 1812 remarks of John Sevier to his son. "There is not the least confidence to be placed in savages," decried the old Indian fighter. "I would not trust neither Chickasaws, nor Cherokees too far." As for the Creeks, Sevier summed up his attitude by declaring them "as great a set of villains as ever lived." The reality of the situation, however, painted a different picture. In an effort to get the US government to stop whites from trespassing on Creek land, one chief contacted President James Madison in 1809 with a litany of complaints concerning white incursions: stealing cattle, cutting timber, killing game—all in Creek territory. The chief also cited the extreme poverty in which the Creeks were living, with very little clothing and ammunition. To its credit, the federal government did make some attempt at rectifying the dire circumstances by forcibly removing white squatters from Creek lands—two thousand in 1809 alone. These and earlier attempts, however, never seemed to stem the tide of white encroachment.[7]

Tennessee's hunger for Indian land was insatiable, and, as far back as territorial status, it was apparent most white Tennesseans agreed on the complete elimination of Indians from their state. Statehood in 1796 did little to appease Anglo-American appetites. The Cherokees held at least 25,000 square miles of land within the chartered limits of the state, while the Chickasaws possessed over seven million acres of land, mostly between the Tennessee and Mississippi Rivers. Secretary of War James McHenry received a letter from one of his treaty commissioners, Alfred Moore, in 1799 stating that Tennesseans "burn with indignation at the restraints put upon their avidity for the Indian lands." State officials, observed Moore, "want all the land and not a part." Tennesseans actually instigated war with the Indians, and "whoever shall have the address to effect this," Moore noted, "will rise high in the estimation of his countrymen." Governor John Sevier, lamenting in 1800 over the fact that the Cherokees held valuable, fertile lands within the state, not to mention the access of navigable streams, expressed his disgust with the "Indian hordes . . . composed of the little tawny murdering tribes that were our earliest and most poisonous enemies." At the opening of the nineteenth century, the Cherokees found themselves vainly struggling to keep their lands, although promised by Tennessee officials that no more cessions would be asked of them. Certain Cherokee chiefs received bribes in the form of concessions—money, guns, and such—to promote further cessions, thus creating rifts within the Cherokee leadership.[8]

Justification for Indian removal in the early 1800s constituted a clear and logical argument, at least for white Tennesseans. To most Americans, Indians were "wasting" land that could be put to good use by whites who could better cultivate it. No matter that Indians *did* practice agriculture; the farming they did was simply not enough. As a result, Indians impeded the progress of "civilized" Americans. Indian claims presented a legal obstacle in Tennessee's quest to rid the state of nonwhite elements. Removal to the West would alleviate that problem. Tennessee officials, such as Governor Willie (pronounced "Wylie") Blount, therefore made Indian relocation a top priority in their administrations. In March 1811, Blount indicated he would "work cheerfully" to promote Indian settlement west of the Mississippi. Not only would tangled land claims be resolved, but also removal would better guard against foreign "tampering" with Indians. True, the Indians claimed rights to the land by virtue of their nativity, but, as Blount expressed it, "I have doubts whether a tribe . . . should have, and hold, a good title to a large unsettled Country . . . [there] ought to be some limitation to their bounds." From the beginning of his administration, Blount worked to extinguish Indian titles to lands within the state—urging removal as *the* solution—and doggedly continued this policy throughout his three terms (1809–15).[9]

While land west of the Mississippi River held little interest to Anglo-Americans in the early 1800s, the Mississippi River itself represented the lifeblood of the Old Southwest. Daniel Smith defined two issues threatening the existence of the Tennessee settlements: invasion by southern Indians and the denial of free access by river to the port of New Orleans. "The western people consider the navigation of the Mississippi as the light of the sun, a birth-right that cannot be alienated," professed Smith in 1793. Because of its geographic location, it seemed natural for Americans to have access to this river, despite the fact that Spain claimed navigation rights. According to one Tennessee politician in 1795, free access to the Mississippi was all the people needed to become numerous and wealthy. So adamant were Tennesseans about their navigation privileges that the state constitution of 1796 included in its Declaration of Rights, "That an equal participation of the free navigation of the Mississippi, is one of the inherent rights of the citizens of this State; it cannot therefore, be conceded to any prince, potentate, power, person, or persons whatever."[10]

The waning Spanish empire looked at the Mississippi River as the last bulwark between their fading dreams of a North American empire and the onslaught of Anglo-American settlers pressing on Spanish borders. "From the moment his Majesty loses dominion of the Mississippi," warned a Spanish official, "an equal fate will be decreed for the Kingdom of Mexico." With the Louisiana Purchase of 1803, Tennessee now rested in the geographic center of the nation, providing the state with a false sense of security. "What a proud pre-eminence of situation do we hold in the union," declared one Tennessee politician, "no longer considering ourselves as the outskirts of the nation, trembling at every hostile appearance of our neighbors." Although the United States obtained free navigation on the Mississippi through the Louisiana Purchase, Americans were constantly aware of the precarious hold they had on the waterway. Potential enemies still waited in the wings to seize the opportunity to stifle western commerce. A toast given at an 1808 Fourth of July celebration in Greeneville, Tennessee, reiterated the river's importance to the state: "The navigation of the Mississippi—The life and soul of the commerce of the Western Country."[11]

The Mississippi River, while certainly the key outlet for western commerce, was not the only waterway westerners valued. The river systems emptying into the Spanish province of West Florida also tantalized Tennessee and other southern states. (West Florida extended from Baton Rouge on the Mississippi to St. Marks on the Gulf of Mexico—the land east of St. Marks comprised East Florida). As early as the 1780s the river outlets of the Floridas held a special appeal to future-thinking westerners. The acquisition of Louisiana (with the exception of New Orleans) paled in comparison to the value placed on West Florida. Federalist Alexander Hamilton, while applauding the addition of Louisiana in 1803, nevertheless indicated the Floridas were "obviously of far greater value to us than all the immense, undefined region west of the river." Many of these rivers emptied into the Gulf of Mexico in West Florida, taking a north–south course through what is now Alabama-Creek territory in the early nineteenth century. The Mobile River, in particular, became second only to the Mississippi in importance to commerce in the Old Southwest.[12]

Governor John Sevier, in his 1801 message to the Tennessee legislature, alluded to the control of exportable rivers "without the attainment of which, it is almost impossible that the state of Tennessee can long exist in any degree of credit and political respectability." Simply put, river traffic saved money. Products shipped from East Tennessee to Nashville cost one hundred dollars per ton by land, but only thirty dollars by river. Overland goods moving to the Atlantic often resulted in shipping costs ranging from 300 percent to 500 percent more than the manufacturers' costs. Indians claiming the land surrounding the river systems—claims Tennesseans felt had no validity—presented the only obstacle. State officials implored the government to extinguish these entitlements and secure navigation rights. The westerners, typically taking matters into their own hands, balked at making repeated requests to the federal government for action, particularly regarding the salient matters of expelling contentious Indians and jealous foreign neighbors.[13]

The outbreak of the Creek War in 1813 provided Tennesseans with the perfect means to an end they had been seeking for more than a decade. In his October 15, 1813, letter to Brigadier General Thomas Flourney, Governor Willie Blount exposed the real reasons for conducting a war against the Creeks: "I persuade myself to believe, that, in the course of the coming fall and winter, that the Creeks will be not only whipped, but that the floridas, will be ours. . . . Those objects once effected, each southern and western inhabitant will cultivate his own garden of eden, and will, through the natural channels placed by a wise and just Creator, convenient for his use, export his own produce, and import such comforts as he may think desirable, by the shortest routes of communication with the ocean. And, moreover, he will be no longer disturbed, either by the British, Spaniards, or Indians." But Big Warrior, speaking on behalf of the Upper Creeks in an April 26, 1813, letter to Benjamin Hawkins, implored the Indian agent to advise the whites to stay out of the Creek Nation. "You mean to destroy us, on these waters, in trying to make use of it, when we don't allow of it," Big Warrior warned.[14]

The domestic and foreign intrigue surrounding the "Lower Country" set the tone for the so-called Burr Conspiracy of 1806–7. Aaron Burr designed a plan in the early nineteenth century to create an independent nation in the West, although he insisted it would be a colony of two thousand Tennesseans and Kentuckians in northern Louisiana that could spearhead a predicted war with Spain. His plan involved planters, politicians, and army officers, including General James Wilkinson and Andrew Jackson. Burr contracted Jackson to build five boats after Burr made several trips to Tennessee to drum up support for an "expedition" in late 1806. Jackson, as major general of the state militia, became suspicious of Burr's intentions (perhaps because of Jackson's intense distrust of Wilkinson), but ordered out the militia in October 1806 in preparation for war with Spain nevertheless. Then President Jefferson issued a proclamation against Burr, implicating Jackson because of his connection to Burr. Jackson, in defending himself, became particularly vehement against Jefferson and Secretary of War Henry Dearborn for trying to exploit the subsequent Burr trial as a "political persecution" against him. Jackson used the occasion of Burr's trial to personally blame Jefferson for his overly pacific attitude toward British impressment, publicly saying, "Mr. Jefferson can torture Aaron Burr while England tortures our sailors."[15]

The significant consequence of the Burr Conspiracy was the treasonous label it put on the state of Tennessee. Before his arrest, Burr was feted in Nashville on September 28, 1806, with a dinner at Talbot's Inn, attended by "many of the most respectable citizens of Nashville," according to a Nashville newspaper. Toasts and songs accompanied the affair. The local newspaper described Burr as "the steady and firm friend, of the state of Tennessee." By the year's end, however, Burr was accused of treason, and, on the evening of January 2, 1807, the population of Nashville burned him in effigy, the newspaper now branding him a traitor. "We have the utmost confidence in assuring our Atlantic brethren," the editor pronounced, "that the idea of separation is spurned with indignation and horror." The press in Tennessee constantly filled their 1807 editions with accounts of Burr's treachery and his subsequent trial. At the Fourth of July dinner in Springfield (Robertson County) that year came this revealing toast echoing the concerns of Tennesseans concerned over the fallout from the state's involvement with the deceitful Burr: "The western country—Ever willing to assist the sister states in the detection and punishment of lawless combinations and traitorous conspiracies."[16]

The defensive posturing in the Old Southwest over Burr evidenced the thin skin westerners wore regarding their place in the Union. The decade previous to the Burr Conspiracy witnessed another "plot"—this one to seize Spanish territory in Florida and Louisiana with the aid of Great Britain and allied Indians. US senator (and former Southwest territorial governor) William Blount narrowly avoided impeachment by Congress in 1797 for his role in the conspiracy. Blount and others, however, viewed the "conspiracy" more like a business transaction, blaming federal apathy in the Southwest as a justifiable excuse for action-taking westerners who sought some sort of legitimate authority on the frontier that would guarantee land titles, support internal improvements, and defend settlers. Of course, Blount's suffering from great debt at this time obviously played a part in his motives, but an isolated Tennessee seemed to understand his plight. After Blount evaded impeachment by refusing to appear before Congress, forgiving Tennesseans promptly elected him to the state senate.[17]

One British observer noted that if the Union were ever to be broken, the split would occur in the West, as that region was "notoriously full of gamblers, speculators and adventurers of all sorts." When Congress debated on allowing a delegate to represent the territory of Louisiana in 1804, Tennessee's William Cocke unhesitatingly approved the measure, spouting, "I love and venerate these people—they live in the west." Within the state of Tennessee itself, there persisted a spiteful rivalry between the two grand divisions of East and West Tennessee. In his assessment of both regions, Daniel Smith contended in 1793 that the "commercial connections" of the Holston and Cumberland areas were so different (East Tennessee connected to the Atlantic, West Tennessee connected to the Mississippi) that "their situation will probably induce the inhabitants of those districts to employ themselves differently, for the most proper or profitable productions in one settlement, may not be the most profitable in the other." To be sure, the Cumberland settlements were so fearful of domination by East Tennessee that they initially rejected statehood in the mid-1790s.[18]

No greater slight on the prestige of East Tennessee occurred than the shift of the state capital from Knoxville to Nashville in 1812. After a special session had been held in Nashville in September 1812, some members of the legislature made an attempt in the following month to move it back to Knoxville. When that failed, a compromise was offered (but rejected) to make the town of Sparta (as a halfway point) the capital. The new capital "city" of Nashville came from humble roots. At the turn of the nineteenth century, the main square of the town sported only three small brick houses, a large rough stone building used as a courthouse, and a one-story log structure serving as a jail, with a whipping post nearby. The most notable buildings were Talbot's Inn and Ropers Tavern ("The inhabitants of this town use a great quantity of spirituous liquors," one observer noted). By 1805, the town was described as a place "in a state of rapid improvement," consisting of four hundred homes, with still only a handful constructed of brick. By the time of the War of 1812, with a population well over one thousand, Nashville began to resemble a place of distinction, even offering theatrical performances in a crude theater constructed from a one-room, vacated salt warehouse on Market Street. Other cultural venues included a library, a debating society, a dancing school, and such events as a "philosophical oration" in the courthouse by a lecturer on the subject of "Conscious; or, the Moral Consciousness." More unsophisticated entertainment could be found at Talbot's Inn, where tightrope walkers performed for an admission fee of fifty cents, or at the Nashville Inn, where a live animal show featured apes and rare birds. City planners passed an ordinance in 1812 making sidewalks along the public square twelve feet wide and paved with brick. At the same time, an act was passed to build a toll bridge across the Cumberland River.[19]

On the day Nashville newspapers announced that the United States declared war on Great Britain, one could find advertisements for salt, iron and nails, bricks, groceries, writing paper, corn-shelling machines, as well as a fifty dollar reward for the capture of a runaway slave. Such advertisements for escaped slaves were common in southern newspapers of the day. There was little hope for a slave except escape, unless a grateful owner emancipated him. Even under the pretense of due process of law, slaves had little chance of receiving justice. What of the status of free blacks in Tennessee? In West Tennessee, the number of free blacks in 1800 was fifty-one; in 1810 it was 809, reflecting the rapid overall population growth in the region. In Nashville, the free black population went from fourteen in 1800 to 130 in 1810. Free blacks operated businesses and joined the militia, with some acquiring wealth and land titles. Robert Renfro, known as "Black Bob," became a citizen of note in Nashville, owning and operating a tavern on the north side of the square. Renfro, along with at least three other free blacks, were enrolled in the militia company of Davidson County at the outbreak of the War of 1812. On the surface, there seemed to be little outward signs of racism. Despite certain restrictions, Tennessee was the only southern state (besides North Carolina) that permitted free blacks to vote in the early decades of the nineteenth century. Yet to maintain control over free blacks, measures were enacted to regulate their lives (such as registering the names of free blacks in order to monitor their movements). Removing free blacks from the scene was also an option, for as early as 1816 legislators were endorsing a congressional plan to establish a settlement for free blacks in Liberia.[20]

There is no evidence that Tennessee free blacks participated in any great numbers in the War of 1812. One exception was Major Jeffrey Locklelier, who apparently served in the militia during the War of 1812 ("Major" was a given name, rather than a military rank). It was said that Andrew Jackson and John Coffee (Jackson's close friend and military right-hand man) were acquaintances of his. Coffee also befriended another free black, Phillip Thomas, who operated a barbershop in Nashville. Thomas, writing to Coffee in January 1815, congratulated the general on the successful campaign in New Orleans, adding that "nothing but my Complexion and my great desire to make money restrains me from participating in the great actions of the Army of Tennessee!!!" Why the reluctance to enlist free blacks into military service? It could be that the idea of placing weapons in the hands of a black man— *any* black man—was anathema in a slave-based society. Ironically, more Tennessee slaves probably served in the war than free blacks. Since some runaway slaves escaped to Indian country where they learned the dialect, they were often used as interpreters during the Creek War. One such slave was "Thomas Bruner's blackman Bob" who served as linguist at Fort Williams in 1814. Other slaves stayed with their masters under the designation of "waiters" during the war. During the Creek War, John Coffee used four of his slaves as waiters and took three with him for the campaign at New Orleans. His most trusted slave, Ben, was probably with him the entire time. Tennessee muster rolls from the War of 1812 reveal that "waiters" were paid for their services, but it is doubtful they received any of the actual wages.[21]

Just as blacks, free or not, were expected to "know their place" in society, whites also lived within an ordered pattern of social structure. Frontier elites had the difficult task of maintaining their status as those expectant of deference from their subordinates in the midst of an environment that idealized individual liberty and freedom. In the 1780s and 1790s, men such as John Sevier and James Robertson won their laurels on the basis of their ability to fight and control Indians who disturbed the settlements of the early pioneers. They won the respect of their followers through bold and decisive actions, usually ending in the spilled blood of the offending Indians. By the first decade of the nineteenth century, with the Indian menace virtually removed, frontier society progressed to the next level of civilization: peaceful inhabitation of an agricultural republic, marked by limited manufactures and unlimited commercial possibilities. The men who earned deference would be those whose virtues included a profound dedication to making those possibilities a reality—merchants, politicians, speculators, even the unpopular lawyer. These forward-looking individuals were bent on creating a society based on order and controlled progress. The War of 1812 interrupted development on the frontier, producing men like Andrew Jackson, a stiff-necked warrior of the kind Tennessee once paid homage to in the 1790s. Determined to subdue the enemy at any cost, Jackson represented more of the past than the future. Indeed, the story of the War of 1812 is more often about looking back than looking ahead.

For many in the United States, ominous and unsettling portents of war began in 1811, with disasters wrought by nature: devastating floods of the Ohio and Mississippi Rivers in the spring; a widespread summer drought resulting in substantial crop failures; destructive storms off the Atlantic coast in the fall; and a horrifying fire at a Richmond, Virginia, theater in December that killed seventy people, including the governor of the state. War with Great Britain seemed imminent, as the Twelfth Congress met in Washington to hammer out resolutions intended to involve the nation in an armed conflict with its old nemesis. In early November, forces of the US Army, led by Indiana territorial governor William Henry Harrison, clashed with Indians at Tippecanoe, sparking what some labeled as the first battle of the War of 1812. A Saint Louis newspaper editor made the grand understatement when he wrote, "On the whole, [1811] has been an uncommon year."[22]

Equally uncommon was the appearance of a comet in the skies throughout the latter part of 1811. The comet—with its head a million miles across and tail one hundred million miles long—was first sighted in August and receded in December, being the brightest in October. No mere astronomical curiosity, a comet had traditionally been interpreted as a portent of dark times. One Tennessean recalled the first sighting of the comet "caused a deep sensation in a crowd, all of whom had been taught to look upon comets as harbingers of impending calamity." Isaac Clark, a self-styled poet from Sumner County, penned the deep concerns of the times in verse:

After Comets come in our sight,
The nations rage and often fight
The sound of war we constant hear,
Destruction flows both far and near.

Another Tennessean related how the comet caused the local population to believe "the roar of battle and sounds of cannon could be heard in the skies."[23]

The disappearance of the comet in December 1811 brought little relief to the superstitious population, for in the early hours of December 16 an earthquake rocked the West and sent individuals literally running into the streets in fear and bewilderment. From this date until the middle of March the following year, a series of earthquakes—an estimated two to three thousand tremors—struck the Ohio and Mississippi valleys, forever changing the region's landscape. The New Madrid earthquakes, named after the Missouri epicenter of activity, altered the topography of thirty to fifty thousand square miles in present-day southeast Missouri, northeast Arkansas, and western Tennessee and Kentucky. Vibrations shook the ground in a region encompassing nearly two million square miles, south toward New Orleans, north to Detroit, and east to Boston and Charleston. Miraculously, despite the gaping fissures, landslides, and flooding waters, estimates suggest only a dozen deaths occurred. The region lying along the New Madrid fault was sparsely populated, and the rudimentary wooden structures in the towns lessened the possibility of fatalities that might have resulted from toppling brick buildings.[24]

The citizens of Carthage, Tennessee, awoke at three in the morning on December 16 to find the walls of their homes fiercely shuddering and the ground forcefully quaking. "Imagination cannot point out the horrors it produced on the mind!" the *Carthage Gazette* reported, "The uncommon darkness of the night . . . the houses shaking and tottering—the earth reeling and quivering to its center." Reuben Ross was in a Stewart County field looking for a lost horse when a second series of tremors erupted at sunrise on the morning of December 16. Fleeing toward his house, he was startled to see many of his neighbors ("a pitiable and terror-stricken crowd," as he described them) flocking to his house, where they sought spiritual comfort from his father, the local preacher. The stunned group remained at the house throughout the day and night. The tops of chimneys fell off in Columbia, Tennessee, where one man, whose one-story house was shaking, thought it might be hogs rubbing up against the blocks underneath the structure.[25]

In fact, the earthquakes generated a host of explanations, among them volcanic activity, electricity, vibrations from the moon, underground fires, and even the comet that mysteriously disappeared about the same time as the arrival of the earthquakes. Most individuals, however, interpreted the earthquakes (as they did the comet) as a portent of evil—a sign of God's displeasure with the current state of affairs. The earthquakes affected the nation's religious climate, resulting in an initial surge of pietistic passion, then, once the earthquakes had subsided, a subsequent decline in devout fervor. This was particularly true on the frontier, where the transitory, unsteady, and sometimes-violent nature of its people affected their religious associations. A Davidson County man remembered how alarmed he and others were and that "many professed religion," while he himself took up "prechen." A resident of Kingston, Tennessee, believed the earthquakes to be a positive influence. "There is now in parts of this state," he wrote in April 1812, "where perhaps there was never before since its first settlements, a prayer heard, meetings, fasting and prayer, religious societies in which they frequently sit up all night." This religious fervor came out of a conviction that God wanted his people to repent of their sins.[26]

Another significant event of 1811 solidified the notion that war was inescapable. On November 7, 1811, at the confluence of the Tippecanoe and Wabash Rivers in the Indiana Territory, US forces clashed with an Indian confederation led by Tenskwatawa (the Prophet). American militia and US Regulars, commanded by Governor William Henry Harrison, were attacked in the early morning hours outside Prophetstown where they were awaiting a meeting with tribal leaders. Although the tribal forces took the army by surprise, their assault was eventually repulsed when their ammunition ran low. Harrison's army then managed to destroy Prophetstown and scatter its inhabitants. As in the frontier wars of previous decades, American savagery at Tippecanoe matched those of the Indians, as soldiers scalped the bodies of dead Indians and fixed the scalps to the muzzles of their guns for display. While it is true American forces suffered greater casualties (about sixty killed), the battle at Tippecanoe served as a symbolic victory for the United States. Although Harrison did not have any official governmental sanction for his attack at Tippecanoe, he afterward drew President Madison's approval for his actions. Harrison, a transplanted Virginian nabob, had previously proved himself a loyal disciple of Jeffersonian principles by strategically negotiating with numerous Indian tribes to transfer millions of acres of land to the United States.[27]

The confederacy of Native American tribes, formed in the Old Northwest in the early nineteenth century, represented a serious threat to the security of the United States' frontier. Initially led by Tenskwatawa, the Indian movement gradually fell under the leadership of the Prophet's brother, the Shawnee Tecumseh. Under his guidance, the confederation came to include followers from several different tribes. Tecumseh's vision of a pan-Indian alliance led him to journey south to enlist the aid of the Southeast tribes. Having little success, with the notable exception of the Creeks, Tecumseh was on his way back to Prophetstown when Harrison's forces made their unauthorized attack. Tradition has it Tecumseh told the Creeks that when he reached home, he would stomp his foot on the ground and shake every house in Tuckabatchee (a Creek village where Tecumseh delivered a vehement anti-American speech in October 1811). The earthquake of December 1811 fortuitously played into the Shawnee leader's hands, reiterating his thunderous declaration. The significance of this coincidence weighed heavily on the upcoming conflict between the whites of the Old Southwest and the Creek Indians, as the latter turned more and more to their shamans for spiritual inspiration—a condition leading to intertribal conflicts. Furthermore, some Creek warriors journeyed north to join Tecumseh's cause and fought with him in his war against the Americans.[28]

Western reaction to the events at Tippecanoe exemplified that section's frustration with the federal government's hesitant policy to deal with the Indian "problem" head on. "Will our government act; or will they always sleep?" proclaimed the Cincinnati *Liberty Hall*. "Surely this is enough to rouse them from lethargy." When the news of Tippecanoe arrived in Knoxville on the first day of December 1811, it was accompanied by a false report of the death of 180 soldiers, and a force of 1,200 Indians rampaging unchecked through Kentucky. Several days later, Tennessee governor Willie Blount wrote to a friend in Boston that it was now time to teach the "Savages on the Wabash" a lesson in American superiority. The *Carthage Gazette* referred to the "treacherous attack" of the Indians on Governor Harrison's troops as "a powerful incentive to citizen soldiers who pant for an opportunity to avenge the numberless scenes of savage barbarity." And the Nashville *Clarion* announced that "savage hell-hounds are unchained upon our frontiers." The *Clarion*'s remark was appropriate to the estimation of the Indian movement under the Prophet, who John Sevier once referred to as "an artful, cunning dog."[29]

One of the Tennesseans panting for vindication was Andrew Jackson, who scribbled a letter to William Henry Harrison in late November 1811, pledging military support. "The blood of our murdered Countrymen must be revenged," an angered Jackson spewed. "That banditti, ought to be swept from the face of the earth." (Jackson would express the same sentiments on the eve of a war with the Creek Nation nearly two years later.) According to him, the hostile Indians were "excited to war, by the secret agents of great Britain." Jackson was not alone in this assumption. The fact that British arms and ammunition were discovered at Tippecanoe, along with other British-manufactured goods, lent credence to the idea of English subterfuge. Governor Harrison even insisted the opposing force of Indians was better armed than the Americans because they had been equipped by the king's forces at Malden (a British post in southwest Ontario). Those eager to draw the link between Indian hostility and British interference paid scant attention to the reality that American-made weapons were also found at Prophetstown. The *Aurora*, a hawkish Philadelphia newspaper, insisted that 25,000 British troops were in Canada helping the Indians "to complete the work which their prophet, like another Mahomed, commences in massacre and blood." The headline of the *Aurora*'s December 5, 1811, issue declared: "WAR! WAR! WAR!—The blow is struck."[30]

President James Madison, in his June 1812 declaration of war, made little mention of British instigation of Indians. Still, because of the widespread belief in America of this duplicity, and the fact that British "intrigue" played such a vital role in western thought, the connection between the British and Indians is worthy of closer examination. The key to British strategy involved the security of Canada and its lucrative fur trade. Using Indians as a buffer zone against any American intrusion, British policy involved a tricky balancing act of securing the Indians as allies, while at the same time trying to restrain them from overtly enticing American retaliation. The great distance between the Foreign Office in London and the Canadian frontier made it virtually impossible to oversee strict control of such a situation. The autonomy displayed by British Indian agents gave them inordinate leverage in Anglo-Indian relations in that they had the responsibility of putting instructions from superiors into a language Indians could understand. Agents did this without adequate supervision and, thus, their own prejudices could often make or break official policy.[31]

The notion that the British were to blame for Indian depredations across both the northern and southern borders of the United States gave westerners motivation for declaring war in 1812. Tennessee representative John Rhea, in a March 1813 letter to Kentucky governor Isaac Shelby, expressed his hope that William Henry Harrison's army would "be able to give the enemy a blow which will make him feel for the wrongs he has done, and more especially for exciting the Indians to war against the United States." In that same month, President Madison presented his second inaugural address and emphatically spoke of British involvement with the Indians: "They have not, it is true, taken into their own hands the Hatchet & the knife devoted to indiscriminate massacre; but they have let loose the savages armed with these cruel instruments; have allured them into their service, & carried them to battle by their sides: eager to glut their savage thirst, with the blood of the vanquished, and to finish the work of torture and death, on maimed and defenceless [sic] captives." Madison's unusually harsh tone came as a response to the events of January 1813 when approximately sixty wounded American prisoners, captured at the River Raisin (near present-day Detroit) were murdered by Indian allies of the British, who failed to protect the prisoners from the victorious Indians' wrath. The episode provoked rage across the nation, particularly in the West, as the victims were Kentucky militia led by a Tennessee commander, General James Winchester. "Remember the Raisin" became a rallying cry for Kentuckians during the remainder of the war. The River Raisin incident also sparked official sanctions against British-inspired Indian depredations against American citizens. A little-known public act, passed by Congress in March 1813, granted authority to the president to retaliate, in kind, against violations of the laws and usages of warfare by those acting under the British government's protectorship. In other words, it legally condoned committing atrocities as a response to enemy atrocities.[32]

The congressional codifying of such sanctions stems from a history of producing countermeasures to Great Britain's attempts to stifle America's commercial interests. The war between England and France in the early nineteenth century caused American relations with both nations to deteriorate, as the United States became collateral damage in the life-and-death struggle for the control of Europe. Blockades shut down most European harbors to American vessels, as both England and France seized American ships they felt were in violation of their commercial restrictions. The British system of impressment aggravated the situation even more. Not wishing to go to war, the Jefferson administration convinced itself the United States had the power to coerce the European belligerents into submission through economic methods rather than military might. As a result, a series of embargoes, beginning in 1806, restricted American ships from engaging in foreign trade. The Non-Importation Act of 1806 refused entry of many British goods, while the Embargo Act of 1807 prohibited all American ships from departing for a foreign port. The act was an economic disaster for merchants and shippers, particularly in the coastal states. In the wake of a depression, rising unemployment, and a surge of smuggling operations, Jefferson repealed the much-hated embargo shortly before leaving office in 1809. In its place, the Non-Intercourse Act (1809) opened American trade to all countries except England and France. This act, however, proved to be as ineffective as its predecessor. In 1810, the new administration under Madison acknowledged the failure of economic pressure to coerce the European powers and engineered a desperate measure known as Macon's Bill Number 2. Trade to both England and France was now thrown open with the caveat that if either power would rescind their restrictions on American commerce, the United States would reapply nonintercourse against the power opting to refuse. The belated repeal of Britain's Orders in Council served as small reward for America's efforts at economic arm twisting.[33]

As a result of Jefferson's embargoes, American foreign trade fell 90 percent between 1807 and 1814, causing one historian to label it as "perhaps the most painful economic shock the United States ever experienced." Although farmers did not feel the economic crunch as greatly as merchants, farm prices were already in decline by the time the embargoes were put into place and dropped even further right before the declaration of war. Citizens of Montgomery County, Tennessee, petitioned Governor Sevier in 1808 to call a special session of the legislature to deal with the problems the embargo caused. The lack of markets for surplus produce meant Tennesseans could not free themselves of debt; furthermore, the stagnation in trade created a scarcity of specie. The lack of hard money also raised its value, which, in turn, gave an undue advantage to the "monied and creditor class of [the] community" over the debtor class. Reacting to this situation, the legislature enacted laws in 1809 postponing payments of debts and staying legal executions.[34]

Notwithstanding the obvious pitfalls of the embargoes, Tennesseans generally supported both administrations' directives; in fact, some thought the restrictions too lenient. "The non-importation act & those who supported it," toasted one Robertson County citizen in 1806, "may more energetic measures be pursued next session; if the great Leviathan of the deep does not treat our flag with more respect." Some Tennesseans found the conduct of New Englanders, who resorted to smuggling to lessen their economic losses, as traitorous. James Winchester lamented in 1808 over the fact that "the Strong arm of Government" failed to coerce "the insurgents in New England to obedience." Some, like the editor of the *Carthage Gazette*, followed the party line and insisted that no matter what the positive or negative effects of Jefferson's embargo, it had been adopted by Congress "and by an administration in whose wisdom and rectitude of intention we place much confidence." While most westerners supported the embargoes in theory and practice, they did so with reluctance, preferring action to paper diplomacy. In late 1809, a group of prominent Nashville citizens, including James Robertson, Andrew Jackson, and Felix Grundy, drafted a resolution showing their approval of Madison's embargo policy, adding that if Congress decided to take arms "against those, who have so often insulted, and injured us, we will risk our lives and fortunes to support the cause of our country." These were no idle words, as the men who expressed them firmly believed that a nation's honor, once insulted, deserved the same consideration as if one's personal honor had been injured.[35]

In 1807, the national honor of the United States came under intense scrutiny as a result of the *Chesapeake* affair. On June 22 the British warship HMS *Leopard* attacked and boarded the American frigate *Chesapeake* off the coast of Norfolk, Virginia. The *Leopard* had been dispatched to search for British deserters, but when the *Chesapeake* refused to be inspected, the British warship fired on the American vessel, killing three and wounding eighteen. The British then boarded the frigate and found four Royal Navy deserters among the *Chesapeake* crew—one was British-born and the other three were American citizens who had served in the Royal Navy. The British citizen was later hanged, one of the Americans died in a Halifax hospital, and the other two were eventually freed. The British minister to the United States, David Erskine, expressed his concern over America wanting to go to war over the episode. In a July 1807 letter to the British Foreign Secretary, Erskine estimated that while America would not go to war over commercial disputes, "the passions of the people might be worked upon to any extent by an appeal to them on the Ground of National Insult." Erskine's analysis of America's reaction to the *Chesapeake* affair was right on target. The perceived British insult provoked rage across the nation. In Tennessee, mass meetings were held, newspapers condemned the incident, and Governor Sevier put the state militia on alert. Some were of the opinion that armed conflict should be the only redress. One Sumner County resident addressed his fellow citizens with a harangue against Great Britain, declaring that despite his aversion to "the effusion of human blood, and the accumulation of burdensome taxes," he felt sure there was no other course than war in this case. In July 1807, citizens met in Nashville to express their outrage at a meeting chaired by James Winchester. Judge John Overton delivered a stirring speech denouncing the affair, calling it a "horrid catastrophe." A committee adopted resolutions declaring the attack an act of war and encouraged President Jefferson to take steps toward avenging the insult. Instead of declaring war on Great Britain, however, Jefferson and his administration settled for economic sanctions via embargoes that served only to divide the nation at a time when it could have united in a common cause.[36]

At the July 1807 public meeting that took place in Nashville, a secretary kept minutes of the event. "Upon this occasion every member of the meeting seemed to fire and burn," he recorded. "The *amor patriae* of '76 seemed to animate every countenance, to glow in every feature, and trill through every fiber." This reference to the patriotism of 1776 became a key component in the rhetoric and ideology of the second-generation revolutionaries. Unsure of their role and place in history, they went to great lengths to associate themselves with their epoch-making peers. In order to prove they were not a "degenerate" race, Americans of the 1812 generation insisted that the revolutionary spirit had not dissipated. What better way to prove the merit of a son than to emulate the deeds of the father? The War of 1812 provided an opportunity for the second generation to prove their worthiness in a manner the revolutionary generation could appreciate: through martial deeds. Nathaniel Macon of North Carolina, speaking on the House floor of Congress in March 1814, proclaimed, "The object of this war and that of the Revolution is the same. . . . The object of both is to prevent oppression and to maintain our rights." Proponents of the war in 1812 began to refer to it as the "second war of independence." Not only was this a cry for justification, but it also offered a solution to the perceived abasement in society. "The love of country . . . destroyed by the love of wealth," confirmed one wartime minister, "will be revived by *this second war of independence.*"[37]

In hindsight, seeking a war against Great Britain in 1812 in order to disprove a nation's degeneracy may seem a reasonably esoteric explanation, but it is only one of many answers to the question *why* the United States fought the War of 1812. Twentieth-century historians produced a myriad of explanations concerning the war's causation, including maritime rights, national honor, land hunger, the Indian problem, territorial expansion, Anglophobia, and western exports hampered by British Orders in Council. In the second half of the twentieth century, historians placed more attention on the Republican Party's rise to power in Congress and Republicans' subsequent desire to take aggressive action in restoring their honor, as well as America's. Some historians go so far as to claim Federalist extremism was the critical factor in Republicans declaring war in 1812, not the actions of the British.[38] Suffice it to say, all of these explanations hold water, but isolating it to one main cause has proved impossible. There are some key issues, however, that deserve more consideration than others. The topics of impressment, territorial expansion, national honor, party politics, and the Indian situation (the latter, particularly, from a western point of view) encompass the most germane interpretations under consideration. A closer examination of these points rounds out the fuller picture of what led America into its second war of independence.

It has been said that the War of 1812 was "an unhappy byproduct of the world war launched by Napoleon." On the surface, it may seem a stretch to tie a conflict raging in the ancient capitals of the Old World to the backcountry "wilderness" of the southern frontier. After all, it was a time when it took months for news to cross the Atlantic and weeks to disseminate it throughout the United States, making the world seem more remote than it really was. But the affairs in Europe played a vital role in America's commercial ventures, and newspapers of the day followed the mighty struggle between England and France with keen interest. There was more than commerce at stake: to many, England represented a familiar nemesis, while French aid during the American Revolution earned that country a token of gratitude. Still, it must be remembered that Great Britain supplied America with most of its manufactured goods and imported most of America's raw materials. To be sure, the war in Europe sparked a boom in the American economy, due mostly to increased shipping and favorable terms of trade. This was particularly true of the years between 1793 and 1808, before Jefferson's embargo put a damper on American shipping. The volume of cotton exports illustrates this prosperity, jumping from 18,000 pounds in 1800 to nearly 94,000 pounds by the end of the decade. Some American merchants, despite the blockades and edicts, continued to trade with England after June 1812 through a complicated network of smuggling. It is a significant fact that America provided flour to the English army on the Iberian Peninsula during most of the War of 1812.[39]

The French had been also violating American commerce for years. Beginning in 1793, French privateers assaulted American shipping in response to France's desperate need of supplies due to the war in Europe. By 1798, hostilities between the two nations broke out at sea. This "quasi war" terminated in 1800, although French depredations continued until 1813. The issue of British impressment of American sailors, however, supplied enough fuel for the fire in portraying England as the sole enemy of the United States. It has been estimated that in the twenty-year period from 1792 to 1812, approximately 10,000 seamen were impressed, the majority of them during the 1802–

12 time frame. Yet Britain perceived the very act of America declaring war on England as support to France. "The time of declaring the war had stung them more than the act itself," wrote American envoy James Bayard in 1814. "They considered it as an aid given to their great enemy at a moment when his power was most gigantic and most seriously threatened the subjugation of the continent as well as of themselves." The stinging England felt may also have something to do with the idea that because of all the American embargoes, nonintercourse, and nonimportation acts, Britain did not seriously believe the United States would actually go to war. There are indications that the Madison administration maneuvered toward war based on a strong sense of injury from *both* France and England.[40]

When America's attention was not focused on maritime feuds, it remained on land—the one resource the nation had plenty of, yet seemingly never enough. The Louisiana Purchase would have satisfied even the most gluttonous land speculator, but at the time the prairies were deemed too sterile for occupation. The need for fresh territory by land-sapping pioneers initiated the drive to acquire Canada—Britain's key dominion in North America. British ownership presented an obvious obstacle but, in the scheme of things, it was a man-made impediment. After all, God himself "marked our limits in the south, by the Gulf of Mexico; and on the north by the regions of eternal frost," according to one Republican expansionist. On the surface, Canada seemed to be easy pickings, the population of British North America being one-tenth that of the United States (600,000 versus 6,000,000). Furthermore, of the total population of Upper Canada (the territory nearer the head of the Saint Lawrence River) in 1812, 60 percent were recently arrived Americans. However, the majority of Americans in Canada were sympathetic to the Federalist causes in the United States and could not envision Americans abandoning their comfortable homes to fight the battles of "Napoleon, Madison, and Co[mpany]." As it turned out, American offensive operations were hampered by difficult winter conditions and the great expense of time and money required for military exploits.[41]

The motivation for taking Canada involved more than merely the acquisition of territory. Depriving Great Britain of Canada would affect British capacity to exercise its commercial and naval powers against the United States. When the American embargoes of 1807–9 cut off Britain's supply of lumber, livestock, and wheat (which were reexported to the West Indies for coffee and sugar), Great Britain looked to Canada to fill the void of American raw materials. England began a program of economic growth in Canada after 1808, and Americans (especially New Englanders) started to use Canadian markets as outlets. The financial interests of the northern borderlands overshadowed any patriotic impulses initiated by Jefferson's embargoes or the declaration of war, particularly when trading with the enemy turned out to be good business. By 1812, Canada became an integral part of British access to American resources, and to strip Britain of its North American possessions represented a definitive means of obstructing British trade. On the eve of the War of 1812, James Monroe stated the administration's position on Canada: "In case of war it might be necessary to invade Canada, not as an object of the war, but as a means to bring it to a satisfactory conclusion."[42]

"The acquisition of Canada and Florida would add much to the probability of a peace being lasting," Nathaniel Macon intimated in 1813, "for while these remain in the possession of any European Government, that Government will most assuredly manage the Indians so as to force an Indian war on us whenever it pleases." Macon played into the apprehensions of western constituents, convinced of British chicanery in every isolated Indian attack on the frontier. The Charleston *City Gazette* of July 14, 1812, expressed its approval of the war with a condemnation of Canada, calling it the "den of corruption, the nursery of spies, and the Indian intriguer, the smugglers' resort, the refugee's asylum, and the British footstool." These condemnations seemed to be verified after the brutal massacre of American prisoners at the River Raisin. John Long, a resident of Rogersville, Tennessee, upon hearing of the disaster, crossed into Kentucky to join that state's militia. In a December 1813 letter, Long explained why he enlisted there: "my object of going out was to Serve My Country, Retalliate for the River Raisin, See proctor Surrender his Sword, kill tecumsy [Tecumseh], take Malden and restore Detroit." In hindsight, the frontier population greatly exaggerated the Indian menace. While the danger from Indians may have been real on remote outposts of the backcountry, in reality, Indians only early on threatened the existence of white settlement in the West. President Madison devoted just one paragraph (two long sentences, really) in his war message of June 1812 to the topic of Great Britain inciting Indians on the frontier. Nevertheless, to those inhabitants of the backcountry (such as Tennessee), where a legacy of border warfare permeated the consciousness of public memory, the issue of marauding Indians, spurred on by British intrigue, remained an important motivating factor for war.[43]

With the United States being outmanned on the seas, Canada became a logical offensive goal—a throwback to the Revolutionary War mentality that Canada must be secured to eliminate any British threat. The mystique Canada held in the military minds of Tennesseans is striking. As early as 1809, a Tennessee newspaper, hinting at an imminent war with England, noted that Canada would be "a great and fair field for military glory." The

War of 1812 provided the golden opportunity to make these dreams of glory come true. In early September 1812, William Carroll and Andrew Hynes (both to be key officers in the war) introduced a memorial in the Tennessee General Assembly authorizing a regiment of militia "to march and aid in the subjugation of Canada." A year later, the Assembly would be clamoring to send regiments of Tennesseans to subjugate the Creek Indians, but at the start of the War of 1812, most of the attention focused on Canada. Returning from his abortive mission to the Mississippi Territory in April 1813, Andrew Jackson tendered his services to Secretary of War John Armstrong to fight in Canada. "I have a few standards wearing the American Eagle," Jackson boasted, "that I would be happy to place upon the ramparts of malden." Tennessean Thomas Hart Benton, an officer in the Thirty-Ninth US Infantry, best expressed this overwhelming urge to fight in Canada, where "Montcalm, Wolfe, and Montgomery have rendered the ground classic to the soldier." "I look towards Quebec as a Mohametan [sic] towards Mecca," a starry-eyed Benton wrote, "a holy spot where I must see once in my life, and see it too in all the pomp and glorious circumstance of war." Benton, like most Tennesseans, would never get to fulfill his military fantasies on the walls of Quebec, although some Tennesseans who served in the US Regular Army (especially the Twenty-Fourth US Infantry) did see service in the northern campaigns.[44]

The expectation of fighting on the same sacred ground as the military men of lore exposed the close distance between the warrior culture of the day and a sense of manhood. The respect accorded to martial deeds far exceeded that of most any other activity, particularly in the Old Southwest. Honor, tied to coming of age, implied a demonstration of one's independence and self-vindication. Significantly, the rhetoric of the American Revolution used honor as a motivating factor, linking it to manhood (vengeance against an oppressive "parent"). A nation going to war over issues of honor should never be underestimated. In his 1812 public address to the Tennessee militia, Colonel James Henderson prodded their sense of pride by insisting he would not tolerate any cowards among them. "What is life to that man who forfeits his honor?" he asked. "He lives a disgrace to himself, and dishonor to his children" (Henderson would later die in the campaign at New Orleans). Andrew Jackson proclaimed "Death Before Dishonor" as his personal motto.[45]

If honor was the key to one's existence, then it stood to reason that a nation's honor was central to its survival. Duels solved personal disputes regarding honor in the early republic, while nations resorted to wars. Clergyman Noah Worcester's 1815 pamphlet, "A Solemn Review of the Custom of War," made this telling statement: "Public wars and private duels seem to be practiced on similar principles." With the honor of the nation at stake, the War of 1812 could be compared to a gentlemanly duel where insult followed insult until there was no recourse left, without losing face, except that of war. "The aggressions, insults and outrages upon our lawful commerce and rights of sovereignty," the governor of the Mississippi Territory reminded his legislature in 1812, "were borne with until longer forbearance would have constituted the crime of submission." For many Americans, Great Britain had cast too many affronts without having been properly rebuked. It was simply a matter of honor.[46]

The first session of the Twelfth Congress opened on November 4, 1811 (a month earlier than usual at the request of President Madison). On the following day, Madison presented his third annual message in which he left little doubt as to the administration's view of Great Britain's refusal to repeal her maritime sanctions. Using such phrases as "derogatory to the dearest of our national rights" and "maintaining the honor of the American flag," Madison stopped short of insisting on a declaration of war; instead, he warned Congress it was time for the United States to wear "an armor and attitude demanded by the crisis." The chief leaders of the prowar faction of the Republicans in the Twelfth Congress were mostly westerners—in particular, Henry Clay of Kentucky and Felix Grundy of Tennessee. Clay, as Speaker of the House, and Grundy, an important figure on the influential House Committee on Foreign Affairs, engineered a program whereby the United States could wage war and still be seen as a peace-loving nation. To do this, they decried the evils of war, insisting the confrontation they promoted was a "defensive" one. They also had to show that war *should* be declared, that there was sufficient cause for it, and that it would be worth the cost. Furthermore, the war would have to give the nation an opportunity to prove its "manhood." The rhetoric of the War Hawks stressed Britain's hostile conduct toward the United States, while revealing that she was systematically trying to destroy America as a commercial rival and reduce the United States to a colonial state once again. By the close of 1811, the War Hawks felt secure in predicting a declaration of war was near at hand. Felix Grundy wrote in January 1812, "If War is not resorted to, one thing is certain to my mind, this nation or rather their representatives will be disgraced." Grundy may have been trying to placate the growing impatience in the West, where many were tiring of the tardy movement of Congress. "Words, words, words appear still to be the rage," one westerner complained of the Twelfth Congress. Yet to a man the War Hawks held out that war could be avoided *if* Great Britain would revoke her Orders-in-Council (maritime sanctions). Even before the Twelfth Congress met, Henry Clay stated that war was "inevitable" unless England rescinded her maritime restrictions. But after attending the British parliamentary debates in early 1812, American envoy Jonathan Russell concluded the British were inflexible on revoking the orders. "I no longer entertain a hope we can honorably avoid war," a somber Russell wrote in February 1812. (Ironically, the British Government *did* repeal the Orders-in-Council at approximately the same time as America declared war.)[47]

Congressman Felix Grundy, raised in the backcountry of Virginia and the Kentucky frontier, came to Tennessee about 1807 and established a thriving law practice in Nashville. Leading the pack of War Hawks in the Twelfth Congress that pressed for war, Grundy used the oratorical skills honed in the theatrical atmosphere of the western courtrooms. Grundy spoke eloquently and passionately on the "experiment" the United States was about to conduct if Congress declared war. He listed the grievances against Great Britain, focusing on the maritime sanctions levied on American shipping and, most importantly for the West, the instigation of the Indians on the frontier. The nation's honor had been insulted and no course of action besides war could right it. "I prefer war to submission!" Grundy loudly proclaimed in true western braggadocio. Yet like most vociferous War Hawks, Grundy appeared willing to drop the whole matter if Great Britain rescinded its Orders-in-Council. Grundy abhorred war but feared an unjust peace even more. But if war *were* to come, Grundy promoted the idea that Canada be the main target. The congressman referred to the Canadians as potential "adopted brethren," cleverly adding that annexation would have the political benefit for the North of offsetting the South's desire to claim the Floridas for the United States.[48]

Eventually, on the first day of June, 1812, President Madison delivered a war message to Congress behind closed doors. Madison addressed the issues of impressment and violations of commercial rights with a brief mention of Indian intrigues—conspicuously absent was any discussion about the acquisition of Canada and/or Florida. Madison challenged Congress by asking if the nation should "continue passive under these progressive usurpations and these accumulating wrongs, or, opposing force to force in defense of their national rights, shall commit a just cause into the hands of the Almighty Dispenser of Events." Two days later the House Committee on Foreign Affairs released its War Manifesto as a positive response to the president's message. The House immediately voted for war by a margin of 79 to 49. The Senate debated for two more weeks before ultimately giving its approval with a 19 to 13 vote. President Madison signed the declaration of war on the next day— June 18. On that day, Tennessee's George Washington Campbell, who had championed for war in the Senate, wrote to Governor Willie Blount: "The die is at length cast—the day of retribution is at length arrived, and the people of America, have an opportunity afforded them to avenge the wrongs they have been enduring for so many years." On the next day, Grundy penned an open letter to his Tennessee constituents, reminding them of their moral obligation to the revolutionary tradition. "Are we a degraded and degenerate race," he challenged, "or is the mighty spirit of our fathers in us?" "We shall prove ourselves worthy to be called Freemen," answering his own question, "by which we shall show that our fathers have not bled in vain." War had finally come. Upon receiving the official notification of the declaration of war, Governor Willie Blount penned a response to Secretary of War James Monroe assuring the Madison administration of Tennessee's support and loyalty to the cause: "I view this declaration of war by our government in the light of a renewal of the previous declaration of American liberty and independence, which, I doubt not, the whole people of the Untied States are determined to hand down to posterity unaltered except by their exertions, to make them shine more brightly." Congressman John Rhea of Tennessee later summed up what he felt America was fighting for: "We are contending for our rights, liberties, constitution, and Government and Soil—Great Britain is contending to destroy our rights and liberties, to subvert our constitution and Government, and to reduce and subdue our Soil to his own use." Rhea painted a simple picture in black and white that no-nonsense westerners could relate to—it only remained now to see if America could pass the test of war.[49]

2

The Nashville *Clarion* publicized the news of the declaration of the "second war for independence," appropriately, on the Fourth of July. An express rider thundered into the state capital the evening before, with President Madison's proclamation in hand. The significance of the news arriving on the eve of the Fourth of July was not lost on the *Clarion*'s editor. "It was this day 36 years ago that the American people declared themselves free from the tyranny of George the third," he articulated, "and we are highly gratified to find this second declaration proves that the people of the present day have still some of the spirit of their forefathers, and are determined to fight for the rights acquired by them." A timely letter from Felix Grundy accompanied the news. "The national legislature has done its duty," Grundy trumpeted, "It now remains for the people of the United States to show themselves Americans." The announcement of war set off wild celebrations across the state—parades, bonfires, rifle salutes, and, of course, the obligatory toasts, like that of Governor Willie Blount, who saluted the memory of George Washington and the heroes of '76. George Wilson, editor of the *Knoxville Gazette*, reported citizens enthusiastically shaking hands with each other and meeting at the Globe Inn to raise a glass (or two) in honor of the occasion. "The American Eagle has risen from her nest of peace," Wilson gloated, "& the British lion with his allies of the forest will tremble beneath her soaring."[1]

Tennessee land speculator Moses Fisk, formerly of Massachusetts, chastised his minister brother for delivering a sermon back home condemning the unjustness of the war: "None, as it seems to me, was ever juster. . . . The British government (favorites of Heaven you call them, I call them anointed felons) are responsible for all the mischiefs [*sic*] to result from the war." Moses accused the New England clergy (including his brother) of siding with Great Britain. "This is a new way of praying for enemies," he spewed. This brand of Anglophobia permeated the writings and musings of most Tennesseans leading up to the war. A few months before the June 1812 declaration, one Tennessean, labeling himself "Americus," pronounced the clear advantage of a war with England: the annexation of Canada in the North and the Floridas in the South. "Americus" saw the expulsion of the British from the North American continent as "a great national object." Thus the expansionist tendencies of the western Jeffersonians were directly tied to an imbued hatred of Great Britain.[2]

As the Twelfth Congress forged legislation leading the nation to war in early 1812, it became apparent a large army of volunteers and militia would be necessary to conduct any sizeable military campaigns. The Volunteer Act of February 6, 1812, authorized the president to accept companies of volunteers not exceeding 30,000 men for a year, unless discharged earlier. Officers of units already organized were to remain at their posts; while officers of newly organized units were to be selected in accordance with state militia laws (this was later modified so that the president could appoint all company and field officers). In April 1812, Congress also authorized the president to require the governors of the states to call out 100,000 militiamen for a period of six months. Since all eligible men were, by law, already in the militia, volunteers had to come from those same militia ranks, thereby greatly affecting state organizations. Coupled with existing militia laws, the resulting confusion proved to be disastrous in terms of enlistment periods, as a frustrated Andrew Jackson would bitterly discover in late 1813.[3]

In the meantime, the Volunteer Act provided the initial opportunity for Tennesseans to join the fray. In announcing the February 6 act, Major General Andrew Jackson issued his divisional orders in late July 1812 with the idea his troops would be fighting in the South rather than in Canada. "Behold in the province of West Florida, a territory whose rivers and harbors, are indispensable to the prosperity of the Western, and still more so, to the eastern Division of our State," Jackson declared. Furthermore, West Florida, he added, was the "asylum from which an insidious hand incites to rapine and bloodshed, the ferocious savages," referring to supposed British instigation of the Creek Indians. A month later, when the secretary of war informed Governor Blount that Tennessee troops might be called into service on the northern frontier after all, Jackson quickly issued orders reflecting a possible change in plans. "Do not stand to stipulate for the theatre on which you are to fight," Jackson affirmed. "It is enough for a brave man to know that his country needs his services; no matter whether against the Creeks in the south, or the Showaneese [Shawnee] in the north; whether against the blacks at Pensacola, or the British in Detroit." To Jackson and many Tennesseans, it did not matter *where* the fight was as long as they could participate in it. Moreover, it seemed not to matter *who* they were fighting as long as they could brandish their swords against an enemy.[4]

Longing to win laurels on the field of battle, most Tennesseans seemed more than willing to do their duty. Peer pressure, via the press of the day, played a huge role in sustaining this sense of obligation. In late 1812, a Nashville newspaper published the names of men in Warren County who enlisted in a company led by Captain George W. Gibbs. These were men, according to the account, who showed "that they will serve in any station when their country require[s] their personal exertions." A Knoxville newspaper echoed the same sentiment when it reported on the mustering of a regiment of cavalry in early October 1812, where each man "felt the throbs of patriotic anxiety beat high in his bosom." When the regimental officers had asked for volunteers, only two men refused to step forward. The newspaper labeled the two shirkers as those "whose love of domestic enjoyments prevailed against that elastic courage which breaks from the shade of tranquility and peace." By appealing to the 1812 generation's fear of too much leisure and luxury, the newspaper challenged the men to act as their "fathers" had done. Colonel James Henderson of the Second Division broached the subject with less subtlety. "Every one that has tendered his services, as a volunteer, to the President, and now refuses to shoulder his gun, will draw on himself the contempt of unborn thousands," Henderson admonished in a published address. The fact that most men in a captain's company of volunteers or militia knew each other as friends, neighbors, or family relations must have influenced enlistment numbers, not to mention camaraderie in the field.[5]

This "camaraderie" sometimes found itself overshadowed by the concern that one's neighbor might be a British informer. In the initial stage of the war, British aliens posed a more immediate threat to the security of the United States than British soldiers—enough so that legislators felt obligated to assess the danger by reviving the 1798 Alien and Sedition Acts in which unnaturalized British males over the age of fourteen had to register with the federal government. In the 1812 version of this act, all male "enemy" aliens fourteen years of age and older had to report to the nearest US Marshal. The marshal compiled the names, ages, occupations, length and places of residence in the United States, the number of people in a family unit, and whether or not the individual had declared his intention to become an American citizen. The officer also supplied information about the alien's potential for causing trouble and forwarded his report to Washington. Most of the statistics found their way into the Navy Department files—an indication that the biggest fear revolved around collaboration with British naval squadrons operating off the Atlantic coast. Some ten thousand British males reported to US marshals and, in March 1813, the government ordered the relocation of certain aliens (including those engaged in the maritime trade or who had come to the United States since the outbreak of hostilities) to designated interior locations at least forty miles from the coast. All other categories of British subjects were permitted to remain in their usual places of residence, but their status was subject to monthly review.[6]

It is difficult to assess how the Alien Act affected Tennesseans, as there was no obvious naval sabotage to consider. Still, the notion of foreign subterfuge lent an air of paranoia concerning British "spies" in the state. A contributor to a Knoxville newspaper, calling himself "A Militia Man of 1808," sent out this near-fanatical warning: "England has her advocates, her supporters, and her spies—they are dispersed through our country, under different characters, pursuing different occupations—endeavouring to acquire the confidence of the people, that they may delude them—*enquire for them! Mark them! Watch them!!*" Records indicate that the federal marshals of East and West Tennessee did make an effort to register British aliens, but not without protest from some of the intended parties. In a published letter to the marshal of West Tennessee, English-born George Foster of Franklin County protested the Alien Act, saying he had come to America in 1790 at the age of seventeen and had fought in the Indian wars. He subsequently married, raised nine children, and made his living as a farmer and Baptist minister. "I feel as willing to support the government and fight in defence of the country as any man that can be found," Foster challenged. As a peaceful American, he believed the act violated the Constitution and his essential rights.[7]

Foster's profession of his loyalty to the United States may also have been for the benefit of his neighbors, whose Anglophobia reached new heights after the declaration of war in 1812. Those who opposed the war, whether British or not, were dubbed "Tories," a throwback to the term applied to Loyalists during the American Revolution. "A short life, and a hard death to all tories," went one volunteer toast at a Carthage, Tennessee, Fourth of July celebration in 1812. *Wilson's Knoxville Gazette* ran an article in October 1812 titled "The Hanging Party," declaring that all Tories deserved "elevation to the ridge pole of the gallows." In a Nashville newspaper, a piece written by "Long Tom" extended the distrust of tories to a pronouncement of treason: "I believe that any man whose sentiments are not now wholly with the general government, is a Tory; and that the moment he puts his sentiments into the form and feature of opposition, he is a TRAITOR." "For the first complaint, a simple dose of Tar and Feathers is recommended as an infallible cure," Long Tom hinted, "But for the second, Hemp is the most sovereign specific."[8]

Long Tom's allusions to tar and feathering, as well as hanging, harkened back to the American Revolution, when Loyalists suffered such indignities and crimes, causing some to exodus to Canada. Founding Father Thomas

Jefferson likened those opposing the War of 1812 to the Tories of the American Revolution. In 1810, Revolutionary War veteran John Sevier predicted another war with Great Britain, admitting that "we shall have to cope again with the old Tory party." In a July 1812 letter to Governor Blount, Lieutenant Colonel John Anderson of Bledsoe County suggested that all militia officers be required to take an oath of allegiance, as there are "many old Tories and fools" in the county. Anderson suggested that "a few waggon Loads of them to Quebeck" would alleviate the problem. The volunteer spirit of Tennessee may have been partially sparked by a need to demonstrate one's uncompromised patriotism to his peers.[9]

Despite the unabashed enthusiasm states such as Tennessee exhibited, the Volunteer Act of 1812 proved to be "extremely unproductive," according to President Madison in August of that year. Still, Madison knew he must rely on volunteers "who may be presumed will cross the line without raising constitutional or legal questions." In order to understand the nature of Madison's predicament, one must examine the structure of the militia as it existed in the period of the early republic. Basically state controlled, the militia lacked a uniformity, which stifled concerted efforts to mobilize them into the war effort. To be sure, the state governors wielded more power over the militia than the president. Short enlistment terms and lack of training plagued the militia, making it an ineffective force. In addition, the US Regular Army suffered from recruiting difficulties that were never resolved during the war, that is, a lack of reorganization, broken logistical systems in supplies and weapons, and, especially, poor leadership. In 1813 a Tennessee militiaman named Jesse Denson published a small book on science and history in which he defined "Militia Men" as those who "should strive to acquire military knowledge, be obedient to their officers, and accustom themselves to bodily exercises." A militia signified citizens taking their obligations seriously and behaving with public virtue. Militia participation reinforced a masculine self-identity by sustaining a unified white male community, excluding "others" such as women and minorities. Muster days enforced this combination of solidarity and exclusion. Social status usually determined the selection of the militia officers—those being landholding neighbors who had the reputation for getting things done and, thus, demanded respect and homage. Once gained, military titles were retained with pride and preferred over political ones. (George Washington preferred to be called "General" even after elected president, as did Andrew Jackson.) The discipline militia officers sought reflected the order and deference required in a hierarchical community. The wording of an 1813 document commissioning a captain in the Tennessee militia indicated the officer "is hereby required to obey his superior officers lawful commands; and all officers and privates under his command are to be obedient to him as captain." Yet obedience in a democratic, frontier society often came reluctantly, as the officers of the militia and volunteers were soon to find out in the War of 1812.[10]

The Uniform Militia Act of 1792 provided the basis for militia organization in the United States throughout the nineteenth century. According to this act, all able-bodied white males between the ages of eighteen and forty-five (with some exceptions) were required to enroll in their state's militia, furnishing their own stand of arms. The act allowed individual states to organize and train their militia in their own fashion. Militiamen called into national service were limited to three months service per year. Volunteer companies could be authorized by the president (up to thirty thousand men) if they provided their own arms and equipment. This volunteer service was to last one year from the mustering date, and it was this act that Congress reapproved in February 1812. Repeated attempts to remodel the 1792 act resulted in failure, and it remained basically intact throughout the nineteenth century.[11]

Regimental musters occurred once a year, with not much in the way of actual military training taking place at the annual event. Often meeting at the county seat, the muster became the basis for tax collecting and elections—many state and national elections were held on muster days—thus becoming an occasion for political meetings, other social events, and even drunken brawls. Because officers were elected by popular vote, there was no guarantee they would be qualified to train the men in the proper military fashion. It is little wonder, then, that Governor Blount encouraged the Tennessee General Assembly in September 1812 to purchase military handbooks, emphasizing that "such books are much wanted here at a crisis like the present and would at any time be useful in the hands of the militia."[12]

Statistics show that Tennessee claimed 29,183 active members of the state militia in 1812—the first year the state filed such a report to the federal government. Interestingly, less than half of that number possessed firearms, a refutation of the myth of the sharp-shooting frontier backwoodsman. Volunteer companies, operating under the same rules as other militia companies, comprised a small but significant component of the state militia system, as they enjoyed a certain amount of autonomy: holding their own elections, choosing their own uniforms, and fixing the time and place of musters. Each regiment of militia could organize one volunteer company of light infantry, and in 1807 the legislature authorized a company of volunteer riflemen to be raised in each county. Most of the staff and rank of volunteer militia units were upper-class citizens who had the time, affluence, and social prestige to devote to "soldiering." The units adopted names such as "Nashville Blues" (signifying the color of their tailor-made uniforms) and acted as much as a social organization as a military one. Rufus Morgan, a successful merchant in Knoxville, organized (at his own expense) a company of "choice lads" in September 1813 to march against the Creek Indians. These volunteer militia units reflected the class divisions existing in antebellum America in that the connotation of a "volunteer" carried more prestige than a "drafted" militiaman.[13]

Militiamen absent from regimental musters were fined by a court-martial, but offenders generally ignored the penalty. A nineteen-year-old Tennessean from Sumner County named Palemon Winchester actually challenged the fine. A regimental court-martial in February 1814 at Cairo fined Winchester for nonperformance of a draft for a tour of duty during the Creek War. Palemon's father, Stephen Winchester (brother of James Winchester), petitioned, on his son's behalf, circuit court judge Thomas Stuart in March 1814 on the basis that Governor Blount had no constitutional right to call out the state militia during the Creek War. At issue was Section 36 of chapter one the Tennessee militia law of 1803, which read: "That in case of actual invasion or incursion, or an invasion threatened or premeditated, against this state or any part thereof, then it shall be lawful for the governor for the time being, or any officer by him directed, to order into actual service all or such parts of the militia as the exigency may require." Since the Uniform Militia Act of 1792 specified that only the president could call out the militia in such circumstances, Winchester contended that Blount had exceeded his authority. Furthermore, was it lawful to send the militia outside the boundaries of the state to fight the Creek Indians? "The King Can do no wrong," Winchester sarcastically wrote of Blount's unconstitutional power. Judge Stuart gave his opinion in a reply of March 11, 1814: "It seems to me the Governor is by law made the judge whether an invasion is premeditated or not and that it would be subversive of all military order and discipline to suppose the soldiers if they thought differently from the Governor on that point. . . . I think the Militia ought to presume the order to be legal unless it manifestly appears to be illegal and unconstitutional on the face of it." Addressing the question of sending the troops beyond the limits of the state, Stuart asked and then answered the question: "Is it lawful to order the militia beyond the limits of the State? I know of no law which prohibits it. . . . Might not the intended invasion be most effectually expelled and prevented by attacking and destroying the enemy in their own country?" Stuart went on to point out that the president did, indeed, call upon the Tennessee militia in 1812 (although not for an invasion of the Creeks) and the Creek Nation was within the limits of the United States. Curiously, despite Stuart's lengthy opinion, he hesitated in making a final decision on the case, opting for the state Supreme Court to do so (no such case has been found; perhaps the war concluded before a decision was reached).[14]

The case is remarkable for the fact that someone would actually refute the governor's actions indicates not everyone agreed with the state's eagerness to wage a war. Judge Stuart's firm opinion on the matter sided with the governor's, yet the judge's reluctance to make a final decision shows a lack of commitment to the finality of the militia laws (or, perhaps, a sign of deference to Stephen Winchester, an important citizen of Sumner County). Also, the case shines a light on the ambiguity of constitutional law regarding the militia. During the War of 1812, Massachusetts and Rhode Island initially refused to commit troops to the war effort—an obvious contradiction to presidential powers—and Connecticut constantly bickered with President Madison over the use of state militia in federal service. These snubs illustrated the vital role states played regarding the militia, yet it was Congress that supposedly had the final say in all matters pertaining to the militia. The situation was different on the frontier, whose history of border warfare included a denunciation against the lack of federal intervention in protecting exposed settlements to Indian attacks. As a result, the tradition of the militia as the bulwark of democracy remained entrenched in the thinking of most backcountry settlers (who participated in the militia system in one form or another).[15]

In October 1812, Secretary of War William Eustis provided the impetus for Tennessee's first organized efforts in the War of 1812. Instructing Governor Willie Blount to call out and equip 1,500 of the state's militia, Eustis requested that Blount order these troops, and any volunteers, to make their way to New Orleans for the defense of the "lower country." The men were expected to provide their own arms and equipment, while the government supplied all other camp equipage. One Tennessee volunteer summed up the subsequent Natchez Expedition of 1812/13, fifty years after the fact. He recalled enlisting under General Andrew Jackson and descending the Cumberland, Ohio, and Mississippi Rivers to Natchez and "after remaining there some time, marched back by land, and were discharged at Columbia, Tennessee, without having achieved any exploit worthy of communication." "I never knew the object of the expedition," he acknowledged, "but supposed it was to have a force within easy distance of New Orleans, in case the enemy made an attack on that city." At the time, however, the pomp and circumstance of the expedition provided the press with an opportunity to exploit the state's patriotic fervor. The Nashville *Clarion* provided a glowing account of the troops rendezvousing at Nashville for an expedition most of them thought would take them to New Orleans and then to Mobile and Pensacola. The appointed day, December 10, 1812, was bitterly cold, with piercing northeast winds and snow continually falling during the day. Beginning before eight in the morning, troops amounting to 1,800 men started to come into Nashville, pitching their tents on the hills overlooking the town. The newspaper claimed no complaints were registered, despite the frigid weather and lack of blankets (one for every three men) and tents (nine or ten men per tent). The following day an additional two hundred men came, and for three days all endured the most dismal of conditions, yet "no men ever did or ever can put up with the hardships with a more cheerful acquiescence than these volunteers." The emphasis was on order, harmony, and hardiness. Neither inclement weather nor a lack of supplies would deter "Columbia's true sons" (as Andrew Jackson described them) from doing their duty.[16]

But cracks began to appear beneath the surface of this spotless canvas. In addition to the bad weather and inadequate supplies, a shortage of bank funds to convert the soldiers' pay of government notes into specie added to the woes of the proposed mission. In order to kick-start the expedition, Jackson convinced the bank at Nashville to issue one-third of the funds needed in specie to district paymaster Alpha Kingsley, with the remainder in post notes. In addressing the troops on the last day of 1812, Jackson reminded the volunteers they had tendered their services "from the most patriotic motives" and not pecuniary ones. "Take care how you indulge this restless disposition, least the world should say that you are *ostensible* patriots, but *real mercenaries*," he warned. A few isolated desertions notwithstanding, the troops rendezvousing at Nashville that winter of 1812 answered the call of their country, leaving their homes and occupations to volunteer for service in a remote section of the nation. Governor Blount, addressing them on December 19, expressed his gratitude for their volunteering spirit, which "affords certain proof that you are not only true citizen-soldiers in principle, but further prove, that you are the patriotic sons of the patriots of the revolution now at your posts, ready to defend your rights and privileges which the heroes of the revolution obtained for you." Blount thrust the specter of the American Revolution in front of the volunteers' faces, knowing phrases such as "patriotic sons of the patriots" resonated confidence in their minds that they had taken the proper action. "This army is composed, of citizens, of the best families in the state," the *Clarion* pointed out—the deference paid to the volunteers illustrating the need to sustain the social order of the day.[17]

Finally, after the payment of the troops had been resolved, the grand expedition departed for Natchez (Mississippi Territory) where they were to await further orders from Brigadier General James Wilkinson in New Orleans. The First Regiment, led by Colonel William Hall, embarked from Nashville on January 9, 1813, joining Colonel Thomas Hart Benton's Second Regiment at

Robertson's landing (six miles below Nashville) later that day. On the next day, January 10, the flotilla began its water-bound journey that would traverse the Cumberland, Ohio, and Mississippi Rivers. The army arrived near its destination on February 15, 1813, after a voyage marked by frigid weather, ice blocks in the river, sinking boats, a lack of provisions, and desertions. Two soldiers died during the voyage, both from the Second Regiment. According to Andrew Jackson Edmondson, a volunteer in Captain Thomas Williamson's company, Private John Rogers died of heart pleurisy on January 23, having been unable to speak for three days prior to his demise. General Jackson instructed that the body be laid out "in the neatest clothing he has" before interment at Fort Massac (on the Ohio River) on January 24. On that day, Rogers's body was taken to the fort and buried during an impressive and solemn ceremony. The regimental musicians accompanied the service with the mournful strains of an old Scottish tune known as "Logan Water." It rained during the burial. Just a few days prior to his demise, Rogers penned a poem intended for his wife back in Nashville. It was ironically titled "The Farewell":

> Hark! Hark my dear, the trumpet sounds,
> 'Tis honor calls to war;
> Now love I leave, perhaps for wounds,
> And beauty for a scar.
> But ah! Suppress those rising sighs,
> Ah! Check that falling tear;
> Lest soft distress from lovely eyes,
> Create a new-born fear.
> My life to fame devoted is,
> No fear my fair I know,
> And if [I] now desert that cause;
> Ah! whither shall I go.
> It is not fame alone invites,
> Tho' fame this bosom warms;
> My country's violated rights
> Impel my soul to arms.

Rogers's widow would be the first of hundreds of Tennessee wives to know the dire consequences of having their husbands hear "the trumpet sounds."[18]

Aside from the pathos of the circumstances surrounding the poem, the writing is interesting in that it expresses *why* some Tennesseans took up arms in the War of 1812. An inner drive for "fame," along with the motive of his country's rights having been violated, animated Rogers's actions. In the first instance, the quest for "fame" (or glory) was strong among males of the early republic—sometimes to the detriment of their familial relations. "Do not My beloved Husband let the love of Country fame and honour make you forget you have me," Rachel Jackson once implored her glory-seeking husband.[19] John Rogers was willing to risk his life for the ephemeral laurels that war offered. The other motivation of "violated rights" indicates the success of the War Hawk rhetoric Tennessee politicians espoused and the Republican press propagated. Rogers voluntarily joined other like-minded "patriotic sons" to defend his country's (and, in a sense, his own) honor, no matter what the cost.

The chroniclers of the voyage missed no opportunity to wax poetic on the epic significance of the flotilla. Sailing down the Cumberland River, near Eddyville, Kentucky, Methodist preacher Lerner Blackman performed a religious service on the roof of one of the boats. A contemporary writer portrayed the scene with an allusion to Anglo-American superiority: "Thirteen companies of infantry with officers, a general, his staff and, suite, were formed on the tops of a number of boats floating together. A Minister of the Christian religion, stood upon a pulpit in the midst of them; and the gospel morality of Christ was heard to resound upon the bosom of a river and upon the spot, where, within the memory of several present, the Buffalo had come to drink; the Indians to way-lay the solitary travelers, and the enterprising whiteman had cautiously crept along, in continual peril of his life." The image of a Christian minister exhorting the Word to his flock amid a gathering of boats on a majestic river no doubt inspired even the basest of men. But even inspiration has its price: on one occasion, Reverend Blackman was preaching on the roof of Captain Williamson's boat when the roof caved in, causing the minister and a dozen others to fall through in mid-sermon "to the great astonishment of the Prea[c]her and others." A shaken-but-still-inspired Blackman finished preaching aboard Captain Isaiah Renshaw's boat, which was lashed to Williamson's unlucky vessel. Blackman conducted future prayer services in a canoe where he stood in the center with a soldier on each side of him, while a steersman kept the boat steady.[20]

As Jackson's flotilla made its way down the western watercourses, Colonel John Coffee's cavalry and mounted infantry took a land route to the Lower Country. In a January 2, 1813, letter to his young wife, Mary, Coffee's strong sense of duty explained *his* reasons for joining the Natchez Expedition: "[I] have resolved to do my duty at the sacrifice of my dearest interest and wishes, and I know you will, like a true patriot, applaud my resolution." Coffee's mounted men left Franklin, Tennessee, in mid-January 1813 and reached the Tennessee River on January 25, marching at a rate of 20 to 23 miles per day in severe rains and snow. Taking two days to cross the river at Colbert's Ferry, the regiment entered "enemy" territory but experienced no difficulty in traversing through Indian country. On the contrary, Coffee noted the Indians they encountered were "remarkably accommodating" to his troops, feeding both troops and horses. Surprisingly, Coffee discovered that many Indians left their homes on hearing the approach of his army, as many of them were under the impression the troops would seize their property without any compensation. One rumor even had the Americans planning to assassinate George Colbert, "half-breed" owner of the ferry at the Tennessee River. Taking the well-traveled Natchez Trace, it took the cavalry four weeks to arrive near Natchez—February 16—amazingly on the same day as Jackson's flotilla disembarked at the town.[21]

Upon arrival, Jackson issued regimental orders warning the men not to indulge in "profane Swearing"—something of a paradox considering that Natchez had a reputation for being a place where blasphemers, adulterers, and fornicators were tolerated. "The eyes of the American Nation are upon us," he reminded them, "we are the forlorn hope of the militia of the Union." Once all of the components of Jackson's army rendezvoused, they made their way to Fort Washington, an encampment located near the capital of the Mississippi Territory, several miles from Natchez. There, Jackson and his men found the fort in a state of decay, "the houses rotting down, and a collection of as much filth that with one week's sun would create a plaige [sic]." Jackson opted to pitch his army's tents west of the capital where there was a plentiful supply of wood, good water, and an open field for military exercise and training. Once settled, the army proceeded to await further orders from New Orleans—instructions that never came. Jackson penned a letter to James Wilkinson, informing him he had arrived and would be ready to move his troops at a moment's notice. "My wish is to keep them employed in active service, as Indolence creates disquiet," Jackson wrote, "I have marched with the true spirit of a soldier to serve my country at any and every point where service can be rendered." Jackson did not know (nor Wilkinson, for that matter) that a brief communication from the War Department, dated February 5, 1813, was making its way to the Mississippi Territory, instructing Jackson that his army's services were no longer required and that they were now dismissed. In the meantime, Jackson conducted several communications with Wilkinson at New Orleans, who insisted Jackson remain where he was, as he had no orders from the War Department specifying exactly what Jackson's army was to do. An impatient Jackson waited out the weeks and frustratingly wrote on March 4, 1813: "I am here without any advice orders or directions, as to my future operations—no enemy to face—or any thing to do."[22]

Jackson's officers shared his frustration in playing the waiting game. John Coffee wrote to his wife in late February that the troops were in fine health, but with no orders to march. "We consented to the sacrifice of leaving our homes, our families and all our individual interest," Coffee lamented, "but in that hope I now suppose all will be disappointed." Another officer reiterated Coffee's estimation, adding: "I wish from my soul and I believe almost all the army wish it too, that we had been ordered to Canada, where we could have been of more service than we shall be here." Frequently fighting boredom, the Tennessee troops sometimes succumbed to the temptations held out by neighboring Natchez. When four Tennessee officers were arrested for visiting a brothel in Natchez, Colonel Thomas Benton personally chastised one of the offenders, a lieutenant, with a scathing reprimand: "For an officer to go contrary to orders . . . as you have done to go to such a place as Under-the-Hill as it is called, the place where Hell reigns on earth, where the refuse of creation assembles—this sir is a thing that pains me to think about & which I never want to talk in public again." Reverend Blackman continued to sermonize to the troops and even tried his hand at forming a Bible Society, but, as Ensign Edmondson related, "soldiers here [are] not the people to give such encouragement to such an institution."[23]

James Wilkinson rightly predicted to Secretary Armstrong that an order for Jackson's army to disband "will come like a thunder clap on Jackson." Then, on March 15, Jackson received the secretary of war's February 5 message dispersing the Tennessee Volunteers and instructing the army to hand in all its arms and supplies. A vexed Jackson immediately fired off several letters expressing his intense frustration. In a strongly worded letter to Secretary Armstrong, Jackson reminded him what a precarious position the orders placed Jackson's army in: eight hundred miles from home, with no supplies, and being forced to march through the "barbarous clime" of Indian territory. Jackson frankly stated it was an order "to consign to destruction a well organized detachment of near two thousand men." Jackson wrote to congressman Felix Grundy on the same day, calling Armstrong "this new incumbent who must have been drunk when he wrote [the order]." To his wife, Rachel, Jackson took on a kindlier persona, vowing "to act as a father to the sick and to the well and stay with them until I march them into Nashville." He then wrote Governor Blount to see if the state government would cover the expenses for the return march to Nashville from Colbert's Ferry. Jackson pledged to personally cover the expenditures to that point, keeping some supplies for the sick (who were transported by eleven baggage wagons, a few packhorses, and some officers' horses).[24]

The Tennessee Volunteers left Camp Jackson on March 25 and set a course up the Natchez Trace for a journey few would ever forget: heavy rains (producing mud up to the soldiers' knees), hot, blistering weather where oxen gave out under the heat, broken wagons, waist-high swamps and creeks that had to be crossed, and the constant threat of rattlesnake bites. Several men had to be left behind because of severe illness. On April 20, after an exhaustive march home, the troops were mustered out at Columbia, Tennessee. Many of the men arrived in Nashville two days later to the plaudits of a thankful citizenry. The *Clarion* made sure to emphasize that many of the volunteers extolled the virtues of Jackson, saying he was truly a "father" to them, giving his own riding horse to the sick. At Clover Bottom, near Jackson's Hermitage home, the cavalry paraded before being mustered out, significantly shouting out three loud huzzas of "Canada and Victory" before disbanding. Jackson, attempting to put a positive spin on the unproductive expedition, felt he had succeeded in instilling discipline and subordination into raw troops taking the field for the first time. This estimation justified the remark he made regarding December 10, 1812—the day the volunteers rendezvoused at Nashville—when he proclaimed it "the proudest day of my life." Jackson also declared December 10 to be "the proudest [day] for *West* Tennessee, reflecting the distinction between the two rival divisions. Yet the true significance of the Natchez Expedition may be that once again the federal government displayed an utter lack of urgency to western needs—a circumstance that encouraged Tennessee to stand on its own when it came to military matters.[25]

At the same time West Tennesseans were congregating on the tented fields outside of Nashville, a similar expedition was afoot across the state, but with a different destination. On December 3, 1812, John Williams of Knoxville, a lawyer and soldier of fortune, wrote to Secretary of State James Monroe asserting that since the government "will shortly wish to occupy the Floridas, I determined to collect some military force and march directly to that Quarter." Williams indicated that 165 mounted men had responded to his call and would march on the next day, "where it will afford us pleasure to execute the orders of the President." Madison must have raised his eyebrows when he read the final statement in Williams's missive: "In executing your orders not a man in this corps will entertain constitutional scruples on the subject of *boundaries*." The specific target of Williams's proposed expedition—East Florida—was a region bogged down in international intrigue, and soon to become a diplomatic nightmare for the United States. (As a matter of fact, when John Shaw [commander of the New Orleans station for the US Navy] learned of Congress declaring war on Great Britain in June 1812, he expressed surprise the United States had not declared war on Spain rather than England.)[26]

In January 1812 Congress passed a secret act authorizing the president to take possession of the Floridas in the event that foreign powers should attempt to confiscate them or if Spain surrendered them. In that same month, Secretary of State Monroe sent a two-man delegation—General George Mathews and Colonel John McKee (both of Georgia)—to negotiate with Spanish authorities and carry out the intentions of the undisclosed act. The "foreign powers" Monroe alluded to actually came down to one: Great Britain. In his November 2, 1811, communication with a British envoy, Monroe summed up the administration's stance on East Florida: "Situated as east Florida is, cut off from other possessions of Spain, and surrounded in a great measure by the territory of the United States . . . and having also an important bearing on our commerce, no other power could think of taking possession of it, with other than hostile views." Mathews, a former governor of Georgia, raised a group of Georgia volunteers (labeled as the "Patriots") who, in turn, established an independent Republic of Florida, hoisting their flag on the Florida side of the Saint Mary's River (the northern boundary of East Florida) at Amelia in March 1812. The Patriots, supported by US gunboats and troops, took over the town of Ferdinand and then laid siege to Saint Augustine in April 1812. Paradoxically, the Spanish residents of Saint Augustine, suffering from an economic depression, initially welcomed the Patriots, but the Americans, instead of conducting a coordinated take over of the town, idly wasted their time, creating havoc and destroying property.[27]

In the meantime, under pressure from Federalists and some northern Republicans who withheld their approval of the "revolt," Monroe apologized to the Spanish, admitting Mathews had exceeded his authority, and vowed to remove all American troops from East Florida. The Milledgeville *Georgia Journal* thought differently: "Isn't it better that our government should take St. Augustine, Pensacola, and Mobile while they are weakly garrisoned and not able to make formidable resistance or wait until they fall into the hands of the British and are strongly garrisoned?" Mathews, already disavowed by the federal government, died in August 1812. Georgia governor David B. Mitchell assumed control of the situation and arranged amnesty for the Patriots, a move bound to anger Spanish officials. In the fall of 1812, responding to rumors the Spanish had encouraged Indian and slave insurgency against Americans in East Florida, Governor Mitchell addressed the state legislature to take under consideration the occupation of East Florida. The Georgia legislature, however, deemed any such measure by the state, without federal approval, as unconstitutional. It was at this juncture that John Williams and his Tennessee Volunteers came onto the scene.[28]

In addition to territorial expansion, the situation in East Florida presented two looming issues: Indian depredations and runaway slaves—very often the two were interrelated. Although the figures are unclear, thousands of slaves from Georgia and South Carolina fled to East Florida during and right after the Revolutionary War. Always a haven for runaway slaves, it was estimated that at the time England retroceded East Florida to the Spanish in 1783, there were approximately nine thousand blacks residing there. Intermingling with the Seminole Indians, runaway slaves in East Florida lived under better conditions than their southern counterparts and fought with desperation during the Patriot War because they had more to lose than the Spanish or Indians. Armed Indians and blacks fighting together presented a formidable enemy, militarily and psychologically, to American whites. In reality, some of the East Tennessee "patriots" may have been lured by the prospect of plunder—especially the capture of black women and children to be sold into slavery.[29]

In July 1812, the Seminoles, reasoning that the Americans would soon be attacking them, went on the offensive and raided white plantations along the Saint Johns River with a force that included black Seminole warriors. In the following month, Americans responded with 250 volunteers led by Major Daniel Newman of Georgia on an ill-fated expedition to destroy the Alachua towns of the Seminoles—a campaign marked by devastating hunger and illness. The failure of this campaign, coupled with reports of large numbers of free blacks fighting in Florida, spread alarm throughout the region and up into East Tennessee. By November 1812, John Williams began making "some stir here," according to one East Tennessean, "endeavoring to collect some force, who will, on their own expences [sic], march to East Florida." In that month, Williams circulated a broadside, declaring the proposed expedition to be a "glorious opportunity" for East Tennesseans "to evince their patriotism, and preserve their right to the liberty they enjoy." Predictably blaming England for the current unrest among the Indians, Williams used the standard ploy that Great Britain "[has] enlisted under their banners, the savages, those hell hounds fitted only for deeds of ferocity, who seek victory by the indiscriminate slaughter of all ages and sexes." Williams called on his fellow East Tennesseans to volunteer in sharing "the dangers and glories of the field" rather than face "the slow formality of being dragged from home by compulsory orders." "Freemen ought to risk something," he challenged, "let us go on our own expenses . . . if we can be useful to our country, we will be more than compensated." Williams also called for each soldier to bring his own horse and arms. Unlike the Natchez Expedition of West Tennessee, where payment of troops represented a stumbling block from the onset, the campaign conducted by the East Tennesseans became totally self-supporting—a factor that may have been the difference between a force totaling only two hundred men versus two thousand. Nevertheless, both expeditions boasted that their forces comprised the best men of the region. Williams's broadside proudly mentioned that John Cocke, major general of the East Tennessee militia, had "patriotically enrolled himself as a common soldier." John Cocke's father, the sixty-three-year-old Judge William Cocke, served as a private on the campaign. The importance of all of this rested on the fact that *something* was being done. "I am anxious East Tennessee should do something—not in boasting, but in fighting," decried one East Tennessean, "I am sick of newspaper heroes, of 4th July toast-makers, & town-meeting volunteers."[30]

The East Tennessee Volunteers rendezvoused at Knoxville on December 1, 1812, and left for East Florida three days later. Trekking through the Carolinas, the army traveled anywhere from twelve to twenty-five miles a day before reaching Georgia two weeks later. The march was marked by supply shortages, an occasional fistfight, and a few accidental shootings. One volunteer from Greene County attempted to desert and found himself drummed out of the ranks to the fifer's tune of the Rogue's March, after having one side of his face and head shaven in the presence of the army. Williams stopped at Sparta, Georgia, where he sent word on December 25 to Brigadier General Thomas Flourney (at Saint Marys) concerning the approach of the East Tennessee army. On January 5, 1813, Williams received Flourney's reply, instructing him to advance. Five days later the Tennessee Volunteers arrived at the mouth of the Saint Marys River. With a population of about six hundred, the town of Saint Marys was a center of trade between the Americans and Seminoles—the latter providing beef, pork, venison, and furs in exchange for ammunition, guns, shirts, cloth, pots, and beaver traps—thus proving that no matter how much Americans and Seminoles distrusted one another, both depended on each other for their economic well-being. Across the shores of the Saint Marys River lay East Florida and Williams's "glories of the field."[31]

On February 2, 1813, Flourney directed Williams and his East Tennesseans to attack only those Seminoles hostile to the United States—specifically the Lotchaway tribe—but under no circumstances were they to engage with any Upper Creek Indians. The orders also specified to execute any captured blacks carrying arms, take all others prisoner, and burn all property that could not be transported back to base. On February 7, Williams united his Tennessee Volunteers with a regiment of US Regulars under the command of Colonel Thomas A. Smith, rendezvousing thirteen miles outside a Seminole stronghold known as King Paynes Town. At daylight the next day the Americans (now totaling about six hundred soldiers) charged into town with drawn bayonets but found the village deserted, as the Seminoles had fled on approach of the army. The frustrated Americans spent the night in the abandoned town and set the village on fire the next day, before setting out for another Seminole stronghold known as Bowlegs' Town, but it, too, proved to be deserted. However, on February 10, the Americans encountered a force of Indians and blacks outside of Bowlegs on an elevated tract of land referred to as the "Hammock" (hummock). The Americans unsuccessfully tried to lure out the concealed enemy, losing one officer in the process, while another officer received a severe wound in the hip in the act of bayoneting an Indian. The Americans spent the next several days destroying crops and villages, while confiscating as much property as they could. Williams cited burning 386 houses and absconding 250 horses, along with 300–400 cattle. Thus the East Florida Expedition concluded with very little fighting, some village burning, and a lot of confiscated plunder.[32]

By early March 1813, the East Tennessee volunteers were headed for home, having accomplished little militarily, but having established a reputation for themselves and their state. At Saint Marys, one resident mentioned the "Tennessee Volunteers" in a March 1813 letter, noting they had caused the Seminole Indians "to be quiet" as a result of the late expedition. William Cocke, the sixty-three-year-old volunteer, related to President Madison that the expedition had been "a feast to me to See the young men of my Country Vie with each Other who Should excel in Noble deeds." The fact that a body of Tennessee mounted gunmen, enlisting at their own expense to serve their country, played no small role in helping to foster the tradition of the Volunteer State. The expedition to East Florida presented an opportunity for East Tennesseans to prove their worth on the battlefield, especially in light of the West Tennesseans being offered the chance to do the same in the Mississippi Territory. It is highly significant that John Cocke, as a major general, would encourage East Tennesseans to seek their own "glories in the field" during the Creek War, illustrating yet again the competitive nature of the two divisions of the state. In Florida, the East Tennesseans *did* see a degree of action, albeit of a limited nature, allowing them some bragging rights. Many of the expedition's officers served in a similar capacity in the coming Creek War of 1813–14—some as volunteers and some in the Regular Army. The knowledge they gained in organizing, outfitting, and marching their troops to a distant outpost provided them with invaluable military experience.[33]

As to the so-called Republic of East Florida, the United States kept up a guarded policy after the 1812 "invasion." In January 1813, the Senate proposed a bill authorizing the president to occupy the land west of the Perdido River in West Florida, along with East Florida. After lengthy debates, that congressional body agreed to strike out the part concerning East Florida. The Senate's mind may have been changed by James Monroe's report indicating there was no evidence to support the claim that British troops had landed in East Florida, thus depriving the United States of a "legitimate" reason for invading the region. Yet because of the Napoleonic Wars, it was assumed Spain was now under the control of Britain, leaving the United States to adopt a wait-and-see attitude. The diplomatic snarl created by the uncertain American policy in East Florida—initially instigating a "revolution," then disavowing it—caused Tennessee senator George Washington Campbell to write Monroe in October 1813: "Our wavering policy respecting E. Florida, has brought on it, all the mischief, that usually attends such counsels."[34]

In summarizing East Tennessee's role in the Patriot War of East Florida, several factors must be examined. First, the expedition launched by John Williams exemplified the volunteer spirit of the state—a condition spawned from a history of subverting federal approval before taking independent action. When Williams wrote his December 1812 letter to President Madison, informing him that East Tennesseans were rendezvousing at Knoxville for an armed expedition into East Florida, Williams chastised the Georgia legislature for balking at sending its militia to East Florida without the federal government's go-ahead. "A considerable part of the Georgia Militia it is said have refused to afford relief to the troops of the United States Stationed at St. Johns from a fatal exposition of the constitution relative to the militia," a disapproving Williams wrote, insinuating that Tennesseans apparently had no such qualms. At the same time, Senator Joseph Anderson of East Tennessee introduced a resolution in Congress calling for a committee to consider legislation authorizing the president "to occupy and hold the whole or any part of East Florida." Legitimately or not, Tennessee seemed determined to make sure that East Florida did not fall into any other than American hands. This attitude stemmed from the Madison administration, which considered East Florida to be "essentially a British province" after 1812. America's manifest destiny in the Southeast during the period of the War of 1812 was largely based on obtaining territory before its enemy (Britain, more often than not) did; hence, even remote Cuba found itself under the eager eyes of expansionist Americans fearful of any type of British control over American commerce. Despite the general view that the land in East Florida was relatively worthless, Georgians and Tennesseans knew better. The region between the Saint Marys and Saint Johns Rivers was particularly alluring to Americans, as it had been settled by Virginians, Carolinians, and southern Georgians beginning in the 1790s, when Spain adopted a liberal land policy for Americans to revive settlement in East Florida. Subsequent commercial restrictions caused unrest among American settlers, who were willing to extend their allegiance to any government that would endorse their commercial enterprises.[35]

The southern theater of war in late 1812/early 1813 witnessed a generous outpouring of patriotic fervor, but little in the way of military contests. Martial-minded Tennesseans turned their direction to the North where the main thrust of the war operated. The initial invasion of Canada, led by Brigadier General William Hull in the summer of 1812, resulted in a miserable failure marked by the surrender of Hull's army (consisting mostly of American militia) in mid-August. Hull preceded his campaign with a proclamation issued in July 1812 informing the Canadians he possessed a force "prepared for every contingency" and had no doubt of his success. He warned the Canadian population that if they took part in the fighting, they would be treated as enemies, "and all the horrors and calamities of war will stalk before you." Furthermore, he promised a war of extermination if Indian allies were brought into play. "The first stroke of the tomahawk, the first attempt with the scalping knife, will be the signal of one indiscriminate scene of desolation," he threatened. "No white man found fighting by the side of an Indian will be taken prisoner; instant destruction will be his lot." Later, when Hull found himself surrounded at Detroit by British and Indian forces, British general Isaac Brock mockingly wrote to Hull: "It is far from my inclination to join in a war of extermination, but you must be aware, that the numerous body of Indians who have attached themselves to my troops, will be beyond my control the moment the contest commences." Hull, fearful of an Indian massacre, surrendered the next day.[36]

In truth, the American army under Hull, composed chiefly of Ohio militia, vastly outnumbered the opposing British and Indian forces, but Hull surrendered practically without a fight. The poor quality of Hull's troops, the rampant sickness in his army, and the lack of a steady supply of provisions all contributed to his decision. Still, American reaction to the disaster at Detroit was vehemently stacked against General Hull—some claiming treachery on the part of Hull as the only explanation for such a military calamity. Henry Clay revealed his contempt in a September 1812 letter: "It is impossible to give you an adequate idea of the sensations excited in this Country by the mortifying event at Detroit. . . . I do not think it worth investigation whether the act is to be attributed to treachery or cowardice. It was so shameful, so disgraceful a surrender, that whether it proceeded from the one or the other cause he deserves to be shot." Writing from Monticello, a fuming Thomas Jefferson agreed, insisting Hull be "shot for cowardice and treachery." The

Niles' Weekly Register pronounced that the whole nation was incensed "by the shameful surrender of general Hull." The Madison administration attempted to put a positive spin on the affair when James Monroe announced to Jefferson that "this most disgraceful event may produce some good . . . it will rouse the nation." Monroe's prediction nearly came true in Tennessee, where the legislature pondered over a memorial prepared by William Carroll and others seeking permission to raise a regiment to go to Detroit to aid the troops there—the state legislature to provide supplies and ammunition. However, the memorial landed on a committee desk with no further action taken.[37]

The attempt to recapture Detroit brought Tennessean James Winchester onto the war's northern theater of war. The sixty-year-old Revolutionary War veteran became a brigadier general in the Regular Army in April 1812, confined mostly to recruiting duties. After Hull's defeat, President Madison appointed him commander of the forces of the Northwest Army, a position William Henry Harrison claimed by right of his higher rank of major general in the Kentucky militia (despite the fact that Harrison was not a resident of that state). Extremely popular with his men, the younger Harrison agreed to accept a commission of brigadier general in the US Regulars if he was placed in overall command. Winchester, still outranking Harrison by date of commission, consented to an arrangement proposed by Harrison that they share the command, but the obvious rivalry between them caused a debilitating rift in the army's operations. Referred to as a "supercilious officer" by the Kentuckians, James Winchester nearly caused a mutiny in camp when the Kentucky troops learned of his appointment to command them. Winchester found himself the butt of practical jokes that bordered on cruelty: the men once sawed a pole used to sit on at a latrine so that it broke and the general fell into the filthy sinkhole. There may even have been a plot to thwart the success of Winchester's command by withholding supplies to his army. To be sure, Winchester's men were often barefoot, clad in rags, and dying by the dozens in his camp, resulting in mutinies and desertions by late 1812.[38]

Despite these setbacks, Winchester's army of 1,100 made its way near Frenchtown (present-day Monroe, Michigan) on the River Raisin in January 1813 to await the arrival of supplies and reinforcements from Harrison. While there, Winchester received a distress call from the village, claiming a force of five hundred British and Indians were about to besiege it, leading Winchester to dispatch five hundred men to Frenchtown where they took control of the village on January 18. Winchester fortified the town as best he could, but a British/Indian army of 1,200 attacked the Americans, cutting off any avenue of retreat, and Winchester was forced to surrender. Although the British colonel, Henry A. Proctor, promised to protect the captured

American prisoners, the Indians brutally murdered approximately sixty-five of them. Initial reports coming out of Kentucky indicated that one thousand Americans had been "cut to pieces, or taken prisoners, and the heart of Gen. Winchester cut out" (other reports stated Winchester had been tomahawked and scalped, with his entrails and tongue cut out). In reality, Winchester had been taken prisoner and spent the next year in confinement near Quebec, until his release by the British in April 1814.[39]

While the humiliating defeats were occurring in Canada, the fighting men of Tennessee were either languishing in camp in the Mississippi Territory or trudging through the swamps of East Florida vainly searching for an elusive enemy. Upon hearing of Winchester's disaster at Frenchtown, John Coffee wrote to his wife: "I would to God we had been with him, we would have changed the scene with those rascals—I expect we shall have to go there yet before they can be flogged." Coffee knew the nation's honor had been challenged and disgraced. Only a good drubbing of the British and their "hell hound" allies would put things straight.[40] The early months of 1813 had been calamitous: many Americans were chomping at the bit to fight, but indecisive leadership and diplomatic niceties stalled any positive efforts. When they did actually have the chance to battle, they were poorly supplied and indifferently led. The war had taken a torturous course in its early phases, causing its supporters to shake their heads in frustration and disbelief over the turn of events, while the war's detractors had the smug satisfaction of seeing their doubts realized. In Tennessee, there was a unanimity concerning the war's rationale, but little fortuity to flex the state's military muscles. That opportunity would come in the fall of 1813 and would launch Tennessee (and Andrew Jackson) headfirst into the fighting.

3

On Sunday, September 12, 1813, an express rider arrived in Nashville to hand Governor Willie Blount a shocking report "of the dreadful slaughter of several hundred of our fellow citizens by the Creek Indians." The dispatch referred to the massacre that had taken place on August 30 at the fortified stockade known as Fort Mims, located in a remote region of the Mississippi Territory (about forty miles north of Mobile in present-day Baldwin County, Alabama). The annihilation of hundreds of settlers by the warring faction of the Creeks—the Red Sticks—ignited a panic throughout the southern frontier.[1] Within a month of the incident, Tennessee declared war on the Creek Nation and initiated plans to conduct a coordinated campaign with Georgia, the Mississippi Territory, and elements of the US Regular Army to chastise the offending Creeks. But for various reasons the Americans' strategy never materialized and Tennessee took on the brunt of the 1813–14 struggles that came to be known as the Creek War.

Of the five tribes of Indians affiliated with the Old Southwest—Cherokee, Chickasaw, Choctaw, Creek, and Seminole—the Creeks were considered the most powerful at the onset of the nineteenth century. Geographical advantages made up much of this prestige; that is, the easy access to the Gulf of Mexico, their control of east–west routes, and their possession of highly prized land. Europeans had long recognized the key role the Creeks held and energetically sought their support or neutrality. Since the seventeenth century, the Creeks had been traditionally divided into the Upper Creeks (those towns situated along the Alabama, Coosa, and Tallapoosa Rivers) and the Lower Creeks (towns on the Chattahoochee and Flint Rivers). By the mid-eighteenth century, the Upper Creeks had increased in population and power, due in part to the avoidance of large-scale warfare and the adoption of the Natchez, Shawnee, and other refugee tribes. By 1764, the Upper Creek portion of the Creek "confederacy" consisted of thirty-nine towns with a population of nine thousand (by the War of 1812, the Creek population grew to twenty thousand, including five thousand warriors). Historically, the union of the Upper and Lower Creeks came about as a response to powerful outside forces that threatened them. Many of their languages were related but not mutually intelligible, and the confederation was merely one of convenience, as the real power lay in the individual villages. Thus the Creeks were composed of various tribes each with their own language and customs, structured by a kinship system based on matrilineal class and a clan system that helped to counter any factionalism. This cultural and ethnic diversity of the Creeks created a flexible political structure that proved to frustrate whites seeking land concessions and treaties.[2]

The transformation of Creek culture due to ties with European trade has been well documented.[3] Based primarily on the exchange of goods (particularly guns and cloth) for deerskins, the economic bond between the Creeks and the British reveals a sophisticated trade operating from the late seventeenth century forward. Creek political elites of the early, precolonial period used certain prestige goods to exercise dominance over their people. After contact with Europeans, individual households gained more access to these goods, as well as metals, thus enlarging their influence over all aspects of Creek social life while undermining the elites' monoploly of authority. European intervention also created an atmosphere of intense pressure between Indian societies competing for the highly sought European merchandise. White contact altered the economy of the Creeks by creating new roles for females (spinning cloth, for example), while the males adopted agriculture by which the Creek warriors felt subjugated, thus creating tensions between genders. In the decades following the American Revolution, when the deerskin economy began to fade, the Creeks adopted new conceptions of property—cattle, slaves, cotton—that fomented controversy about what kind of economy and leadership they should have, with many Creeks viewing these innovations as symbols of decay. More ruinous to Creek tradition than white intrusion was the establishment of wealthy half bloods, set apart from the rest of the tribe by accepting white ways, producing a class of people who became potential enemies within the tribe. Anti-American prophets, such as Josiah Francis, gradually succeeded to leadership roles. This eventually led to a civil war among the Creeks, spilling over into a conflict between Indians and white settlers, and giving US authorities an excuse to justify their policy of Indian removal.[4]

Federal policy after the American Revolution involved setting up a "factory" system (trading posts) designed to keep the Creeks dependent on American goods, but like trade with the British, the Creeks soon found themselves in debt, particularly after the decline of the skin trade at the end of the eighteenth century. As the price of goods rose, so did the Creeks' deficits—a condition President Jefferson took advantage of. The American solution demanded land cessions as payment while "civilizing" the Creeks through the introduction of mass agriculture so that they needed less land for hunting. The person assigned to mediate with the Creeks was Benjamin Hawkins of North Carolina, a revolutionary soldier and United States senator before being appointed an Indian agent by President Washington in 1796. He remained at his post, on the Flint River in Crawford County, Georgia, until his death in 1816, twenty years later. By all accounts, Hawkins was a dedicated and honest agent who genuinely looked out for the concerns of the Creeks—some whites saying he took interest in their affairs to an extreme. One observer noted: "Col. Hawkins I am convinced is a Man of great benevolence and seems strenuously disposed to better the Condition of Indians and to bring about an interchange of good office between them & white people, but I doubt if he will be able to effect this because the Georgians seem determined to get More Land from the Indians." Hawkins's loyalty to the cause of white settlers would be questioned throughout his tenure as Indian agent.[5]

At the onset of the American Revolution, the Creeks attempted to adopt a neutral stance until pressure from the British, in the form of an embargo, led the Creeks to conduct raids on the Americans, mostly on the Georgia frontier. In the aftermath of the Revolutionary War, most Creeks remained faithful to the British. "The Creeks are not disposed to have much intercourse with white people, especially foreigners, except with the English," wrote geographer Jervis Cutler in 1812. "Their prejudice is strong in favour of that nation, and they still believe 'the Great King over the water' is able to keep the whole world in subjection." In fact, the intertribal rivalry that precipitated the Creek War was caused, in part, by some key chiefs siding with the Americans in council disputes. One such leader, Big Warrior, actually led a pan-Indian movement in the first decade of the 1800s, but came over to the American side after the Red Stick movement gained ascendency. As a chief from the Upper Creek town of Tuckabatchee, in Creek councils he always stressed the futility of warring against the Americans. At one point, Big Warrior had even advocated the assassination of Tecumseh.[6]

Rumors of the Shawnee chief Tecumseh's visit to the southern tribes in the fall of 1811 had further acerbated the tension between the Creeks and Anglo-Americans. With his plan of an Indian confederacy in tow, Tecumseh left to visit the South in August 1811, returning in January of 1812. Having had limited success with the Chickasaws and Choctaws, he found more favor with the Upper Creeks, especially among the younger warriors. The Shawnees had lived, hunted, and fought with the Creeks in the past (Tecumseh's brother was killed in a raid on the Cumberland settlements in 1788), and both shared cultural intrusions by the whites. Furthermore, both nations felt British aid would help rid them of the Americans. The fact that Tecumseh and his party had to travel through western Tennessee (a region ostensibly under the control of the Chickasaws) to reach their destination alarmed an already-wary white population. Indeed, the state's plans to acquire western Tennessee were partly based on eliminating the routes between the northern and southern tribes. Concerned over reports of Tecumseh's visit, Governor Willie Blount wrote to the secretary of war on May 1, 1812, suggesting that troops and rangers be sent to the area between the Mississippi and Tennessee Rivers to cut off the line of communication between the northern and southern Indians. But before Washington received Blount's request, an incident occurred on the Duck River in West Tennessee that would change the course of affairs between the Creeks and Tennesseans and "set in motion a train of events that led to the expulsion of the last Indians from Tennessee," as one Tennessee historian has noted.[7]

The Duck River passed through Humphreys County (formed in 1809), an area freed from Indian claims by 1805, at which time a population surge began to fill the region. Suffice it to say that if Tennessee was a frontier in 1812, then Humphreys County was the "frontier" of the frontier. Because of its bordering on Indian territory, the county was subject to infrequent attacks. In May 1812, Creek Indians broke into the home of Jesse Manley, who was absent at the time. In the cabin were his wife, a neighbor's wife named Martha Crawley, and five children. Also on the premises was a young man asked by Jesse Manley to look after the families while he and John Crawley (Martha's husband) were on an errand to obtain some supplies. The details of what happened vary, according to what source is consulted—the only agreement being that Indians had killed several whites and abducted Martha Crawley.[8]

Put together from a variety of accounts, the "facts" are as follows. On the morning of May 12, 1812, a small party of Creek Indians (anywhere from five to sixteen) attacked the residence of Jesse Manley at a site known as McSims Bottom, about four miles above the mouth of the Duck River. A young man who was asked to protect the premises while the men were away became the first victim—he was killed in the yard outside the cabin. Upon hearing gunfire in the yard, Martha Crawley raised a loose plank from the cabin floor and hid at least one of her children. She then tried to bar the door with her back but it was soon tomahawked down. One of the intruders held Martha, pleading for her life, while the others ransacked the home, severely wounding Mrs. Manley, who had been recuperating in her bed from a recent birth. Her newborn baby, just several days old, was brutally dashed against the cabin wall (one account has the baby being thrown into the fireplace after being scalped). One of the Manley children tried to escape, but the dogs accompanying the attacking party supposedly tore the child to pieces. In all, five children were murdered and scalped (three belonging to the Manley family), along with Mrs. Manley who was shot in the knee and jaws, scalped, and "indecently and cruelly mutilated." She managed to live long enough to relate the incident to those who eventually came to the Manley house. After the butchery ended, the Indians took Martha Crawley and traveled southwest through Chickasaw country and, after two weeks' travel, arrived in the Creek Nation, where they proceeded to exhibit Crawley in several towns. In late June, Crawley managed to make a daring escape and, after three harrowing nights, came upon a blacksmith named Tandy Walker who was employed at the Indian agency at Fort St. Stephens. Walker took the beleaguered woman to St. Stephens and from there Crawley was escorted back to the Tennessee River. Stories arose about her captivity with the Creeks that had her being whipped and made to strip naked in front of dancing warriors. Significantly, however, her own deposition discloses no incidents of violence toward her during captivity, other than being forced to prepare food during the trek to the Creek Nation.

The murders on the Duck River and the abduction of Martha Crawley triggered a speedy but ineffective reaction within the state. Brigadier General Thomas Johnson dispatched a detachment of five hundred men within forty-eight hours of the affair, proclaiming his men were "burning to avenge the cruel depredations." After crossing the swollen Tennessee River and entering Chickasaw territory, the small army encountered rugged terrain and supply shortages, compelling them to abandon the chase. At the same time, orders were issued in the nearby counties of Dickson, Rutherford, Williamson, and Davidson for the militia there to begin preparations to join General Johnson. A makeshift expedition, led by Colonel William Pillow, followed the trail all the way to Fort Hampton on the Tennessee River, near where the Creek party had passed. Pillow's men captured a straggling Creek and tried to force him to reveal the whereabouts of the renegade Creeks. When the prisoner attempted to escape, he was immediately shot in the back. Then one of the enraged soldiers ran up to the victim, "gave him some stabs with a knife, and tore the scalp from his head yet convulsed with the agonies of death." Pillow's band of men soon returned to Tennessee, having accomplished little on their "daring project," as one newspaper called it. In commenting on the death of the Creek prisoner, the newspaper crassly declared that "one Indian more or less in the world, is a matter of no moment."[9]

Andrew Jackson, away on a business trip to Georgia when the Duck River incident occurred, returned to Nashville on June 4 and immediately sent a letter to the governor upon hearing the news of the affair. In his letter, an animated Jackson insisted the perpetrators "must be punished" and sought Blount's approval to march into the Creek Nation. Jackson wanted to make a swift thrust, before much resistance could be gathered, in order to demand the perpetrators be handed over. If the Creeks refused, Jackson insisted that the Tennesseans "lay their Towns in ashes." Despite Jackson's fervent plea to the governor, state authorities withheld permission to invade, knowing of the illegality of such a maneuver without the consent of the federal government. Instead, Governor Blount ordered a company of rangers to the region between the Mississippi and Tennessee Rivers in the face of Chickasaw Indian agent James Robertson's protests. Robertson's concerns were well founded. In July, the company of rangers, under Captain David Mason, mistakenly fired on a Chickasaw hunting party, killing one of them. Robertson faced the daunting prospect of trying to soothe the outraged feelings of the Chickasaws over the accident. On July 22, the brother of the Chickasaw victim killed a lone white traveler out of revenge. Fortunately, Chickasaw chiefs quickly told Robertson that this incident was in no way to be viewed as an act of hostility toward the United States. Robertson promised compensation to the family of the killed Chickasaw, as well as restitution for property losses sustained by the other members of the hunting party. A bill authorizing the sum of fifty dollars was presented to the Tennessee General Assembly in October 1812, but was eventually rejected.[10]

Newspapers took advantage of the Crawley affair by sensationalizing the details and using it for their prowar propaganda. Grisly aspects of the episode—the killings, scalpings, and mangled babies—coupled with the sexual image of a naked white woman whipped and paraded before dancing warriors made for a potent blend of yellow journalism and Indian-hating bombast. More importantly, coming on the eve of the declaration of war, the Duck River murders provided those newspapers that supported the war with a link (although without foundation) between British intrigue and the southern Indians. When the *Niles' Weekly Register* reprinted the account of the Duck River incident, this editorial comment accompanied it: "Our opinion as to the cause of these horrible murders has been frequently expressed. It arises from our good friends at Amhertsburg and Malden in Canada." The Nashville *Clarion*, more than any other newspaper, used the Crawley incident to fan the flames of war within the state. By the end of June 1812, the *Clarion* had run editorials designed to promote a war against the Creek Nation. In one such piece, "War with the Creeks," the newspaper listed the reasons for such a showdown: the Creeks' habitual horse stealing, their reception of Tecumseh in late 1811, and, of course, the Crawley abduction. As far the *Clarion* was concerned, the Creeks had already declared war. The only question remaining was what were Tennesseans going to do about it? Federal intervention was too slow and too conciliatory, while direct negotiations seemed too unreliable. Since the state had been "invaded," with more attacks impending, military preparations should begin immediately in order to "repel the invasion" and put an end to a Creek war by the middle of August. The editor suggested a flag of truce be dispatched to the Creek Nation demanding the perpetrators of the Duck River murders and the return of Martha Crawley in order to pacify the federal government, but cynically added that no positive benefits should be expected from such an action.[11]

On July 3, an irate Andrew Jackson informed Governor Blount he would wait no longer than July 25 for the Creeks to deliver Mrs. Crawley and her captors (although she had been rescued by then, Jackson did not know this); otherwise, he would lay waste to their villages, burn their houses, kill their warriors, and take women and children as captives. On July 8, Jackson wrote another letter to Blount, expressing his dissatisfaction of the secretary of war's response to the Crawley incident—the secretary having instructed Blount on June 22 to enlist the aid of Benjamin Hawkins to secure Crawley's release. To Jackson, the government treated the abduction the same as if "a party of Creeks had Killed an old sow and her litter of pigs, and drove one off to the nation." Jackson believed the administration should have, at the least, authorized a military campaign unless the captors surrendered. Two days later Jackson penned still another letter to Blount conveying his eagerness "to carry fire and Sword into the heart of the creek nation" if Crawley and her abductors were not given up. Jackson even offered to put up his own money for expenses to supply an army of four thousand men, asking Blount to convene the state legislature during the first week of August so that an army could be put into the field by the end of that month. The general also reminded the governor that other Indian tribes would be watching how Tennessee reacted, and that if the Creeks were not punished "we will have captives in their nations to demand, and many murders of our frontier citizens to deplore." Blount, in theory, totally agreed with Jackson's assessment of the Creek situation. However, as chief executive of the state, he was powerless to grant authority without the permission of the government in Washington. Had he been vested with this power, Blount told Jackson, thousands of Tennessee "peacemakers" would be marching into the Creek Nation.[12]

The Creek depredations in Tennessee in the spring of 1812, coupled with Tecumseh's visit in the fall of 1811, aroused Anglo-American distrust regarding the other tribes on the southern frontier. Many felt the Choctaws and Chickasaws should have taken some action against Tecumseh while the Shawnee leader traveled through their lands. Furthermore, the fact that the rebel Creeks carried their prisoner, Martha Crawley, through Chickasaw territory cast suspicions on that tribe's motives. Andrew Jackson, contacting the Chickasaw chief George Colbert in early June 1812 solicited his aid in locating the perpetrators of the Duck River incident. He warned the Chickasaw chief not to allow "any more scalps or stolen horses" to pass through their territory, otherwise the whites might kill some Chickasaws "through mistake" (possibly alluding to the Chickasaw killed by Mason's rangers). Jackson then prophetically impressed upon Colbert what would happen to the Creeks if they did not deliver the murderers to the whites: "The whole creek nation shall be covered with blood, the fire shall consume their Towns and villages; and their lands shall be divided among the whites." In fact, Colbert *had* seen the Creek party from the Duck River pass through Chickasaw territory. In a May 24, 1812, letter to Brigadier General Isaac Roberts, Colbert stated he encountered the Creeks near Bear Creek with a white woman prisoner he referred to as "Mrs. Crawfort." The Creek warriors told Colbert they were taking their prisoner and looted property back to the Creek headmen. Colbert admitted to Roberts that he was helpless to do anything about the situation and advised that a complaint be lodged with Benjamin Hawkins.[13]

That Hawkins should be consulted seemed a logical course of action. As Indian agent to the Creeks, Hawkins had developed a sense of trust within the nation, especially with the Lower Creeks. Unfortunately, that trust did not extend beyond the Creek boundaries. Hawkins had the unenviable duty of trying to institute a government-sponsored "civilization" plan among the Creeks while placating land-hungry and Indian-hating whites at the same time. After the Crawley affair, most Indian agents came under suspicion when it was learned the Creeks went through Chickasaw lands; Hawkins, in particular, came under intense scrutiny. Tennesseans, demanding a speedy retaliation, wished to take punitive action "for it seems useless to write to Col. Hawkins," as the *Clarion* noted. In fact, some blamed Hawkins's loyalty to the Creeks as an impetus for Creek atrocities. Ferdinand L. Claiborne, brigadier general of the Mississippi Territory militia, expressed no surprise over the recent conduct of the Creeks in June 1812, "when it is known that Col. Hawkins (our agent) is a principle chief of that nation." The *Clarion* intimated that Hawkins be considered "an accomplice of the savages in concealing this hostile conduct of the Creeks from the government of the United States."[14]

Backcountry settlers, knowing how slowly the wheels of government turned and not trusting the Madison administration to respond to the needs of the frontier, preferred to eschew any "amicable adjustments," as one Tennessean put it. The safe return of Martha Crawley did not lessen Tennessee's thirst for revenge. Hawkins had to pressure a clique of Creek leaders to track down and punish the Duck River murderers. When Hawkins later reported that four of the murderers had been put to death, Tennesseans were leery of the veracity of the news. The *Clarion* insisted there was no concrete proof of the victims being the Duck River murderers; rather, they were merely Creek Indians butchered "in the course of the orgies to which all savages are subject." Benjamin Hawkins, according to the *Clarion*, stood by the report in order to please his superiors in Washington. "Although these people had lost their lives in private reencounters and drunken squabbles," the *Clarion* insisted, "he [Hawkins] does not hesitate to represent it as an act of national justice inflicted on criminals who had murdered the whites.[15]

Curiously, when the Tennessee legislature convened in early September 1812 for a special session, they failed to agree on what steps should be taken to punish the Creeks. A resolution authorizing ten thousand state militiamen into service on the frontiers of East and West Tennessee lay on the table of the Senate in October—it would remain there. The resolution, introduced by John Cocke, also called for a message to be sent to the Creeks, demanding a prompt surrender of the murderers of Tennessee citizens within twenty days after the message was delivered. If the Creeks did not comply by the proscribed time, an armed force would be sent "to exterminate the Creek nation." Lastly, the resolution sought to have Benjamin Hawkins removed from the Creek Agency. The failure of the state legislature to mobilize the militia left Governor Blount powerless. In a letter to the secretary of war, Blount confessed that "our opinions as to what amounts to a ready compliance . . . widely differ." Why did the legislature balk at taking military action against the Creeks? The House side of the legislature passed the resolution, but the more conservative Senate did not. By the time of the Ninth General Assembly, Martha Crawley was back in Tennessee, the Creeks had made some attempt to bring the killers to justice, and the expense of supplying ten thousand troops no doubt made some legislators think twice about marching into Creek territory. Most importantly, the state did not have the federal government's approval to take such a step.[16]

By the end of 1812, Tennesseans were preoccupied with other military endeavors—West Tennessee geared up for the expedition to the Lower Country, while East Tennessee joined the Patriot War in East Florida. For the Creeks, however, the end of 1812 brought on an economic crisis within the nation. As the deerskin trade declined even further, the federal government and trading firms took cessions of land as payments for debts. In November, the Creek tribal council agreed to pay off a $22,000 debt to the British-based Forbes Company by handing over tribal annuities from the United States, which amounted to $10,500 per year. To further complicate matters, the American customs collector at Fort Stoddert had stopped Indian travel on the Tombigbee River by making Indians pay duties on imports and exports to Spanish Florida. The faction of Creeks dismayed at seeing their culture transferring itself to a market economy from the traditional forms of reciprocity and redistribution, witnessed their nation becoming too attached to American interests. In one sense, the Creek War was a reaction to these pecuniary concerns.[17]

In early 1813 another depredation further divided the Creek Nation. A band of Creek warriors, returning from a mission to see the Shawnee Prophet and the northern Indians, murdered several families at the mouth of the Ohio River. A report stated the victims were cruelly mangled—one pregnant woman had been cut open and her baby speared on a stake. Hints of cannibalistic rites having taken place accompanied the reports. Benjamin Hawkins, rightly concerned over the repercussions of this latest incident, expressed his frustration to the Creek chiefs in late March 1813 with a scathing letter that predicted the demise of the Creeks as a nation via a war against the Anglo-Americans. "And what will the war bring us?" Hawkins rhetorically asked. "An army, who will destroy our towns, kill our warriors, drive our women and children into the swamps to perish, and take our whole country to pay the expenses."[18]

In April, the Creek chiefs responded to Hawkins's warning by assuring him that they would "kill all of our red people that spill the blood of our white friends." When the chiefs kept their promise and summarily executed nine Creeks involved in the deaths of the whites in Tennessee and Ohio, the Red Stick faction sought revenge. Assistant Indian agent Alexander Cornells communicated to Hawkins in late June that the Red Sticks planned to kill the executioners, particularly the old chiefs, as well as Hawkins. "After this they would be ready for the white people, who could do them no injury, if they came among them," Cornells reported, "as the prophets would draw circles around their abode, and render the earth quaggy and impassable." The Creek shamans also vowed that any Indian town refusing aid to the Red Sticks would be sunk by earthquakes or buried by hills turning over on them. Cornells's account indicates just how deeply the Red Stick movement became steeped in spiritual overtones. In early July Hawkins sent a final admonition, and prediction, to Peter McQueen, one of the Red Stick leaders, simply stating: "If the white man is in danger in your land, you are in danger; and war with the white people will be your ruin."[19]

By July of 1813, a civil war erupted among the Creeks creating apprehension in the nearby white settlements, where residents felt sure that hostilities would spill over into their domain. The increase of Indian depredations—house burnings, cattle killing—caused some residents to comment on the Creeks' alarming conduct. "Tension is mounting, murderous acts and burnings are increasing," wrote one Indian missionary. Rumors circulated throughout the Tensaw and Tombigbee regions of a mass Indian attack involving the Creeks, Choctaws, and Seminoles against the whites (including a plot by the Upper Creeks to invade Tennessee). "All is confusion here," some residents wrote in July 1813. "We shall be in a dangerous situation here without assistance." Tennessee governor Willie Blount received a letter (dated July 23, 1813) from Captain Eli Hammond of the US Rangers painting a grim picture of Creek unrest: whites were being murdered, corn and cattle were being destroyed, and hundreds of "friendly" Creeks were fleeing to the Cherokees for protection. There was even a report that General James Wilkinson had been taken prisoner. Judge Harry Toulmin of the Mississippi Territory notified the government of the situation, but, as usual, federal authorities were slow to react. Brigadier General Thomas Flourney provided a token amount of ammunition and weapons, leaving the territorial militia (550 US volunteers under General Ferdinand Claiborne) to protect the scattered settlements.[20]

Rumors of a joint British/Spanish attack in the Mississippi Territory also surfaced in the summer of 1813. The eagerness of Americans to constantly tie foreign intrigue with any Indian uprising lent credence to such hearsay. In actuality, the Red Sticks alienated Spanish officials and British traders at Pensacola by demanding arms and ammunition. The Forbes Company refused to give into the commands of the Red Stick contingent, led by Peter McQueen. A Forbes Company spokesman complained that the Creeks "have all gone Stark mad." The Spanish governor, however, was more amenable and supplied McQueen with one thousand pounds of gunpowder (later used at Fort Mims). Territorial militia assaulted McQueen's party on their return from Pensacola at a site called Burnt Corn Creek in late July, creating the basis for Creek retaliation at Fort Mims.[21]

After Burnt Corn, the government in Washington decided to take some steps to counter the outbreak of Creek hostilities. Envisioning a coordinated plan among Tennessee, Georgia, the Mississippi Territory, and the US Army, Secretary of War John Armstrong wrote to Governor Blount on July 13 on the subject of raising 1,500 Tennessee troops. Blount replied on July 30 that Tennessee could put as many as 5,000 men in the field—an army he promised to assemble in twenty days. Interestingly, the federal government was concerned about states such as Tennessee actually raising *too* many troops by state drafts, which would confuse the issue of the United States act for volunteers. The War Office responded to Blount on August 20 by stating that since there was a combined operation afoot, a 1,500-man force from Tennessee would be enough. Furthermore, there was some question as to who would command the forces. On August 31, James Monroe wrote to President Madison questioning the wisdom of leaving the command of the southern troops up to the governors of Tennessee and Georgia, suggesting General Thomas Pinckney of the Sixth Military District "might not be better . . . than [Andrew] Jackson, or other militia generals." Madison agreed and placed Pinckney in overall command of operations, despite the fact that the Creek Nation overlapped both the Sixth and Seventh Military Districts.[22]

Meanwhile, many of the Red Sticks within the Creek Nation moved out of their towns to live in temporary camps to await the invasion of the Americans. Some new towns were built as defensive locations, including Econochaca (Holy Ground) and Tohopeka (Horseshoe Bend). Many existing towns also fortified themselves in anticipation of raids. Then, as Americans exchanged communications about raising troops and bickered over leadership issues, a force of several hundred Red Sticks launched an attack on Fort Mims on August 30. At the time, the reports of the number of whites, blacks, and métis killed at Mims reached as high as six hundred—a more accurate figure puts it at between 250 and 275 men, women, and children. Whatever reactions Anglo-Americans experienced in any prior depredation paled in comparison to the response the slaughter at Fort Mims generated. Crowds of terrified settlers in the Mississippi Territory hurriedly packed up their belongings and headed toward the nearest town or stockade, if it was not already abandoned. Many families fled their farms in the middle of the night, leaving their houses, crops, and herds behind, in what came to be known as "the Great Mississippi Panic of 1813." Tennesseans shared in the alarm the Mims massacre brought on. Methodist circuit rider Isaac Conger noted in his diary that many of his constituents in Lincoln County were "very much in fear of being Killed by the Savage." Exaggerated reports, coming from Huntsville (Alabama), indicated eight thousand Creeks were launching a three-pronged attack—the targets being Georgia, Tennessee, and the Mobile settlements. Even though the *Nashville Whig* reported this story as "having since been contradicted in part," rumors such as these left much of the population in terror and apprehension. Colonel Peter Perkins, writing from Huntsville, communicated to Governor Blount that two thousand Creeks were about to attack Huntsville, adding: "It is not uncommon to see a hundred persons at one time, some on foot, others in carriages, wagons or carts, flying to Tennessee for protection."[23]

Leading citizens from Davidson County and surrounding counties congregated in Nashville on September 18, 1813, in response to pleas coming from the Mississippi Territory. The group of fifty or sixty individuals—including John Coffee, William Hall, John Alcorn, William Martin, and Thomas Williamson (all future military officers in the Creek War)—met to debate what actions might be taken against the offending Creek Indians. Reverend Thomas Craighead, acting as chairman, designed his opening remarks to appeal to the audience's public memory of past Indian wars: "Hundreds of our fellow-brethren of the Mobile have fallen beneath the Savage Tomahawk. . . . The martial sons of Tennessee do well recollect the time when they and their fathers were isolated from the rest of the American family, and exposed to the incursions of the same barbarians that now depredate on the Mississippi Territory. You can remember how many members of your individual families have fallen in defense of their altars and firesides." Craighead's oration alluded to the days of Tennessee's frontier wars, when Indian attacks were a common occurrence, and the state felt removed from the rest of the nation. To be sure, the Tombigbee settlements, isolated and hemmed in by hostile Indians and the Spanish, believed the federal government had ignored them— a situation all too familiar to the once-beleaguered Cumberland inhabitants. To Craighead and his audience, Fort Mims represented a glaring and painful reminder of those forlorn days. The meeting produced a committee of several men charged with making a final recommendation. Their report, delivered on the next day, suggested a regiment of cavalry and three hundred to five hundred mounted riflemen be immediately marched into the Creek Nation "to give immediate check to their ravages; exterminate their Nation and abettors; and save thousands of the unoffending women and children on our frontier." It was agreed that the regiment of cavalry—to be led by Colonel John Coffee—be sent to the Mobile region as soon as possible. Coffee timidly indicated his regiment would be ready to rendezvous *if* his men were paid for their former service during the Natchez Expedition of late 1812/early 1813. Paymaster Alpha Kingsley obtained money only after Andrew Jackson and others had underwritten it. Coffee's men gathered at Clover Bottom (near Jackson's estate) to receive their pay and, while there, heard the rumor that Huntsville was under threat of Creek attack. Jackson subsequently ordered Coffee to march to that point post haste.[24]

Legislative wheels were spinning at the same time that military preparations were underfoot. The first order of business for the Tenth General Assembly, meeting in Nashville on September 21, 1813, was "an act to repel the invasion of the state of Tennessee by the Creek Indians, and to afford relief to the citizens of the Mississippi Territory," passed on September 24. Chapter one of the ensuing legislation authorized the governor to organize up to 3,500 men paid from a loan of $300,000 to be (hopefully) repaid by the federal government—if not, a tax would be levied on all taxable property in the state to pay off the debt by the next session of the legislature. (The original bill called for five thousand men and unlimited funds at the governor's disposal to foot the bill, with the state assuming all the expenses.) The wording of the act is unique in that it proposes to launch a military campaign into Creek territory based on *defensive* motives—the title of the act indicates it is designed to "repel" an invasion of Tennessee. (It should be remembered that the mission of the Natchez Expedition of late 1813/early 1814 was for the "defense" of the Lower Country, even though it was apparent the Madison administration saw it as a potential opportunity to take West Florida.) One assemblyman informed his constituents that the declaration of war against the Creeks was "prompted by the dictates of humanity, *self defence*, and patriotism." Tennesseans had flocked to the banner "to repel a threatened invasion of our own frontier." Brigadier General Isaac Roberts of the Fifth Brigade of Tennessee militia, upon receiving orders from Major General Jackson to solicit volunteers from his brigade, called upon the men to help "in repelling the Savage." These proclamations echoed Andrew Jackson's theory of "defensive" border warfare. "It is by waging the war in the heart of the Enemy's country," Jackson once stated, "that effectual protection is to be furnished to our frontiers." Similarly, William Henry Harrison once spouted in 1811: "In Indian warfare, there is no security but in offensive Measures."[25]

The wording of Tennessee's declaration of war may also have something to do with events on the national scene. The federal government's use of the militia came into play in 1812 in certain New England states that resisted federal control by insisting the war was an "offensive" war, and thus it did not meet the criteria for federal use, which proscribed calling out the militia for "defensive" purposes *unless* there was a threat of invasion. Some New England states feared the federal government controlling state militias for its own purpose. These conditions led the rest of the nation to denounce those New England governors for refusing to offer the services of their militia. Judge Harry Toulmin, concerned about efforts to get outside help to the Mississippi Territory threatened by the Creeks, penned a letter to territorial governor David Holmes just days before the Mims disaster, asking: "Has the New England spirit diffused itself over any part of the Mississi[ppi] Territory—and are the militia not only to be confined to their own state, but to a particular section of their state or territory?" By implying the state of Tennessee was under threat of invasion, the General Assembly could justify sending troops into the invader's territory in order to check their progress.[26]

Prowar advocates outside of Tennessee found the state's initiatives worthy of applause. The Washington *Daily National Intelligencer* reported on the declaration of war against the Creek with the headline "Patriotism of Tennessee." The newspaper declared the act to be "genuine patriotism of a Republic—prompt, energetic, without alloy." More important to Tennesseans than the approbation of a Washington newspaper was President Madison's sanctioning of the state's actions. On October 16, Secretary of State James Monroe informed George Washington Campbell that the administration gave its official approval to Tennessee's act of September 24 calling out 3,500 men to march against the Creeks. This, in effect, meant the federal government would shoulder the financial burden for the war. Lawmakers in Tennessee let out a collective sigh of relief upon hearing the news—the *Clarion* reprinted Monroe's letter under the heading "Good News!"—knowing the financial strain the Assembly's actions would have put on the state. Campbell dutifully thanked Monroe for the administration's support, acknowledging that the president's consent was "highly gratifying" to the Tennessee legislature and "calculated to continue and strengthen the confidence hitherto reposed by them in the present administration." Campbell's words represented more than plain lip service to the Madison administration. They echoed the sentiments of Tennesseans in the era of 1812: critical of the federal government, whom they viewed as being sluggish in taking necessary actions, but never disloyal to the union. Besides, the state now had a full-fledged war to concentrate on—one in which Tennessee's longtime enemy, the Creek Indians, would finally reap the "rewards" of past injuries to the founding settlers.[27]

Brigadier General Thomas Flourney, commanding the Seventh Military District, planned to use a concerted army of Tennessee volunteers, Mississippi Territory militia, and Choctaw Indians to proceed into the Creek Nation. Throwing Georgia forces and US Regulars into the mix only served to complicate the situation in terms of nightmarish logistics and leadership disputes. In the end, the hoped-for merger of these diverse forces never really materialized. "About the best that can be said for the cooperation existing among these armies is that they did not fight each other," one historian has quipped. Instead, individual state-sponsored campaigns made periodic stabs at the heart of the Creek Nation. In September 1813, Colonel John Coffee issued regimental orders for his cavalry to rendezvous at Camp Good Exchange, near Nashville, on September 24 (the same day the state legislature passed the war act), ready to participate in a "short and vigorous" tour of duty. Coffee advised the men to bring no more than one change of clothing and ten days' worth of rations (to be compensated by the government). Coffee also called for an additional four hundred to five hundred mounted men to join his regiment. Meanwhile, Andrew Jackson prepared a letter to Coffee on September 29, advising him to maneuver his cavalry unit toward the Mobile region, where Jackson was convinced a mass force of Creeks would strike with their British and/or Spanish allies. Jackson, still recuperating from a near-deadly brawl at a Nashville inn on September 4 with the Benton brothers—Thomas and Jesse—rose from his sickbed to take overall command of the campaign. It was the moment he had been waiting for, and a bullet lodged in his left shoulder was not going to prevent him from claiming his day in the sun.[28]

West Tennesseans responded to Jackson's call with an enthusiasm akin to that of December 1812, when the Natchez Expedition had been formed. In Jackson County, one youth and his friend ran away from home in a canoe they drifted down the Cumberland River to join a company of volunteers in Gainesboro. In Maury County, the students at Mount Pleasant Academy were "strongly aroused to vengeance" as a result of the Fort Mims massacre. Yet one of the students admitted the urge was due "more to the opportunity of escaping present restraints on the far off dream of distinction." So many volunteers offered their services in Maury County that a draft or lottery had to be initiated to determine which ones would get to serve. David Crockett, in Franklin County, heard the news coming from the Mobile region and thought "the Indians would be scalping the women and children all about there." Crockett believed he had to fight the Creeks, despite his wife's protests. "The truth is," Crockett later confessed, "my dander was up, and nothing but war could bring it right again." Not all Tennesseans were as enthusiastic as Crockett about leaving their homes and families to fight in the Creek Nation. In some instances, thoughts of family safety overrode patriotic considerations. William Woods, a major in the Giles County militia, wrote to President Madison in 1812 that the men in his county were reluctant to leave home and fight "till setch times as our wives and Children is made safe from the hands of those our enemies the Creek Indians."[29]

Jackson issued orders for two thousand volunteers to rendezvous at Fayetteville (eighty miles south of Nashville and thirty miles north of Huntsville) during the first week of October. Jackson arrived at the rendezvous point, dubbed Camp Blount, on October 6, where he found fewer men than expected, and those who did show up were not very well equipped. Responding to rumors of a possible Creek attack on Huntsville, Jackson feverishly gathered more supplies and personnel and pushed off into the Mississippi Territory, approaching Huntsville on October 12, where he learned the rumors proved false. Meanwhile, with a force numbering up to 1,300 men, John

Coffee set out from "Camp Coffee" on the south side of the Tennessee River on October 13 in search of Creeks to annihilate. After scouting the region in vain for the enemy, he stumbled onto several Creek towns along the Black Warrior River (near present-day Tuscaloosa), "where Mrs. Crawley was carried." He found the villages deserted, however, and settled for their destruction by the torch, after pillaging what supplies of corn he could carry. "I am now convinced that the Indians will never meet us in action," a disappointed Coffee wrote his wife. "There has not been a gun fired, by either an Indian or a white man." Coffee rejoined Jackson's army on October 24, anticipating a rendezvous with an army from East Tennessee in order for the whole to move together against the Creeks.[30]

John Cocke, commanding the East Tennessee division of militia, made preparations for a strike into Creek territory, much like his counterpart in West Tennessee. On September 6, 1813, Cocke put the first brigade of militia on alert, warning of a potential assault by the Creeks. In the event of such an attack Colonel Ewen Allison (at Greeneville) was instructed to "Instantly order a Competent force not only to repel them but to Chastise and as far as in your power utterly destroy them & persue as far as prudence will dictate." Cocke cautioned Allison, however, not to molest any friendly Indians, "but treat them with hospitality & friendship so long as their Conduct is proper." After Tennessee's declaration against the Creeks, Jackson sent a letter to Cocke, dated September 28, warning him "that the whole of the Creeks [was] in motion." He wanted to know when Cocke could expect to move his division and when supplies from East Tennessee could be shipped. Cocke then issued division orders, calling for 2,500 militia to take the field, reminding his men of the Indian mode of warfare, where "the mother and her infant are more the objects of their hate than the husband or the father." "You whose lives have been preserved only by the valor of your ancestors, know these things full well," he added, as a tribute to the Frontier Fathers.[31]

Typical of the East Tennessee units marching to the Creek War in October 1813 was the company led by Captain Jacob Hartsell. Hartsell served as a tax assessor and magistrate in Washington County before enrolling his volunteer company in Colonel William Lillard's Second Regiment of East Tennessee Volunteer Militia. Hartsell's line of march started in Jonesborough, proceeded to Southwest Point at Kingston, then to the Hiwassee Garrison (Rhea County, Tennessee), and next across the Tennessee River to Camp Ross. Established by General James White in October 1813, Camp Ross was located at the foot of Lookout Mountain near the mouth of Chattanooga Creek. The camp lay on high ground between the creek and the river near the trading post of Daniel Ross. As a rendezvous point, Camp Ross became the East Tennessee equivalent of Camp Blount at Fayetteville for the West Tennessee troops. Leaving Lookout Mountain, Hartsell looked back in awe at one thousand well-armed men in a line of march three-quarters of a mile long. After Camp Ross, the East Tennessee army snaked its way to Turkeytown, a Cherokee village located in the bend of the Coosa River (present-day Cherokee County, Alabama). The army next proceeded to Fort Armstrong (on the border between Georgia and Alabama) and finally to Fort Strother (in present-day St. Clair County, Alabama), where Jackson's army had established its headquarters in November 1813.[32]

The armies of West Tennessee traversed a different path to Fort Strother. After leaving the main rendezvous point at Camp Blount, the West Tennesseans trekked south toward Huntsville and crossed the Tennessee River at Ditto's Landing. Andrew Jackson Edmondson, whose company was at the vanguard of the army, crossed the river and, as his unit touched the south bank, he looked back to see the rear of the army waiting on the north bank. "It was a clear pretty day," recalled Edmondson, "& it looked a pretty sight to see the string [of soldiers] clear across the stream." Others, such as junior officer William Trousdale, found the crossing to be more perilous than stimulating. Plunging into the river's strong currents, Trousdale relied on his horse to keep him alive (Trousdale could not swim), as the horse alternately stepped on rocks or sank headlong into the water. After a laborious crossing of the river, the army set up Camp Coffee on the opposite shore, atop a bluff about one thousand feet above the river. From there, the army had to cross the treacherous Raccoon Mountains before reaching the depot for storing provisions that would become Fort Deposit, twenty miles from Ditto's Landing. Along the way, Jackson's army encamped at several points, such as Camp Gibson (at Seven Mile Creek) and Mountain Camp (on top of Raccoon Mountain), then descended to the mouth of Thompson's Creek at the southernmost point of the Tennessee River in Alabama, where they constructed Fort Deposit. From Deposit, the army took a southeastern course to a spot on the Coosa River known as Ten Islands. After arriving on November 4, Jackson used this site as his main headquarters during the bulk of the Creek War, constructing a military installation to be named Fort Strother.[33]

That Jackson expected support from the East Tennessee army and Georgia is evident in a mid-October 1813 letter to Mississippi Territory governor David Holmes, in which he expressed his desire "to penetrate the heart of the Creek nation." "But I begin to be apprehensive that [the other armies] movements will be too slow for mine," Jackson declared, "I cannot bear to remain idle." Striking out for the Ten Islands, where reports indicated the Red Sticks were congregating, Jackson reorganized his army on the last day of October.

The First Regiment of Infantry Volunteers, commanded by Colonel Edward Bradley, joined with the Second Regiment of Infantry Volunteers, under Colonel William Pillow, to form the First Brigade with General William Hall at its head. The First and Second Regiments of Militia (under Colonels John K. Wynn and Thomas McCrory, respectively) formed the Second Brigade, led by General Isaac Roberts. The mounted gunmen previously attached to Colonel John Coffee's old volunteer cavalry from the Natchez Expedition became a separate regiment, commanded by Colonel Newton Cannon. Colonel John Alcorn took over Coffee's cavalry and the two units formed a brigade of 1,200 under the newly promoted Brigadier General John Coffee. Jackson's total manpower now reached 2,500 men.[34]

Jackson's strategy for total destruction of the enemy did not allow him to become foolhardy enough to take drastic measures—at least not in late 1813. Ever cautious of enemy surprise attacks, Jackson's general orders for his men while at Fort Deposit included a line of posted sentinels and the requirement that every soldier sleep with his arms. No one was permitted to leave the encampment except two men from each "mess"—one for wood and the other for water—and, only then, under protection of a guard. Jackson also addressed his troops as to "the consternation [the Creeks] shall be able to spread through our ranks, by the horrid yells with which they commence their battle." Jackson knew the psychological effect the piercing shouts of several hundred Indians might have on raw, inexperienced soldiers. Not only were the men to ignore the fearful shrieks of the Indians, but they were also ordered never to retreat from the battlefield. Speaking of himself in the third person, Jackson admonished his men: "Never while he commands you shall you have any practical understanding of that word."[35]

Jackson had the manpower, the willpower, and the weaponry—including a fine brass 6-pounder cannon—to strike a blow at the enemy, but one adversary above all others worried him the most: "There is an enemy whom I dread, much more than I do the hostile Creek . . . that meager-monster 'Famine.'" Jackson had made this statement to the wealthy residents of Madison County (Mississippi Territory) in an attempt to secure some corn meal for his famished troops, already down to a mere two days' supply of breadstuff by late October 1813. John Reid, Jackson's aide, concurred with his general's plight by pointing out that Fort Deposit had been established as a depot for provisions, "but where those provisions are to come from, or when they are to arrive, God almighty only knows." "I speak seriously when I declare," a distressed Reid wrote, "[that] we shall have to eat our horses." With no sure source of supplies, Jackson set out for the Ten Islands on October 25, leaving Fort Deposit under the command of Lieutenant Colonel Perkins of the Madison County militia. Hopefully, the Creek towns he intended to destroy would provide Jackson's men with the subsistence they so desperately needed.[36]

Upon approaching the Ten Islands, Jackson dispatched Lieutenant Colonel Robert Dyer, with two hundred of the cavalry, to attack the Creek town of Littafuchee (or Litafatci), south of Fort Deposit on Big Canoe Creek. Dyer returned on October 28 with thirty prisoners in tow, having burned the village. Dyer reported finding a considered quantity of corn and "beeves" in the neighboring fields, but inexplicably failed to bring any of it back to camp. Nearing the Ten Islands on November 2, Jackson instructed Coffee to take one thousand men from his brigade and, with half of them, cross the Coosa River to destroy Tallushatchee, a Creek town south of the Coosa. The other half of Coffee's men were ordered to proceed to the Ten Islands "to scour the intervening country of all hostile Creeks," thus forming a cover for Coffee's raid. Coffee, who once feared his troops would never see an Indian—let alone fight one—now had his chance.[37]

Coffee surrounded the town of Tallushatchee on the morning of November 3 by placing Alcorn's regiment on the right and Cannon's regiment on the left, about one-quarter of a mile apart. Captain Eli Hammond's company of rangers, in front of Alcorn, made a charge at the village to draw the Creeks out from cover and then quickly retreated while Alcorn's men continued to march around the village until they linked with the left wing. The village now being completely surrounded, the men dismounted and charged the trapped Creeks, who "fought as desperately as ever men did upon Earth," according to one witness. As the Creek warriors retreated to their village, one Red Stick leader climbed on the roof of a structure and exhorted the Creeks to stand and fight, insisting spirits would deflect the bullets fired by the whites. The advancing Tennesseans quickly shot him down. Once inside the confines of the village, Coffee's men raced from hut to hut, killing every Creek warrior they could find; in the frenzy of the action, some women and children became victims of their rage. David Crockett, one of the attackers, recalled seeing a large number of Creeks running into a house where a squaw sat in the doorway with her feet against a bow. The woman took an arrow, raised her feet, and drew back with all her might, letting the arrow fly toward the oncoming Tennesseans. The arrow struck and killed one of the soldiers—the first man Crockett had ever seen slain by a bow and arrow. So enraged were the Tennesseans that they fired on the woman until at least twenty rifle balls blew through her. "We now shot them like dogs," Crockett recalled, as they set the house on fire with over forty persons in it. Crockett saw a boy about twelve years old, wounded with a broken arm and thigh, trying to crawl away from the flaming structure. "He was so near the burning house that the grease was stewing out of him," Crockett remembered. When the carnage was over, 180 dead Creeks lay strewn about the village, with eighty women and children taken as prisoner. American casualties amounted to five killed and about forty wounded.[38]

The news of the victory at Tallushatchee reached Ten Islands on November 4, the same day of Jackson's arrival. Jackson immediately ordered five hundred men to reinforce Coffee. John Reid volunteered to go and was sickened by what he saw at the battle site. "I cannot imagine, much less describe a more horrid spectacle," he wrote in his journal. "Most of the dead bodies I saw were parched up by the burning of the houses over them after they were killed." The shocked Reid came within sight of four or five wounded squaws, but "I could not feel in my heart to go up to them." Another spectator to the aftermath of the battle, Andrew Jackson Edmondson, noticed several women and children lying dead on the ground. "One little fellow was tugging at his Mothers breast," Edmondson somberly noted, "& her Stiff & cold." David Crockett, returning to the scene of the battle, recalled some of the famished soldiers eating potatoes they found in the cellar of one of the burned houses— the potatoes were covered with "grease" from the incinerated Indian corpses. Days later, when Jackson's army marched to another Creek engagement at Talladega, they passed through Tallushatchee. Richard Call, a young enlistee, remembered the grisly sights in detail: "We found as many as eight or ten dead bodies in a single cabin, sometimes the dead mother clasped the dead child to her breast, and to add another appalling horror to the bloody catalogue, some of the Cabins had taken fire, and half consumed bodies were seen amidst the smoking ruins. In other instances dogs had torn and feasted on the mangled bodies of their very masters. Heart sick I turned from the revolting scene." For Call, Crockett, Reid, and others, the grim reality of such warfare must have dampened their ardor for killing Indians. Almost as an afterthought, Richard Call spoke of the carnage of the Creek War in these terms: "I remember an instance of a brave young soldier, who after fighting like a Tiger until the engagement was over, fainted at the sight of the blood he has helped to spill." Some veterans of the rout at Tallushatchee would later refer to it as the "Big Bloody."[39]

The *Nashville Whig* reported that the Creeks "fought until every *man* of the Indians were killed; and unfortunately some *women & children* were killed in the houses." While expressing some remorse for these acts, the newspaper declined to specify how many victims at Tallushatchee were not warriors. The action at Tallushatchee represented the first victory for the Tennesseans in the Creek War, and the state extended its enthusiastic approbation. In Knoxville, citizens gathered at a "brilliantly illuminated" church to hear a Reverend Nelson read Coffee's official report of the battle from the pulpit. Nelson then delivered "an expressive, eloquent and patriotic sermon suitable to the occasion." At Camp Ross, where the East Tennessee army awaited orders to proceed to the Creek Nation, Captain Hartsell recorded in his journal on November 7 how the troops received the news of the victory at Tallushatchee: "the hole army whare we lay Shot and Drunck tell midnight for joy, which made much Noise." General Jackson, writing to Governor Blount from Ten Islands, simply boasted: "We have retaliated for the destruction of Fort Mims." But the retaliation did not stop at Tallushatchee.[40]

On the evening of November 7, while constructing Fort Strother at his headquarters at Ten Islands, Jackson received a plea for help from a village of friendly Creeks and their families at Lashley's Fort (present-day Talladega, Alabama), thirty miles below the Ten Islands. The besieged Creeks, threatened by a contingent of Red Sticks, managed to sneak out a messenger who made his way to enlist Jackson's aid in staving off the encroaching Red Sticks. By midnight, Jackson had 1,200 infantry and 800 mounted men in a line of march, leaving Fort Strother in the care of a skeleton force in anticipation of General James White's advance unit of the East Tennessee army arriving soon at the Ten Islands. The army crossed the Coosa River a short distance above Fort Strother, with each mounted man taking an infantryman on horseback until all had traversed the five-hundred-yard-wide river. The march continued across harsh mountainous terrain, where the supply wagons, pulled by horses and mules, frantically tried to keep pace with the flanking columns of troops. "The movement was slow and exceedingly difficult," remembered Richard Call, "often the faithful team would balk or fall to their knees, trembling with the stressing effort to advance, under the whip and cheering whoops of the driver, which echoed and reechoed from rock to rock and rang with deafening note through the wild mountain gorge." The rugged landscape prevented Jackson from bringing along his 6-pound cannon—Captain David Deaderick's artillery company carrying muskets instead.[41]

On the night of November 8, Jackson had his army encamped six miles from Talladega and sent out Indian spies to reconnoiter the area. They returned an hour before midnight with a report that the main body of Red Sticks lay situated a quarter-mile north of Lashley's, but they could not give Jackson any accurate information as to the enemy's strength. At the same time, Jackson received a communication from General White with the shocking news that Major General John Cocke had retrograded White's orders to proceed to Fort Strother. Since Jackson had been counting on White's forces to man Fort Strother and protect the rear of the West Tennesseans, the news of White's failure to appear there left Jackson in a quandary. He decided to attack immediately. By 4:00 a.m. on November 9, the army was in motion: the infantry in three columns with the cavalry and mounted men in the rear and flankers on each side. Colonel Edward Bradley led the right wing of infantry, the center was led by Colonel William Pillow, and the left by Colonel Thomas McCrory. Colonels Alcorn and Cannon commanded the right and left wings of the cavalry, respectively. The advance unit, headed by William Carroll (recently promoted to inspector general), consisted of Captain Deaderick's artillery company, along with riflemen under Captain Anthony Bledsoe and Captain George Caperton. Captain John Gordon's company of spies marched four hundred yards in front of the army.[42]

They arrived a mile from the enemy at 7:00 a.m., at which point Jackson ordered the cavalry and mounted men to advance on the right and left of the infantry to enclose the enemy in a circle. Jackson placed 250 men in the rear of the center, under Colonel Robert Dyer, as a reserve. Hall's brigade on the right and Robert's brigade on the left were then ordered to advance by heads of companies. In completing this circle, however, too great a space was left between the rear of the right wing of cavalry and Hall's brigade. The Red Sticks, concealed in thick shrubbery, fired on Jackson's advance units when they got to within eighty yards—the time was 8:00 a.m.—and after receiving a heavy fire, the Tennesseans charged, only to retreat back to the center to draw the Creeks out into the open. The Red Sticks rushed forward "as if legions of demons had broken loose upon the earth" while "rending the air with the most terrific yells." For Andrew Jackson Edmondson of Colonel Pillow's regiment, it was the first time he ever leveled a rifle at a human being. "Never will I forget my feelings when I raised my gun to fire," Edmondson recalled. "I had heard my father say his first effort he could not get his gun to his shoulder for trembling—I drew mine up & I thought took pretty fair aim." The right wing of Robert's brigade let out one round of fire, but three companies of militia retreated in panic. To fill the gap, Jackson ordered up Colonel Bradley's regiment of volunteers, but the enemy had advanced too rapidly, one soldier recalling, "the balls and arrows flew fast over our heads." Jackson called up Dyer's reserves to check the oncoming Creeks. The fleeing militia restored their courage upon seeing the reserves dismount and fight. They returned to their former position "and within fifteen minutes the enemy were seen flying in every direction."[43]

The Red Sticks who had escaped through the gap ran for the mountains, a distance of three miles. The Tennesseans pursued them with a vengeance, killing as many as they could catch. Major James McEwen and a "friendly" Indian named Fields found themselves in an ambush while pursuing the fleeing Creeks. An arrow struck down Fields, but McEwen managed to carry the wounded man back to safety, where he had the regimental surgeon treat him. Another overeager volunteer, chasing a wounded Creek, outran his own men and was killed and scalped—supposedly the only Tennessee soldier to be scalped in the Creek War. Jackson reported 299 Creek bodies found slain, but felt there were many more bodies undiscovered in the fields leading to the mountains. He estimated the Creek force at 1,080 warriors. American losses consisted of fifteen killed and approximately eighty-five wounded. In a moment of unrestrained bragging, Jackson wrote: "I believe that no impartial man can say that a more splendid result has in any instance attended our Arms, on land, since the commencement of the war."[44]

In summing up the battles of Tallushatchee and Talladega, John Coffee estimated the Tennesseans had killed five hundred Creeks and at least that many wounded. With confidence in his men's fighting ability, Coffee felt assured that although the Red Sticks were "a desperate enemy when they have conquered," they were "very soon put to flight by one resolute stand or charge." A Tennessee soldier who participated in both battles, in writing a letter home to his father, made the claim that "the history of Indian warfare does not furnish an instance of . . . two better fought battles than those of Tallushatchee and Talladega." A story, probably apocryphal, told to Jackson by Choctaw Indian agent John McKee, states that a Creek who survived the battle at Talladega supposedly said: "God damn Genl. Jackson kill Creek too much." But the slaughter was only beginning.[45]

More formidable to the Tennesseans than any Creek warrior yelling and rushing into their lines was the enemy Jackson feared the most: hunger. The Talladega campaign had taught the Tennesseans the value of a secure supply line. Most of the men on the march from Fort Strother and back subsisted on parched corn and some flour taken from the Indians. The return to Fort Strother after a four-day march brought little relief. No available bread awaited the weary troops. In fact, some troops resorted to cooking the corncobs the horses had previously eaten and left lying in dung. In desperation, the men tried to boil rawhides or feast on calf guts. Jackson had to send part of his army to Fort Deposit in the hopes of finding stored provisions (there were some, but not enough to feed an army). At one point, Jackson gave the men permission to head out to meet some incoming supply wagons crossing the Coosa Mountain. As the starving men encountered the wagons, a barrel fell from the back of one of the vehicles and broke open. In a mad scramble, the men grabbed up handfuls of dry flour to eat, trying to satisfy their gnawing hunger. These wretched conditions bred the seeds of disgruntlement that were soon to explode in Jackson's camp. On November 14, Colonels William Martin and H. L. Douglass sent Jackson a communication warning that the First Brigade might conduct a mass desertion—a condition, they said, brought about by a shortage of provisions and the lack of clothing for a winter campaign. By mid-November, it appeared Jackson's foray into the Creek Nation might come to a screeching halt.[46]

Another source of discontent sprang from the camps of the East Tennessee army, where Major General John Cocke stirred up the already-existing rivalry between the two divisions of the state. Prior to the battle at Talladega, Jackson had expected to rendezvous with the East Tennessee army, hoping to obtain much-needed supplies. Cocke, in need of stores for his own army, believed that joining the West Tennessee army would only make the situation worse. The advance unit of Cocke's army, under General James White, attempted to rendezvous with Jackson at Ten Islands in early November through forced marches. On November 7, White asked Cocke to push his own troops to join him, as White felt he was "really presenting a strange spectacle" by advancing his army in enemy country with much of his effective force far behind him. White's unit also included about four hundred Cherokee Indians who were "anxious to go on." Yet on the day before, Cocke had sent instructions to White *not* to rendezvous with Jackson. "If we follow General Jackson's army we must suffer for supplies," Cocke reasoned, "nor can we expect to gain a victory—let us then take a direction in which we can share some of the dangers and glories of the field."[47]

That "direction" led the East Tennesseans to the Hillabee villages, where it was rumored a force of Red Sticks lay. The Hillabees, a Creek tribe occupying four villages, resided in the vicinity of Hillabi Creek, a western tributary of the Tallapoosa River (sixty miles southeast of Fort Strother). Fearful of reports that a Georgia army was on the move to destroy them, the Hillabees sent a communication on November 13 to Jackson, indicating they would lay down their arms and maintain a peace with the United States. Jackson's response of November 17 spelled out the conditions under which hostile Creeks could surrender: restore all prisoners and property taken from whites and friendly Creeks, furnish Jackson with supplies, and join Jackson's army in fighting the Red Sticks. Jackson promised "to carry a war of destruction through every part of the Creek nation that remains unfriendly," adding they would long remember Fort Mims "in bitterness and tears." Jackson forwarded a message to John Cocke on November 18 informing him of the Hillabees' surrender, little knowing that General White attacked the unsuspecting Indians on that same day.[48]

White's army consisted of mounted infantry under Colonel Samuel Bunch, cavalry led by Major James Porter, and a contingent of Cherokees commanded by Colonel Gideon Morgan. Per Cocke's orders, the unit marched toward the Hillabees on November 11, equipped with four days' rations. At Little Oakfuskie, they captured five Creeks and burned the village of thirty houses. They then proceeded to a town named Cenalgo (consisting of ninety-three houses), destroyed it, and then marched on to Nitty Chapicca, which White did not burn, as he thought it might be of some future use. The army approached the main Hillabee town on the evening of November 17 and dismounted within six miles of the village. Colonel Bunch led the advance party, along with the Cherokees, surrounding the town, in preparation to make an attack the next morning. The surprise was complete—of the three hundred Creeks there, sixty were killed and the rest taken prisoner. There were no American casualties. After burning the village, White's army proceeded to Fort Armstrong, reaching it on November 23 after being delayed by rough terrain, wet weather, and the transportation of prisoners. White's official report singled out Bunch, Porter, and Morgan for their efforts, making no mention of who did the actual fighting.[49]

Gideon Morgan, leading the Cherokees of White's army, insisted that his Cherokee force did the brunt of the fighting on November 18—except for one Creek a white soldier killed, Cherokees inflicted all the other casualties. Morgan related that his warriors advanced on the town more rapidly than the Tennesseans and, consequently, took advantage of the surprised Hillabees. Morgan credited Cherokee chief Major John Lowrey with killing six Creeks in battle, and singled out Major John Walker for capturing fifty-four prisoners. "Will not shame redden the face & silence mute the tongue of those who have pretended to doubt the attachment of the Cherokees to our Country," Morgan boasted with not too little a touch of cynicism.[50]

Jackson showed remarkable restraint in not condemning Cocke's decision to attack the Hillabees. Historians have made much of Cocke's "blunder," pointing out that the betrayed Hillabees became the Americans' fiercest opponents for the rest of the war. Yet Jackson's view of friendly Indians was not all that much different from his attitude toward hostile Indians. To be sure, Jackson was probably more upset with Cocke for disobeying his orders than for chastising the Hillabees. Later, when the friction between the two commanders escalated, Cocke would claim that the Hillabee surrender was a "hoax" propagated by Jackson's jealousy over the East Tennessee army's overwhelming victory. "It was planned and executed without his aid; it was too much for his noble soul to bear," Cocke asserted, "hence the story of unconditional submission."[51]

As the Tennessee armies rolled across the Creek Nation piling up one victory after another, a Georgia army under the command of General John Floyd added to the ever-growing list of Creek defeats. On November 29,

1813, Floyd's army struck at a Creek stronghold situated at Autosse, on the east bank of the Tallapoosa River below the mouth of Calebee Creek (in present-day Mason County, Alabama). A Georgia militiaman, James Tait, left an account of the battle in his journal. Before sunrise on the morning of the twenty-ninth, the enemy began firing from their huts at Floyd's army of nearly one thousand militia and four hundred friendly Indians. The Georgians responded with eighteen rounds of cannon fire, "shattering their miserable huts to pieces." Most of the Red Sticks then "scampered like so many wild ants" and retreated to the bank of the river where they rolled into the stream after being shot, while others were killed as they tried to swim across. Tait expressed amazement over the behavior of some of the Creeks who "remained in their houses quite passive during the battle, suffering themselves to be slain without resistance." Tait ended his account by noting, "mercy was asked by some of the poor devils, but none shewn." Tait's concluding remark echoed the battlefield report sent by *Nashville Whig* editor Joseph Norvell on November 4, after the engagement at Tallushatchee: "Our orders are now to shew no quarters to the warriors." For the Creeks, it now became obvious the Americans were bent on a war of complete and total destruction.[52]

4

With the initial phase of the Creek War completed, Major General Thomas Pinckney began pressing Jackson to link the East and West Tennessee armies in order for them to march to the junction of the Coosa and Tallapoosa Rivers—a site known as the Hickory Ground—and establish a garrison there. Consequently, Jackson instructed John Cocke on December 6, 1813, to dispatch 1,500 men to Fort Strother by December 12. True to Jackson's request, Cocke marched his men into Fort Strother on that day, only to find an almost-deserted camp. The situation revolved around the dispute between Jackson and his volunteers, many of whom had enlisted on December 10, 1812, for the Natchez Expedition. Having enlisted for one year and dismissed in April 1813, the men were called up again in September 1813, when the Creek War broke out. The troops believed their enlistment period expired in December 1813, but Jackson insisted that time not spent in the field did not apply. In addition, the militia units that signed on with Jackson at the onset of the Creek War had done so with the understanding that their enlistment was for three months, which was fast drawing to an end. Jackson's appeals to Governor Blount to intervene went unheeded, the governor refusing to believe the men would mutiny: "I cannot somehow think that any of your army would be willing to return home before the Creeks are whipt and well whipt." Blount thought wrong, as would soon be seen.[1]

For Jackson, this mutinous conduct stung deeply, especially coming from the men who had shared the hardships and frustrations of the Natchez campaign with him. Jackson blamed the lack of supplies for the troops' disgruntled attitude, especially after the officers in Hall's brigade requested Jackson to allow the men to march back home to prepare for a further campaign—if not, they would desert. "Such a determination was not expected from those who had been trained & disciplined under my command," a slighted Jackson complained to Governor Blount. "I did think they would have followed me through every danger & hardship without a murmur—

they are the first to desert me." Jackson made a drastic error in judgment when he assumed the men he commanded shared the same fanatical zeal for war that he seemed to possess.[2]

Colonel William Martin, acting as spokesman for the perturbed volunteers, verbally sparred with Jackson in late November and early December 1813 through a steady stream of messages. In one lengthy letter to Martin, dated December 4, Jackson reminded the colonel that the troops who had enlisted for one year in December 1812 were technically "dismissed," not discharged, by him in March 1813. Officially, they were to serve until June 10, 1814. Only the president (through the secretary of war) had the power to discharge the men, yet Martin later revealed that Jackson had, in fact, issued certificates of "discharge" to the men in April 1813. In an emotional appeal, Jackson insisted he loved his men "as a fond father loves his children." But Martin did not buy into Jackson's demonstrative pleas. Samuel Bains, one of the volunteers, observed the tug-of-war between Martin and Jackson and praised the former for contending for the rights of the soldier by pointing out that "Martin is in as high estimation as the Genl. was in the last tour."[3]

It is clear from Jackson's correspondence that he blamed the officers, with a few exceptions, for stirring up the mutinous disposition of his troops. "Where sedition, mutiny or discontent exist in a camp, it originates with the officers and not with the men," Jackson later reflected. "This was fully proven on the night of the 9th of December [1813]." The showdown came on that night when Jackson called out the volunteers to parade in front of Fort Strother. There, Jackson ordered the militia, also on parade, to disarm the volunteers at the point of a cannon muzzle. Jackson implored the men to stay until replacements arrived within a few more days—then he would release them. It must have been a strange sight: Jackson aiming artillery at the men he referred to as "the first pride of my life" and commanding the militia to disarm them, while he entreated them to stay just a few more days. Jackson later referred to the incident as "a grating moment of my life."[4]

On that same evening, Jackson scribbled a note to John Coffee, then in Huntsville, telling his old friend that a mass mutiny might take place at Fort Strother. If so, and if Coffee should encounter any officers or men without written authority to return home, he was to arrest them and escort them back to Fort Strother. Should they resist, Coffee was authorized to "Immediately fire on them and continue the fire until they are subdued." Alternately blaming the lack of supplies and Colonel Martin for the "mutiny," Jackson again expressed his amazement that these volunteers should be "the last Troops on earth who would have asked to go home so long as an enemy was in front." In spite of Jackson's impassioned pleas and threats, many of the volunteers did leave and, as Jackson predicted, made their way to Huntsville. Out of sheer numbers, Coffee was helpless to try to stop them. Peter Perkins, who commanded the Madison County volunteers, complained to Jackson on December 16 that the deserting men were creating havoc in the town. Some of the residents of Huntsville, as well as Perkins own men, aided the deserters so that there was "almost a civil war at this place."[5]

In the meantime, the East Tennessee troops—1,450 in number—arrived at Fort Strother on December 12, as planned. Jackson, in a more jubilant mood, described them as "as fine looking Troops as you ever saw." A relieved Jackson saw an opportunity to immediately revive his campaign against the Creeks. "It would be treating the Holsten Troops, who I know are brave, impolitely, not to give them a fandango, before the time of service of part of them expires," Jackson lightheartedly wrote. The major general's elation quickly turned sour, though, when he learned that most of the East Tennesseans' enlistments were soon to expire on different dates—December 23, December 29, and January 1—and that they, too, were determined to go home. "If I advance, and get into the midst of the Indians," an exasperated Jackson wrote, "[I am] liable to be deserted, by Half my force."[6]

The East Tennesseans soon got caught up in the enlistment quarrels going on at Fort Strother. Jacob Hartsell noted there was more confusion there than he had seen anywhere else in his life, with all the men cussing and swearing. Displeased at being there, the East Tennessee troops preferred to fight the Creeks as soon as possible—some even threatening they would kill Jackson rather than stay three months more. Provisions and supplies were meager at best. Hartsell's entire company had only one tin bucket to cook in, while some of his men were even using a tin cup instead of a bucket. The estranged relations between Jackson and Cocke kept them literally at a distance, Jackson staying in his marquee inside Fort Strother while Cocke (with his Life Guard around him day and night) remained with the East Tennessee troops outside the fort.[7]

Jackson commiserated to his wife, Rachel, on the plight he faced in mid-December with his troops infested with "home mania," as he termed it: "Here I am within sixty-five or seventy-five miles of the whole hostile strength of the Creek Nation with no force that I can count on to march forward to chastise them, and no information from Gov. Blount whether any force is to be sent to enable me to carry on the campaign. Should it stop here, I fear for the scene that will be transacted on our frontier. The Creeks, conquered and beaten, on a retrograde of our forces, will give them vigor, and full confidence in their prophets, and we will have to fight them on our frontier." John Coffee, writing to his father-in-law John Donelson, painted an equally grim picture of the situation: "You can have no Idea of the clamor of the men, all disorder and daily desertions. . . . Each man seems to keep his Calendar before him and the very moment his three months expires, he demands his discharge."[8]

With January 4 as the date for discharging the West Tennessee militia, Jackson desperately needed a fighting force of men. Dispatches to Governor Blount proved to be frustrating. Beginning in early December 1813, Jackson communicated frequently with the governor about the militia enlistments. Personally, Blount felt the militia had signed up for a six-month tour of duty, but he had no authority to discharge *or* replace troops, needing to hear from Washington for a decision of that sort. Blount wrote to the secretary of war on December 10, explaining the complicated enlistment situation in Tennessee, citing three components: the volunteers who had enrolled under the acts of Congress, the militia detached under a requisition from the War Department, and volunteers who had answered the state's call to arms to repel a Creek invasion. The first believed their term expired on December 10, 1813; the militia felt their term should be no more than three months; and the third group also insisted on a three-month tour of duty. Blount needed some answers to the questions of how long the terms of enlistment should be for these three groups and how they should be replaced. Secretary of War John Armstrong gave his opinion on January 3, 1814, indicating that the militia must be considered to have been called out under the law that limited service to three months. Armstrong quoted President Madison as having based this decision on the supposition that "the spirit and patriotism" of Tennessee would provide the necessary substitutes needed to carry on the campaign. In the meantime, Blount informed Jackson in a December 15 letter that William Carroll had enlisted some replacements and that Jackson should dismiss the volunteers, with the understanding that there would be no provision for their being paid. Jackson relayed a copy of Blount's letter to General William Hall's volunteer infantry on December 23, giving them permission to leave, but "taking upon yourselves all the consequences & responsibility of such a measure."[9]

While Tennesseans hashed out the complexities of the enlistment acts, troops from Georgia and the Mississippi Territory were chalking up victories against the Red Sticks. After General John Floyd's Georgia militia soundly defeated the Creeks at Autosse in November 1813, the Red Sticks suffered another loss in the next month at a site know as Econochaca, or, the Holy Ground (on the Alabama River near the present-day town of White Hall, Alabama). The location had a particular significance for American forces, as it was a sacred spot for the Creeks (who considered it impervious), as well as the stronghold for William Weatherford and the Red Stick prophet Josiah Francis, two of the plotters of the Fort Mims massacre. General Ferdinand

Claiborne's army consisted of 700 Mississippi Territory volunteers, 150 Choctaws under their leader Pushmatawa, and the Third US Infantry commanded by Colonel Gilbert C. Russell—a total of 1,100 men. On December 23, the Americans tried unsuccessfully to surround Econochaca, but did manage to coordinate a three-pronged attack that caused the Red Sticks to hastily flee. American losses amounted to one killed and twenty wounded, while thirty-three lost their lives on the Creek side, including twelve African Americans fighting as allies of the Red Sticks. Besides being a morale booster, the battle netted thousands of barrels of corn—a welcome sight for troops who had been living on bread alone for the past eight or ten days. Before burning the village, the American troops found about three hundred scalps hanging in the public square of the village, many of them supposedly taken from the victims at Fort Mims. The Americans also discovered some correspondence between the Red Stick chiefs and the Spanish governor at Pensacola, providing evidence of a link between the two. Furthermore, the battle shattered the predictions Red Stick prophets made that the Holy Ground contained a magic barrier that would strike dead any white man who tried to pass through it.[10]

The news of the victory at the Holy Ground, coupled with the rout at Autosse by the Georgia troops, must have frustrated Jackson even more. After all, he had once complained that the other armies he was supposed to rendezvous with were too slow in their movements. Yet here he was mired in the middle of enlistment disputes, desertions, supply problems, and low morale. Governor Blount had added insult to injury by politely suggesting that Jackson temporarily give up the Creek campaign. In a lengthy reply to Blount, written in the midnight hour of December 29, an aggravated Jackson spelled out the reasons why he should *not* abandon the campaign. Putting the onus on Blount, Jackson reminded the governor that the state had mustered 3,500 men to repel the Creeks, a measure the president approved. Since no length of service was indicated, it was up to the governor to make sure 3,500 soldiers should always be in the field until the goal of complete extermination of the Creeks had been accomplished. Jackson chastised Blount for not doing his duty, noting that he had caved in to the whims of "those fawning sycophants or cowardly poltroons." Jackson also reminded Blount that the original plan for invading the Creeks called for a junction with the Georgia army—a circumstance that had not yet transpired. Thirdly, the Cherokees and friendly Creeks were counting on American protection, and to retreat now would be to expose them to destruction, which would be a sign of treachery on the part of the Americans and potentially add at least five thousand warriors to the strength of the enemy. If any of these arguments failed to move Blount, Jackson concluded with the bold claim that he would never retreat: "I will perish first. . . . If you compel me to retrograde the awful consequences must and will be ascribed to you, and you are politically damned forever. I shall do my duty. I will retain the post or die in the struggle." Armstrong's letter of January 3, 1814, supposedly settled the issue as to the length of enlistment term for the militia, but, of course, neither Jackson, Blount, nor the troops, knew of it at the time.[11]

Jackson's stance, noble at it was, still required an army that would fight. William Carroll and Brigadier General Isaac Roberts both returned to West Tennessee in December 1813 to drum up as many men as could be had. Instead of drafting the troops needed, Roberts ordered into service four companies of riflemen—from Maury, Lincoln, Bedford, and Giles Counties—in the Fifth Militia Brigade. The units rendezvoused at Fayetteville, then proceeded to Huntsville and were mustered somewhere south of Ditto's Landing. They halted two miles from Fort Strother, suspecting Jackson meant to compel them to serve six months rather than three. Roberts went on to Fort Strother to confront Jackson with the news that his men only wanted to serve three months. An argument ensued and Roberts stormed off to his tent to initiate a flurry of letters between the two men during the night. Roberts attempted to bring his men in on the next day, but they still refused and left for home, with the exception of Lieutenant Nathan Davis and a few others. Jackson later dispatched Lieutenant Davis to try to persuade his company to return. Davis actually managed to bring many of them back after a month's absence. But Jackson later blamed the desertion of Roberts's brigade for not ending the Creek War sooner than anticipated.[12]

In Nashville, William Carroll published a plea to the "Citizens of West Tennessee," urging them to join Jackson's army: "Are you not anxious to participate in the glory that awaits the patriot and brave? Come on then— hesitate not to share in the laurels nearly won." Apparently, most West Tennesseans were not that anxious, as Carroll's efforts only netted two small companies of volunteers (a total of nine hundred men), but only on the condition they served for *sixty* days—even less than the normally proscribed three months of the militia. In a December 15 letter to Jackson, Carroll complained of the "fireside patriots" in Nashville who talked a lot about the war but did little to aid the cause. "I had thought that Tennessee had patriotic citizens—I am mistaken, the storm of winter has cooled their ardour," Carroll grumbled. Carroll marched his green troops to Huntsville, wisely encamping them four miles from the town so that "the new troops might not be contaminated by the old." Carroll then spent the bulk of his time getting the men battle ready. In Huntsville, Colonel Peter Perkins amassed 250 mounted men and officers, but Coffee told Jackson the men were "of a mongrel kind," one-half of them being volunteers and the other half being drafted. Coffee was even less impressed with Carroll's sixty-day recruits, stating, "they are very clamorous and I fear will not do much good."[13]

Jackson was stunned when he learned that Carroll's recruits had enrolled for only sixty days. Jackson confided to Coffee that he had no authority to accept these terms or to pay them on that basis, yet he was in no position to turn the recruits away. It would now be even more difficult to get Coffee's men to rejoin Jackson, knowing the situation of the sixty-day volunteers. Coffee's men crossed the Tennessee River on December 28, despite Coffee riding after them to read Jackson's orders—Coffee called the occasion "this unhappy moment of our army." As his men began to desert in droves, Coffee, much like Jackson, resolved to remain firm at his post. "Let others do what they may," he wrote his wife, "it shall never induce me to do an act that will reflect on me when enquired into." Then, in a desperate move, Coffee intercepted Carroll's recruits in Madison County and tried to incorporate the two regiments into his brigade. The mounted volunteers protested, insisting they be led by William Carroll and taken to Jackson's headquarters at Fort Strother to "place ourselves under the immediate command of our valiant and esteemed Gen. determined to conquer or die under his standard." With that, Coffee took no more action on the matter.[14]

Between Carroll's sixty-day recruits, the remnants of Coffee's brigade, the Madison County volunteers, and a few stray units, such as Captain Eli Hammond's rangers and Captain John Gordon's spies, Jackson felt confident enough to launch another campaign into Creek territory. Manpower was stretched incredibly thin—in early January 1814 there were only fourteen men available to man Fort Strother—so much so that Jackson actually padded the figures for the sake of the troops' self-confidence. Jackson later admitted that he only had 767 men (including officers) when he set out on the new campaign, a lower count from those originally mustered. Some of the deficiency was due to sickness and the "coose fever." He did not reveal the real number out of concern it would demoralize the men. Fortunately, Jackson's army picked up at least two hundred friendly Creeks and sixty-five Cherokees at Talladega after leaving Fort Strother on January 17. Three days later, the army neared the mouth of Emuckfau Creek on the Tallapoosa River, where a force of Red Sticks (estimated at nine hundred strong) had assembled. Before leaving Fort Strother, Jackson addressed the volunteer regiments of Colonels Nicholas Perkins and William Higgins to try to persuade them the campaign ahead was not as dangerous as they might think—the Creeks being deficient of weapons and ammunition. He advised the men to be "cool and collected" in moments of action and to fire with deliberation, "making every shot tell." As for the Indian yells, Jackson reminded them "that yells never killed anyone, and to keep moving on the charge." Then, almost as a premonition, Jackson warned the men that if they ever found themselves in disorder and retreat—a situation he most dreaded—he reminded his men that the Creeks were excellent in using "the tomahawk and war club upon a scattered and flying foe."[15]

On January 21, 1814, Jackson's army camped on an eminence in an open forest where the ground in front was level for more than half a mile and level on all the other sides for about two hundred yards. The rear sloped to a deep valley through which Emuckfau Creek flowed. The army formed a hollow square with the horsemen forming the internal lines, while the artillery (the 6-pounder was brought along), allied Indians, horses, and baggage occupied the enclosed space. Sentinels were placed about two hundred yards in advance of the square. The watchword that night was "Stick to it."[16] The Tennesseans had little rest, as the picket guards frequently fired on Creek spies, now aware of Jackson's presence, reconnoitering the camp. About 4:00 a.m. on January 22, as the army awoke to prepare its breakfast, the alarm sounded and the guards came running back into camp, hotly pursued by the Creeks "yelling like demons." Jackson's raw troops responded with élan: "Every man in a moment, in the twinkling of an eye, seized his arms & was ready for the combat." The onrushing Creeks came within such a close distance to the campfires that some of them fell into the fires as they were shot. Jackson ordered a countercharge on his left, supported by Colonel Higgins's regiment and Captain Larkin Ferrill's company, and the repulsed Creeks took on heavy casualties as they were chased for two miles.

During the lull, Jackson instructed General Coffee to take four hundred men and the force of friendly Indians to burn the Creek fortifications on the Tallapoosa. Coffee's scouts reported the breastworks were too formidable to attack, and Coffee sent word back to Jackson that it would take the concerted effort of the whole army to take the stronghold. (The site was at Horseshoe Bend—a location Jackson would revisit two months later.) Upon Coffee's return, the Creeks renewed their attack, this time on the right (some accounts say the rear), and Coffee had to counterattack with Jackson's Life Guard (nicknamed the "Black Corps" from the number of servants attending their masters). Jackson instinctively held back the rest of his army, believing the Creek assault was a feint for a main thrust on the left. Jackson's perception proved correct as, in a few moments, there appeared on the army's left a Creek chief "in his war costume well mounted, with a bearskin cap, and horns as long as a half grown bullock," shouting out commands to his warriors. William Carroll now led a countercharge against this main attack on the left, while Coffee contended with superior forces on the right, as he only had about fifty men due to some misunderstanding of orders. Coffee recieved a wound during the fray and his aide (and brother-in-law), Major Alexander "Sandy" Donelson, was shot in the head. The men placed Donelson on a horse in front of a rider who took the body back to safety. As the horse and rider approached, one of Donelson's friends recognized the body as "the blood ran down his pale cheeks." Jackson came riding up to the scene and cried out "Sandy!" but Donelson (Rachel Jackson's nephew) was already dead. Jackson bluntly remarked, "well, it is the fortune of war."

Jackson next ordered Jim Fife, one of the principle commanders of the friendly Creeks, to take one hundred of his warriors and go to Coffee's aid. Upon being reinforced, Coffee launched a general charge and routed the enemy, whom they pursued about three miles, killing at least forty-five. William Carroll had successfully repulsed the main Creek attack and sent the Creeks into flight. At one point, some of the retreating Creeks sought cover in a canebrake, from which they could hold off any attackers. Colonel Richard Brown of the Cherokees and about twenty-five of his mounted men rode parallel to the canebrake in order to draw the fire of the Creeks, whose smoking guns revealed their exact position. The Cherokees charged into the morass and dispatched the Creeks with tomahawks before the Red Sticks could reload their rifles. By early afternoon, the battle was over.

Jackson decided to retreat to Fort Strother, yet knowing and hoping the Creeks would be lured into another fight. In addition, there were scant supplies available for the allied Indians he had picked up on the way to Emuckfau. In the meantime, the army would camp on the night of January 22 at the battle site. The American dead were buried with brush burned over the graves to prevent the Creeks from later digging up the bodies and scalping them. Soldiers assembled litters to carry the wounded, which included John Coffee, who had been wounded in his right thigh. The men also constructed a makeshift log wall around the camp in anticipation of a night attack. The evening was punctuated with so many repeated false alarms of sentinels running into the camp that it was impossible for the men to sleep. The gloom and anxiety of the night became temporarily broken by a frightened sentinel racing blindly into the camp and hitting a tree so hard as to almost knock himself out. He had been sleeping at his post and dreamed the Indians had attacked and were engaged in hand-to-hand combat. This comic episode brought rounds of laughter from the men and helped relieve the tension.

At ten thirty the next morning, Jackson's army began their return march to Fort Strother, stopping at nightfall two miles south of Enitachopco Creek.[17]

Jackson had a road cut to Enitachopco to draw the enemy after him, rather than risk being caught in an ambush. The army had trudged along, slowed down by the wagons, artillery piece, and the twenty-three litters that had to be carried over the uneven terrain. Each litter consisted of a blanket stretched between two poles and hitched to a horse in front and behind (the head of the rear horse hanging over the wounded soldier). This method required three healthy men to assist—one for each horse and one to attend to the wounded man. This meant that one-fourth of the troops would thus be occupied.

Most of the men had no tents, and a heavy rainfall that night made for a miserable experience. After an uneventful night, except for the occasional false alarms by the picket guards, the army left their campsite about 10:30 on the morning of January 24 and began to cross Enitachopco Creek. The front guard and part of the flank column had already traversed the stream, the last litter was climbing the opposite embankment, and horses were in the act of pulling the 6-pounder across, when the firing of the alarm gun sounded in the rear. Jackson heard the alarm with pleasure, rather than fear, as he had anticipated the attack to occur. "He turned to me as if what he wished the most was about to take place," John Reid recalled. But Jackson's smug look of satisfaction soon turned into absolute shock when he saw his rear guard "flying in wild confusion." The Creeks, in attacking Jackson's rear position, caused panic within the ranks, and soon the whole rear guard, with the exception of about two dozen men, fled in terror toward the stream. The thrust of the Creek force (about eight hundred in number) swooped down on those who remained, as the men heard the whine of bullets near their faces and felt the shots tearing into their uniforms.

The storming Creeks, yelling and pouring a destructive fire on the petrified troops, pushed through the rear guard and neared the Enitachopco Creek. Jackson, in vain, implored the men to stand and fight, trying desperately to draw his sword with his crippled left arm, nearly breaking the arm in the attempt. The artillery corps unlimbered the cannon from the horse, swung the cannon out of the water's edge and hauled it up to a small mound just in time to confront the enemy, then about thirty paces away. John Reid witnessed the action and passionately wrote about it three weeks later: "There they withstood, with the few brave who would not quit that side of the creek, & with those who individually rushed across to their relief, the whole brunt of the enemy for several moments. . . . I never saw such unbending and relentless bravery. Most of the artillery boys were in tears—but they were not shed for their dear comrades who were falling beside them—it was the expression of a determination which nothing but death could conquer." Fending off the

Creeks with their bayonets, while getting off two rounds of cannon fire, the artillery crew began to fall: Lieutenant Robert Armstrong, by the side of the cannon with a wound to his thigh; his friend, Bird Evans, sunk beside him; others fell wounded or killed, including Captain William Hamilton, an East Tennessee officer who, alone, had stood by Jackson during the December enlistment crisis. At one point, when they were about to fire the cannon, the men discovered the rammer and picker of the cannon had been left tied to the limbers in the confusion of the moment. Craven Jackson of the artillery corps pulled out the iron ramrod of his musket, used it as a picker, primed the cannon with a cartridge, and fired it. Constant Perkins, also of the artillery, pried off his bayonet, used his musket as a rammer, drove home the load with the muzzle of his musket while Craven Jackson again used the ramrod as a picker and the cartridge as a powder horn, firing the cannon once more. Lieutenant Armstrong fell just after the first firing of the cannon, exclaiming as he lay gravely wounded, "my brave fellows, some of you must fall but you must save the cannon."

The heroics of the artillery corps, or "Nashville Volunteers" as they were sometimes called, bought Jackson's army just enough time to regroup. John Coffee raised himself from his confinement on one of the litters to lead the rally. With the Creeks in front and on both sides of the Tennesseans, all seemed lost, until a charge of mounted men dashed across the creek and put the enemy to flight, pursing them for two miles. In the end, according to Andrew Jackson, twenty-six Creeks were found dead in the field—at least one of whom was killed by sixty-five-year-old Judge William Cocke, who had enlisted in the army as a private. (William Cocke was the father of General John Cocke, Jackson's East Tennessee rival. In his report, Jackson singled out Judge Cocke for killing an Indian and saving the life of a fellow soldier.) It was left for the Tennessee army to gather its dead and wounded, break camp, and head back to Fort Strother—a three-day march. The American dead were initially carried from Enitachopco by mounted men who held the bodies across their horses, waiting until the army camped on a level ground that first night in a dense forest. Richard Call, one of those who stood with the artillery corps in their moment of glory, remembered the burial of the dead in eerie detail: "It was a gloomy night, made so by the sad task of burying our dead, which work we did by torches. The flickering and uncertain light of which, added to the funereal gloom of the scene—increased by the doleful sound from the treetops, as the winter's wind swept over them, making a fitting requiem over the graves of the lamentable dead." For some, the journey back to the headquarters on the Coosa was nearly as grueling as the battles of January 22 and 24. Many had lost their baggage and equipment and had to lie on the ground at night without a fire or blanket for comfort, waking up nearly frozen each morning.

Arriving at Fort Strother on the evening of January 27, Jackson and his army—no longer green, raw troops—sat down to recuperate, reflect, praise, and incriminate. After the official reports were composed and sent out, Jackson and Coffee had the painful duty of notifying their families of Sandy Donelson's death. On January 28, Coffee penned a letter to Sandy's father, John Donelson. Never one for sentimentality, Coffee simply stated that Donelson's son had died by a gunshot to the head and then used the occasion to complain of the undisciplined troops he had to lead into battle, speculating that he could have driven the enemy off the field if he had had his old regiment of cavalry. In his letter to his wife, Mary (Sandy's sister), Coffee broached the subject with a bit more sensitivity. "I received a wound myself in my right side but not dangerous," Coffee informed her, "and your Brother Sandy is no more, a few minutes after I was wounded, he was shot through the head, and fell." Andrew Jackson notified Rachel of her nephew's demise by recounting the battle at Emuckfau and noting, "amongst the dead was our friend Major Alexander Donaldson [sic] who bravely fought and bravely fell." This news, coupled with Jackson's close call at Enitachopco, caused Rachel to go into a deep depression accompanied by illness, sleeplessness, and constant prayer.[18]

While Jackson had nothing but praise for the artillery corps, whom he referred to as "my little Spartan band," he condemned the actions of Colonel Nicholas Perkins and Lieutenant Colonel John Stump (commanding the right flank of the rear guard at Enitachopco), who he said "ought to be shot." Court-martial proceedings against the two officers were held at Fort Strother at the end of January, with Colonel William Higgins presiding. The charges were disobedience of orders, cowardice, and abandoning their posts. Subsequent testimony showed that Perkins had ordered his men to dismount and fight, but most of them fled in fright. The court absolved Perkins of all charges, but found Stump guilty and cashiered him out of the army.[19]

The campaign had been a close call for Jackson—too close. Although estimates of the Creek fighting force reached as high as eight hundred to a thousand, there were probably no more than five hundred warriors at Enitachopco. One military historian remarked that "had the Red Sticks been there in strength, Jackson might have gone down in history with Braddock and Custer." Nevertheless, the Tennesseans came through Emuckfau and Enitachopco relatively unscathed—casualties, according to Jackson, were four killed and several wounded in each battle. He estimated the Creek dead at roughly two hundred. The cowardly display of the rear guard at Enitachopco troubled Jackson more than anything else. Raw, undisciplined troops, led by pusillanimous commanders such as Lieutenant Colonel Stump, had to be avoided at all costs if the war was to be brought to a speedy termination. "The disorder that prevailed amongst officers & men in our late excursion," Jackson concluded, "was a striking example, and as sufficient warning never to enter the country of our enemy with troops not reduced to some kind of obedience & order." From this point forward, Jackson obsessed over the problem of discipline within his ranks—from contentious generals down to an insubordinate private—and would take drastic (in some cases too drastic) measures to ensure he had the army he needed to pursue his dreams of glory.[20]

In February 1814, Andrew Jackson learned of a large gathering of hostile Creeks at the bend of the Tallapoosa River near Emuckfau. He knew the place as the same one that General Coffee decided not to assault on January 22, a site known to the Americans as Horseshoe Bend. Jackson also heard that the Creeks fortified there were determined to defend the place to the last warrior. Jackson instinctively knew that a defeat of the Creeks at Horseshoe could spell an end to the Creek War. "This will be the hotbed of the war until destroyed," Jackson informed General Pinckney. By early March, Jackson wrote his wife from Fort Strother: "I am buried in preparations for a movement from this place . . . after I make a movement I shall put a speedy end to the Creek war, which as soon as it is done I shall without delay return to your arms." But before Jackson could return to Rachel's embraces, he had to coordinate plans for putting together an army he could rely on to conduct the campaign with precision and discipline. Getting help in gathering such an army was the first order of business. At the end of January 1814, William Cocke vowed to do what he could in hastening troops and supplies from East Tennessee, per Jackson's request. Next, Governor Willie Blount made a call for troops in February 1814—2,500 men from West Tennessee and 2,000 from East Tennessee. The long-held rivalry between the divisions reared its ugly head yet again when Major General John Cocke informed one of the East Tennessee regiments to return home while on their way to Fort Armstrong. Cocke insisted the troops had been enlisted illegally, leaving the East Tennesseans in a state of confusion. Jackson, having had enough of Cocke's interference, had the general arrested on charges of mutinous conduct. Jackson had reached his limit of tolerance—a quality he had no abundance of—and now acted with retribution.[21]

In Jackson's Second Division of militia, the assigned quotas of infantry remained delinquent. Brigadier General Thomas Johnson blamed the regimental officers for not holding courts-martial to inquire into the deficiencies. "I know the militia are brave," he reassured Jackson, "and we are marching to join the brave who have proved themselves as such." Such discouraging reports were offset by the loyalty shown by other officers such as Captain John Gordon and his company of spies. Gordon issued orders for his company to rendezvous at Huntsville on March 7, "well equipped for active and immediate service." He also encouraged enlistees "to come forward and share in the dangers and honors of the field." Jackson also welcomed the addition of a contingent of US Regulars to his army—the Thirty-Ninth US Infantry led by Colonel John Williams of Knoxville, who had coordinated the expedition into East Florida in late 1812. With a complement of six hundred men (mostly East Tennesseans), the Thirty-Ninth represented a regiment of disciplined, trained soldiers to round out Jackson's growing army and, perhaps more importantly, to help quell mutiny within the ranks.[22]

Jackson had another obstacle to overcome: supplies. Unreliable contractors forced Jackson to comment: "Contractors are the greatest curse to an army—and many times from their failures, [they] prevent movements that would prove fatal to an army." Jackson was determined the Horseshoe Bend campaign would not fail due to lack of provisions. "The source of all my fears are the want of supplies," he confessed before the March 27 battle. From Fort Strother, Jackson subcontracted with the Huntsville firm of Pope and Brahan, ordering a deposit of rations for forty days to feed three thousand men. He then ordered a similar deposit at Talladega and one at the junction of the Coosa and Tallapoosa Rivers (the future site of Fort Williams). Cost was to be no object, as he indicated to his contractors: "All I want is that my army should be furnished regularly and plentifully; and that must be done if any means in my power shall enable me to effect. This is a moment in which the least delay may prove ruinous to my hopes and to the Campaign. God forbid I should ever again see discontent and mutiny in my camp." Jackson's overall commander, General Thomas Pinckney, cautioned Jackson in February 1814 not to gather *too* large an army, as it would be difficult to keep it supplied.[23]

Obtaining the supplies did not solve the problem of getting them to the troops. Footpaths, trails, rivers, and streams crisscrossed the Creek Nation landscape, but few actual roads existed. In order to transport his much-needed supplies, Jackson relied on waterways (when he could) and the construction of new roads for supply wagons. The men assigned to do this back-breaking task were dubbed "pioneers"—whole battalions or regiments being used. Hacking a road out of the wilds took a tremendous amount of time and effort, as a battalion from Colonel Richard Napier's regiment discovered in February 1814. Nevertheless, Inspector General William Carroll became annoyed with Napier's lack of progress in road making. "He is like ninety nine officers out of a hundred in the service, *no energy*," complained Carroll. On March 22 Jackson entreated Colonel Robert Steele to expedite the building of the boats to get the supplies transported. "Hurry the contractors—hurry the boat builders—hurry every man on whose exertions the army has to depend for its supplies."[24]

While provisions and equipment beleaguered Jackson, manpower continued to come in from various quarters. One source—the Cherokee Indians—proved to be as dependable as they were fearless. The Cherokee forces fought alongside the Tennesseans in many of the engagements in the Creek War—most notably at Horseshoe Bend—wearing a deer tail or white plume in their hair to distinguish them from hostile Creeks. Despite their bravery in battle and the loss of life occasioned during the fighting, the Cherokees seldom received the credit due them in the official reports and newspaper accounts. Random acts of vandalism and robbery committed by the East Tennessee troops on Cherokee land became the biggest source of complaint from the Cherokees regarding their treatment by the white soldiers. Indian agent Return Meigs sent a strong protest to Secretary of War Armstrong regarding the wanton destruction of cattle and hogs by the troops, as well as the theft of Cherokee horses. The monetary claims placed on these depredations, mostly for stolen and butchered livestock, totaled nearly $6,000.[25]

Regardless of the fractured relations between the Tennesseans and the Cherokees, Colonel Gideon Morgan's regiment of warriors shared Jackson's enthusiasm for fighting. In late February 1814, Morgan sent a message to Jackson from Fort Armstrong, where the Cherokee regiment languished, advising the general of the frustration shared by the Cherokees over not being able to finish the job because of supply shortages. Lagging spirits were lifted when Jackson ordered the regiment on to Fort Strother, to rendezvous with his army. John Ross, a lieutenant in Morgan's regiment, urged all Cherokees "who wish to signalize themselves by fighting & taking revenge for the blood of the innocent" to step forward and join the ranks. At Horseshoe Bend, the Cherokees would sacrifice eighteen of their warriors in battle while thirty-six of them returned home wounded.[26]

The Cherokee contingent, five hundred strong, joined Jackson's army at Fort Strother, where Jackson's massive army of nearly four thousand men gathered. Leaving about five hundred men under Colonel Robert Steele at the fort, Jackson set out on March 14 with a force of about three thousand (in addition to the five hundred Cherokees and one hundred friendly Creeks). Before departing, Jackson had a young volunteer by the name of John Woods executed by a firing squad in the presence of the entire army. Woods had been found guilty of disobedience of orders, disrespect to his commanding officer, and mutiny—charges that demanded the death sentence, which, in most instances, was commuted by the commanding general. In this case, however, Jackson approved the sentence of the court-martial and instructed that Woods be shot by a detail of twelve men from the Thirty-Ninth US Infantry. In a letter to General Pinckney, written on March 14, Jackson informed Pinckney his army would be marching that day, beginning at noon. "They have been detained a little this morning—mutiny having again shewn itself in my camp," Jackson reported. "A private (John Wood) having been sentenced by a court martial to suffer death by shooting," Jackson continued, "that ceremony is now in the act of execution." The letter belies the later story that Jackson could not bring himself to witness the execution and, thus, rode out of camp while the firing squad did its duty. Actually, Jackson exceedingly regretted "that Genl. Doherty's Brigade is not present to witness it." The execution no doubt had a sobering effect on Jackson's troops, as they crossed the Coosa River on the first leg of their journey into Creek territory.[27]

While Jackson marched the bulk of his army southward, he had his supplies, accompanied by the Thirty-Ninth US Infantry, transported down the Coosa River. Most of the mounted men were to move out later and overtake Jackson, with instructions to march in the center of the flank columns in order to prevent the enemy from turning the army's flanks. The rifle company making up this center position, considered Jackson's Life Guard, had as its head Lieutenant Nathan Davis, handpicked by Jackson to command the detachment. The favoritism Jackson showed sparked jealousy among the other rifle companies, who refused to march with Davis. After an uneventful trek through Creek territory, Jackson's army reached the halfway point on March 21 at the mouth of Cedar Creek on the Coosa River (in present-day Talladega County, Alabama). Here, he began construction of a fortified depot named Fort Williams, in honor of the Thirty-Ninth Infantry's commander. On March 22, Jackson wrote to Colonel Robert Steele back at Fort Strother to hasten the delivery of the army's supplies. Miraculously, Williams and his regiment, along with the army's provisions, arrived by boat on that same day.[28]

Jackson ordered a detachment form General Thomas Johnson's brigade to scour the area and burn any neighboring Creek villages, "killing all the warriors and making prisoners of all the women and children." The detachment returned the following day, having found only empty, abandoned villages, along with a number of white scalps. On March 24 Jackson prepared his army to move out of Fort Williams heading to Horseshoe Bend. Not wishing to get caught in another Enitachopco-like disaster, a cautious Jackson ordered one hundred men from General George Doherty's brigade and another hundred from Johnson's brigade to reconnaissance for seven miles in order to spot any large parties of Indians. He placed Colonel Ewen Allison in command of the detachment, calling him "a good woodsman and an officer of experience in Indian warfare."[29]

Addressing the army before departing, Jackson admonished his men to be cool and collected in battle ("let every shot tell"); ignore the yells of the Indians; and, most importantly, to never retreat: "any officer or soldier who flies before the enemy without being compelled to do so by superior force and actual necessity—shall suffer death." The army consisted of six hundred men from General Doherty's brigade, six hundred from General Johnson's brigade, all of the Thirty-Ninth US Infantry, all of General Coffee's mounted men (including the Cherokees and friendly Creeks), the artillery company, and Lieutenant Davis's company. All were given twenty-four rounds of ammunition and eight days' worth of rations (four days of bacon, four days of jerked beef, and "bread stuff"). General Johnson stayed behind at Fort Williams, with approximately four hundred men, to guard the newly built stockade. The army moved out at 5:00 a.m. on March 24. It would be a grueling journey of over fifty miles across unmapped, hilly terrain. Once encamped for the evening, no fires were allowed; sentinels were posted and ordered to be extremely vigilant, but "not to fire at shadows"; and reveille was to be at 4:00 a.m. each day.[30]

More than fifty miles to the east, the Red Sticks waited for the Anglo-Americans at a fortified location at a bend in the Tallapoosa River known to the Creeks as Choloco Litabixee ("Horse's Flat Foot"), nearly one hundred acres in a U-shaped bend on the river enclosed by an ingeniously constructed breastwork crisscrossing its way across the neck of the peninsula. Composed of five large, horizontal logs ranging from five to eight feet in height, the works appeared to be remarkably strong and compact. Double rows of portholes were strategically arranged so that an approaching enemy would be exposed to a deadly crossfire. Jackson admitted that "the skill which they manifested in their breast-work, was really astonishing." The fortifications were situated on an area of high ground that sloped down to the river, where a village (Tohopeka—Creek for "wooden fence" or "fort") of one thousand Creek warriors and their families lived. In charge was the Creek chief, Menewa, who forewent the usual procedure of removing the women and children from a battle site, perhaps indicating the Red Sticks' determination to be victorious or die in the process.[31]

Early on the morning of March 27, 1814, Jackson's army lay encamped only six miles from Tohopeka. The general dispatched Coffee's brigade (with the

Indian allies) on a route that would take them three miles below the Creek encampment, on the opposite side of the Tallapoosa, to prevent any escape via the river. By 3:00 a.m. Coffee began rousing his cavalry and mounted men—seven hundred in number, along with six hundred Indians—in preparation to move out. At 6:30 a.m. Coffee's force was on its way. Meanwhile, Jackson took the main body and approached the village up to the point of the breastworks. Jackson planted his artillery pieces—one 3-pounder and one 6-pounder—on a small rise about eighty yards from the nearest portion of the Creek fortifications. He then positioned his army in front of the works: behind an advance guard was Colonel John Williams's Thirty-Ninth US Infantry; General George Doherty's East Tennessee militia was on the right (led by Colonel Samuel Bunch); while the West Tennessee militia (under Captain James McMurry) held the left position, along with Captain John Gordon's company of spies.[32]

Between 10:00 and 10:30 a.m., Jackson's artillery began to probe the strength of the Creek fortifications with shots directed at the log walls. Behind the works, Creek warriors taunted and shouted at the soldiers, periodically exposing themselves to return fire on the Americans. Salvo after salvo failed to penetrate the breastworks to any sizeable degree—about seventy rounds being expended. Meanwhile, Jackson's exposed troops lay flat on the ground. General Doherty and Colonel Williams twice implored Jackson to allow the militia and regulars to storm the breastworks, but Jackson refused, hoping the artillery would eventually breach the fortifications.

As the artillery hammered on the walls of the Creek compound, Coffee's men on the opposite side of the Tallapoosa were growing equally restless, especially his Cherokee troops. The Indians lined the banks of the river for the whole extent of the bend, while Coffee's cavalry acted as a guard on the high ground to defend the rear from any attack. Coffee described what happened next: "The firing of [the] cannon and small arms in short time became general and heavy, which animated our Indians, and seeing about one hundred of the warriors and all the squaws and children of the enemy running among the huts of the village which was open to our view, they could no longer remain silent spectators, while some kept up a fire across the river (which is about 120 yards wide) to prevent the enemy's approach to the bank, others plunged into the water and swam the river for canoes that lay on the other shore in considerable numbers, and brought them over, in which crafts a number of them embarked, and landed on the bend with the enemy." At this point, Colonel Gideon Morgan made his way across the river downstream to report to Major Lemuel Montgomery, who commanded the left wing of the Thirty-Ninth US Infantry, of the progress made by the Cherokees. Upon his return, Morgan found that nearly two hundred Cherokees had made their way across the Tallapoosa and were engaging the enemy in the village, fighting their way to the high ground that was midway between the river and the breastworks. Morgan then crossed the river himself, along with thirty others, to join the fight. He received a severe wound above his right eye during the ensuing battle, rendering him unconscious. When Morgan came to, he found his right arm and leg partially paralyzed, and he eventually lost sight in his right eye.

Jackson, now realizing the breastworks had to be stormed to be taken, finally consented to Doherty's and Williams's third imploration to charge the works. Shortly after the noon hour, the fourteen-year-old drummer of the Thirty-Ninth sounded the long drum roll for an attack. John Reid recalled the intensity of that moment: "Never were men more anxious to be led to the charge than both our regulars and militia. The long roll was sounded, and they moved forward to the charge with an undauntedness which was altogether astonishing. . . . I never had such emotions as while the long roll was beating, & the troops in motion. It was not fear, it was not anxiety or concern for the fate of those who were so soon to fall, but it was a kind of enthusiasm that thrilled through every nerve, & animated me with the belief that the day was ours, without adverting to what it must cost us." As the onrushing soldiers collided with the breastworks, a brief contest ensued as the muzzles of the white soldiers' muskets clashed with those of the Indians' through the portholes—so close that many of the Indians' musket balls were welded to the bayonets of the Americans' muskets.

Tradition has it that Major Lemuel Montgomery was the first one to scale the breastworks, dying in the process. Montgomery, a twenty-five-year-old officer in the Thirty-Ninth US Infantry with good family connections and a promising law career back in Nashville, led the charge to the wooden walls of the fortifications and was in the act of climbing over the breastworks, calling for his men to press on, when he was shot through the head and immediately expired. Yet John Coffee later related that Montgomery reached the works, fired his pistol through a porthole (slaying an Indian in the process), but received a fatal shot through the same opening, instantly killing him. Interviews conducted years later about the battle indicated a soldier named James Love may have been the first one over the walls. Just as Love was in the act of leaping down, a Red Stick hurled a tomahawk, striking Love in the face (leaving a huge scar for the rest of his life). Still, the image of Montgomery atop the breastworks—"waving his hat and huzzaing when he received the ball in the head which instantly killed him"—remained fixed in the public's memory of the battle. Montgomery's death is mentioned in practically every account of the battle, official or otherwise.

Once the works had been overtaken, the Creeks found themselves pinched between two assaults: one from the front by the US Regulars and Tennessee militia that came spilling over the breastworks; and one from the rear, where Jackson's Indian allies successfully managed to infiltrate the village by way of the river and were making their way to the high ground. There was no escape. Coffee's men and the Cherokees waiting on the opposite shore cut down those Creeks who tried to swim the Tallapoosa to safety. The Americans left no vacant spot on the riverbank, and the fleeing Creeks "fell an easy prey to their vengeance." Indeed, one participant described the Tallapoosa as "a River of blood."

At the breastworks, the combat turned hand-to-hand as the US Thirty-Ninth clambered over the walls. Twenty-one-year-old Ensign Sam Houston scaled the works and hit the ground when a barbed arrow struck deep into his thigh. Houston tried to pull the arrow out, but failed. He cried out to his lieutenant to extract the arrow and, after two painfully futile attempts, Houston raised his sword and demanded the officer try it one more time, "and if you fail this time, I will smite you to the earth." The panicked lieutenant frantically yanked on the arrow, tearing the flesh as the arrow finally came loose. A bright stream of blood gushed from the open wound and Houston recrossed the breastworks to have a surgeon bind the gash. General Jackson, checking on his injured, spotted the young ensign and ordered him not to return to battle, despite Houston's pleas to do so. Ensign Houston, however, disregarded Jackson's orders and once more rushed to the breastworks to rejoin his comrades. Other officers, including William Carroll (who received a wound), got caught up in the frenzy of the onslaught and left their positions in order to participate in the battle. Jackson recalled that "it was difficult to detain the artillery men at their posts, although 10 had been previously wounded."

The Creeks on the high ground retreated to a second line of defense—makeshift breastworks of fallen timber, cut underbrush, and mounds of earth—fighting with whatever weapons they had. The next five hours would be the severest part of the battle, and despite the fact that "the Creeks fought with their usual desperation . . . the slaughter was great." Still the Creeks fought on, asking for no quarter and giving none. The Creek prophets exhorted their warriors to fight on and most of them did, even after being wounded, fearing a more painful death if they were taken prisoner by the white troops. The Creeks were systematically cut to pieces. "The whole margin of the river which surrounded the peninsular was strewn with the slain," recalled Jackson. In the heat and fury of the battle, the Tennessee soldiers displayed deeds of unselfish courage, as well as despicable acts of atrocity. Lieutenant Jesse Webb testified to being hit in the right arm by a Creek bullet when a second bullet lodged in his left groin. Then, a third shot struck him in the right breast. Webb fell to the ground and lay there bleeding as a Creek warrior ran up and smashed his war club across Webb's chest, breaking his breastbone. The Indian was about to take Webb's scalp when a fellow soldier bayoneted the Creek. Webb tried to get out of danger, but every time he would try to rise up, he would fall headlong onto the ground. Losing more blood each time he fell, Webb was near death when Captain Moses Davis braved a hail of bullets and arrows to drag the gravely wounded Webb to safety. In the Creek village, an old Indian sat pounding corn meal oblivious to the yelling and screaming of women and children, the zigzag firing between the Indians and whites, and the roaring flames of the burning buildings. A Tennessee soldier went up to the old man and shot him, presumably so he could tell the folks back home that he had killed an Indian. Another soldier rushed up to a young Creek boy, about five or six years of age, and crushed his head with the butt of his musket. When an incredulous officer demanded to know why he did it, the soldier crassly replied, "Oh, it is all the same, he will make an Indian someday."

Surrounded, and with no possible means of escape, the Creeks continued to fight to the finish. Jackson advanced near an angle of the second breastworks with his interpreter, George Mayfield of Captain Gordon's spies, taking cover behind an oak tree. Jackson instructed Mayfield to request that the Creeks surrender, assuring them they would be treated humanely. When the Creek warriors heard Mayfield call out to them in their language, they halted their firing long enough to hear his words. But their reply consisted of several shots at Jackson—one bullet glancing off the bark of the tree near Jackson's head and hitting Mayfield's right shoulder.

The battle continued with renewed ferocity until sundown with one last stronghold remaining for the Creeks: a section of the secondary breastworks built over a ravine in the form of a roof with narrow portholes from which musket fire could be kept up. The terrain was too rugged for Jackson's artillery to be brought up, so he called for volunteers to charge this last remnant of Creek resistance. When no officer ventured forward to lead the advance, Ensign Sam Houston, still crippled from his wounds, called upon his platoon to follow him toward the ravine. Their hesitation prompted Houston to seize a musket from one of the men and plunge forward alone. Amid a storm of arrows and bullets, the ensign advanced within five yards of the portholes when he received two rifle balls in his right shoulder, disabling his arm. Houston finally collapsed to the ground, continuing to implore his still-reluctant troops to make the charge. Finally, the soldiers decided to set fire to the logs and underbrush in an attempt to dislodge the Indians. As the sun set on Tohopeka, the flames of the burning brush illuminated small groups of Creek warriors scurrying from the inferno only to be shot down by the waiting Tennesseans. The killing continued until it became too dark to see.

As nighttime hid the battlefield, sight gave way to sound, as the groans of the wounded and dying knifed through the air. "It was the darkest night of my life," recalled the severely wounded Sam Houston. After the surgeon removed one of the balls in Houston's right shoulder, he told the young ensign there was no use extracting the other, as he would probably not last the night. "Everybody looked on me as a dying man," Houston grimly remembered. Houston, of course, somehow survived. Lieutenant Jesse Webb also endured his ordeal, having lain on the ground most of the night unattended. In all, thirty-two Americans were killed and ninety-nine wounded during the battle; the Cherokees lost eighteen killed and thirty-six wounded; and the allied Creeks had five killed and eleven wounded. As for the Creeks, estimates vary as to how many escaped the slaughter at Horseshoe Bend. Jackson and his staff claimed no more than twenty or thirty managed to evade their deaths, although the figure is probably much higher.

On the morning of March 28, the Americans turned their attention to the numbers of Creek slain that lay on the battlefield. The tips of the noses of each dead body were cut off to ensure an accurate count—557 tips being collected. In doing this deed, the Americans were adding insult to injury, as the punishment for the crime of stealing in Creek society called for the slitting of the offender's nose (and ears). Whether knowing it or not, the Americans desecrated the bodies of those warriors who fell in battle by physically mutilating their bodies and psychologically labeling them as thieves. Among the dead were "two or three women and children . . . killed by accident," according to Jackson. In addition to a count of enemy dead on the battlefield, Jackson wanted an estimate of those killed while trying to cross the Tallapoosa. Consulting with officers stationed along the river during the contest, Jackson felt secure in reporting an extra 250–300 enemy dead to his overall count. Thus the Creek fatalities at Horseshoe Bend reached as high as nine hundred, making the battle one of the most devastating losses for Native Americans in North American history.[33]

Yet the carnage was still not over. A small group of hostile Creeks, about sixteen in number, took refuge in one the caverns dug out of the bluff of the riverbank for extra protection. Attempts to dislodge them by gunfire proved futile and dangerous. Not wanting to sacrifice any more American lives, someone suggested a more elaborate, yet effective, plan: "A ditch about three feet deep was dug along the edge of the bluff, entirely across the shelving part. A row of long sharpened pine stakes was then driven deep along in the bottom of the ditch, at intervals of about eighteen inches apart. The soldiers by this means at last succeeded in splitting off the entire mass of earth forming the shelving bluff, which falling upon the lurking warriors beneath, completely buried them alive." While the sixteen Creeks were being smothered to death, some Tennessee soldiers were engaged in the age-old tradition of combing the battle site for souvenirs. Lieutenant Benjamin Wright of the US Thirty-Ninth pilfered some silver ornaments from the body of an Indian he slew the day before. He later had them fashioned into forks and spoons, which his family preserved for generations. Wright also discovered an infant boy in the bushes by the river, whom he brought back to Tennessee to raise, naming him Roses. Some of the soldiers took home more grisly souvenirs, such as bridle reins made from long strips of skin cut from dead Indian bodies.[34]

As to their own dead, the Tennesseans had the grim task of disposing their fellow soldiers' bodies. With the exception of Major Montgomery, the bodies of the slain were sunk in the Tallapoosa River to prevent the Creeks from mutilating the corpses (some of the American dead at Emuckfau had been found stripped and scalped). Montgomery's corpse was buried on the battlefield with precautions taken to make sure no Indian would discover its location—the dirt dug up was carried to the river and brush was burned over the fresh soil to conceal the grave. The wounded were placed on litters hitched to a horse from the front and behind. Many of the wounded suffered greatly from the excruciating, three-day journey back to Fort Williams, several of them dying along the way. Arriving at the fort, accommodations were made to provide for the wounded, as the exhausted soldiers swapped their tales of combat with those who had remained at the fort. Lieutenant Benjamin Cloud, left on guard duty, heard the sorrowful news that his younger brother, William, had been killed at Tohopeka, his body wrapped in a blanket, and sunk in the Tallapoosa River. Benjamin had asked to take his brother's place on the line of march to Horseshoe Bend—tragically, his request had been denied.[35]

Historians have labeled the Battle of Horseshoe Bend as the climax of the Creek War, but, at the time, the Tennesseans were sure the conflict required at least one more punishing blow on the Red Sticks. John Coffee's letters to his wife during the first week of April 1814 indicated that blow would be leveled at the site known as the Hickory Ground (Hothlewaule), near the junction of the Coosa and Tallapoosa Rivers in the heart of the Creek Nation.

Knowing the enemy to be starving, Coffee felt the hostile Creeks could not hold out much longer. Coffee expected to be home that summer, when Tennessee's army of three thousand would join with the Georgia troops and put an end to the war. Despite heavy rains and short supplies, Jackson marched his army to the Hickory Ground, arriving on April 17, only to find the town deserted. Soon, as droves of starving Creeks poured into Jackson's camp to surrender unconditionally, Jackson came to the realization the Creek War was, indeed, at an end.[36]

Word of Jackson's victory reached welcome ears in Tennessee and beyond. Tennessee congressman John Rhea told his constituents that the decisive battle at Tohopeka "will long be remembered; and will instruct tribes of Indians to confide in the United States and not to be seduced by a foreign power." Kentucky's old Indian fighter, Isaac Shelby, wrote to William Henry Harrison about Jackson's published report of Horseshoe Bend. "He is eclipsing every thing that has been before him in respect to Indian fighting—at least in killing them by [the] hundreds," Shelby confided with glee. "Those miserable wretches will have Occasion long to Mourn the day they listened to Tecumseh's talks." A Saint Louis newspaper, bemoaning Missouri's own Indian problems, cried out: "The BLOOD of our citizens cry aloud for VENGEANCE. The general cry is let the north as well as the south be JACK-SONIZED!!!"[37]

Approximately 8,200 Creek refugees, starving and homeless, poured into the Creek agency and US forts in the summer of 1814, seeking rations. One North Carolina soldier, recently stationed in Alabama, wryly commented: "It appears to me that we came to feed more than fight them." Jackson was seemingly more sensitive to their sufferings. "It is enough to make Humanity shudder to see the distressed situation of the Indians," he told Rachel, "eight thousand are kept alive, being fed by the Government daily." In a later letter, Jackson referred to the Creek refugees as "the most distressed wretches you ever saw," adding: "Could you only see the misery and wretchedness of those creatures perishing from want of food and picking up the grains of corn scattered from the mouths of the horses and trodden in the earth—I know your humanity would feel for them, notwithstanding all the causes you have to feel hatred and revenge against."[38]

For Tennessee and the rest of the nation, the Creek War seemed to be at an end by April 1814. Creek villages lay in smoldered ruins, while flags of truce were being waved at Jackson's army. General Thomas Pinckney arrived at Fort Jackson with troops from the Carolinas to relieve the Tennesseans expected to leave for home by the end of the month. "Thus the creek war is ended," John Coffee wrote on April 25. Disturbing reports coming from the Mississippi Territory, however, cast doubts on whether the Creek War was, indeed, finished. In early May 1814 the Nashville *Clarion* proudly bore a headline "The Creek War at an End," but a month later the newspapers announced "The Creek War Not Over." The abrupt change came as a result of rumors that the Spanish were supplying the Creeks with arms and ammunition at Pensacola. Commenting on the rumors, the *Clarion* proclaimed: "We have often said it, and still repeat the remark, there is as much friendship in the Creeks as in the Spaniards who are under British influence. A later report stated there were one thousand Indians at Pensacola, well supplied by the British, who provided 17,000 stands of arms. To add to the angst, it was believed the British sought to arm runaway slaves as well. The *Clarion* predicted another bloody campaign with the Creeks: "We make no other calculation than that many valuable lives will be lost before a permanent peace will be made."[39]

As the summer progressed, so did the magnitude of the rumors of a British invasion on the Gulf Coast. George Strother Gaines, writing from St. Stephens, related to his brother in Hawkins County, Tennessee, that the "high spirits" raised by Jackson's victory at Horseshoe Bend had been cut in half by reports coming out of Pensacola of the British landing with 22,000 stands of arms, hundreds of British troops, and the eventual arrival of several thousand black soldiers from the West Indies. "If all this be true we shall have even a warmer summer than the last," Gaines gloomily wrote. Tennesseans were taking time that summer to celebrate their victories over the Creeks and welcome home their hero, Andrew Jackson. On his way back to Nashville, Jackson and his officers were feted in Huntsville on May 7 with a dinner and ball, after being escorted into town by the citizens. Jackson's entourage arrived in Nashville on May 14 to a welcoming committee comprised of Captain Deaderick's artillery, a company of Cumberland College students, and a detachment of the US Twenty-Fourth Infantry. There followed several days of dinners, balls, speeches, toasting, and the firing of musketry. On one particular occasion, Jackson set the tone for what was to become the political climax of the Creek War: "We have laid the foundation of a lasting peace to those frontiers which had been so long and so often infested by the savages we have conquered. We have added a country to ours, which by connecting the settlements of Georgia with those of the Mississippi Territory, and both of them with our own, will become a secure barrier against foreign invasion, or the operation of foreign influence over our Red neighbors in the south." The dream of linking the regions of the Old Southwest was about to become a reality. It only remained for the Americans to figure out the means by which the Creeks would defray the expenses of the Creek War.[40]

The anticipated treaty with the Creeks raised the hopes of southerners eager to profit, one way or another, from the acquisition of Creek territory. As early as February 1814, George Strother Gaines informed his brother in Tennessee: "Should the Alabama lands fall into the hands of our Gov[ernmen]t & I will not doubt it, you must come out & select you a tract of land & bring all our friends with you if possible." "Alabama will be the garden of America ere many years," Gaines predicted. The much-awaited treaty with the Creeks took place in early August 1814 at the site of the newly constructed Fort Jackson, the earth-and-wood structure standing on the east bank of the Coosa River, just north of where it joined the Tallapoosa. As an operation of the federal government, Secretary of War John Armstrong appointed Major General Thomas Pinckney of the Sixth Military District, along with Creek Indian agent Benjamin Hawkins, to conduct the negotiations. The selections could not have been more upsetting to the martial-minded westerners, who viewed both individuals (especially Hawkins) as too forgiving of the Creeks. The *Clarion* pronounced Hawkins to be a man who, on every occasion, has "manifested a spirit of hostility to the interests of this state." "He is a man the citizens of Tennessee have no confidence in," declared the newspaper. John Coffee and other Tennessee officers bitterly complained about having no voice in the terms of peace "after we have under all the privations undergone, conquered the Country and reduced them to unconditional terms." Their fears of a pacifist treaty were confirmed when they learned of the initial conditions of the treaty—as proscribed by the War Department—calling for a land cession from the Creeks only large enough to compensate the United States for the cost of the war.[41]

It was obvious to practically every westerner that Andrew Jackson should be involved at the treaty proceedings. As fate would have it, timing favored that very scenario. Partly as a reward for his victories in the Creek War, Jackson received a commission of major general in the US Army with the position of commander of the Seventh Military District, replacing Thomas Flourney. Opponents of Pinckney and Hawkins eventually secured their removal as chief negotiators, making way for Jackson to dictate entirely new terms to the Creeks. Jackson held little regard for parlaying with Indians, having very clear ideas on how the treaty at Fort Jackson should transpire. In mid-May 1814 he had indicated to General Pinckney that the primary function of the treaty should be the connection of the settlements in Georgia to those of the Mississippi Territory and Tennessee, and, therefore, lands west of the Coosa River and north of the Alabama River should be included in the truce. In the same month Jackson suggested to James Monroe that the government grant preemption rights to potential settlers of the newly acquired land and, also, "to give to the officers and soldiers a preference who conquered it." "The sooner this boundary is fixed the better," an impatient Jackson told Colonel John Williams.[42]

Jackson forecasted the Creeks allied to the Americans might become hostile over the newly proposed boundary lines of the treaty, but that did not stop him from gathering nearly three dozen of their leaders to Fort Jackson and coercing them to cede twenty-three million acres of Creek land (the majority of Red Stick leaders having been killed or fled to the Floridas). In addition to the loss of land, the treaty demanded the Creeks "abandon all communication, and cease to hold any intercourse with any British or Spanish post, garrison, or town," or admit any agent or trader not licensed by the United States. The treaty also gave the United States the right to establish military posts and trading houses, to open roads within the territory, and "a right to the free navigation of all its waters." Lastly, the treaty called for "the capture and surrender of all prophets and instigators of the war, whether foreigners or natives . . . if ever they shall be found within the territory guaranteed to the Creek nation." The wording of the document cleverly put the onus of the war clearly on the Creeks, calling it "an unprovoked, inhuman, and sanguinary war, waged by the hostile Creeks against the United States."[43]

As predicted by Jackson, the friendly Creeks vehemently protested the terms of the treaty. Big Warrior, addressing the proceedings on August 6, stated the reason for the Creek War as being the shedding of white blood by the Red Sticks—a faction that had not yet been entirely defeated. Big Warrior suggested the government wait until the hostiles were terminated and then discussions about compensation could begin. On the next day, Jackson replied to Big Warrior by insisting there was more to the causation of the war than the shedding of white blood. Jackson blamed *all* the Creeks for not turning in Tecumseh when the Shawnee leader was spreading his message among the Creeks. "If my enemy goes onto the house of my friend, and tells my friend he means to kill me," Jackson reasoned, "my friend becomes my enemy, if he does not at least tell me I am to be killed." As for the Creek War not being over, Jackson readily agreed, stating why it was important to conclude the treaty at that point in time: to keep the friendly Creeks separate from hostile ones so that the United States could protect them. On the day the Creeks signed or put their mark on the treaty—August 9, 1814— Creek leaders petitioned the government for redress, viewing the proceedings as unfair: "We do not deem the exchange as equivalent." On the next day, Jackson bragged to John Coffee about the land cessions acquired from the treaty, alluding to it as "the best unsettled country in America." Jackson then quickly left the distraught Creeks behind in Fort Jackson, making his

way to Mobile via the Alabama River. Floating past the lands now in possession of the United States, Jackson imagined "elegant mansions and extensive
rich & productive farms" lining the banks of the Alabama , which would add
"greatly to the wealth as well as the security of our Southern frontier." "This
acquisition of territory cuts off all direct communication between Spanish
agents and the Creek tribe," the *Clarion* echoed, "and enables our government
to connect the white settlements of Georgia and the Mississippi territory."[44]

Within a year of the Treaty of Fort Jackson, settlers from the Mississippi
Territory were already encroaching on Creek lands—planting corn, taking over Indian homes, and threatening Creeks—even before the boundary
lines had been run. Surveyor John Strother complained to Jackson in June
1815 of the difficulties surveying the Creek treaty line, citing interference by
Benjamin Hawkins, who stressed to the commissioners that full and ample
remuneration should be made to the Creeks for their losses before the lines
could be laid out. Strother referred to Hawkins as a "notorious hostile chief."
Jackson responded in a letter dated September 4, 1815, warning the Creek
chiefs not to interfere with the survey: "Listen I tell you that line must and
will be run, and the least opposition brings down instant destruction on the
heads of the opposers." Although the treaty was submitted to the Senate in
November 1814 and referred to a select committee in December, there seemed
to be great resistance to its ratification until Jackson's victory at New Orleans.
The treaty was then ratified unanimously on February 16, 1815. In the end,
the Creeks gave up approximately 60 percent of what is now Alabama and
20 percent of Georgia.[45]

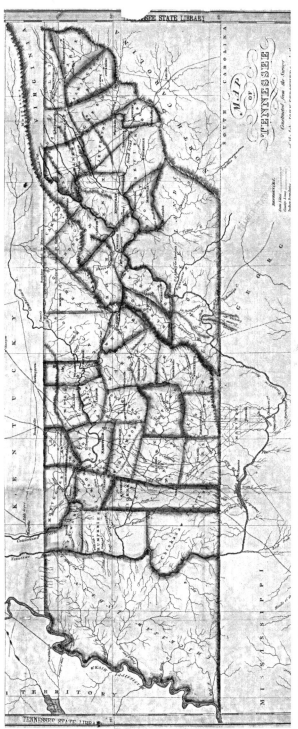

1. Map of Tennessee. This 1818 map by John Melish shows the counties in the state as they existed about the time of the War of 1812. Note the land within the state occupied by Indians—a source of contention that Tennesseans were determined to reverse. (Courtesy Tennessee State Library and Archives)

2. Andrew Jackson (1767–1845). This image, taken from a John Wesley Jarvis portrait, is one of the more unflattering likenesses of Jackson. Born in the backcountry of the Carolinas, Jackson moved to Tennessee in the late 1780s, where he quickly made the right political connections and married into one of the elite Tennessee families. Yet it was his ambition and tenacity that propelled him into the national spotlight via his victories in the War of 1812. (Courtesy Tennessee State Library and Archives)

3. Felix Grundy (1775–1840). Coming to Tennessee in the first decade of the nineteenth century, Grundy already had a reputation as one of the West's finest lawyers. He served as a US congressman from Tennessee in the Twelfth and Thirteenth Congress, becoming one of the most fervent spokesmen for war against Great Britain. Opponents insisted "James Madison, Felix Grundy, and the Devil" caused the war. (Courtesy Tennessee State Library and Archives)

4. John Coffee (1772–1833). Tennessee soldier and surveyor, Coffee became associated with Andrew Jackson early on in Jackson's business ventures. Loyalty marked Coffee's friendship with Jackson, as Coffee accompanied Jackson on every campaign of the War of 1812. Coffee married Rachel Jackson's niece (Mary Donelson) in 1809 and, after the war, became one of the wealthiest planters in the newly formed state of Alabama. (Courtesy Tennessee State Library and Archives)

5. William Carroll (1788–1844). This Washington Bogard Cooper portrait shows Carroll near the end of his life. A much younger Carroll came to Nashville with impressive credentials (his father was business partner in Pittsburgh with Albert Gallatin, President Madison's secretary of the treasury). Carroll quickly found himself in Jackson's circle of friends and rose rapidly through the ranks during the War of 1812. After the war, Carroll had a successful political career, serving more terms as Tennessee's governor than anyone before or since. (Courtesy Tennessee State Library and Archives)

6. Willie Blount (1768–1835). Governor of Tennessee, 1809–1815. Coming from the highly influential Blount Family of North Carolina, Willie Blount was stepbrother of William Blount, former governor of the Territory South of the River Ohio (1790–96). Willie Blount served as Tennessee's governor during the entire War of 1812, supporting Andrew Jackson and always maneuvering to extend Tennessee's landholdings through Indian removal policies. (Courtesy Tennessee State Library and Archives)

7. Major Ridge (ca. 1771–1839). As a young warrior, this Cherokee chief fought against the Anglo-Americas on the Tennessee frontier, but later joined Andrew Jackson in the Creek War as part of a Cherokee alliance. He served with distinction and later became a wealthy planter. He was assassinated in Oklahoma during a vicious dispute over communal Cherokee lands. This portrait was done in 1834 by artist Charles Bird King. (From Thomas L. McKenney and James Hall, *The Indian Tribes of North America* [1836])

8. Menewa (ca. 1 765–ca. 1835). Originally called Hothlepoya, or "The crazy war hunter," for his feats as a marauder on the Tennessee frontier, this Upper Creek warrior became one of the leaders of the Red Stick faction that bitterly opposed the intrusion of Anglo-Americans on Creek land. He led the Creeks at the doomed Battle of Horseshoe Bend, which he survived, only to die during the final removal of the Creeks in the 1830s. (From Thomas L. McKenney and James Hall, *The Indian Tribes of North America* [1836])

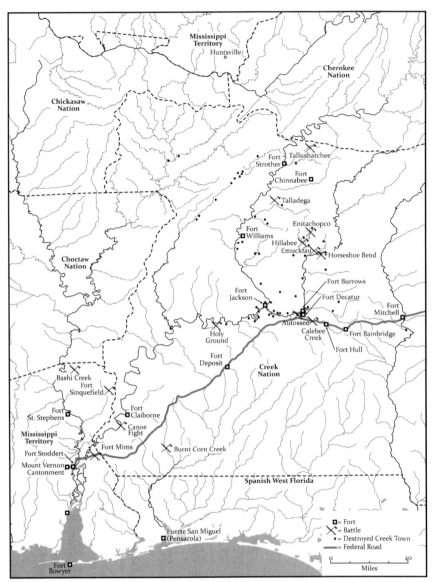

9. General Jackson's campaign against the Creek Indians, 1813–14 (Adapted by Sarah Mattics, Center for Archaeological Studies, University of Alabama, from Record Group 77, CWMF, Misc. 11, 1813 and 1814. National Archives and Records Administration [Washington, DC]. Reproduced from Kathryn E. Holland Braund, ed., *Tohopeka: Rethinking the Creek War and the War of 1812* [University of Alabama Press, 2012], xiv)

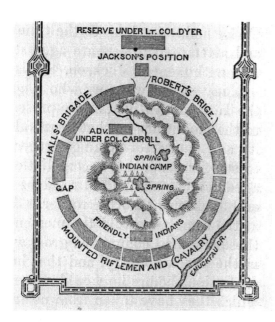

RESERVE UNDER Lt. COL. DYER

JACKSON'S POSITION

ROBERT'S BRIGE.

HALLS' BRIGADE

ADv. UNDER COL. CARROLL

SPRING

INDIAN CAMP

GAP

SPRING

FRIENDLY INDIANS

MOUNTED RIFLEMEN AND CAVALRY

EMUCKFAU CR.

10. Talladega Battle Plan. The plan Andrew Jackson used against the Creeks on November 9, 1813, was the same method he tried to use throughout the Creek War: surround the Creeks with over-whelming forces and then elimi-nate as many warriors as he could. (From Benson Lossing's *The Pic-torial Field-Book of the War of 1812* [1869])

11. *Jackson Quelling Mutiny.* This nineteenth-century depiction shows General Jackson standing behind his horse, pointing a rifle at mutinying troops during the Creek War. Actually, Jackson had his militia ready to fire on the volunteers who were determined to march home, believing their enlistment terms had expired. It was galling for Jackson to deal with these disputes; he felt his Tennesseans looked up to him as a father figure. (Courtesy Tennessee Historical Society Pic-ture Collection)

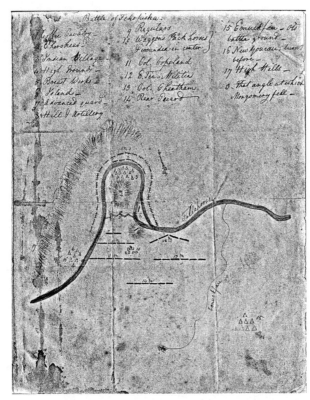

12. Map of Horseshoe Bend. This March 27, 1814, engagement marked the beginning of the end of the Creek War, when Jackson's forces killed approximately nine hundred Creek warriors, making it the greatest loss for Native Americans in North American history. Tradition has it that Jackson personally drew this map, but that has never been verified. (Courtesy Tennessee Historical Society Miscellaneous Files)

13. *Fortifying New Orleans.* This nineteenth-century print shows General Jackson giving orders as slaves work in the background on the fortifications on what became known as Line Jackson. Records show that Jackson used local slaves extensively to construct the breastworks that lay near Rodriguez Canal on the Chalmette battlefield and at other fortifications in the area. (Courtesy Tennessee State Library and Archives)

Fortifying of New Orleans.

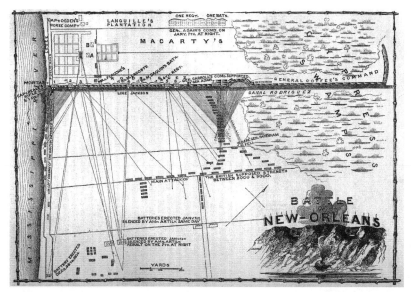

14. Battle of New Orleans. This diagram illustrates the attacking lines of the British against Line Jackson on January 8, 1815. The attack resulted in a miserable failure for the British and an astonishing victory for the Americans, even though the battle was fought two weeks after the signing of the peace treaty in Ghent, Belgium. (From Benson Lossing's *The Pictorial Field-Book of the War of 1812* [1869])

15. Jackson at New Orleans. This mid-nineteenth-century engraving depicts the image of Jackson that most people associate with him: astride his horse, near the famous breastworks of New Orleans, with an oversized American flag in the background. The Hero of New Orleans engineered his huge popularity from the War of 1812 to catapult himself into the presidency. Indeed, January 8 was celebrated as a holiday in many parts of the nation. (Courtesy Tennessee State Library and Archives)

5

James Rhea, a merchant in Blountsville, Tennessee, had a disturbing dream in late June 1814, so troubling that he jotted down this entry in his diary on June 27: "Last night I, James Rhea, dreamed I saw in the Northern Region many Streaks as Red as Blood—broad—pointing downward—this dream may be a sign of war." His concern mirrored the news coming from Europe that Napoleon had been defeated, thus freeing up forces to invade the United States. Rhea, whose brother John served as a US congressman, portentously foresaw the destruction of the nation's capital when, in August 1814, British troops ransacked and burned several federal buildings, including the presidential mansion and the Capitol itself. The Nashville *Clarion*, "with mingled emotions of shame and indignation," announced the British capture of Washington by couching the news with western defiance and resolve: "The slave of a madman has set his myrmidons to work to lay waste a city named after a veteran who put to shame the pride of Britain; but his attempts are [in] vain—his ignoble ambition may only aspire to plunder and burn the town, if that be his object he may be gratified; but if he thinks by any act of his to obscure the remembrance of the Americans of what was done for them by Washington, he is mistaken, as well might he impiously attempt to eclipse the noon-day sun." Andrew Jackson surprisingly kept his anger in check and reacted to the news with a positive attitude, calculating that the burning of Washington would "have the happy tendency to arouse the people, to a vigorous and united effort, in the defence of the country."[1]

No matter how much resolve Americans infused into the situation, however, the fact remained that Great Britain had unleashed its hitherto-occupied army on the mainland of the United States. British strategy, from the beginning of the war, revolved around the protection of its Canadian provinces, but as early as November 1812, the British envisioned a diversionary expedition in the South, to relieve the pressure of the northern campaign. Plans called for the use of Indian and black forces, but England never followed up on this strategy until after the Creek debacle at Horseshoe Bend. At that time, Vice Admiral Sir Alexander Cochrane became commander of the North American station and set a plan in motion to gather the refugee Creeks in the Gulf region. In May 1814, Captain Hugh Pigot, with a complement of British men and arms, landed near the mouth of the Apalachicola River to contact the chiefs in the area, who agreed to the issuance of British arms. Pigot had the assembled Creeks and Seminoles drilled and trained by British officers, reporting to his superiors that 2,800 Indians could be mustered in, along with a Choctaw force he mistakenly thought would join. Pigot planned to take his army of Indians, supported by a small detachment of British soldiers, seize Baton Rouge, and swoop down on New Orleans (where he counted on eight hundred Baratarian pirates to enlist in the British cause). Pigot's report influenced Cochrane to the degree that the latter informed the Admiralty in June 1814 that with two to three thousand troops he could land at Mobile, rally the Indians, black slaves, and disaffected Frenchmen and Spaniards around him, then drive the Americans out of the Floridas and Louisiana. As jumping off points, Mobile and Pensacola remained crucial to British plans.[2]

General James Wilkinson had predicted to Secretary of War William Eustis in March 1812 that England would attempt to use Pensacola and Mobile as launching sites for an invasion of New Orleans. Eustis responded by announcing those towns should become American possessions "in the event of an attempt to occupy them by any foreign government." But the occupation of Mobile and Pensacola involved more than a military chess game between the United States and Great Britain. Spain, although allied to England in the Napoleonic conflict, officially remained neutral in the war between the Americans and the British. The Spanish relied on the British in seeking protection from American advances in the Floridas but at the same time counted on the United States for supplying flour and other necessities for the Peninsula campaign in Spain.[3]

Looking from the Spanish point of view, their North American holdings presented a financial and logistic nightmare. Spain once held the area west of the Mississippi River, along with the Floridas, by virtue of treaties conducted in 1763 and 1783, yet the vulnerability of this region made it an easy mark for neighboring powers. France sought to regain Louisiana and did so under Napoleon; the British trade in the Upper Mississippi Valley compromised Spanish authority there; and American expansion constantly pressed against Spain's North American borders. Surrounded by "enemies," Spain could not possibly man its territories properly—it cost five times as much to maintain regular soldiers in America than in Spain. In effect, Spain was losing money in trying to retain its holdings. Ironically, Spanish officials had similar problems in ruling their provinces as the Americans had in the Old Southwest, that is, runaway slaves from Spanish owners, trouble with marauding Indians, and low troop morale due to isolation and sickness. The anti-Spanish feelings that festered in the Americas weighed in heavily on the inherent weakness of the Spanish empire. The tradition of Spanish bigotry and cruelty, known as the Black Legend, which had taken root in the religious wars of sixteenth-century Europe, crossed over to the New World by the Protestant English who labeled the Spaniards as mean and crafty, as well as proud and insolent. Symbolized by the rapacious conquistador and the inhumane treatment of Indians, Spain appeared to be immersed in feudal attitudes and slavish Catholicism that continued to color the judgment of Europeans (and, later, Americans) against the Spanish into the nineteenth century. There is no doubt an ethno-religious emotion of Spanish phobia played a part in the United States striking at the Floridas. "I hate the Dons," Andrew Jackson ranted in 1806. "I will die in the last Ditch before I would yield a foot to [them]."[4]

By the time of the War of 1812, practically all the settlers coming into West Florida were Americans, mostly from the South (who brought their slaves with them), lured by the untapped land. In time, Americans comprised five-sixths of the province's population, dominating the commercial traffic between West Florida and the United States in the process. As long as the Spanish Crown guaranteed cheap land and a stable regime, local residents in West Florida remained content. When those guarantees faded, as they did by 1810, so did local loyalty. The problems that led to this situation were twofold: first, a perceptible rise in crime—West Florida was, after all, a frontier borderland where criminals could cross back and forth across national lines; and, second, the Spanish restriction of their land policy (which had favored farmers wanting small grants) made it more difficult for foreigners to obtain land. Under these circumstances, an American takeover of West Florida seemed imminent, or, as one observer noted, "the people are as, ripe fruit; waiting the hand that loves to pluck them; and with them all [of] florida." It came as no great surprise when a group of American filibusters took over the weak Spanish command at Baton Rouge in September 1810 and promptly declared independence. The newly elected "governor" of West Florida, Fulwar Skipwith, left no doubt in anyone's mind about the true mission he had toward West Florida in his inaugural address when he alluded to his allegiance to the United States: "The blood which flows in our veins, like the tributary streams which form and sustain the father of rivers, encircling our delightful country, will return, if not impeded, to the heart of our parent country." Skipwith's words echoed the anthem western expansionists resonated in previous decades: the permanent safeguarding of the Mississippi and the acquisition of the other river systems flowing down through the Floridas and into the Gulf of Mexico. Ignoring Skipwith's "revolution," President Madison, while loath to incur the wrath of Spain, Britain, or France, authorized the possession of West Florida (except for Mobile) in October 1812, from the Perdido River to the Mississippi, based on the American interpretation of the Louisiana Purchase. This policy of openly encouraging American citizens to immigrate into Spanish-held territory and then covertly encouraging them to overthrow Spanish rule reflected the Jeffersonian concept of manifest destiny, that is, acquiring territory without actual military conquest (filibustering). The notion of taking of the Floridas came under the heading of self-defense—the same justification Tennessee adopted in its declaration of war against the Creek Indians.[5]

Justifiably upset over the American takeover of Mobile and West Florida, the Spanish governor in Pensacola loudly complained to American authorities in the Mississippi Territory just prior to the Creek War. In July 1813 the territory's governor, David Holmes, informed Tennessee governor Willie Blount of the Spanish demands for the return of Mobile and West Florida, adding: "It is not improbable but that the British may have an agency in the measure; if so, this business may eventuate into something serious." Should it come to a war with the Spanish, Holmes knew he could count on "the physical force and unalloyed patriotism of Tennessee." A few months later, when the Creek War began in earnest, westerners turned the tables on Spain, accusing the Spanish as aggressors for instigating the Red Sticks on the unprotected American frontier. And most agreed with Andrew Jackson, who declared Pensacola to be "the Hotbed of the war, and the asylum of our enemies." Situated about seven miles from the Pensacola Bay, with the Escambia Bay to the east, Pensacola served as an ideal port for commerce and naval activities on the Gulf of Mexico. At the time of the War of 1812, the town's population numbered at least three hundred families living in houses mostly made of wood, supporting five hundred to six hundred Spanish troops. A more detailed report, submitted in September 1814, revealed Pensacola's defenses to consist of five hundred Spanish troops, four hundred citizens, 130 British marines, and 450 Indians. Actually, there may have been as many as seven to eight hundred Creek warriors at Pensacola, representing the majority of Creeks that escaped the aftermath of the Creek War. The official Spanish policy allowed the British and the Indians to operate within West Florida, provided they recognized Spanish control of Pensacola. The Spanish population of the town, besides the military force, consisted of lower-level bureaucrats and their families—inhabitants that Major Howell Tatum of the

Tennessee army referred to as "dirty, indolent, indigent people," in the true Anglo-American fashion of Spanish stereotyping.[6]

In January 1814, Governor Blount informed John Sevier that the Spanish governor in Pensacola was openly dealing with the Creeks, a circumstance that, according to Blount, needed to be resolved by removing the governor and putting someone of American authority in his place. In that same month, Andrew Jackson, in the midst of trying to defeat the Creeks with his shrunken army of sixty-day recruits, vowed that the campaign would end successfully with "Pensacola burnt or I fall in the attempt." Jackson had popular support for his plans to raid Pensacola. Responding to the rumor that 17,000 stands of British arms had been delivered to Pensacola in July 1814, the *Niles' Weekly Register* declared: "If this armament has been permitted at *Pensacola*, there can be no doubt as to the course we should persue [sic]." In October 1814, Louisiana governor William C. C. Claiborne recommended the Madison administration approve the taking of Pensacola, citing that the port was "in every sense of the word an enemy's Post." Claiborne based his reasoning on three points: Pensacola was an asylum for marauding Creeks, it served as a supply depot for the British, and it was a logical spot for the British to launch an attack on Louisiana. Claiborne urged the government to set Jackson's army loose on the Spaniards in order to remedy the situation.[7]

Officials in Washington, however, expressed more caution over entering neutral foreign territory with a force of arms. A July 18, 1814, letter from Secretary of War John Armstrong gave Jackson veiled permission to attack Pensacola by instructing Jackson to carefully ascertain the intentions of the Spanish, adding: "If they admit, feed, arm and cooperate with the British and hostile Indians, we must strike on the broad principle of self-preservation." Yet Jackson did not receive this letter until mid-January 1815. (There is strong evidence that the letter was purposely withheld.) Armstrong, blamed for the burning of Washington by the British, was forced to resign as secretary of war in late August 1814, replaced by Secretary of State James Monroe, who now held two important cabinet positions. Monroe's subsequent instructions to Jackson, dated October 21, 1814, signaled a definite shift in policy toward the Spanish Floridas. "Take no measures," Monroe directed Jackson, "which would involve this Government in a contest with Spain."[8]

Exaggerated rumors bombarded Jackson's headquarters at Mobile in late summer 1814. Reports such as the one that 25,000 British troops, along with large quantities of arms, had landed at Pensacola and elsewhere in the Floridas, prompted Jackson to fire off urgent messages to Washington, pleading for permission to strike at the Spanish. "How long will the government of the United States tamely submit to disgrace and open insult from Spain," an exasperated Jackson demanded in an August 25, 1814, letter to John Armstrong. Two days later, Jackson admonished Armstrong with another challenging communication, expressing his regret that the government would not grant permission to seize Pensacola. "Had this been done," Jackson insisted, "the american Eagle would now have soared above the fangs of the British Lyon [*sic*]." The change of the secretary of war post from Armstrong to Monroe did not seem to faze Jackson. Monroe's October 21 letter, specifically instructing Jackson *not* to invade Spanish territory, would have made little difference to Jackson—even if he had received it before he attacked Pensacola in early November. Instead, Jackson penned a letter to Secretary Monroe on October 26, informing him he would soon be taking Pensacola, even at the risk of having the president dismiss him from the army. "I shall have one consolation," Jackson wrote in anticipation of a reprimand, "a consciousness of having done the only thing which can, under present circumstances, give security to this section and put down an Indian war; and the salvation of my country will be a sufficient reward for the loss of my commission." Five days later, on October 31, Jackson informed Washington he was about to "expel" the Indians and the British from Pensacola "in a very short time."[9]

What steeled Jackson's resolve to invade West Florida at this juncture in 1814? Amid all the wild rumors circulating that summer of the British landing in West Florida with men and matériel, the British actually *did* land a force at Pensacola under the command of Lieutenant Colonel Edward Nicholls of the Royal Marines in mid-August, although the numbers were miniscule compared to what American reports indicated. Nicholls arrived with about one hundred officers and enlisted men, bringing two thousand muskets, two thousand swords, and two field pieces. The plans included raising a force of five hundred blacks and Indians in order to scout the countryside for possible assault routes to New Orleans. British officials cautioned Nicholls to avoid any diplomatic entanglements with Spanish authorities, but to move against Mobile and New Orleans should hostilities break out between Spain and the United States. Nicholls arrived at Pensacola in mid-August 1814 only to find starving Creek Indians and fearful Spanish officials expecting an American attack. The British garrisoned themselves in Fort San Miguel, north of the town's main plaza on the summit of Palafox Hill, where English and Spanish flags flew side by side.[10]

Colonel Nicholls, with a blatant lack of tact and diplomacy, literally took over the town of Pensacola. He began by controlling commerce and travel in and out of the town and jailing anyone he deemed suspicious. He further alienated the population by recruiting Indians and local slaves, then arming, drilling, and uniforming them while permitting them to patrol the area.

Of the one hundred slaves Nicholls enlisted, some of them were from local Spanish residents, who resented losing their property. The British enlistment of blacks was part of an overall strategy devised by Alexander Cochrane, commander of the North American Squadron, who issued a proclamation in April 1814 promising slaves their freedom and land in the British Colonies if they fought against the Americans. The British employed Indians to distribute this proclamation throughout the Southeast, principally because of their knowledge of the terrain and their ability to blend into the surroundings. No image could have been more apocalyptic to white southerners than Indians, at the behest of the British, attempting to stir up a slave rebellion. "This will be one of the most frightful events which ever occurred in America," predicted one citizen, "a powerful savage and negro army, joined by slaves of the Country, who if not met and drove into the Sea without delay will Carry fire and sword thro' that devoted Country."[11]

Nicholls believed a successful attack on the Americans would bolster the confidence of his Indian allies, even though his orders confined him to aiding the Indians and laying the groundwork for a larger British expedition. In mid-September, Nicholls, in concert with his naval counterpart, Captain William H. Percy, attacked the American post of Fort Bowyer near Mobile. Captain Percy convinced Nicholls, with his five hundred Indians and one hundred blacks, that Mobile would make an easy prize. Situated on Mobile Point, a four-mile-wide peninsula thirty miles south of Mobile, Fort Bowyer consisted of a low, wooden battery of weak strength, manned by 160 men under Major William Lawrence. It looked like a perfect target for a combined land and sea assault. Nicholls, too ill to lead the land attack, placed Captain Robert Henry of the marines in command, while Percy's naval force reached Mobile Bay on the morning of September 12. Two days later, Henry's force of about 250 marines and Indians assaulted Fort Bowyer but were repulsed. Percy's two British ships of war found the waters of Mobile Bay entirely too shallow for their attack, causing one of the frigates to be abandoned and burned during the engagement. The British, with a land force too small and ships too large for shallow waters, evidenced an underestimation of American military prowess—a common British trait of the times. Major William Lawrence's Spartan band consisted of well-disciplined Regulars, trained in the use of the fort's artillery. The British failure at Fort Bowyer had one pronounced effect, however. It led Andrew Jackson to believe the main British thrust would be at Mobile, not New Orleans, and, consequently, he resolved to drive the British once and for all from nearby Pensacola.[12]

Jackson had been playing a diplomatic cat-and-mouse game with Spanish governor Mateo Gonzalez Manrique through a series of communications that Jackson took to be of a debasing nature. Manrique admitted he had been arming the Creek Indians at Pensacola, but only as a defensive measure against American "insults." Jackson, in a September 9, 1814, letter, reminded Manrique that the Americans would adopt "an Eye for an Eye Tooth for Tooth, and Scalp for Scalp" policy with the Spanish. Jackson then pointed out that a British flag flew over a Spanish fort at Pensacola and facetiously told Manrique he expected the Spanish governor to "provide for my troops and Indians a Fort in your Town, should I take it into my head to pay you a visit." Jackson assembled his army at Fort Montgomery (in present-day Baldwin County, Alabama) at the end of October. The troops gathering at the fort (which lay near the killing fields of Fort Mims), represented a hodgepodge fighting force: Mississippi Territory dragoons, companies from the Regular Army (the Third, Thirty-Ninth, and Forty-Fourth US Infantries), Captain Deaderick's small company of Nashville artillery, six to eight hundred Choctaw Indians, a regiment of West Tennessee militia, and John Coffee's brigade of mounted gunmen. Coffee had spent the summer at home in Rutherford County with his wife and infant child, until getting the call from Jackson to rendezvous his mounted men at Fayetteville in early October. By the end of the month, Coffee and his men were at the "Cut Off," a stretch of land connecting the Tombigbee and Alabama Rivers, four miles above their junction (in present-day Clarke County, Alabama). Because of the difficulty of providing forage for the horses, half of Coffee's brigade (totaling more than one thousand men) had to march on foot in order to rendezvous with Jackson's forces.[13]

Jackson led his main army out of Fort Montgomery on the first day of November, linking with Coffee's forces at Fort Mims on the next day. Bones from the August 1813 massacre were still to be seen there, as one Mississippi Territory soldier named George Downs testified, creating a "melancholy spectacle" for the Anglo-Americans. Yet, the hurried, last minute preparations for the campaign left little time for contemplation. "In such a scene of bustle and preparation, it would take a Plato to collect his ideas," Downs commented. "Nothing is to be heard but cannon, drums, fifes, trumpets, and almost an incessant fire of musketry—all eager for the expected fight." Downs informed his brother that his next letter would be dated "from within the walls of Pensacola, should I steer clear of Spanish Bull Dogs." From Mims, Jackson's massive army of three thousand men plodded its way toward Pensacola through the piney barrens and savannahs of West Florida in a march that one volunteer remembered as being one mile wide and three miles long. The army arrived on the outskirts of Pensacola on the evening of November 6, delayed by the breakdown of the ammunition wagons along the way. As the American army neared Pensacola, Lieutenant Colonel Nicholls frightened the population into believing Jackson's forces numbered seven thousand men who would be granted twenty-four hours of pillaging once the town capitulated. Obviously outmanned, Nicholls took the precaution of removing the Indians across the bay to safety and taking down the British flag at Fort San Miguel. Leaving the Spanish to basically fend for themselves (except for several British ships in the harbor), Nicholls threatened to level Pensacola if the Spanish lowered their flag in the face of the Americans.[14]

Private James McCutchen, one of General Coffee's mounted gunmen, recorded this terse entry in his diary on November 7, 1814: "we marched into Pensacola & took possession of the town & they surrendered the fort unto us." Typical of enlisted soldiers' accounts, McCutchen summed up American activities at Pensacola in the most understated fashion. Other reports provide a much more detailed version of the battle.[15] Approaching Pensacola from the west, where the main roads leading into the town were located, Jackson halted his forces about a mile and a half from the outskirts of town. Jackson then dispatched Major Henry Peire of the Forty-Fourth US Infantry to Fort San Miguel bearing a large flag of truce and a communication for Governor Manrique. Peire, after selecting six or eight soldiers as an escort, advanced toward the Spanish post. As the party neared, cannon from the fort sent a shot in Peire's direction, which Peire misinterpreted as a signal for him to enter the fort. He left his escort and started toward San Miguel, still bearing the flag, when a second round of fire passed over the heads of the escort party, immediately followed by a third shot. It was now apparent, even to Major Peire, that he was not welcome.

As Peire and the advanced troops retreated to a safer distance, the guns of San Miguel continued to fire, despite Peire making one last attempt to approach the fort. Jackson then removed his army about two miles outside of town to set up camp. He next sent a Spanish sergeant, captured by the Americans the day before, with a dispatch for Manrique in an attempt to set up a line of communication. The sergeant made his way past San Miguel and found the Spanish governor, who allowed the sergeant to return to the American lines with permission for Major Peire to enter Pensacola. While negotiations were going on in the town, Jackson took the opportunity of inspecting the fort, using his telescope. He could plainly see San Miguel manned by both Spanish and British troops. It was well after dark when Peire returned to Pensacola, carrying Jackson's message to Governor Manrique. Jackson's dispatch explained that the Americans had come to Pensacola because the Spanish had allowed the British "to take possession of your fortifications and fit out expeditions against us," while giving "asylum to the savages hostile to the U[nited] S[tates]." Jackson demanded the possession of Fort Barrancas, the main installation guarding the entrance to the bay, as well as the other Spanish fortifications, adding that if there were any bloodshed it would be on Manrique's hands. Major Peire came back to the American lines with Manrique's reply in the early morning hours of November 7. The governor defiantly acknowledged the American general's "ill-grounded demand" with the suggestion that any spilled blood would be on Jackson's hands, not his own.

In addition to Manrique's reply, Major Peire returned with valuable information concerning the defenses at Pensacola. The officer learned, for instance, that several British vessels were anchored in the bay just off shore, with the bulk of the British forces on board. Furthermore, the British-equipped Indians no longer posed a threat, as they had been removed to the opposite side of the bay. Jackson realized that Pensacola could now be readily taken, but he sent Major Peire with one final communiqué to Manrique, repeating his original demands. The message gave the Spanish governor until 6:00 a.m. (November 7) to reply. About 7:00 a.m. Manrique's tardy answer arrived, the Spanish governor still refusing to give up the fortifications. Manrique insisted that the British and their Indian allies no longer presented a confrontational factor to the Americans, and, therefore, there was no reason for Jackson to launch an attack. He also explained that it was on Lieutenant Colonel Nicholls's orders that the troops of Fort San Miguel fired on Major Peire and his escort. Jackson, unfazed by this last communication, set his army in motion. Although the Americans were encamped on the west side of Pensacola, Jackson knew from previous reports that the town's weakest defenses lay on the east side. Jackson decided to route his main force through the woods a mile above Pensacola in order to approach the town from the east—a march of about three miles. To mask this ruse, he left behind about five hundred men under the command of Colonel Thomas Butler, whom he ordered to make a feint down the main road into town while the bulk of the army struck from the opposite side. Jackson split his main army into three columns: the Regulars, led by Majors Joseph Woodruff and Henry Peire, made up the bulk of the left; the Choctaws, commanded by Major Uriah Blue, were on the right; and Coffee's dismounted Tennessee volunteers, under Colonel Thomas Williamson, composed the center. During the march to circumvent the Spanish, Coffee received word from Lieutenant Jesse Bean, whose company of spies kept up a constant fire at Fort San Miguel to divert attention, that the enemy was advancing from the fort to attack them. Coffee quickly dispatched two hundred men under Lieutenant Colonel James Lauderdale to counterattack the Spanish, who soon retreated to the safety of their fort.

Three main streets ran through Pensacola, parallel to the bay. On the center thoroughfare, Parafox Street, the Spanish planted two pieces of artillery near a blockhouse to impede the Americans. Jackson's left column, composed of the Regulars, entered the center street while Williamson's volunteer gunmen took the street to the right of Parafox. The drafted militia entered the street to the left, while the Choctaws passed along the back part of town to the right of the three roads. Before the final advance, Coffee received orders to form the mounted men at the brow of the hill above town and wait for further instructions. Jackson's ploy worked, as the British vessels in the bay—on the left of Jackson's army—failed to fire on the Americans. The Spanish battery on Parafox Street represented the only real obstacle to taking the town. Jackson ordered Captain William Laval of the Third US Infantry to lead a company of men to storm the battery. Before Laval's men could overtake the artillery, the Spanish managed to fire three rounds at the onrushing Americans, the second of which struck Lieutenant Alfred Flourney (Forty-Fourth US Infantry) below the knee of his left leg, while the third volley of grapeshot felled Captain Laval, shattering his thigh bone to pieces (rendering him a cripple for life). One naive Tennessean told his fellow soldiers he would stop and pick up one of the cannonballs as they came rolling down the street. At the last second, he was jerked back by a more experienced soldier, as they both watched the ball strike something on the ground and explode six feet in the air. As the Regulars overpowered the battery, they contended with sporadic fire from the nearby gardens and houses that lined the streets. Meanwhile, Governor Manrique approached Colonel Williamson's volunteers, frantically waving a white flag of surrender. Williamson immediately reported the capitulation to Jackson who, in turn, met with the governor and other Spanish officials at the intendant's office on the public plaza to conduct a formal surrender.

As negotiations proceeded, the British commenced firing from the vessels in the harbor, as well as from some small, armed barges anchored slightly off shore. Although the shelling had little effect, Jackson ordered Lieutenant Richard Call of the Forty-Fourth to take the captured Spanish cannon and implement a return fire. Call had the pieces hauled to the beach and managed to stave off any further British interference. The barges retreated from the shoreline, while one of the larger vessels put to sea. Call remembered that "had she not run I must have done so the next moment," as he was just about out of ammunition. At the same time, shots were heard in the direction of Fort San Miguel. In spite of Manrique's directive that the commander of the fort, a Colonel Sotto, surrender the post to the Americans, the Spanish fired on Major Thomas Hinds's Mississippi dragoons and the

Choctaws, wounding two of Hinds's men and two Choctaws. The meeting between Jackson and Manrique now turned into a strongly worded lecture by Jackson on Spain's breach of neutrality concerning the Creeks and British. Jackson insisted the Americans immediately occupy all the military installations at Pensacola, including Fort Barrancas and Fort Santa Rosa (the two posts that guarded the entrance to the harbor). The forts were to remain in American hands until the Spanish could furnish a competent force to protect the neutrality of West Florida. Manrique issued signed orders for delivery of the various forts in accordance with Jackson's demands. However, Colonel Sotto refused to surrender Fort San Miguel. As a result, Jackson initiated preparations to attack the fortress.

That evening a call went through the American camp for volunteers to assault San Miguel in the event an agreement for surrender could not be reached. "At night we proposed to take the fort by storm with scaling ladders," recalled Private William Trousdale of Colonel Williamson's regiment. "Volunteers were called for—I answered the call affirmatively—had my ladder leaned against a pine tree close to my tent and was on the eve of moving in execution of the scheme when the fort surrendered." On the morning of November 8 Colonel Sotto had finally come to terms with Manrique's directive and let the Americans enter Fort San Miguel—the Spanish flag remained on the ramparts so as not to encourage fire from the British, who had been busy with their own preparations. During the night the British blew up Fort Santa Rosa and were about to do the same to Fort Barrancas, fourteen miles to the west. The military importance of this installation was apparent to both British and Americans: from this point, ships could not pass into the bay without being subject to firing and, more importantly to the British, vessels already in the bay could not escape. The British frigates anchored off Pensacola now raced toward Barrancas, and, around 2:00 p.m. on the afternoon of November 8, the Americans heard several explosions coming from the vicinity of the fort. The British had ignited a storehouse, said to contain about three hundred barrels of gunpowder. Two American detachments were sent to investigate, and, as expected, they found Fort Barrancas in ruins. The British had made their getaway.

The English did not leave empty handed. According to residents living near Fort Barrancas, Spanish soldiers and as many as three hundred slaves, belonging to the inhabitants of Pensacola, could be seen on board the British ships. That the British had proved themselves to be ineffective in their aid to the people of West Florida created a rift in future Spanish/British cooperation. From their point of view, the British noted a great reluctance on the part of the Spanish to participate in its own defense of Pensacola, citing jealousy as the main factor for refusing British aid and forbidding the English to attack the American army. Nicholls later claimed that Manrique asked for direct assistance on November 6, when it was too late, as the British had already relocated its Indian forces across the bay. Before leaving, the British destroyed Fort Barrancas in order to ensure that the Americans could not use the guns of the fortress to fire on British ships in the harbor. With the possession of Barrancas made impossible by its destruction, Jackson deemed his mission to be concluded. He had successfully dislodged the British from Pensacola and removed (at least temporarily) the Indian threat. Food and supplies were gathered on November 9 for the return trip to the Mississippi Territory, and, at about 4:00 p.m. on that day, Jackson commenced his march home, his "visit" to Pensacola at an end.

Jackson left behind a legacy of goodwill with the residents of Pensacola, particularly in the wake of the haughty treatment of the British and the false apprehensions of American barbarity. "Instead of the Massacre & pillage which was anticipated, Gen. J[ackson] & his army have obtained for themselves a lasting name for their humanity & good order," one resident observed in a November 10 letter. "Not a single excess was committed." John Coffee noted that the respect accorded to the Spanish population "had an astonishing effect on their feelings toward us." Equally impressive was the civil conduct of the Choctaws, from whom the Spaniards expected much abuse, especially after having suffered some casualties at the hands of the Spanish troops. Howell Tatum noted that the Choctaws acted "far more *decent* & correct than the *British soldiers*, though savages." In fact, the population expressed apprehensions about the British returning to Pensacola after the Americans evacuated. Besides the Spaniards' goodwill, the American forces departed from Pensacola with the two Spanish pieces of artillery that felled Laval and Flournoy, removing the weapons to Mobile. The Americans also made off with some articles from the Catholic church in Pensacola, as well as the Spanish flag that flew at Fort San Miguel. Jackson expressed his regret about these oversights in a November 16 letter to Governor Manrique, indicating the church artifacts and the flag would be immediately returned (but not the cannons). After all, the articles of capitulation on November 7 had specified the Spanish flag would "remain flying" in the fort. Besides, Jackson's official stance of the march on Pensacola was based on the principle that the Americans were attempting to aid the Spaniards in maintaining their non-aligned stance in the war.[16]

Back at his headquarters in Mobile by mid-November, Jackson informed his superiors of his campaign at Pensacola. Despite his seemingly diplomatic intentions, Jackson had clearly violated Spanish neutrality by invading West

Florida without the express consent of his own government. Jackson realized the culpability of his actions, but justified them on the basis that Spain had violated its own neutrality by harboring the British and their Indian allies. Writing Secretary of War Monroe on November 14, Jackson explained: "Not having the sanction of my government, or the means of repairing the fortifications, I determined not to occupy them, restore Fort St. Michael [San Miguel] to the Spanish governor as I found it, and withdraw my troops to this point for the protection of the frontier, but before I did this I had the satisfaction to see the whole British force leave the port and their friends at our mercy. . . . Thus Sir I have broken up the hot bed of the Indian war and convinced the Spaniards that we will permit no equivocations in a nation professing neutrality." Interestingly, Monroe responded on December 7, 1814, to an earlier letter of Jackson's (October 26, 1814) advising the Tennessee general that the president still wished a confrontation with the Spanish to be avoided, *but* if Jackson had already made the attack, then he was instructed to withdraw his troops from Spanish territory, declaring he had entered it for the sole purpose of freeing it from the British. Jackson had gotten away with a potentially dangerous international situation, receiving his government's (albeit cautious) approval after all. For the people of the Old Southwest, however, Jackson had accomplished a long-awaited chastisement. Governor Willie Blount summed up this attitude in a grand understatement: "Genl. Jackson did a good act towards this section of the Union when he entered Pensacola."[17]

The reason for the Madison administration's lack of concern over Pensacola centered on the bigger issue of the safety of New Orleans. British plans for the inevitable capture of the city came to light through a series of letters coming out of Havana. The author of these letters, a Massachusetts merchant named Vincent Gray, had relocated to Havana where Lieutenant Colonel Edward Nicholls stopped in August 1814 en route to the Gulf Coast. Gray began to piece together the British plan from what he heard and observed and hastily wrote Governor W. C. C. Claiborne, James Monroe, and James Innerarity (of the Forbes Company) about British preparations for the Gulf. Gray's information was as accurate as it was alarming—he correctly forecasted that Nicholls was bound for Pensacola to incite the slaves to join him, as well as the discontented Indians there, telling the Creeks their lands taken through the Treaty of Fort Jackson would be returned. Gray also indicated that Nicholls expected a large number of Louisianans to join the British cause, promising them a return of Louisiana to Spain. Finally, Gray knew of the British intentions to capture the mouth of the Mississippi, as well as the forts at Mobile and Baton Rouge, thus effectively isolating New

Orleans. Innerarity apparently met with Andrew Jackson in late August to confer on these revelations and, in the next month, the Madison administration advised Jackson to make preparations to defend New Orleans. Jackson, however, did not believe the British would attack New Orleans, perceiving the British recruitment of Indians and blacks at Pensacola as a continuation of the Creek War. By merely securing the Gulf Coast, he felt the war in the South could be concluded.[18]

Before Jackson could turn his attention to New Orleans, he wanted to make sure he had conclusively checked the Indian threat in the region. From Fort Pierce, in mid-November 1814, Jackson issued orders for Major Uriah Blue of the Thirty-Ninth US to take command of the Tennessee units under Major William Russell and Major John Childs, as well as the friendly Choctaws, Chickasaws, and Creeks, plus some of Coffee's brigade (a total aggregate of about one thousand men). Blue's orders were to "march and scour the Escambia [River]" on both sides and destroy or capture any hostile Creeks, make prisoners of any women or children, confiscate all cattle and corn, and burn or destroy all Indian villages the army came upon. Major Blue was also instructed to attack the Seminoles, if supplies held out, but supplies did not hold out. Furthermore, severe weather hampered the success of the expedition. In the end, Blue's force managed to kill about fifty hostile Indians and capture some two hundred prisoners, destroying several Indian camps in the process. Although the expedition never fully realized Jackson's expectations, it held the hostile Indians in check while Jackson made preparations to attend to the more pressing matter of defending New Orleans.[19]

On December 23, 1814, Edward Palfrey, a Bostonian transplanted to New Orleans, wrote to his father that the people there were daily expecting a British attack on the city. "It is fully believed that Lord Hill commands the expedition but if ever he lands here I'll engage he never will see England again," Palfrey gloated. "I shall enroll myself in some Company today to go and see the fun, and have a hand in it if possible." Palfrey was mistaken in assuming Lord Hill would be at the helm of the British invasion, but the British did, indeed, launch an offensive operation against the city on the very day of Palfrey's correspondence. Having come to Louisiana with his father and brothers a decade earlier, Edward Palfrey represented the new type of citizen in Louisiana: American born and American bred. This was a drastic change from the French-based population that previously dominated the region. At the time of the Louisiana Purchase, there were seven French to every American in Louisiana; by the time of statehood in 1812, however, the ratio had declined to three to one. The drastic influx of Americans caused a rift in the cultural relations between the two peoples. In truth, the French faction in the Territory of Orleans opposed the annexation of West Florida in 1811, fearing it would numerically strengthen the American faction in the region. One émigré to Louisiana in the early 1800s observed that political differences in the state were based more on language and heritage. "We are neither Federalists nor Democrats," he observed. "We are either French or Americans." The transition from territorial status to statehood did little to alleviate the collective presumption of distrust between the various factions. In 1813, a toast made in New England evinced a feeling that Louisiana would contribute little to the nation: "The state of Louisiana—The fifth wheel of a Waggon!" New Orleans's reputation as "a place of speculation, dissipation, debauchery, and revel," as noted by an American visitor on the eve of the War of 1812, did little to assuage the bitterness between the incoming Americans and their native rivals.[20]

Added to this unfair stereotype was the Creole population—those descended from colonial settlers in Louisiana, especially of French or Spanish descent—who often found themselves in political and economic competition with the French-born Louisianans, as well as the Anglo-Americans. The Creoles were labeled as ostentatious, vice addicted, and poorly educated. One Frenchman described them as "rude, envious . . . avaricious, and presumptuous," as well as "notorious romancers" whose "ignorance exceeds all human credibility." Not content with these slanders, he continued his diatribe by referring to Creoles as infamous liars "devoid of moral energy." "They yield themselves to pleasure in excess," another French critic wrote. "Feasting and gaming occupy all their attention. . . . The Creole women are passionately fond of dancing." Anglo-Americans were quick to agree with these unfair assessments. One Philadelphia woman, recently resettled in New Orleans, related to a friend that among the Creoles "the pursuit of wealth and love of dancing seem to supersede almost every other thing." Interestingly, Andrew Jackson was said to have made a similar comparison when reflecting on the campaign at New Orleans. Relating how the population of New Orleans panicked upon the initial approach of the British in December 1814, Jackson supposedly tried to calm the anguished crowds by promising them he would die in their defense. "I went on my way to duty [while] they went off to dance," Jackson snidely recounted.[21]

The transference of governments (French, Spanish, and American) over the years complicated efforts for unity among the populace in Louisiana. The Americans viewed themselves as more energetic and sophisticated, politically and economically, than their French and Creole rivals. In turn, the French and Creole citizenry displayed resentment toward the American style of constitutional self-government thrust upon them. But the most obvious drawback to solidifying relations between the diverse Louisianan populations was the language barrier—at Fourth of July celebrations, for instance, orators recited the Declaration of Independence in French. The state's legal system kept court records in English, but the pleadings and evidence often had to be translated into French, Spanish, or even German. When there were no interpreters available, French members of the jury would leave the courtroom while an English-speaking lawyer presented his argument, and the American jurors would retire when French was spoken.[22]

A racial element constituted another potent factor in assessing the cultural climate in New Orleans. In 1805, for example, 8,222 inhabitants resided in the city—3,551 whites, 3,105 blacks, and 1,566 free blacks. The latter category comprised a significant element of the city's social structure. During Spanish occupation (1762–1802), the free black militia became an essential instrument for political expression, as well as an avenue for social advancement and a means to gain honor and prestige. After the transition to American rule, the leading free blacks of New Orleans petitioned Governor William C. C. Claiborne in 1804 for permission to form two militia companies—a situation that caused concern among American officials. White opposition to such a proposal forced Claiborne to compromise: the free blacks obtained permission to form the units, but white officers were appointed to command them (in the following year, territorial legislators forced the inactivation of the units, heightening racial tensions). The formation of free black units also hinged on the men providing their own arms and horses, and in some cases, only those with property valued at one hundred dollars or more could join.[23]

The violence of the Haitian Revolution (1791–1804) acerbated the fears whites had of arming black troops in Louisiana. The black insurrection aspects of the revolution, which concluded with the elimination of slavery in the French colony of Saint-Domingue and the formation of a Haitian republic, instilled alarm in Americans, who were exposed to the horrible details of the insurrection via newspaper accounts. Recognizing the potential for similar revolts, many slave states adopted legislation to keep out Caribbean slaves, even abolishing the slave trade, in fear of radical ideas being spread by "French negroes." Most of the refugees from Saint-Domingue—a large portion being free blacks—gravitated toward Louisiana because of its geographic proximity, its Gallic culture, and its lenient laws concerning free blacks. Thousands of refugees poured into New Orleans, doubling the city's population in the 1790s, offering a continuance of French Creole culture in the face of expanding Anglo-American settlement. In 1804 French citizens petitioned the New Orleans City Council to take some action against the arrival of slaves and free blacks from the Caribbean "with their hands still reddened with the blood of our unfortunate fellow countrymen . . . perhaps tomorrow their smoking torches will be lighted again to set fire to our peaceful homes."[24]

Still, the fears elicited through slave insurrections did not outweigh the "necessity" of bondage. The sugar boom of the late eighteenth/early nineteenth centuries in Louisiana—by 1815 the state was producing ten million pounds of sugar annually—intensified the demand for slave labor through the production of sugar cane. Between 1790 and 1810, nearly 18,000 slaves from Africa, the Caribbean, and the United States came to lower Louisiana, making New Orleans one of the principal slave markets in North America. Even after the ban of the importation of slaves into the United States in 1808, smugglers such as Jean Laffite based much of their lucrative trade on slavery. In fact, a Louisiana slave insurrection in 1811 was thought to have been instigated by slaves smuggled into the territory by men like Laffite. By the time of the campaign at New Orleans, all these elements—slaves, free blacks, smugglers—would play an integral role in the military strategy of both the British and Americans.[25]

Vice Admiral Sir Alexander Forester Inglis Cochrane, commander in chief of the North American Station, held a distinct contempt for Americans. The Royal Navy officer had effectively blockaded the East Coast of the United States, witnessed the burning of Washington, and reluctantly withdrew from Baltimore after his bombing vessels ("and the rockets red glare") failed to bring Fort McHenry to its knees. Writing from Maryland in September 1814, Cochrane noted "that like Spaniels [the Americans] must be treated with great severity before you ever make them tractable." Cochrane's sentiments, which may have had something to do with the fact that his brother had been killed at the Battle of Yorktown, merely echoed the regard that many British espoused when discussing the American scene. From his base in Bermuda, Admiral Cochrane had the task of successfully landing British forces in order to capture the key port of New Orleans. Initially, it was thought the city's defenses were such that an assault of warships up the Mississippi River in concert with an army debarking from vessels on Lake Pontchartrain would be effectual, as long as the forces were in proportion to that of the Americans. British commanders, such as Cochrane, based their conjecture that New Orleans would be an easy target largely on a report completed in early 1813 by Captain James Lucas Yeo, whose observations, communicated to the First Lord of the Admiralty, indicated a prize ripe for the picking: "The City of New Orleans is not fortified, nor furnished with the means either for Hostile or Defensive operations. . . . There is nothing but

Faction and discontent, and the American Party is by far the weakest. The Indians are implacably hostile to them, which, added to their internal discord, would operate much against them. . . . I am persuaded there is nothing that would cause more alarm and consternation than the bare apprehension of our Black Troops being employed against them." Cochrane's subsequent actions bear out the importance and validity the British high command placed on this report.[26]

Anticipating an enemy who might outnumber his own force, Cochrane realized the significance of Yeo's conclusions and set about on a plan of action to enlist the aid of the malcontents designated in the report, yet in each instance, the scheme fell far short of British expectations. First, Cochrane tried to take advantage of the cultural divisiveness evident in Louisiana by issuing a broadside in the summer of 1814, claiming "the american *usurpation in this country* must be abolished." In addition to Yeo's observations, Captain James Stirling, writing in March 1813, remarked that the Louisianans were "unconnected by blood or long fellowships with the other States of America. . . . there can be no doubt but a considerable party might be formed in favor of a separation from the United States." These assumptions led the British to anticipate little opposition from the population once on Louisiana soil. "I should think we shall not meet with any resistance at New Orleans," wrote a British captain on the eve of the campaign. "But on the contrary they will most likely be glad to put themselves under our Govmt [*sic*] as soon as they know we are approaching." Yet the welcome the British expected from the French Louisianans never materialized. "In fact," another British officer observed in January 1815, "not a white man of even the lowest description has joined us since we landed, nor have our generals or the Admiral succeeded in obtaining information of the most trivial nature." This inability to collect accurate data on the layout of the terrain, or on American troop strength and other reconnaissance-like information, proved to be a huge detriment for the British at New Orleans.[27]

Cochrane next tried to enlist the aid of the remnants of the warring Creek faction by issuing a proclamation in early December 1814 to the Creek chiefs and other Indian nations professing the support of the British "Father" to his "Indian children." In return for their assistance, Cochrane promised the Creeks "the restoration of those lands of which the People of Bad Spirit have basely robbed them." The British did manage to lure several Creek chiefs— escorted by Lieutenant Colonel Edward Nicholls—to accompany the campaign against the Americans at New Orleans, but no significant body of Indians fought for the British. The one minor exception was a small contingent of Choctaw warriors who saw some brief action in late December 1814.[28]

Captain Yeo's recommendation that a regiment of black troops be employed in the South, based on the inherent paranoia of slave owners, prompted the British command to enroll the West India regiments. Mostly African born, these troops evolved from the British experience during the Caribbean revolts of the 1790s. Many were illiterate former slaves who spoke little English and exhibited poor morale and even poorer discipline. Traditionally, the British never congregated these black troops into large units and, for the most part, they were assigned remote posts. Yet the West Indians were thought to be less vulnerable to tropical diseases and, hence, could prove to be valuable fighters in the sultry climate of the American South. Unfortunately for the West India regiments, Louisiana experienced an unusually cold spell in the winter of 1814/15, and the black soldiers, without proper blankets or clothes, suffered immensely. One British officer commented that the black troops "were reduced to such a state of torpidity as to be absolutely incapable of the smallest exertion." The extremely cold weather even caused several deaths within the regiments. Regarding the Louisiana slaves, British strategy called for recruiting them for service, rather than for inciting insurrections. Cochrane placed high hopes on raising armed slaves "from their Hatred to the citizens of the United States," adding they would be more terrifying to the Americans than any British troops. Louisiana slave owners misinterpreted British recruitment of slaves as an attempt to foment slave uprisings, and this created a near-hysteric atmosphere in the plantations surrounding New Orleans, where slaves outnumbered their white owners by a twenty-five to one ratio. The fact that at least two hundred slaves escaped to the British proved to be a source of frustration to planters who tried, unsuccessfully, to reclaim them after the war ended. Yet the British plan to use runaway slaves as a fighting force, as in the case of the Indians, never panned out.[29]

That Britain intended New Orleans to be a strategic war goal was confirmed in August 1814 when Albert Gallatin, an American envoy at the peace negotiations in Ghent (Belgium), informed Secretary of State James Monroe that he sensed British intentions to carry on the war were more serious than he had anticipated. "It appears to me most likely that their true and immediate object is New Orleans," Gallatin advised. "They well know that it is our most distant and weakest point, and that if captured it could not be retaken without great difficulty." Amid rumors of the British landing large numbers of forces at Pensacola that summer, with more troops expected, New Orleans residents grew extremely apprehensive, many hiding their gold and other valuable possessions from the British invaders. "The whole country here appears to be in a stir, many scared almost to death," wrote one woman from a nearby plantation, "some have already made their escape." Especially uneasy about the potential British invasion of Louisiana were the merchants of New Orleans, already chafing under the yoke of the embargo that deterred cotton speculations. The firm of Talcott and Bowers, New Orleans cotton brokers, expressed their concern of a British attack in a September 5, 1814, letter to one of their clients, admitting the principle defenses of New Orleans consisted of "mud, musquitoes [sic] & Climate."[30]

This tongue-in-cheek estimation by Talcott and Bowers reflected the reality of the situation: the defenses of New Orleans *were* inadequate to an aggressive British attack. Most of the forts and batteries that protected the city showed definite signs of disrepair and lacked supplies. Lieutenant Colonel William MacRea, who commanded New Orleans, outlined a grim picture in his September 1814 report to Jackson. According to MacRea, most of the military installations lacked barracks, powder magazines, and cannon platforms—those that existed were in poor condition. Six lone gunboats, along with some smaller vessels, all under Commodore Daniel T. Patterson, made up the entire American naval defense. To add to the residents' consternation, the aftershocks of a devastating hurricane that struck the Mississippi delta in mid-August 1812 still plagued the region. Upwards of a hundred homes were destroyed in New Orleans and thousands of roofs were literally torn off, producing "a solemn, unaffected gloom on the countenances of the inhabitants of the country," according to one naval officer. Besides a considerable loss of life, the hurricane destroyed shipping and broke the levee, flooding the city. Rumors of slave uprisings increased the already-thick tension.[31]

By late August 1814, Claiborne felt obligated to inform General Andrew Jackson that the population of Louisiana lacked the loyalty and unity needed for a spirited defense. "Americans, Native Louisianans, Frenchmen, and Spaniards (with some Englishmen) compose the mass of the Population," Claiborne explained. "Among them, there exist much Jealousy, and as great differences in political sentiment, as in their language and habits." Shortly afterward, Jackson received a more blunt assessment from another Louisiana inhabitant who sensed "rottenness in the people," predicting disunity and flight should the British invade the state. "The militia of this state cannot be relied on," the informer avowed. These communications caused Jackson to believe he would be dealing with a population not to be trusted; indeed, their unreliability might even lead to traitorous activities. Suspicions of this type played into Jackson's already paranoid nature, as evidenced by his response to Claiborne, warning him to be wary of spies and conspirators ready to corrupt the morale of the population. "You ought to have every avenue well watched with confidential patrols," Jackson advised. "We have more to dread from Spies, and traitors, than from open enemies." Jackson's decision to declare martial law in New Orleans in mid-December no doubt stemmed from this apprehension. He later indicated that he believed "hordes of spies and British emissaries lurked in the city" after the British landed in Louisiana.[32]

Jackson found himself in a difficult, though not unfamiliar, situation. He needed fighting men and needed them badly. Despite his rank of major general in the US Army, there were very few Regulars he could call on, due to their spread-out distribution. Furthermore, strained relations between the army and navy prevented Jackson from ordering Commodore Patterson to transport troops to Jackson's command post at Mobile. Patterson refused on the grounds that he was not under Jackson's direct command. With only the Louisiana militia and Mississippi Territory volunteers at hand—units Jackson believed to be wholly inadequate in experience and morale—Jackson had only 2,000 men available to thwart an invasion he anticipated to number 35,000 British forces. From Mobile, Jackson sent out urgent messages to Tennessee for aid in late August 1814. Jackson instructed his adjutant general, Colonel Robert Butler, to issue a call for East and West Tennessee troops, as well as the Cherokees, emphasizing, "there is not a moment to be lost in Pushing on the Troops and supplies." Jackson expected a British landing on the Gulf Coast within the next month, even giving credence to the wild speculation that Russia had committed to furnishing fifty thousand troops to the enemy. Recently appointed secretary of war James Monroe provided Jackson with further impetus to depend solely on Tennessee when he informed Jackson, in a late September communication, "that on the militia of Tennessee your principle reliance must be."[33]

Jackson would lean on his old standbys, the Second Division of Tennessee Militia, for the support he felt he lacked in the South. The ever-faithful John Coffee and many of his mounted gunmen stayed by Jackson's side throughout the post–Creek War period, participating in the takeover of Pensacola in early November 1814. William Carroll had succeeded Jackson as major general of the West Tennessee Militia in October 1814, handily defeating Brigadier General Thomas Johnson in a military election. General Carroll reorganized the Second Division into five new regiments and immediately issued a public plea for volunteers to defend Louisiana. Carroll cleverly relied on the time-tested ploy of free commerce on the Mississippi River as a lure for volunteerism: "Should any foreign power obtain a permanent possession of the City of New Orleans and the mouth of the Mississippi we may bid farewell to all our prosperity and anticipated greatness. Let our enemy once get possession of this key of our commerce and we shall be completely locked out from all intercourse with the world . . . let him command the Mississippi river, and we become the most dependent degraded and miserable people on earth." Carroll also appealed to prospective political-office seekers by point-ing out that those individuals "displaying a generous devotion to the cause of their country" would prove themselves worthy of being elected. Carroll, himself a future political fixture in Tennessee, knew the value a military title could bring to a politically minded war veteran.[34]

Having amassed an army of two thousand volunteers, William Carroll set out for New Orleans on November 24, 1814, in a fleet consisting of forty-five flatboats, counter to Jackson's order that the army be transported over-land. With martial music playing and crowds cheering, the fleet left the docks at Nashville, with Carroll's boat, the *Cecelia* (named for his wife whom he married in September 1813), led the flotilla, reminding one over-enthusiastic chronicler of the embarkation of Columbus heading for the New World. As the boats floated down the Cumberland River, Carroll had the companies drilled in squads on board the boats, issuing orders that no firing of guns, bugle blowing, or hollering would be permitted. At night a sentinel stood at the head of each boat. Courts-martial were convened on company vessels, with punishment for minor infractions ranging from having one's whiskey rations taken away to working at the oars for a full day. Bouts of drinking, along with entertainment from the slaves that accompanied the expedition, alleviated the laborious journey. Doctor William Lawrence noted getting drunk on a few occasions and laughing at the Negroes who danced to the music of a banjo player. On the grim side, one soldier recorded the deaths of ten men before reaching New Orleans. The fleet sojourned down the Ohio and into the Mississippi, arriving at Chickasaw Bluffs (future Memphis) on December 4. At this point, heavy rains impeded their progress and the task force landed at Natchez on December 14. Three days later they came to Saint Francisville and, finally, arrived at New Orleans on the afternoon of Decem-ber 20. Carroll's much-needed reinforcements fortuitously arrived just days before the initial landing of the British invasion force. A similar flotilla of 2,500 Kentucky militia followed close on the heels of the Tennessee troops navigating their way down the Mississippi. Marred by supply shortages, dis-abling weather, and several deaths, the Kentucky expedition left Louisville on November 21, 1814, but did not arrive at New Orleans until January 3, 1815. Upon their arrival at New Orleans, the Kentucky troops immediately began breaking down their flatboats in order to construct shelters out of the planks. In addition to camp equipage, the Kentuckians desperately lacked muskets and rifles. The balance of the troops—a full two-thirds—came unarmed and, consequently, were sent to the reserve line of Jackson's army. The remain-ing third, under Brigadier General John Adair, took up a position support-ing Carroll's Tennesseans.[35]

In late November, Andrew Jackson departed from his headquarters at Mobile, leaving the command of the Seventh Military District in the hands of General James Winchester. Jackson arrived in New Orleans on December 1, 1814, and immediately undertook a thorough examination of the defenses in and around the city. His entrance, however, sparked a local debate when he decided to reside at the home of Doctor David Kerr instead of the residence of the wealthy Creole, Bernard de Marigny, as previously planned. This snub of Marigny's hospitality took on exaggerated proportions in the rigid social hierarchy of the Creole aristocracy. (When the Louisiana legislature voted to present a costly sword to Jackson after the war, Marigny lobbied against it.) Jackson's choice of aides—Edward Livingston and Abner Duncan, both successful New Orleans attorneys—further disenfranchised the French and Creole elements of the city, who saw Jackson's selections as siding with the American bloc. Livingston and Duncan seemed a logical fit for Jackson, however, as he personally knew both men: Livingston had served with Jackson in Congress and Duncan had met Jackson earlier in Natchez. Jackson needed Livingston as an interpreter in a city where more French was spoken than English, and, in fact, Livingston proved to be invaluable to Jackson, taking the rank of colonel and writing many of the general's proclamations and dispatches. However, Livingston did have his shady side. As a former US attorney and mayor of New York, Livingston came to Louisiana on the heels of a scandal involving the disappearance of public funds. Intelligent and ambitious, Livingston set up a highly profitable law practice in New Orleans, adding the smuggler Jean Laffite to his long list of clients. Congressman John Randolph of Roanoke once said of Livingston: "He is brilliant but utterly corrupt, he stinks and shines like rotten mackerel by moonlight."[36]

Jackson's relationship with Governor Claiborne was tenuous, at best. While Claiborne had his doubts as to the loyalty of the French and Creole population, Jackson had his own misgivings about Claiborne's leadership abilities. This lack of faith stemmed back to a decade earlier when both Jackson and Claiborne sought the post of governor for the Territory of Orleans. Critics of Jackson deemed him too violent a person for a position requiring diplomatic skills. Jackson, on his part, felt Claiborne to be wholly unqualified for the job (although he never delineated why). Claiborne took offense to Jackson's appointment of Edward Livingston as his aide-de-camp at New Orleans, Livingston being a bitter political adversary of Claiborne's. The governor maintained that the strained relations between himself and Jackson were a result of Livingston's intrigues against him. Jackson's opinion of Claiborne further deteriorated during the New Orleans campaign, when Claiborne showed a lack of military initiative. According to Jackson, Claiborne had an opportunity to lead the troops against the British on at least one occasion, but failed, causing Jackson to comment that the governor was "much better qualified for the great pomp & show, & courting popularity in quiet life . . . than military achievements amidst peril danger."[37]

Claiborne did offer some useful suggestions to Jackson, notwithstanding their shaky relationship. In addition to making Jackson aware of the social and political rivalries festering in New Orleans, he also recommended using the city's battalion-strength free black militia—a move that outraged the slaveholding white population. Faced with what he deemed to be a shortage of manpower, Jackson consented to the idea, issuing a proclamation in September 1814 guaranteeing the same pay and bounty as offered to white enlistees ($124 in cash and 160 acres of land), coupled with the promise that black troops would not "be exposed to improper comparisons or unjust sarcasm." Obviously, the planter/merchant class of New Orleans opposed weapons in the hands of the black population, free or otherwise. The city's press consequently delayed the publication of Jackson's proclamation until late October. Eventually, two battalions of free blacks were formed. In a revealing letter to Governor Claiborne, who had informed him of the intense skepticism concerning the black troops, Jackson confided that he intended to assign the black battalions in the rear of any action "where they will be kept from doing any injury." "If their pride and merit entitle them to confidence, they can be employed against the Enemy," Jackson noted. "If not they can be kept from uniting with him." Regardless of the blatant distrust dished out to them, the free black battalions performed with honor and distinction throughout the campaign, proving themselves to be valuable contributors to the war.[38]

As desperate as Jackson was for additional manpower, he adamantly refused to enlist the services of the pirates lurking in Barataria Bay (fifty miles from New Orleans) and their professed leader, Jean Laffite. Contrabandists by profession, Laffite preferred his band of men be called "privateers," showing great disdain for the word "pirate." Along with his brother, Pierre, Jean Laffite came to Louisiana after the turn of the nineteenth century from mysterious origins and established a well-organized smuggling operation tucked away in the wilderness of bayous and swamps outside of New Orleans. Acting under the guise of letters of marque issued by a number of nations, the Laffites plundered the Gulf of Mexico, reselling the spoils at secret auctions or through "advisors," whose names comprised the elite of New Orleans, including Bernard de Marigny, Auguste Davezac, and Jean Blanque—the latter, a merchant, banker, and former slave dealer, who also held a seat in the state legislature. With such well-connected Louisianans, Laffite enjoyed relative immunity from the law and ungrudging respect from much of the local population. The goods he offered to eager purchasers ran the gamut from cinnamon, linen shirts, and handkerchiefs to canvas and twine, in addition to slaves, who always fetched a handsome price. The Laffites practically became heroes in the eyes of the French population, who despised the Americans for outlawing the slave trade. Prosecution of these smugglers became impossible as long as Frenchmen comprised the majority of juries.[39]

On September 2, 1814, Captain Nicholas Lockyer, accompanied by two other British officers, came to Laffite's headquarters at Grande Terre bearing a message from Lieutenant Colonel Edward Nicholls. The letter, dated August 31, solicited the aid of Jean Laffite and his Baratarians in return for a full pardon of their crimes, lands for Laffite and his followers, and the restitution of any plundered Spanish property, as well as British citizenship and a captaincy for Jean Laffite. The British high command earlier determined that securing the services of the Baratarians would help solidify their plans to control the Gulf region. After hosting the British messengers for two days, Jean Laffite bid the British officers a farewell by asking Nicholls, in a letter dated September 4, for fifteen days in order to make up his mind. Upon their departure, Laffite sent a note (along with the British documents) to Jean Blanque, his agent in New Orleans, informing him of the British offer and his resolve to serve the United States instead, referring to himself as "a true American." The fact that Jean's brother, Pierre, lay in a New Orleans jail may have been a deciding factor in Laffite's decision to back the Americans rather than the British. "I may have evaded the payment of duties to the custom house," Laffite confessed, "but I have never ceased to be a good citizen." As Jean professed his newfound patriotism, brother Pierre staged an escape from jail and tendered his services to Governor Claiborne to defend New Orleans. "I am the stray sheep, wishing to return to the sheepfold," Pierre informed Claiborne in an apologetic letter.[40]

After Jackson's arrival in New Orleans and his inspection of the city's defenses, he eventually came to the conclusion—after further cajoling from Edward Livingston—that he could use all the help he could get, even from "hellish Banditti" (as Jackson described the Baratarians), particularly after the British were sighted approaching Lake Borgne on December 12. Two days later, the British advanced on the lake with three divisions consisting of forty-two heavily armed launches and three unarmed gigs with over one thousand seamen and Royal Marines aboard. Opposing them were five lone gunboats, formed in line of battle, and 182 seamen led by Lieutenant Thomas Ap Catesby Jones. Initially, Jones staved off the assault after one British barge collided with an American gunboat and ensued in hand-to-hand combat, suffering severe casualties. Two more barges became stuck, causing the British to temporarily pull back. During the renewed contest, Lieutenant Jones received a disabling wound and the British soon overtook all the American vessels. The British suffered seventeen killed and seventy-seven wounded and inflicted at least six deaths, wounded thirty-five, and captured eighty-six Americans (including Captain Jones). With this British victory at Lake Borgne, Admiral Cochrane's fleet was now free to push toward New Orleans. In fact, Cochrane used the captured gunboats to protect his troop transports before attacking Jackson's army.[41]

Now, the men and matériel the Laffites offered seemed less of a stigma to Jackson. The vast stocks of ammunition tucked away in secret locations lured Jackson into an agreement with Jean Laffite. Especially appealing were the 7,500 gunflints that Laffite could provide—a commodity Jackson readily admitted he needed for his army. Jackson ordered the release of any Baratarian in confinement who agreed to take arms to defend New Orleans. Governor Claiborne issued a proclamation to those smugglers in hiding that Jackson would petition the president for a full pardon for every man who did his duty. The Laffite brothers met with Jackson, probably on December 22, at which time Jackson granted Jean Laffite a safe-conduct pass and sent him off to help defend Louisiana. The Baratarians who joined Jackson's army—about four hundred in number—were organized into three companies and dispatched to reinforce the forts guarding the main approaches to the city. The only "pirates" to take part in the action of the subsequent battles were Pierre Laffite (who fought alongside John Coffee on December 23 as a guide) and two gun crews on the American breastworks at Chalmette—one led by Dominique Youx, a partner of Laffite, and the other by a Baratarian lieutenant named Renato Beluche. Still, when the campaign at New Orleans finally ended, Jackson went from calling the Baratarians "pirates" and "robbers" to "privateers and gentlemen."[42]

Laffite's material contributions notwithstanding, the lack of arms and ammunition still plagued Andrew Jackson. In November 1814 the federal government shipped 5,000 stands of arms and 30,000 cartridges, along with other camp equipage, from Pittsburgh to New Orleans. In order to reduce the cost of freight, they were sent on three keelboats whose water route demanded they stop at many landings en route, slowing their progress. On December 14 William Carroll's flotilla actually intercepted one of the boats at Natchez and confiscated 1,400 stands of arms that Carroll later delivered to Jackson. The other boats arrived *after* the campaign, including the steamboat *Enterprize*, which left Pittsburgh on December 21 and arrived at New Orleans on January 9, 1815, one day after the climactic January 8 battle. Troops arriving at New Orleans without arms, including Carroll's men, forced Jackson to order a search by civil officials of every house and store in the city for muskets, bayonets, cartridges, pick axes, shovels, and hoes. The arrival of Coffee's men must have comforted the anxious Jackson, as they came fully armed and equipped. Stationed at Baton Rouge, Coffee had received a message from Jackson on December 11 indicating there might be a "fandango" with the British soon. "If so you and your Brave followers must participate, in the frolic," Jackson playfully wrote. Then on December 19, a more resolute Jackson informed Coffee there might be a British attack at any time, "but I am prepared to give them Bloody noses and with the aid of your brave riflemen will bury them all before they can reach the city."[43]

The appearance of Coffee's and Carroll's men came not a moment too soon. After an agonizing trek across swamps, canebrakes, and bayous, the main British army advanced to the plantation owned by General Jacques Villeré on the morning of December 23, 1814. Captain John Tylden of the British Forty-Third regiment described the topography as "intersected in all directions by small ditches of water & is so low that it is scarcely above [the] water mark." (Transporting heavy artillery would be a logistical torture and in no small way contributed to the ultimate defeat of the British.) Just as debilitating was the unusually cold weather; one British captain indicated the weather as being so severe some nights "as to produce ice an inch thick in tubs." The captain acknowledged he had to wear two coats, two pairs of trousers, and three waistcoats to keep warm, even in his tent.[44]

Still, the morale of the British remained high. Although the British knew the Americans had knowledge of their coming, their troops were "in the habits of Victory," as one British colonel termed it. In addition, many of the men believed the expedition would lead to some prize money for the capture of the vast warehouses of cotton stored at New Orleans. This supposition gave rise to the popular notion that the British intended to pillage New Orleans once they overran Jackson's army. According to American sources, the British watchword and countersign on the morning of the January 8 battle was "Beauty and Booty." Newspapers were keen on printing unconfirmed reports stating the British promised their soldiers "forty-eight hours pillage and rapine of the city of New-Orleans!" French counsel Chevalier de Tousard later claimed British prisoners indicated they were "promised the plunder of the city and complete license," differing only in the number of days allowed, some saying three while others saying eight. In reality, there is no evidence to suggest the British government sought any profit from the fall of New Orleans. Nevertheless, Admiral Cochrane was suspected of plunder as the motive for attacking New Orleans, an accusation endorsed by the Duke of Wellington, who believed Cochrane was the type of man who might put booty ahead of duty.[45]

Another psychological factor that played into the fighting at New Orleans consisted of the miscalculations of each side's troop strength. Both Americans and British overestimated the other's total numbers. The inaccuracies reflected the poor reconnaissance abilities of both sides, whose officers often relied on the veracity of prisoners and deserters. When the British first landed in Louisiana, they estimated the American strength to be about 11,000 men, which increased to 14,000–15,000 after the British were repulsed. One British officer who published his memoirs of the campaign in 1821 insisted Jackson's forces totaled 25,000 men. Jackson, on his part, figured his enemy's numbers at 12,000–15,000. Modern estimates place the actual numbers at 7,730 for the British and 7,386 for the Americans. Ensign David Weller of the Kentucky militia wrote to his brother in early January 1815: "It is impossible for me [to tell] how many troops there is in all but the levee and a way out to the swamps is crowded with troops." Weller also commented that "the Creealls [sic] are turning [out] very fast—Jackson has the Negroes a fighting too." Weller's reference to the Creoles and free blacks fighting alongside the Tennessee, Kentucky, and Mississippi troops, as well as the Regular Army (not to mention the Choctaws and pirates), indicates the acute awareness of the soldiers concerning the diversity of forces under Jackson's command in New Orleans. That Jackson made the whole operation function as a unit is a credit to his leadership abilities and his physical stamina. The Creek War had taken its toll on Jackson's body, now wracked with various pains and illnesses. Jackson's decision to reside with Dr. David Kerr instead of wealthy Creole Bernard de Marigny may have been based on the necessity of having a doctor at hand. In fact, Kerr treated Jackson for dysentery throughout most of the general's stay in New Orleans. Furthermore, the city had a reputation for being particularly unhealthy, as yellow fever frequently plagued the population.[46]

Jackson did not allow his physical ailments to interfere with his ability to command. With such a disparate army and an even more dissimilar population to deal with, Jackson presented a strong, authoritarian leadership to all concerned—too authoritarian for some Louisianans. Most residents of New Orleans viewed Jackson's imposition of martial law on the city in mid-December 1814 as a necessary evil, given the impending circumstances. However, the general's refusal to lift the ban once the English had retreated created a severe rift between Jackson and some of the population, leading to an eventual trial for contempt of court. Of course, extreme adversity against a common foe often causes diverse sections of society to form a bond. So it was at New Orleans in late 1814/early 1815. Even before he arrived at New Orleans, Jackson published a proclamation in the *Louisiana Gazette* on October 18, 1814. "Every Louisianian, either by birth or adoption, will promptly obey the voice of his country," Jackson demanded, "[and] will rally around the Eagle of Columbia, rescue it from impending danger, or nobly die, in the last ditch of its defense." For the most part, Louisianans responded affirmatively. "We daily expect the enemy to make an attack upon this place," wrote one New Orleans citizen on December 16, 1814, "we are ready, however, to receive them. . . . There now reigns but one party; all are determined to oppose the enemy." "Nationalities no longer count; we are all Americans," French consul Chevalier de Tousard boasted in early January 1815. Tousard attributed the homogeneous situation to Jackson, who, in Tousard's words "has inspired a confidence that has united all parties and all shades of opinion." Among the troops, Jackson maintained a constant presence, making regular visits (often three times a day) to the fortifications, keeping part of his staff constantly on the lines. He also set up a rigidly enforced line of communications via horse riders at various stations, varying between twelve to thirty miles between stops. Jackson seemed to have all the right elements in place to guarantee a victory for himself and the United States.[47]

6

Private James McCutchen, of Dyer's First Regiment of West Tennessee volunteer mounted gunmen, scribbled this entry in his diary on December 23, 1814, at New Orleans: "we marched 10 miles down to the Battle ground where we had an engagement with the British and lay on the ground all night." In his usual brusque style, McCutchen summed up the critical initial engagement between the British and American forces at New Orleans. Other observers were not quite as pedestrian as McCutchen in their assessments. Another participant, Richard Call, referred to the December 23 engagement as "the greatest, and much the best fought field ever won by General Jackson." Call claimed the magnanimous victory of January 8 eclipsed the importance of the December 23 clash and, yet, the latter contest "enabled [Jackson] to prepare for and to fight the battle of the 8th of January." Jackson himself agreed that this initial clash allowed time to set up a defensive stand and thus save the city. He unashamedly called the battle "the *best* fought action in the annals of military warfare."[1]

Major General John Keane, leading the advance elements of the British army (Sir Edward Pakenham not having arrived in Louisiana until December 25), managed to surprise Jackson and get within several miles of New Orleans; had he pressed forward, the city might have been his. But with only 1,600–1,800 men at his disposal against what he thought was an American army consisting of 20,000, the cautious Keane opted to halt just past Villeré's plantation between the Mississippi River and a cypress swamp. Sometime near two o'clock in the afternoon of December 23, Jackson heard the alarming news that the British were only nine miles from the city. From his headquarters on Royal Street, Jackson responded immediately and, through a flurry of dispatches, quickly gathered all available forces and sent them scurrying southward out of the city. Jackson ordered part of Carroll's Tennessee division, stationed four miles above New Orleans, down the Chef Menteur Road to check any British advance from that direction (the rest of Carroll's division remained in the city during the battle). John Coffee led the left of Jackson's army, along with the Mississippi dragoons and mounted riflemen under Major Thomas Hinds, while Jackson himself led the main thrust, consisting of the Regulars (men of the Seventh and Forty-Fourth US Infantries), Major Jean Baptiste Plauché's New Orleans volunteers, and Major Louis Daquin's corps of volunteer blacks. Choctaws, marines, and artillery comprised the smaller detachments of Jackson's army—a total of about 1,800 men.[2]

As these disparate elements made their way through New Orleans, they encountered a terrified population running pell-mell through the crowded streets. One of Coffee's men, in the first troops marching through the city, recalled "the women crying & screaming for fear of the British." A mounted soldier from the Mississippi dragoons looked up at the balconies overhead, filled with ladies "weeping and wringing their hands." Riding at the head of the Regulars, Andrew Jackson stopped to console a group of distressed women commiserating over the impending invasion. According to a witness, Jackson assured them the British would never make it to the city "without passing over the dead bodies of his slaughtered army." The women, their spirits temporarily bolstered by Jackson's confidence, waved their handkerchiefs in appreciation as the army moved toward the outskirts of New Orleans. Some of Coffee's cavalry were given bottles of liquor as they galloped through the streets, knocking off the top of the bottle instead of trying to uncork it, then taking a drink and passing it on.[3]

Night had already settled by the time the Americans approached the battlefield. Cold, raw, disagreeable weather, with the moon shining brightly, set the tone for what was about to transpire. The men, fatigued from their hurried march from the city, were bathed in sweat and mud, as "the north wind blew furiously," recalled one Louisiana officer. The battleground consisted of a generally flat landscape varying 1,000–1,500 yards between the Mississippi River and swampy woods, intersected with rail fences about five feet high and wet ditches. Large outbuildings and slave huts lay scattered over the terrain. The main road ran parallel to the levee—a mound of earth about four feet high—bordering the river. Near this road, British General Keane, after leaving the Villeré plantation, gave the order to make camp until additional troops could be brought forward. (It has been supposed that had the British advance column continued their march, they could have reached New Orleans before Jackson could react, yet there is no hard evidence the British planned to attack the city that day.) Jackson devised a plan intending to make the British think the best American troops were in the center, so that Coffee's men would then turn the British right flank, while Jackson attacked from the front with the Seventh US Infantry. Commodore Daniel

Patterson, onboard the schooner *Carolina*, was to fire on the British left flank while General David Morgan was to get as many men as possible in the rear of the British lines. Jackson ordered Colonel Arthur P. Hayne to take five hundred men (Hinds's dragoons and two Louisiana rifle companies) to advance against the enemy in order to ascertain his position before the main army could be concentrated. The American advance party tore down all the fences from the levee to the woods, opening the way for the main army, while keeping an alert eye for any British movements. The Americans then waited in absolute silence for the signal to attack.[4]

The famished British were enjoying a much-needed hot meal when, at about 7:30 p.m., they spotted the *Carolina* approaching. At first they thought the vessel might be one of their own cruisers but became anxious when they received no answer after hailing it. The *Carolina* then swung broadside, and a distinct voice shouted, "Give them this for the honour of America!" In the next instant, a deadly shower of grapeshot scattered the panicked soldiers who, after hurriedly extinguishing their campfires, sought shelter behind the earthen levee. The elated captain of the *Carolina* crudely recalled, "there never was a finer time for killing men." With no artillery to counter the *Carolina*'s heavy guns, the British fired off a few Congreve rockets that had no effect on the American vessel. As the men lay huddled near the levee, they discerned musket fire coming from the direction of the British right. Soon they heard a fearful yell and the night skies became illuminated on all sides from the blaze of musketry.[5]

The firing of the guns from the *Carolina* signaled the American land troops to begin their attack. Richard Call, now Jackson's aide, remembered the moments before the initial attack with amazing clarity: "The line of battle in front and on the enemy's right flank was formed in whispered words of command. The moon was bright, the air was still and calm, and a death like, portentous silence reigned over the whole field. At length when all was ready the word was given to advance, and a full band, broke the brooding silence, with the animating all-cheering notes of 'Yankee Doodle.' On we marched. At last the enemy sprang in wild astonishment from their hiding place and formed in haste such a line to receive us, as the best disciplined veteran troops alone could have done." John Coffee, unfamiliar with the terrain, chose Colonel Pierre Denis de la Ronde of the Louisiana militia to serve as his guide—a wise choice, considering the battleground lay on Ronde's plantation. With the additional aid of an interpreter (Pierre Laffite) to instruct the French-speaking troops, Coffee advanced past Hinds's dragoons into the enemy's right flank, while the Regulars and militia attacked the British near the river. In a matter of moments, all hell broke loose, causing Private

M. W. Trimble to recall: "The atmosphere seemed to be on fire, and the very earth trembled." As musket balls whizzed past the exposed soldiers, the shells from the *Carolina* came dangerously close to the American troops, and as the Congreve rockets screamed across the night sky, some of Coffee's men took cover in the ditches traversing the field. One old soldier refused to jump into a ditch, defiantly shouting that the Lord would protect him. Hardly had he spoken when gunfire shattered his arm in several places. When the Americans neared the enemy's center, British bugles could be heard blaring in the darkness, as English officers attempted to regain some order in the terrorized ranks. "Even amidst the roar of battle," Trimble recalled, "we could hear the thud of the balls mowing down their rifles, the cries of the wounded, and the cool and clear orders given by their officers: 'Steady men, steady!' 'Remember you are Britons!' was sounded from rank to rank."[6]

Faced with total destruction or surrender, the trapped British units decided their only course of action was to counterattack the Americans. Rushing from the embankment, the British charged into the scattered American forces. "All order, all discipline were lost," George Gleig, a lieutenant in the British Eighty-Fifth Light Infantry, recalled. In what he termed as "the tumult and ferocity of one of Homer's combats," Gleig described how each officer would collect twenty or thirty men around him and charge into the enemy, fighting with bayonets, swords, and fists. The initial British counterattack forced the Americans to temporarily retreat. Colonel John Gibson, of Coffee's brigade, fell on his back while trying to escape, and a British officer made several attempts to stab him with a bayonet, which Gibson managed to stave off with his hands until he was able to kick the officer in the stomach and make his getaway. Other American officers were not as lucky as Gibson. Colonel Robert Dyer mistakenly strayed into the British lines and received a grievous wound in his leg as his horse fell dead beneath him. Some of Coffee's men found themselves in the rear of the British when a musket ball struck the head of Colonel James Lauderdale, killing him instantly. Extremely popular with his men, Lauderdale's death had a demoralizing effect on the brigade. One account indicates Lauderdale died a hero's death "with his sword firmly grasped in his hand." Yet Lauderdale may have been a victim of friendly fire. In the confusion of the night battle, a company of US Regulars changed their position, encountering a company of Tennessee riflemen and both mistakenly opened fire on the other and even engaged in hand-to-hand combat. Colonel Lauderdale, recognizing the blunder, rushed in between the groups and began knocking down their guns with his sword when he was fatally shot.[7]

During the next hour and a half, the darkness, the smoke of the battle, and the jumbled positions of each army made it impossible to tell friend from foe. The New Orleans Rifle Company became divided and one-half of them marched up to who they thought were Jackson's men, crying out, "huzza for Tennessee," only to be captured by the British. The men in Coffee's brigade began to fire at each other. Major William Kavanaugh, replacing Colonel Lauderdale, asked for volunteers to go out and signal the troops they were firing on Americans. Sergeant Andrew Jackson Edmondson, along with Captain John Donaldson and another man, volunteered for the mission. The three men cautiously advanced about a hundred yards when Donaldson and the other soldier said they would go no further. Edmondson pressed on alone, arriving to within twenty yards of the line of fire, and yelled out they were shooting at their own men. A man came close enough to ask what unit Edmondson belonged to and the sergeant indicated he was in Coffee's First Regiment. Edmondson then asked if the soldier belonged to the Second Regiment and, as the man shouted back, "yes," Edmondson could see white straps on his uniform. Edmondson stopped cold in his tracks, realizing the men opposite him were British soldiers. The uniformed man approached Edmondson, calling him a "damned yankee," and ordered him to lay down his arms. A frightened and embarrassed Edmondson took off running at full speed with British bullets spraying around him, "which did not make me run slower—from the whistling of the balls I thought the whole British army were shooting at me."[8]

In similar fashion, American troops trapped British soldiers by pretending they were British troops—a situation that led either to surrender or fierce hand-to-hand combat. Groups of British soldiers were captured in this manner, including a Major Mitchell, who came upon a Tennessee unit and asked if it was the British Ninety-Fifth Infantry. Lured into thinking he had found his regiment, the shocked major soon discovered his error and was forced to lay down his sword, which Captain John Donaldson immediately picked up and put around his waist. (It was later discovered that Major Mitchell might have been the British officer who put the torch to the Capitol in Washington.) The men of Captain Thomas Jones's company (Dyer's regiment) found themselves cut off from the main force and were fired on from behind by their own men. The friendly fire continued until the troops got to within thirty yards of each other, at which point Jones's men repeatedly shouted they belonged to Coffee's brigade. The attackers replied they could not be sure and ordered Jones's men to lay their arms on the ground. At that point, the assailants were so close that it became apparent they were British soldiers impersonating Americans. Rather than surrender, Jones's men attacked with a loud roar and clashing of swords. In all, Jones's company suffered one killed, four wounded, and three taken prisoner. Of the latter, a junior officer named Daniel Treadwell had the most adventurous encounter of the night. As he was being led away by a lone British guard, Treadwell turned and made a remark about the British being in retreat. When the guard turned to look, Treadwell took out a pistol he had hidden under his coat and shot the tricked British soldier. Treadwell then took the guard's gun and ran toward what he hoped were the American lines. Instead, he ran headlong into the British, who recaptured him. As he was being escorted away again, this time by two sentries, intense firing broke out close by, and as the guards turned toward the direction of the fire, Treadwell seized the moment to knock one of them down and make yet another hairbreadth escape. Treadwell's luck finally ran out when he came across a mortally wounded American officer who begged Treadwell to stay with him. Treadwell complied and, through this act of kindness, was taken prisoner for a third (and final) time by the British.[9]

British lieutenant George Gleig neatly summed up the collision of the two forces that December night when he referred to the battle as more of "a perfect tumult . . . than an engagement between two civilized armies." The contest began to ebb sometime around midnight, with sporadic firing continuing until three in the morning. Ironically, the British wound up in roughly the same position as they started, although they had about two hundred casualties. The survivors lay shivering in the cold air of the frosty morning without campfires, pinned down by the relentless guns of the *Carolina* (joined by the sloop USS *Louisiana*), who kept up a constant barrage throughout the following day, aiming at the British trying to carry off wounded comrades and firing into the house where the British wounded lay (one man had his knapsack, which he was using as a pillow, shot out from underneath his head). On their part, the Americans dropped back a half a mile, taking along their wounded. The Americans had suffered twenty-five killed, seventy wounded, and about seventy-five men taken as prisoners. Sergeant Edmondson recalled spending the rest of the night trying to find his horse. "My patriotism at about sun up was at a pretty low ebb," an exhausted Edmondson wrote. "I felt a good deal like running if an enemy appeared & the boys all said they felt pretty much as I did." Edmondson's morale was temporarily lifted when the regimental commissary officer rolled out some barrels of whiskey and Edmondson helped himself to a full cup, downing it with one swallow. "This warmed me all over," he beamed, "and made me ready for anything that might come." General William Carroll's men, who had been posted at a different location outside the city, came up to reinforce Jackson, and the army pulled back another mile and a half to the position behind an old millrace known as the Rodriguez Canal on the Chalmette plantation. Guards remained on the front line for picket duty, where they stayed all night without a fire or blankets. The watchword that night was "English." Although the pickets could light no fires, the bulk of the retreating Americans, standing in an open field, begged for (and received) permission to kindle a fire for warmth. Within minutes, innumerable campfires blazed up along a line extending from the banks of the Mississippi to the woods, giving the impression that Jackson had more troops under his command than the British supposed. This, plus the fact that some American prisoners taken that night told the British Jackson had 30,000 men at his disposal, led the English commanders to assume the American army was much more considerable than anticipated.[10]

As night dissolved into day, the appalling remnants of the fierce battle, hidden by the darkness, now came into view. "When daylight appeared," Private Trimble remembered, "[British] dead and wounded covered the field." Lieutenant Gleig, with some British companions, went out in search of a friend's body and expressed total shock by the sights he encountered: men shot through the head or heart; heinous, mortal wounds from bayonets, swords, and musket butts; and bodies piled in small groups whose faces "exhibited the most savage and ghastly expressions." In some cases a dead English and American soldier could be seen lying side by side with a bayonet fastened in each other's body. Gleig managed to locate his friend's corpse and have it carted off to headquarters where he oversaw the burial in a garden. While there, Gleig visited the hospital set up in the plantation house and witnessed more dreadful sights. "Every room in the house was crowded with wretches mangled, and apparently in the most excruciating agonies," Gleig recalled. "Prayers, groans, and I grieve to add, the most horrid exclamations, smote upon the ear wherever I turned." In the bitter cold of the morning, the bodies on the frozen field took on a ghostly countenance. One British officer, Lieutenant Benson Hill, later recorded his impressions of the American dead: "These poor fellows presented a strange appearance; their hair, eye brows, and lashes, were thickly covered with hoar-frost, or rime, their bloodless cheeks vying with its whiteness." He also noticed that very few of the bodies were clad in military uniforms; indeed, Hill thought most of them "bore the appearance of farmers or husbandmen." Yet, the British officer grudgingly acknowledged they had died nobly defending their country.[11]

Initially, Jackson wanted to renew the attack, that is, until his scouts informed him of British reinforcements making their way toward the enemy's lines. He then placed his artillery on the levee road near its junction with the Rodriguez Canal so as to sweep the front of any British advance. He left the Seventh US Infantry, Hinds's dragoons, and a unit of Louisiana cavalry on the de la Ronde property to keep abreast of British movements. Jackson next set up a position behind the canal, with a cypress swamp jutting toward the river on the left and the tract of land in front of the canal narrowing to about six hundred yards. About a hundred or so yards behind the canal, the two-storied mansion on the nearby Macarty plantation offered Jackson an excellent vantage point to survey the topography in all directions. Jackson could view the activities of the British through the use of a telescope set up in the dormer window of Macarty's house. Coffee's brigade had the unenviable task of holding down the left end—the cypress swamp—of Jackson's new defensive position. The men labored at cutting down trees, clearing undergrowth for a line of fire, and fixing their tents on platforms to sleep on. All the men slept, when they could sleep, with their clothes on and arms in hand, doing so until the conclusion of the campaign. Many of the men did not have the luxury of tents and had to sleep on floating logs lashed to the trees. On duty, Coffee's men usually stood in knee-deep or waist-high swamp water.[12]

On December 24, the same day American and British negotiators at Ghent, Belgium, signed a peace treaty—Jackson began construction on what has become the most famous breastworks in American military history. Known as Line Jackson, this extended mound of earth stretched a thousand yards in a straight line across an open, level field and then broke at an angle upon reaching the cypress swamp where Coffee's men were situated (Pierre Laffite taking credit for suggesting to Jackson he make an extension into the swamp). Unevenness marked Line Jackson—it being higher and wider in some places than in others. John Coffee depicted the breastworks as "a strong bank of earth twelve feet thick and high as a man's shoulders, on our side and a ditch on the other side [filled] with water." A Kentuckian described the ditch as about ten feet wide filled with twelve to eighteen inches of water. British officers who actually tried to scale the works recalled the line to be from ten to twelve feet wide and anywhere from eight to ten feet high, while the ditch measured ten to twelve feet wide and three to four feet deep, with water coming up to a man's waist.[13]

One of the more persistent myths about the breastworks at Line Jackson was the use of cotton bales to fortify it. Nineteenth-century illustrators of the battle were keen on promoting this idea. In truth, cotton bales *did* play a role in the construction after it was discovered the soggy soil made for poor entrenchment. A French engineer suggested placing cotton bales on the ground and laying wooden platforms on top of them for the batteries that soon appeared on Line Jackson. Sergeant Andrew Jackson Edmondson recalled the bales of cotton (no more than a hundred) being utilized in the first portions of the line, but most of the works consisted of earth and torn-down fence pickets. Realistically speaking, cotton did not make for a suitable material, as it could easily catch on fire. The cotton bales had a more practical use when Jackson's men fashioned them into mattresses. Jackson's impatience to have the breastworks in place as quickly as possible meant conscripting any and all personnel. Dandified French-speaking Creoles supposedly could be seen shoveling next to the unshaven and crudely dressed militia of Tennessee. They were joined by large groups of slaves, loaned out by the local plantation owners. Judging by the amount of correspondence concerning the matter, it is evident that slave labor for fortification projects remained indispensable throughout the campaign. One contemporary noted that Jackson requisitioned six hundred blacks to work on the defensive lines (there were actually two other "lines" situated behind Line Jackson in the event the British penetrated the first). In all, thousands of slaves worked on military fortifications at strategic locations at New Orleans.[14]

Tents were set up between the levee and the Rodriguez house along Line Jackson as shelter for the men, while in front of the line—nearly five hundred yards away—mounted pickets were stationed to watch British movements for daily reconnaissance. Across the fields of Chalmette, the encamped British army lay with its own sentinels keeping watch on the Americans. During the siege of New Orleans, Americans would sneak up to the British lines and kill their sentinels, a practice the Americans facetiously called "hunting parties." The Choctaws were particularly adept at conducting these forays, especially a Choctaw named Poindexter, who, after killing British sentinels and stealing their arms, would sell the rifles to American officers as souvenirs. The British, trained in the strict etiquette of European warfare, expressed their abhorrence of this practice, referring to it as "an ungenerous return to barbarity." One British officer admitted the practice had the effect of creating "considerable anxiety and uneasiness" but considered the Americans as assassins rather than soldiers. Another British officer acknowledged that the scouting parties made the lives of the British miserable, but excused the Americans on the basis they were defending their own land from invasion— the same stance Jackson adopted when the British made a formal complaint.[15]

On Christmas Day 1814, a salvo of artillery from the British camp announced the arrival of Sir Edward Michael Pakenham (sometimes spelled Packenham), commander of British forces in North America. Although not overly pleased by what he found—his force cooped up on a small patch of land between the Mississippi and a large swamp—he decided to continue offensive operations against an enemy he had never faced before and whose determination he severely underestimated. Pakenham's first order of business concerned the devastating enfilading fire coming from the *Carolina* and *Louisiana*. The British set up a battery on the levee consisting of two 9-pounders, four 6-pounders, and two howitzers. On the morning of December 27 the British fired hot shot at the *Carolina*, causing her to catch fire and forcing the crew to abandon ship. Fortunately for the Americans, the *Louisiana* escaped damage by being towed out of range. Then at dawn on December 28 Pakenham coordinated an advance on Line Jackson in two columns: Major General Samuel Gibbs on the right, marching up the main road, and Major General John Keane on the left, taking the levee road. The American outposts, spotting the advancing columns, fell back and the British were able to move forward for about five miles without encountering any resistance. Then, abruptly, the American position came into view about seven hundred yards in the distance, and the artillery on Line Jackson and the guns of the *Louisiana* simultaneously opened up on the British columns with devastating precision. Keane's men halted and sought cover in the ditches and sugar cane stubble on the flat terrain. The British moved up their field artillery to counter the American firepower but found themselves severely outmatched. Even though Line Jackson still did not possess a full complement of artillery, the land guns, combined with those on the *Louisiana*, overwhelmed the British artillery. A British officer described the contest as a "destructive fire of artillery as I ever saw." Caught in a deadly crossfire, some of Keane's men ran toward some outbuildings for protection only to have the Americans fire red-hot shot at the structures, setting them on fire (the Americans having previously filled the buildings with combustibles for such a situation). The entire area became "one grand and terrific blaze," according to British quartermaster William Surtees. Lieutenant Gleig, in typical British reserve, described the scene as "altogether very sublime." He went on to say: "A tremendous cannonade mowed down our ranks, and deafened us with its roar; while two large chateaux and their out-buildings, almost scorched us with the flames, and blinded us with the smoke which they emitted." A second advance by the British infantry also proved ineffective, and, by evening, Pakenham ordered a general retreat after suffering sixty casualties. American losses amounted to eight killed and seven wounded.[16]

Most of the American casualties came on the extreme left, an area removed from the artillery contest. As a diversionary tactic, Pakenham had sent Lieutenant Colonel Robert Rennie to reconnoiter the cypress swamp while the main thrust steered its way toward the center of Line Jackson. To counter this move, Major General William Carroll detached about two hundred Tennesseans under Colonel James Henderson to drive off some of Rennie's troops who had positioned themselves behind a fence and ditch. Henderson's orders specified for him to come up to the right of the British by skirting the swamp and attacking from that angle. But contrary to Carroll's orders, Henderson formed his men in the open plain where the Americans could not fire their cannon without hitting Henderson's men. Carroll tried yelling out the proper orders to Henderson's men, but the splashing of the swamp water through which they marched made it impossible to hear. A desperate Carroll then dispatched an officer to warn Henderson but a British volley killed Henderson and two of his men before the officer could reach them. After Henderson fell, his men retreated and one man got left behind, badly wounded. In great pain, the soldier attempted several times, unsuccessfully, to make it back to the lines when two of Carroll's officers leaped over the breastworks and aided the man to safety while under heavy British fire. Major Howell Tatum, who witnessed the rescue, called it "as great an act of bravery as was witnessed on the lines during the siege." Pakenham's order to withdraw caused Rennie to reluctantly retreat, Rennie later insisting he could have turned the American left on that day. Nevertheless, Pakenham had committed his troops on December 28 to conduct a reconnaissance-in-force, not a major offensive. He set out to explore the Americans' strengths and weaknesses and discovered more of the former than the latter.[17]

After the December 28 clash, both Pakenham and Jackson rapidly came to the correct conclusion that artillery would be the difference-maker in the ensuing contest for New Orleans. Each side spent the remainder of the month bolstering its firepower with as many heavy guns as could be obtained and transported. The Americans had the distinct advantage in that the British did not have enough "heavy" cannon and lacked an ample supply of artillery ammunition. Still, with the weather turning more favorable, the British spent the next few days moving cannon—ten 18-pounders and four 24-pounders—from their ships, dragged with incredible labor by seamen across the morass of bayous. The Americans bolstered Line Jackson with additional artillery and, significantly, set up two batteries on the opposite side of the river (the West Bank) while continuing to throw shots into the British camp with great effect. Both sides soon became familiar with the constant deafening roar of artillery salvos (one American soldier indicating Jackson's batteries could fire fifty-four rounds in one hour). "The report of Cannon is now as familiar to me as eating," an American volunteer related to his father in a December 30 letter. British quartermaster Surtees recalled the abject fear caused by the 32-pounder firing from the American breastworks as it plowed into the British lines. Through the use of a spyglass, Surtees could see each shot as it was fired three-quarters of a mile away, "appearing like a small black spot in the midst of the column of white smoke, and which gradually grew larger in appearance as it approached."[18]

As the Americans continually strengthened and reinforced their lines, the British decided to try to eliminate the American batteries by making use of their own heavy cannon. On the evening of December 31, working as noiselessly as possible, the British erected six batteries of thirty pieces of artillery—using hogsheads of sugar as earthworks—about three hundred yards from the American lines. At daylight on New Year's Day, 1815, a heavy fog accompanied by rain prevented the British from opening fire until nine in the morning. Across the terrain of Chalmette, the unsuspecting Americans could be seen on parade with bands playing and colors flying. One of the American mounted picket guards patrolling near the swamp spotted the British batteries only a few hundred yards away and suddenly felt a cannonball fly so near him "as for me to feel the commotion of the air in my face." He quickly retreated from the scene as "the round shot, shells and rockets, were falling about me as thick as hail." Thus began what was to later be known in the campaign for New Orleans as the great artillery duel of January first. Similar to the plan of December 28, Pakenham's strategy called for a two-pronged assault on the American right and left, with Lieutenant Rennie once again making a feint on the far left of the American line through the woods. Emphasis lay on silencing the American artillery, and once accomplished, the main attack would storm the breastwork by filling the ditch in front of it with fascines (cylindrical bundles of sticks bound together).[19]

The initial onslaught of the British salvos temporarily shocked the unprepared American volunteers and militia. It was a spectacle that none of them had ever seen or experienced. An officer in Jackson's army later wrote to a friend in Nashville how the British "opened upon us the most tremendous fire of shot, shells, rockets, and for a short time, musketry." Inspector General Andrew Hynes, in a January 6, 1815, letter, called it "the greatest cannonading that has been known in America." Even the blasé British soldiers, used to such sieges in Europe, expressed their amazement. One British officer wrote: "New Year's Day afforded us a sight of fire works, popguns, mortars and rockets such as been seldom witnessed even in Lord Wellington's great actions in the Peninsula." The effect of just one shell could be devastating. A single shot from a British battery killed three Americans and disabled a 24-pound cannon. Doctor William Lawrence suffered the loss of hearing in his right ear when a bomb burst near his quarters, knocking him and his surgeon's mate to the ground. The fragments of the same explosion hit another assistant below the knee (the leg had to be amputated later) and killed a horse standing nearby. In the space of ten minutes, more than a hundred balls, shells, and rockets struck the Macarty house, where Jackson had his headquarters, causing Jackson and his staff to abandon it. Amazingly, American casualties were slim—only five recorded deaths—since many of the missiles overshot their mark. "The British let loose their Cannon, and Rockets like hail . . . but to no purpose," enlistee Levi Lee jotted in his diary, "their [cannon] balls generally went over us, and their Rockets generally went over too; and some of them went a hundred yards high." The inaccuracy of the artillery can be attributed to the fact that British guns were mounted on makeshift platforms that recoiled with every shot and on carriages designed primarily for naval vessels.[20]

Soon recovering from their initial shock, the Americans poured forth their own brand of destruction with unabated enthusiasm. Private James McCutchen, of Dyer's mounted gunmen, expressed the situation in his typically clipped fashion: "The British began to fire with redoubled furey [sic] which was returned by us in like manner." The superiority of American firepower now came into play. With precision-like accuracy, the guns on the American line began to demolish the advanced British batteries, which were not as well protected as those behind the American breastworks. By noon, the British began to run out of ammunition and temporarily ceased firing—inspiring the Americans to increase their own shooting, as they let out a loud cheer. The additional American artillery on the West Bank intensified the destruction. Captain Edward Wylly, Pakenham's military secretary, later summed up the predicament in a March 4, 1815, letter to the Duke of Wellington: "After three or four hours of incessant firing it was found that no impression whatever had been made, that our ammunition was almost totally expended, our batteries nearly demolished and our loss in Artillery men so severe that we had no longer the means of pursuing our object." It became evident to Pakenham that his assault would only end in failure as long as the American artillery stood firm. Even Rennie's far-left foray ended miserably when he and his two hundred men found the woods to be too boggy and deep for movement. As a result of the British advances there, however, Jackson decided to augment Coffee's regiment of men on the far left with Coffee's other regiment, which had been stationed in the rear. Jackson's general order for January 1 expressed his good wishes for a happy New Year and appreciation for the men's service, especially the artillery. As a reward, the troops received an extra half gill of whiskey.[21]

The British, who had put too much faith in their ability to destroy the American artillery, faced the humiliating task of retreating once more from the battlefield. The initial redoubts facing Line Jackson—the ones made from the hogsheads of sugar—failed to protect the British batteries. The American guns "knocked the batteries about our ears," recalled English Lieutenant

Robert Aitchison. The British were forced to remove their cannon from their advanced position, a chore made doubly difficult when the weather turned rainy that evening. Aitchison remembered it as "the dirtiest, and most fatigueing [*sic*] job I ever was engaged in." The retreat had two direct effects on Sir Edward Pakenham's future strategy: first, he would wait for reinforcements—the Seventh and Forty-Third regiments being due to arrive soon—and, second, he committed to the idea of securing the right (west) bank of the river in order to enfilade the American position *before* storming the breastworks.[22]

The British spent the next several days in preparation for their final assault on Line Jackson. Reinforcements were slow in arriving—the last of them not reaching the British camp until January 6. In the meantime, Pakenham concerned himself with the dwindling supplies of ammunition and commissary stores. Moreover, the constant harassment of American artillery and "hunting parties" chipped at the morale of the British troops, making it difficult to even enjoy the comfort of a campfire at night. The weather remained cold and wet, and desertion became a serious concern to the British commanders. Pakenham's scheme to take the West Bank evolved into a grandiose plan to pass troops over to the right bank by widening and deepening Villeré's Canal, extending it through the levee of the Mississippi in order to secure a waterway from the advanced base to the river. An amphibious force would then secure the West Bank and establish batteries there. British troops labored incessantly on the project, working day and night in shifts, to the point of physical and mental exhaustion. By January 7, fifty boats of all sizes had been dragged into the new canal. The success of the project depended upon a dam that would have to hold the water of the canal under the boats. When the levee was cut into the river, this dam (built behind the boats) would have to resist the flow of the river. Unluckily, for the British, the dam collapsed and the subsequent delay resulted in the failure of the entire endeavor.[23]

Jackson took advantage of the lull in activity to augment his defensives and shore up any weak spots in them. His men had fought bravely and, in some instances, suffered severely. Yet some officers, such as Captain Isaac L. Baker of the Forty-Fourth US Infantry, had serious doubts as to the tenacity of the American militia. "We are well fortified but not strong enough to give them a field fight," Baker conceded in a letter dated January 5, 1815, adding the Americans believed the English had eight thousand Regulars at their disposal. Jackson, who may have had similar apprehensions, relentlessly repaired and strengthened the breastworks in anticipation of a major field assault. He continued work on two rear lines of defense while authorizing the construction of an advanced redoubt near the river to enfilade any British attack on the Chalmette field. Workers widened and deepened the Rodriguez Canal, filling it with more water. Massive work parties, mostly slaves, carried dirt to the breastworks to thicken the walls, revetted by fence rails collected from miles around. The length of Line Jackson was now over a half-mile, extending into the swamp for some distance and then turning at a right angle in the direction of the city. The breastworks in the swamp consisted of a double row of logs with a two-foot space between the rows filled with earth. The troops stationed along Line Jackson, from the levee to the cypress swamp, consisted of US Regulars and Louisiana militia (1,327 troops), Carroll's Tennessee militia (1,414 troops), and Coffee's men (2,692 troops). More importantly, there were eight batteries consisting of a dozen pieces of heavy artillery positioned along Line Jackson. Carroll's eight hundred Tennesseans lay between Battery #6 and the swamp, supported by seven hundred Kentuckians (who arrived in New Orleans on January 4) under General John Adair. The bulk of Coffee's men, with sixty-two Choctaws, were on the extreme left of the line. The troops positioned between the other batteries included four hundred men of the US Seventh, Major Jean Baptiste Plauché's battalion of New Orleans companies, Major Pierre Lacoste's Louisiana battalion of free men of color, Major Louis Daquin's Santo Domingo free men of color, and 350 men from the Forty-Fourth US Infantry—all under the overall command of Colonel George T. Ross. Behind the center of Line Jackson stood a tall pole with an American flag attached.[24]

Pakenham's plan resembled that of his previous two attempts at penetrating the American lines. The main attack focused on the American left, where Gibbs's troops would hug the edge of the swamp, out of range from the artillery on the West Bank (though not that of the guns on Line Jackson). A second assault, toward the American right, consisted of a two-prong attack under the overall command of Major General Keane. Lieutenant Colonel Rennie's light companies were to dash down along the levee road and overtake the not-yet-finished advanced redoubt, which could enfilade Line Jackson. The bulk of Keane's brigade was to advance to the right of Rennie and attack to reinforce Rennie or Gibbs, according to circumstances. Main bodies of the British Seventh and Forty-Third were held in reserve under Major General John Lambert. Lieutenant Colonel Thomas Mullins, of the British Forty-Fourth, had been instructed to have three hundred of his men carry forward sixteen ladders to be used in scaling Line Jackson, as well as fascines to fill the ditch in front of it. Key to the plan was the timely crossing of the Mississippi by troops led by Lieutenant Colonel William Thornton to capture the American batteries on the right bank. With 1,200 men, Thornton's mission was to seize the American guns before the main attack at Chalmette

commenced, then turn the captured cannon against Jackson's men in an enfilading fire. Feverishly digging a canal to launch Thornton's boats into the
Mississippi became a near-impossible task. Cave-ins along the canal banks
slowed progress by six hours (from midnight to daybreak), and the difficulty of transporting boats from Lake Borgne cut the attacking force in half.
Furthermore, the swift current of the Mississippi carried the boats a mile
farther downstream than originally planned.[25]

Despite the failure to get Thornton's men across the river according to
the original timetable (they were to have landed and captured the American guns long before dawn), no one awoke the British commander to tell
him. Arising at five in the morning, Pakenham learned with dismay of the
long delay involving the West Bank attack. Pakenham still felt obligated to
set the main assault in motion, regardless of this obvious setback. There had
been too many such setbacks, too many demoralizing forays against the un-
couth American forces. The British army was on the field—poised and ready
to storm the American lines. It was time for British pride and courage to evidence itself. After breakfasting at five thirty, Pakenham ordered the signal
rocket fired as daybreak inched its way across the fields of Chalmette. One
British officer described the weather that early morning as "dull, close, and
heavy, the clouds almost touching the ground." The red glare of the Congreve
rocket arched into the shadowy sky, signaling the opening salvo from the advanced artillery of the British. An officer from the British Forty-Fourth, at
the vanguard of the attack, recalled seeing the balls striking the ground in
front of Line Jackson, "causing a sort of blue light." The Americans reacted
quickly. Jordon Noble, the mulatto teenage drummer of the US Seventh Infantry, beat the long roll for battle—it was he who had signaled the attack in
the darkness of December 23. In a matter of moments, Line Jackson erupted
with a thunderous barrage of artillery and small arms, which one Kentuckian understatedly called "a pretty considerable noise." The shattering vibrations from the deafening roar literally shook the ground under the feet of
the Americans at the breastworks, as the continued peal of artillery could be
distinctly heard two miles from the battlefield. The British assistant adjutant
general, Harry Smith, felt his heart sink on observing what happened next:
"The rocket was hardly in the air before a rush of our troops was met by the
most murderous and destructive fire of all arms ever poured upon [a] column."
Smith, a veteran of the Napoleonic campaigns, referred to the American firepower as "the most murderous I ever beheld before or since." To the backwoods Tennessee militiamen, the sight of thousands of uniformed British
troops, marching in perfect order, made an indelible impression. One Tennessean at the breastworks remembered the British advancing "in a most im-

posing order," without a break in rank until the Americans began firing. "The recollection of their scarlet uniforms and martial bearing is as fresh to me as yesterday," the aged veteran recalled over a half a century later.[26]

In hindsight, the British assault appeared doomed from the beginning. One British officer recalled "an evil forboding" in his mind just before the signal to attack, when a dead silence prevailed over the battlefield, along with a thick, lowhanging fog. Most of the fascines and ladders, upon which the British placed much of their strategy, never made it to the breastworks. The advance units of the Forty-Fourth Foot Infantry had been instructed to rush up to Line Jackson as quickly as possible, carrying fascines and ladders in order to fill the ditch in front of the breastworks. They were then to scale the works, thereby allowing a bayonet charge of the American line. The Americans opened fire when the British were approximately seventy-five yards from the breastworks, as three 24-pounders cut a swath through the British columns with grape and canister. "The first objects we saw," recounted Captain John Cooke of the British Forty-Third Regiment, "were the cannon-balls tearing up the ground and crossing one another, and bounding along like so many cricket-balls." After the first discharge of cannon, the rattle of a thousand muskets filled the air. When about forty yards from the American lines, many British soldiers stopped to return fire, instead of proceeding forward with the equipment. In the face of the murderous hail of shot and shell leveled at them, this reaction seemed natural. While some of the advanced British troops fired back at the Americans, others could be seen straggling around in confusion, eventually mixing in with supporting columns marching toward the front. In the hesitation, only a few fascines and ladders made it to the ditch. From his vantage point on the American left, John Coffee witnessed whole columns of British troops wiped out by the American batteries, yet "they appeared to fill their columns as fast as we thinned them until their front in many places reached our ditches." Those men who made it that far paid the ultimate price. On one of the ladders thrown up against the breastworks, four soldiers were killed while trying to scale it. Some of the British removed their shoes in order to better climb the slippery earthen bank, while others stepped upon the shoulders of fellow soldiers to reach the top of the embankment. One British captain athletically leaped across the ditch only to be mortally wounded at the base of the works. The British, temporarily repulsed, renewed the attack with vigor, but with the same outcome. The number of British who actually made it to the breastworks varies according to different eyewitnesses, but it would appear that as many as four hundred managed to reach the American lines, only to be instantly killed or captured.[27]

The bulk of General William Carroll's Tennesseans, backed by the Kentucky troops, waited behind the breastworks, four deep—the best marksmen in front with two rear ranks reloading the muskets and rifles. Once the firing commenced, however, all order seemed to break down as ranks and sections became intermingled, all vying to take a shot at the enemy. "Our men did not seem to apprehend any danger," a Kentucky soldier recounted, "but would load and fire as they could, talking, swearing, and joking all the time." The entrenchments behind which the Americans stood protected them from the British artillery and small arms fire poured upon them, no doubt accounting for the miniscule number of American deaths. One of the recorded casualties may have been a result of friendly fire, as one unidentified Kentucky soldier related: "During the action, a number of Tennessee men got mixed with ours. One of them was killed about five or six yards from where I stood. I did not know his name. A ball passed through his head and he fell against Ensign Weller. I always thought, as did many others who were standing near, that he must have been accidentally shot by some of our own men. From the range of the British balls, they could hardly have passed over the breastwork without passing over our heads, unless we were standing very close to the works, which were a little over breast high, and five or six feet wide on the top." One of the Kentucky officers kept dashing up and down the line, crying out, "We'll pay you now for the River Raisin! We'll give you something to remember the River Raisin!" Like many of the Kentuckians on Line Jackson, this officer had no musket, but he picked up an empty barrel and hurled it at the British as they clamored up the breastworks. He then jumped up on the entrenchment with an iron bar to fling it at the oncoming British.[28]

"The assault was furious, and brave almost beyond example—but was as bravely met and repulsed," one American officer wrote on the following day, "The[ir] column was two or three times repulsed and still returned to the charge—but were ultimately compelled to retreat, being literally mowed down by our bullets and grape and canister shot." The devastation wrought by the American artillery extended beyond the advancing British troops. A sergeant of the Seventh British Foot, held in reserve, testified to having a portion of a soldier's brain splatter his cap while, at the same time, a man behind him had a part of his upper face shot away—"his eyes were gone and the bones of his brow all jagged and dripping blood." The resolve of the British to continue their attack in the face of such destructive firepower made a profound impression on the Americans ensconced behind their breastworks. Major Howell Tatum, one of Jackson's engineers, later wrote: "The effect was astonishing. The enemy were broken three, several times, halted, closed column and advanced again and finally entered the canal with their front platoons. Such destruction of men, for the time it lasted, was never before witnessed. . . . The scene exhibited on the field of action, in front of the line of defence, where the columns advanced & retired, was truly distressing to a feeling mind." Another American soldier commented: "There never was an army more determined and desperate," adding, "and there never was an army more terribly Beaten." Even in death, the British soldiers appeared "brave and firm," noted still another American soldier.[29]

The British had more success at the unfinished redoubt on the American far right. Two days before, Jackson's men began construction on a small, detached flanking redoubt on the extreme right of Line Jackson. It was positioned on the other side of the Rodriguez Canal with a dry ditch surrounding it, accessed by a plank laid across the canal. The station, manned by detachments of the Seventh and Forty-Fourth US Infantries, had two 6-pounders set to rake an approach from the levee road. A company of about one hundred British foot soldiers advanced down the main road toward the redoubt on the morning of January 8, intending to draw fire from the redoubt and the artillery across the river on the West Bank. Although exposed to heavy fire and suffering high casualties, the company pressed forward with such rapidity that they were able to force their way into the redoubt. The company's commander, Lieutenant Colonel Rennie, took two bullets in the head as he climbed into the embrasure. An American eyewitness claimed one of the British officers (Rennie?), who managed to get to the top of the embrasure, called out to the "Yankee Rascals" to cease firing, as he flourished his sword crying, "the enemy's work's are ours!" He was immediately shot down. As the British overran the position, hand-to-hand combat ensued, causing the Americans to temporarily abandon the post. General Jackson, near the scene at this time, observed an English officer brandishing his saber on the entrenchment while British soldiers scaled the rampart. Jackson immediately rode to the spot and demanded to know who gave the order to retreat. When a captain informed Jackson the enemy had overtaken the redoubt, Jackson barked back at him to return and force them out with a bayonet charge. The men of the Seventh US responded and, with fixed bayonets, successfully counterattacked the British who had to relinquish their short-lived prize. One of the Americans lifted a watch and snuff box from Rennie's lifeless body as souvenirs.[30]

As American artillery continued to demolish the ranks of British troops trudging across the Chalmette terrain, English guns spewed their own form of destruction. Several 18-pound cannonballs struck the house that William Carroll occupied as his headquarters, forcing the Tennessee general to flee the premises. As he and his staff ran out of the building, a 32-pound ball took the head off one of Carroll's servants. British artillery also concentrated on the Macarty house, hoping to catch Jackson and his staff there, but the general and his officers had long since retired to their posts along the line, leaving an empty building soon shattered by British cannonballs. Because of the their position in the swampy woods, most of Coffee's troops escaped any harm from the British onslaught; in fact, Lieutenant Edmondson of Coffee's brigade later admitted that all he saw of the engagement was the smoke from the American guns. Amid the roar and din of the battle, British bugles feebly blared out field commands and maneuvers. The Americans, on the other hand, played music incessantly throughout the battle, stationing a New Orleans band behind the center of the line where the American flag waved overhead. The strains of "Yankee Doodle" "sounded along the whole line on the morning of the 8th of January," according to Andrew Jackson, boosting the morale of the men. General Pakenham, sensing his own army desperately needed some inspiration, rode toward the front lines, waving his hat and urging his troops forward. Suddenly a shot penetrated the area above his knee, completely shattering it. Then, while getting on a fresh horse, a fatal ball entered Pakenham's spine, instantly killing him. About the same time, General Gibbs, Pakenham's second in command, fell mortally wounded. Major General John Keane, who led the advance attack, suffered grievous wounds, taking him out of the action. In a matter of minutes, the top echelon of British command at Chalmette was gone.[31]

Across the Mississippi River, the British found themselves in more favorable circumstances. Although Thornton's force of 550-plus men debarked way behind schedule, the attack on the West Bank proved to be a surprising success. Upon landing unopposed on the bank, Thornton saw the British signal flare over Chalmette and proceeded on land toward the American defenses under the overall command of General David Morgan of Louisiana. Morgan had a total strength of about eight hundred men, the majority being Louisiana militia with a contingent of 250 Kentucky militia. The forward American units, under Major Jean Arnaud, took up a line along a canal some three miles below Morgan's main position. Arnaud's men retreated upon the approach of the British, and the Kentuckians were ordered to reinforce. They met Arnaud's retreating men and tried to establish a new position along a drainage ditch. The two groups, both lacking military training and discipline, put up a feeble stance against Thornton's Regulars. As the Kentuckians and Louisianans fell back to the main position, Morgan opened up with his two fieldpieces and one naval gun. Thornton quickly surmised that the American right was vulnerable, being manned only by a few exhausted Kentuckians, and deployed skirmishers on the double to lead a bayonet charge against the exposed flank. The Kentuckians broke and fled with the Louisiana militia soon at their heels. The British pursued the fleeing Americans for two miles but halted as word reached them of the British disaster on the left bank. Upon learning of the potential defeat on the West Bank, Jackson promptly sent French general Jean Humber across the river to assume command, but, astonishingly, the Louisianans refused to accept a "foreigner" to lead them. Jackson then sent Governor Claiborne to personally dislodge the British at all costs. But Claiborne found his troops so demoralized that he did not attempt an offensive move. Fortunately for the Americans, the British did not exploit their success on the West Bank by reinforcing Thornton's expedition. Instead, an ordered withdrawal put an end to any hopes of salvaging the British calamity at Chalmette.[32]

After the deaths of Pakenham and Gibbs, followed by the wounding of Keane, British command fell on Major General John Lambert. In the face of the severe drubbing the English troops endured, Lambert called for a council of war among the officers, the majority of whom determined it best to retreat from the field (and, likewise, call back Thornton's men). The mistaken thought that the Americans outnumbered the British three to one heavily swayed the council's decision. During the council of war, according to Major Harry Smith (Lambert's military secretary), Admiral Edward Codrington, whose duty as captain of the field was to keep the troops supplied with provisions, expressed his concern over the dwindling British supplies. Codrington felt the troops should attack or the whole army would starve. Smith pithily replied, "Kill plenty more, Admiral; fewer rations will be required." Smith was selected as bearer of the white flag, along with a letter to Jackson requesting a cease-fire to bury the dead. Announced by a bugle call, Smith approached Line Jackson, only to be fired on—in fact, a cannon shot struck the ground near his right foot, nearly taking it away. Smith remembered thinking, "it would have been a bore indeed to have lost [it] under such circumstances." The smoke that permeated the field may have obscured the waving white banner, but the wind slowly dissolved the smoke enough for the Americans to spot Smith near the American picket lines. An American adjutant general met Smith and then delivered Lambert's note to General Jackson. It was now about noon. In an exchange of messages between Jackson and Lambert, the former wished to know if Lambert was writing as commander in chief. When Lambert responded affirmatively, an armistice was set for three thirty that afternoon.[33]

Once the smoke had cleared and the din of battle ceased, the fields of Chalmette revealed sights and sounds that would never be forgotten by the men who encountered them. A soldier from Carroll's division tried to describe the aftermath of January 8 in a letter to his father: "I saw several acres of ground covered with their dead, dying and wounded men weltering in their gore! Such sights, groans, and lamentations had never before entered my ears." A Kentucky soldier stated the field was completely red, with dead and wounded lying in heaps. William Carroll likened the fallen British to "the ripened hay before the scythe of the mower." One Tennessee volunteer indelicately remarked how the British lay "like hogs in their bed, pile upon pile." Doctor William Lawrence noted that he could have walked on the dead bodies of the British for a quarter of a mile without stepping on the ground. Perhaps the most moving tribute came from an unidentified Kentucky militiaman: "Individuals could be seen in every possible attitude. Some laying quite dead, others mortally wounded, pitching and tumbling about in the agonies of death. Some had their heads shot off, some their legs, some their arms. Some were laughing, some crying, some groaning, and some screaming. There was every variety of sight and sound. Among those that were on the ground, however, there were some that were neither dead nor wounded. A great many had thrown themselves down behind piles of slain, for protection. As the firing ceased, these men were every now and then jumping up and either running off or coming in and giving themselves up." One of those who gave himself up to the Americans was a young Irish soldier who bounded over the breastworks to surrender. When it was discovered that the young Irishman had been shot through the breast, a few Americans helped him remove his burdensome equipment. As a Tennessee soldier came walking by with a coffee pot full of water, the wounded man begged him for a drink. After swallowing two or three mouthfuls from the spout, the soldier emitted a few grasps of breath and died. Other random acts of kindness on the part of the Americans compelled many of the British to admit the Americans behaved well in the aftermath of the fighting. One wounded British officer even had the privilege of imbibing some choice claret from one of Jackson's staff.[34]

Seeing that the British were making no attempt to tend to their wounded, American militiamen climbed over the breastworks in order to bring them in, ironically using the discarded scaling ladders as makeshift stretchers or even carrying the injured on their backs. Unfortunately, British snipers began to fire on the rescuers, supposedly to prevent any British wounded from being taken as prisoners of war. Captain Joseph Savory led a company of "free men of color" who volunteered to take out the snipers, which they did, but at the cost of ten casualties. When the truce took effect in the afternoon, a British detail came on the scene to remove and bury their dead. Major Harry Smith noted how each body was straightened and the big toes tied together with string before the corpses were thrown into an immense hole. Nearly two hundred bodies were tossed into the opening, "the bodies hurled in as fast we could bring them," Smith recalled. The ghastly wounds of the dead—some cadavers were without heads—sickened the battle-tested Smith. Lieutenant George Gleig of the Eighty-Fifth Light Infantry rode out to the battlefield and saw "the most shocking, and the most humiliating" sight he had ever encountered. British bodies had been thrown by the dozens into shallow holes, "scarcely deep enough to furnish them with a slight covering." Gleig's dismay deepened upon witnessing an American officer smoking a cigar and counting the British dead "with a look of savage exultation," repeating to each individual who approached him that the American loss had been only eight killed and fourteen wounded. The official report of American casualties for January 8 listed thirteen killed, thirty-nine wounded, and nineteen missing. The official British tally, in round numbers, reveals nearly four hundred deaths on the battlefield with nearly five hundred more dying from wounds. In addition, nearly 2,500 British troops suffered some sort of disabling wound on that day, making a grand total of almost 3,500 casualties of one sort or another.[35]

As in most battles of most wars, the victors helped themselves to the spoils. At the conclusion of the fighting, American soldiers could be seen scampering onto the battlefield to collect British muskets, watches, and other "plunder." Pakenham's assistant, Major Smith, observed the Americans looting no article of clothing from the British dead except for shoes. Jackson, in a letter to Secretary of War James Monroe, mentioned his men had recovered some Congreve rockets (which he was forwarding to Washington), as well as numerous swords and bugles. He also informed Monroe that as a professional courtesy he would return to General Keane his sword lost in battle. However, he wished all the other articles to remain in the possession of the Tennesseans. Once the usual souvenir gathering had transpired, the arduous task of removing dead bodies, tending the wounded, and transporting prisoners took place. Cartloads of the enemy's dead traversed the battlefield, as the British hastily deposited the bodies in shallow, watery graves. (The arms, legs, and heads of the corpses could be seen sticking out above the ground in many places a month later.) The bodies of Sir Edward Pakenham and General Gibbs were shipped back to England in casks of rum—a somewhat indignant, yet popular, method of transferring cadavers over a long distance. This primitive method of preservation caused one Tennessee officer to quip that Pakenham and Gibbs had been sent home "in good spirits."[36]

The Americans used carts to remove the British wounded and take them to overcrowded field hospitals, where exhausted surgeons performed numerous amputations. One English officer observed a basket full of severed legs, most of which were still covered with stockings. Messengers were sent into the city to enlist all available doctors, and many of the wounded were transported to the Ursuline Convent in New Orleans. One lone spectator in the city counted forty cartloads of British wounded passing his way. Another spectator in New Orleans witnessed a hundred British prisoners march by his shop, noting they appeared to be "brave and wholesome looking men, well uniformed in Red Coats." The prisoners were being escorted to boats and barges destined to go upriver to the town of Washington, in the Mississippi Territory. A young woman residing on a plantation outside of New Orleans witnessed two barge loads of prisoners on their way up the Mississippi and reacted with shock and disgust upon noticing that some of the prisoners were black troops.[37]

Back at Chalmette, in the days immediately after the January 8 battle, Jackson toyed with the idea of a follow-up attack on the British. Edward Livingston, who now held the rank of colonel, advised against it, as did General John Adair of the Kentucky militia. After consulting with his closest confidant, General John Coffee, Jackson changed his mind upon hearing Coffee's assessment of how American militia might perform outside the confines of Line Jackson. While Coffee acknowledged the bravery of his men, he explained to Jackson that "they are not disciplined, & might not be so efficient in an open plain against veteran troops." Apparently, the British felt the same way, as indicated by a February 1815 letter from Edward Codrington, captain of the fleet, who believed that had the Americans fought the British in the open, they would have received "that dressing which our people are well disposed to give them." In addition, the absence of weapons still plagued the Americans. The victory over the British seemed so fortuitous that "surely Providence has had a hand in the thing," Coffee admitted. William Carroll acknowledged that God had directed the entire campaign "as if with a cloud of smoke by day and a pillar of fire by night." A soldier in Carroll's division accounted for the disproportionate casualties of January 8 by claiming the Americans "were fighting in a cause which the living God approbates; we were in the defence of our land and liberty, the land which gave us birth." "We have taught the English that American independence will ever crush tyranny," bragged Doctor William Lawrence, "and that God and good angels fight on our side, while they in all their pride and boasted strength will fall." That Providence guided the Americans to success at New Orleans became a repeated theme in the weeks, months, and years that followed the campaign—there seemed to be no other logical explanation.[38]

The British had a more practical evaluation of what happened on the plains of Chalmette. At first, the English bemoaned their loss with unmitigated mortification. One British officer referred to the debacle of January 8 as "a disastrous affair from beginning to end," while another officer declared to his wife in a letter written on the next day that "there never was a more complete failure." John Tylden, captain of the Forty-Third Foot Regiment, could not bring himself to detail the defeat in his journal entry of January 8, 1815: "8th Jany—Sunday—Made our attempt to force the enemies lines in which our failure was the most complete I have witnessed. . . . I cannot yet bring my-self to relate them." It was not until three days later that Tylden was able to add any further thoughts on the battle. "I have seen many affairs and some severe ones," he wrote on January 11, "but I never saw so melancholy, heart-breaking business as this." Once the shock of defeat passed, the British began to critique what went wrong. Two schools of thought developed from these evaluations: one, the failure to storm the American breastworks rested on the misplacement of the all-important ladders and fascines, coupled with the British Forty-Fourth's inability to advance in a timely fashion; and, two, the attack on the West Bank should have been completed hours before the ini-tial attack at Chalmette. British author William James, while not calling the Forty-Fourth outright cowards, referred to the regiment's "misbehavior" that clearly caused the life of Pakenham and Gibbs, adding in explanation that the men of the regiment were "chiefly Irishmen." Yet one British officer who participated in the campaign later insisted the ditch in front of the breast-works could have been taken *without* the ladders or fascines. The inability to properly reconnoiter the American defenses prevented any such assessment prior to the attack. "Had its dimensions been known to the soldiery," the of-ficer noted, "the star of the American general would not on that day have shone with such splendor." Admiral Codrington focused on the issues of the West Bank attack, offering the opinion that had there been a flotilla of boats to land the troops on the opposite shore during the night, Thornton could have taken the American batteries and turned them against Line Jackson.[39]

Major Charles R. Forrest of the Thirty-Fourth Regiment of Foot provided the most concise explanation (or, rather, explanations) for the British failure at New Orleans. According to Forrest's analysis, the most serious problem for the British forces was the distance—about seventy miles through diffi-cult terrain—from their supply source. Also, a lack of proper intelligence kept the British in the dark for most of the campaign as to American troop strength and movements, whereas the Americans had an elaborate network of "spies" that kept track of British intentions (although it must be brought out that the Americans were just as guilty as the British in overestimating troop strength). Forrest admitted that Line Jackson was well defended, and being relatively short and strongly posted, it was difficult to overwhelm, not to mention the cross fire from the other shore of the river. Lastly, the local population did not support the British, as they had been led to expect. In any event, the British had been soundly defeated and by an enemy they deemed entirely unworthy of the victory. The magnitude of this American success did not escape the participants at the time. A soldier from Robertson County, Tennessee, described the battle in a February 17, 1815, letter as "a day which time can never wear from the minds of thousands of the fallen posterity of Adam." Thomas B. Johnson, the postmaster of New Orleans, rightly predicted the battle would "form an epoch in the history of the Republic."[40]

The battle had been won, but the British remained in their camps, albeit defeated and demoralized. The decisiveness of the contest eluded the Americans, temporarily at least, who expected the British to commit to one more final assault. Archibald Young, a sergeant in Colonel James Raulston's regiment of Tennessee milita, indicated in a January 12 letter that the Americans "now expect another battle every day and hour." Jackson ordered a constant barrage of artillery fire directed toward the British encampments, which served to heighten the already-depressed state of the English soldiers. "Here we remained in front of the enemy, under a constant fire from the enemy for ten days," recalled one British private, "always accoutered and ready to stand to our arms, as we did not know the minute we [might be] surprised by the enemy." The coldness of the season only added to their miseries. Then, on January 13, Andrew Jackson ordered a mortar to be set up and fired at the enemy every two hours during the night—a signal for all batteries to fire in regular rotation from right to left. This pattern continued for days. The casualties inflicted were light, but disheartening; for instance, a sleeping lieutenant in the British Forty-Third had both his feet shot off by a cannonball one night. During the day, the Americans on Line Jackson gathered to wave flags with slogans such as "Sailors Rights" and shout insulting phrases at the British. A military band would mockingly play "Yankee Doodle" and other tunes, even "Rule, Britannia!," to the discouraged British troops, some of whom began to desert. British colonel Frederick Stovin penned a letter to his mother, expressing his frustration over the "abominable" war. "It is truly repugnant to fight against people who speak the same language," he reasoned, "many of whom are really your countrymen & all who claim their origin so universally from your own Soil."[41]

After the January 8 battle, the British spent nine grueling days constructing a road to Lake Borgne over which the army could withdraw. While General Lambert devised plans for a retreat, Admiral Cochrane made a belated effort to have his fleet force their way past Fort St. Philip, bombarding the fortress for four consecutive days. "I am under the impression they intend to Bombard us for a month," the post commander, Major Walter H. Overton, frustratingly wrote on January 17. "I would agree to lose my right arm . . . if they would come up and fight fairly." The British attack only resulted in the death of one American and perhaps made Jackson a little uneasy as to the true intentions of the British. On the evening of January 18, Lambert managed to pull off a miraculous retreat in total silence, leaving a British surgeon to deliver a letter to Jackson the next morning advising him of the British departure and requesting the Americans care for eighty soldiers too badly wounded to be removed (it took the British three days to remove their wounded to the ships on Lake Borgne). Jackson dispatched Doctor David Kerr to tend to the wounded while he and his staff rode into the abandoned British camp to find cannons and thousands of cannonballs left behind, along with other public and private possessions. News of the British retreat reached New Orleans at noon on January 19, just as postmaster Thomas B. Johnson put the finishing touches on a letter addressed to Dolley Madison, the president's wife: "Intelligence has at this moment been received from General Jackson that the British have evacuated the country. The rear of their army completed the retreat to their shipping last night, leaving behind them many of their men, desperately wounded, besides several pieces of cannon. The city is in a ferment of delight. The country is saved, the enemy vanquished, and hardly a widow or an orphan whose tears damp the general joy. All is exultation and jubilee. What do we not owe a protecting Providence for this manifestation of his favor!" The campaign for New Orleans had ended in total victory for the Americans, who promptly bestowed the title of "hero" on Andrew Jackson and his Tennessee army.[42]

7

On January 24, 1815, the citizens of New Orleans flocked to the Place d'Armes (soon to be renamed Jackson Square) to pay homage to their newly declared champion, Major General Andrew Jackson. The Abbe Guillaume Dubourg, apostolic administrator of the Louisiana diocese, headed preparations for the celebration, which centered on a religious service of public thanksgiving. It was Dubourg who had issued a mandate, on December 18, 1814, to the clergy and laity of New Orleans to pray for the success of the American army led by "the hero of the Floridas." Jackson, perhaps sensing the abbe stood in good with the Lord, wrote to him after the campaign requesting a display of public gratitude on the American victory. Dubourg eagerly agreed and set the date for Tuesday, January 24. The preparations called for a Roman-like tribute to the conquering lion. A temporary arch, supported by six columns, stood in the middle of the Place d'Armes. Two young ladies—one symbolizing Justice and the other Liberty—posed on each side of the arch. Under the arch were two young children, each on a pedestal, holding a crown of laurel. From the arch to the Saint Louis Cathedral stood a range of young ladies, wearing a silver star on their foreheads, all dressed in white and covered in transparent veils, representing the different states and territories. Each female held a flag in her right hand with the name of the state she represented and, in the left hand, a basketful of flowers. Behind each girl was a shield inscribed with the name of the state or territory, suspended on a lance stuck in the ground, linked together with verdant festoons. The best-dressed troops available stood at attention a few steps behind the processional lines. The ceremony called for Jackson and his staff to proceed to the church and pass under the arch, where he would receive the crowns of laurel from the children and personal congratulations from the girl that represented the state of Louisiana. As Old Hickory passed through the arch to be crowned, the "Americans" let out a loud chorus of huzzas, while the French repeated over and over, "*Vive* Jackson! *Vive notre General!*" Abbe Dubourg met Jackson's entourage at the entrance of the cathedral and offered an address, after which he conducted Jackson inside to a seat near the altar. The solemn chant of the *Te Deum* soon spilled out into the streets. Throughout that night the whole town and its suburbs remained splendidly illuminated.[1]

The celebrations in New Orleans continued for several more weeks; they included a sumptuous dinner held in honor of Jackson on the birthday of George Washington. Rachel Jackson, recently arrived in New Orleans as of February 19, wore a fashionable costume selected by the wife of Edward Livingston, as well as elegant jewelry presented to her by the ladies of New Orleans (the same ladies that were to describe Rachel as "short and fleshy" behind her back). Jackson noted the two large glass transparencies that greeted his wife and him upon their entrance—one emblazed with the motto "Jackson and Victory," while the other read "Immortal Washington." It would not be the last time that Jackson's and Washington's names would be linked in the aftermath of the war. In fact, even before the providential victory at New Orleans, the press favored comparing the two military leaders. The *Nashville Whig*, citing a piece published by the *Rogersville Gazette* at the conclusion of the Creek War, acknowledged Jackson's seeming ability "to unite the boldness and stratagem of [Anthony] Wayne, and the prudence and sagacity of [George] Washington." There is no doubt that Jackson, himself, honored the memory of Washington, a man he referred to as "the mighty chieftain," a term that came to describe Jackson, albeit in a more derogatory manner.[2]

The excitement originating from New Orleans rapidly spread throughout the country, as post riders delivered the news of Jackson's success. Ensign John Sevier of the Seventh US Infantry, nephew of Senator John Sevier, flaunted his exaltation in a January 10, 1815, letter to his mother: "I feel young and active and handsome. . . . I believe we in the South have settled the dispute of Nations." Nashville residents, amid the loud booming of cannon, illuminated their front windows with candles in celebration of the news coming out of New Orleans. In East Tennessee, one Blountville merchant predicted Jackson's name would "shine among the great men of the 19th Century." In Washington, as in Nashville, candles shone in every window, while guns fired throughout the night, the news of the victory at New Orleans having reached the anxious city on February 4. In Congress, members congratulated the Tennessee delegation "as though we had been in the action," according to Senator Sevier. "Our army from Tennessee is more talked of here," he wrote his son, "than half the world besides." Even Federalists got caught up in the enthusiasm. A Massachusetts man, visiting New Orleans at the time of the battle, admitted he relished defeating the British, despite his conviction the war had been an unnecessary one. "It makes the world respect

America," he declared, "& I trust will shortly induce the British to consent to an honorable peace." Of course, the British *had* consented to an "honorable" peace *before* the American win at New Orleans—a prospect that left some Americans wondering what might have happened at Ghent had the news of Jackson's victory arrived before signatures were put on the treaty. An express rider left Washington on February 14 and reached East Tennessee six days later, traveling at the thunderous pace of eighty miles in twenty-four hours. Four days later, on February 24, the express reached Nashville, where Governor Blount authorized the rider to procure a horse for the trip to New Orleans. The rider carried a letter from the postmaster general announcing that peace had been concluded between the United States and Great Britain. The news of the treaty eventually arrived in New Orleans on March 6.[3]

The social atmosphere in New Orleans had drastically changed since the ecstatic celebrations of late January. Despite the British retreat, Andrew Jackson had stubbornly refused to loosen the bonds of martial law on the population. With no immediate threat on the city, the local militia and volunteers became eager to return to their homes, while the citizens longed to return to life as it was before the campaign. But Jackson, having no official word that hostilities had ceased, continued to treat New Orleans as a military camp—his camp—and, therefore, all its citizens were "soldiers" under his command. The situation grew tense as resentment built between Jackson and city/state authorities. Actually, the seeds of discontent were planted during the fighting between the British and Americans in late December 1814. At the commencement of the December 28 attack by the British, Jackson heard some disturbing news from his aide, Abner Duncan, who informed the general that Governor Claiborne announced the Louisiana legislature was about to capitulate to the British. An incredulous Jackson demanded to know where this information came from and Duncan replied it was a Louisiana militia colonel (later identified as Colonel Alexander Declouet). Jackson, in the midst of being attacked by the enemy, fired off instructions to Duncan to have Claiborne look into the matter and, if found true, to "blow them up," meaning the legislators. Duncan, in turn, told a Claiborne aide that Jackson wanted the legislative assembly shut down and members prevented from entering. Claiborne complied with what he naturally thought were Jackson's orders and had the doors of the government house locked. Stunned legislators, turned away at the door by armed sentries, decided to look into the matter through a committee of inquiry. Affidavits began to be collected in the days immediately following the January 8 battle. By the end of the month, the committee convened to determine the facts surrounding Jackson's actions. Colonel Declouet testified he had apprehensions of the legislature capitulating based on remarks he heard by several members of the "French faction," who feared Jackson would conduct a "Russian" war and burn New Orleans to the ground before letting it fall into British hands. The French legislators apparently felt the British had more respect for property than Jackson did, indicating the American militia stole more personal property than the English enemy. In the end, the committee put the thrust of the blame on Abner Duncan, who obviously had misinterpreted Jackson's instructions.[4]

Did the French faction of the legislature have grounds to be concerned about a possible Russian defense of New Orleans? Nearly a decade after the campaign at New Orleans, Jackson related an incident that took place a few days after the December 23 night battle, in which several Louisiana assemblymen came to Jackson wanting to know if he intended to destroy the supplies in the city should the British overrun the American lines. An annoyed Jackson, feverishly working to construct a line of defense, told the men that if, indeed, he was compelled to retreat through New Orleans, then the legislature "would have a *warm* session." James Parton, in his 1861 three-volume biography of Jackson, relates an undated conversation between Jackson and his friend John Eaton in which Jackson insisted that if the British had overrun his defenses, he would have "retreated to the city, fired it, and fought the enemy amidst the surrounding flames." Whatever the truth of the matter, the incident left bad blood between Jackson and the Louisianans, a relationship already fraught with distrust and suspicion.[5]

Those misgivings partly stemmed from the frustration of the plantation owners whose real estate and property were affected by the fighting outside New Orleans. Both sides contributed to the destruction of fences, bridges, and slave quarters, as well as some mansion homes. Cattle had been taken and hungry soldiers often stole the stored-up sugar—the campaign having come at the time when the cane had been harvested and processed. Worst of all to the plantation owners was the loss of hundreds of slaves who ran away to the sanctuary of the retreating British army. The owners pled their case to Governor Claiborne who, in turn, sought permission from Jackson in early February to initiate private negotiations with the British for the return of runaway slaves. But Jackson spurned the idea, informing Claiborne that if either he or the Assembly took it upon themselves to interfere with military business, they would be arrested. "I am pledged for the protection of this District," a peeved Jackson reminded Claiborne. "I trust I know my duty and will perform it." As it turned out, Jackson soon afterward sent a three-man delegation (which included Edward Livingston) to the British to negotiate the release of the slaves. The mission, however, proved unsuccessful as the British insisted the blacks had come to the army of their own free will.[6]

The abortive mission took place just as the British were attempting a last-ditch effort to salvage their Gulf campaign. Their target was the town of Mobile, protected by the American installation of Fort Bowyer, guarding the entrance to Mobile Bay. Strategically, the town could be used as a jumping-off point for an enemy to harass the frontiers of Georgia and the Mississippi Territory, and Admiral Cochrane had just such a plan in mind after the rout at New Orleans. Cochrane directed Major General John Lambert to capture Mobile and organize two bodies of Indians and blacks (combined with British soldiers)—one to plague the interior of Georgia, the other body to capture Fort Stoddert (near the junction of the Tombigbee and Alabama Rivers). Both actions were designed to tie down the American militia while prompting another possible attack on New Orleans. Andrew Jackson, acutely anticipating such a move, wrote a letter to Secretary of War James Monroe on February 10 predicting Mobile as the next British target: "It is true Mobile, in point of worth, is a trifling object with the British compared with [New Orleans]. But in point of harassing us, and stirring up the Indians to hostility against us, it is all important—and if once possess[ed] by them, and seconded by Spain, it will cost much blood and treasure to regain it—regained tho' it must be, or the enemy menaces this country constantly." Jackson realized the British could strike once again at New Orleans by taking Mobile and, with Indian allies, penetrate westward into the Mississippi Territory in order to make an attack on Louisiana from the north.[7]

Unknown to Jackson, the British staged an attack on Fort Bowyer as Old Hickory penned his message to Monroe. Lambert landed six hundred men three miles east of Fort Bowyer on February 8 and managed to advance within three hundred yards of the American fortifications before day's, end. The British kept fortifying their position, and during the next three days, maneuvered sixteen guns around the fort to fire in conjunction with the vessel *Etna* anchored in the bay. Short on provisions and nearly surrounded, the American commander of Fort Bowyer, Major William Lawrence, realized any reasonable defense was impossible and agreed to Lambert's demand of surrender on February 11. Major Harry Smith, military secretary to General Lambert, approached the fort with a flag of truce on that day, presenting the demand. He recalled Lawrence acting "as civil as a vulgar fellow can be." Lawrence indicated he would surrender the next day (February 12), providing his army could march out of the fort with their arms before giving them up. A wary Smith agreed but placed a body of British troops just outside the fort in anticipation of some sort of trickery by Lawrence, for, as Smith put it, "by the Major's manner and look under his eyebrows, I could see there was no little cunning in his composition." At noon on February 12, the garrison of

Fort Bowyer, about 370 in number (the majority being the Second US Infantry) marched out of the fort in orderly fashion. The prisoners, which one British officer described as "very dirty, and both in dress and appearance looked much like Spaniards," included twenty women and sixteen children.[8]

The British victory at Fort Bowyer turned out to be a hollow one, as the news of the peace treaty reached the British fleet during their maneuvers. The treaty spared the capture of Mobile and a renewed attack on New Orleans. The three-man American delegation sent to negotiate the return of the runaway slaves, having been detained by the British during the siege of Fort Bowyer, viewed a London newspaper announcing the agreement at Ghent. Upon their return to New Orleans, the Americans spread the good news, and the February 21 issue of the *Louisiana Gazette* pronounced the war over. Jackson, still not having received any official notice of a formal treaty, demanded the editor of the *Gazette* publish a retraction, instructing the people of New Orleans not to believe any rumors of peace until a formal announcement had been made. On the next day, newspapers from Charleston, South Carolina, arrived containing reports of the British ratification of the treaty. The insulted *Gazette* editor complied with Jackson's instructions in the February 23 issue, adding the mocking statement that "we have been officially informed that the city of New Orleans is a camp, our readers must not expect us to take the liberty of expressing our opinions as we might in a free city."[9]

As dissatisfaction and impatience spread among the local militia, some of the French-speaking soldiers discovered a loophole allowing them to obtain an immediate discharge from military service. By applying for certificates of citizenship from the local French consul, they could be absolved from military duty. In reaction to this blatant affront to his authority, Jackson ordered all French citizens possessing such certificates to leave the city of New Orleans for a distance "not short of Baton Rouge" until the British left the region permanently or until the restoration of peace. This slight of the French population angered one Louisiana legislator enough to challenge Jackson through an anonymous letter published in a New Orleans newspaper on March 3. The legislator, Louis Louailler, denounced Jackson's "abuse of authority" while questioning the general's right to declare martial law in the first place. Using the pseudonym "A Citizen of Louisiana of French Origin," Louailler referred to Jackson's martial law as "useless" and "degrading." An incensed Jackson set about discovering the identity of the anonymous author and had Louailler arrested two days later. When federal district judge Dominick A. Hall granted a writ of habeas corpus for the release of Louailler, Jackson had the judge placed under arrest as well. In the meantime, on March 6, a messenger brought the news from Washington announcing peace between the

United States and Great Britain—this was the same letter from the post-master general that Governor Blount had read in Nashville. But, in Jackson's eyes, a letter from the postmaster general was not the same as an official notification from the secretary of war; thus, marital law would remain in effect and Louailler was to be court-martialed on the basis that the Louisiana legislator was a "soldier" in Jackson's "camp." Accused of exciting mutiny, unsoldier-like conduct, and being a spy, Louailler faced a military court-martial headed by General Edmund P. Gaines, who had personal doubts about the legality of such a trial. Much to Jackson's frustration, Louailler was acquitted on March 11, although Jackson immediately overturned the verdict, citing his authority as commanding general in a region under martial law.

On the same day as Louailler's acquittal, Jackson had the imprisoned Judge Hall banished from New Orleans in anticipation a similar verdict be given to the judge if put on trial. Escorted under guard to a point four miles above New Orleans, Hall waited out a brief exile before returning to the city to exact his revenge. On March 13 the letter Jackson had been waiting for finally arrived, carrying the "official" news of the ratification of the Treaty of Ghent. Jackson immediately revoked martial law, much to the relief of the town's population. But amid the jubilation, Judge Hall brought legal suit against General Jackson, charging him with contempt of court for his opposition in the execution of a writ of habeas corpus. On March 27, 1815, the trial of *The United States vs. Andrew Jackson* commenced, with no less than Judge Dominick A. Hall presiding. The trial concluded four days later, resulting in a $1,000 fine levied on Jackson, which he promptly paid and then calmly walked out of the courthouse. Within the following week, Jackson departed the city of New Orleans for home, leaving behind a dichotomous legacy of savior and tyrant.

When Andrew Jackson turned his back on New Orleans on April 6, he left behind more than a duplicitous reputation—the bodies of hundreds of Tennesseans remained in New Orleans, victims of the diseases that spread rampantly throughout the American camps, particularly after hostilities ceased in early January 1815. Dysentery, malaria, and yellow fever decimated the troops stationed in New Orleans. It has been estimated that following the battles, five hundred men died from disease in one month alone, mostly from dysentery. An unidentified officer of the Louisiana militia, who kept a journal during the campaign, noted at least three or four men dying each day by early February. William White, aide to General Carroll, wrote to his wife on February 10 how many of the sickly Tennessee soldiers were "daily paying the last debt of nature" (two hundred of Carroll's division had died by the beginning of February). Kentucky general Isaac Shelby reported that nearly one-third of the soldiers in his entire command were on the sick list, mostly from measles and mumps. General John Coffee's brigade, in particular, suffered from the unhealthy conditions in which they found themselves, sometimes lying in six inches of water when they could not find poles or puncheons to cover the soggy ground. By early March, nearly one out of every three men in Coffee's brigade reported sick or was attending the sick. According to Rachel Jackson, Major John Reid had informed her that nearly one thousand soldiers had lately died in Jackson's army. With hospital facilities stretched to the limit, the sick were transported into New Orleans and even to other towns, such as Natchez, conveyed by the steamboat *Vesuvius*. On one such journey the steamboat carried five hundred sick and wounded on board, with five or six dying daily. It is no wonder, then, that Jackson's army—those who survived—longed for the day when they would be dismissed from service and could return to their homes.[10]

That day came in mid-March 1815, as Jackson's forces prepared for the long march home to Kentucky and Tennessee. On March 15 the army marched to Lake Pontchartrain, where it took several days to get all the troops across. Doctors then determined if a soldier could march and, if so, would he be able to carry his gun and knapsack. Those too weak to march were allowed to ride in supply wagons normally reserved for the officers' private baggage. From the lake the men journeyed to Madisonville and then accessed the Natchez Trace for the trip home. The primitive conditions found on the Trace—one traveler described it as a haven for panthers, wolves, snakes, and devouring mosquitoes—made the trek a long and tortuous one, particularly for the ailing . The mounted men obviously had an easier time of it, although forage for their horses became difficult to obtain. Brigades of infantry straggled up the Trace, stopping at the primitive inns and stands (trading posts), such as Brashears (near present-day Jackson, Mississippi), and private homes scattered along the way. The sick and their attendants usually comprised the rear of the procession. Those too ill to complete the journey were left behind wherever care might be available. One observer noted that "for months we seldom looked up or down the Natchez Trace without seeing passing soldiers." A southbound traveler on the Trace reached Brashears and saw that 150 sick men had been left behind. Farther along, he encountered ten wagonloads of Carroll's sick men heading north.[11]

Such adverse conditions tended to bring the worse and best out of the returning soldiers. Private William Simmons of Colonel Metcalf's regiment, suffering from pleurisy, had his knapsack (containing Simmons's clothes and personal papers) stolen from under his head while he was sleeping at one of the stops on the Trace. Lieutenant Andrew Jackson Edmondson, journeying up the Trace on a tired horse, ran into an old schoolmate named Samuel Hope at Brashears. The bedridden Hope begged Edmondson to take him along, as he felt sure he would die if left behind. Edmondson allowed Hope to ride his horse, while he walked beside them the rest of the distance home. Nashville newspapers were printing reports that over three hundred returning Tennessee soldiers had died already. From Brashears, General Carroll wrote to the press in Nashville, asking them to make a public plea for the families and friends of the ailing soldiers to journey to the Trace with horses and provisions to transport the men home, as supplies could not be had. A man named Brooks traveled from Tennessee down the Trace in search of his two sons serving in Coffee's brigade. Riding south of a place called Crowders, Brooks encountered a throng of Coffee's men plodding the road and, in a tearful reunion, found both his sons alive and well. General John Coffee had more than enough incentive to get home as quickly as possible. A letter waiting at the Choctaw Agency for Coffee informed him he was the father of a baby boy born on March 4. Coffee must have beamed as he read his brother-in-law's description of the infant as having "bold and manly" features, including a high forehead, heavy eyebrows, and a large nose. The letter concluded with the prediction the boy would someday make a fine soldier.[12]

For Andrew Jackson, the journey home consisted of celebratory adulations wherever he stopped. At Natchez, for instance, the citizens planned a tribute to the man they referred to as "the gallant saviour [sic] of the western world." A broadside distributed to the Volunteer Rifle Corps of Natchez in early April 1815 typified the unabashed veneration Jackson elicited during the post–New Orleans victory: "Remember Him, whose dauntless breast was first set to protect you from the bloody scalping knife of the barbarous Creeks! Remember Him, whose presence, on the glorious 8th of January, 1815, roused the brave but undisciplined sons of the west to conquer the brave veteran conquerors of Europe—who saved your property from plunder—your wives and daughters from rapine! Remember Him who, next to your own unparalleled Washington, had aided to elevate your country to the fairest rank among the civilized nations of the earth!" Another individual who received the royal treatment on his journey home was General William Carroll. The young officer—he had turned twenty-seven on March 3—had the good fortune to command the section of Line Jackson where the main thrust of the British attack occurred on January 8. As a result, Carroll joined the pantheon of War of 1812 notables. "The battle of the 8th January," declared the *Nashville Whig*, "has placed him on the list with the names of *Scott, Macomb, Gaines*—has erected to his fame a monument as lasting as *brass*,—as imperishable as *time*." Carroll returned to Nashville about the third week in April, having been preceded by General Coffee the week before. For Jackson, the grand finale came when he approached Nashville on the fifteenth of May to be met by a select committee outside of town. Then, four miles from Nashville, the entourage encountered several hundred citizens with "welcome smiles and loud huzzas" who then escorted Jackson to the courthouse in Nashville where Felix Grundy delivered an address. A cotillion at the Bell Tavern capped the festivities. Jackson, Carroll, Coffee, and the other elite officers of the Tennessee army returned to a number of dinners, balls, and fetes of all kinds before settling back down to their normal routines. The citizens in some counties welcomed the returning volunteers and militia with barbeques and other events. For most soldiers, it was enough just to have made it home. Lieutenant Edmondson, still trudging beside his slow-moving horse carrying the sickly Samuel Hope, approached his family's residence near Nashville unannounced early one morning. Edmondson eagerly climbed the fence and observed some of his family walking in the yard. No one noticed him until he fired his pistol in the air. His sisters and parents ran to him, rejoicing over his safe return. "None but them that have gone through just such a scrape as we had can tell how we all felt," Edmondson later recorded, "for myself I was fully paid for all my trials—my dear old Mother hung on my neck—I was her youngest."[13]

The image of Edmondson's mother clinging to her soldier-son's neck symbolized the feelings of joy and relief most Tennessee families experienced in mid-1815. Hundreds of other Tennessee homes, however, felt the awful loss of brothers, fathers, and sons who never returned from the war or came back crippled or disabled. Charles Coffin, the president of Greenville College in East Tennessee, expressed his admiration for the Tennessee veterans by proclaiming the state's military achievements as topping any other state's. Others agreed—the brilliant triumph at New Orleans, coming at the close of the war, gained Tennessee (and Jackson) a reputation that extended beyond the state's boundaries. (A question historians might ask is what if the victory at New Orleans had occurred say, in 1813, rather than at the conclusion of the war?) When Congress heard the news of the American success at New Orleans, party divisions temporarily healed amid the members' demonstrations of joy, with most of the acclaim directed at "the sons of the west, and particularly [those] from Tennessee," according to one observer. A geography book published after the war extolled Tennessee's patriotism, noting that "from 1776 . . . until the memorable battle of New Orleans, the troops of Tennessee have been at their post, when their country demanded their services."[14]

It was particularly gratifying for Tennesseans to realize that Britain's "choicest veteran troops should be repulsed by our raw and undisciplined troops and with such immence [sic] loss," according to Andrew Hynes in a February

1815 letter to his brother. The perceptions coming from the battlefield indicated the militia had devastated England's elite troops with an overwhelming display of firepower consisting of muskets and small arms. John Coffee, in a letter written less than three weeks after the battle, told how the British advanced in solid columns on the morning of January 8, but "before they reached our small arms, our grape and canister mowed down whole columns, but that was nothing to the carnage of our rifles and muskets when they reached them." A colonel in the Louisiana militia at New Orleans made the assessment that all the cannon fire, shots, shells, and rockets were "only the pomp of war—musquetry [*sic*] we have proven is the thing for execution." British medical personnel aided the misconstruction of the battle by misdiagnosing only a few instances of casualties caused by artillery. The notion of small arms fire winning the battle served to propagate the idea of the militia as the "bulwark" of the nation—a concept that remained unquestioned for well over a century. Finally, historians began to challenge the myth of the American sharpshooter as the hero of the Battle of New Orleans. The evidence was strong: the Americans had heavier guns mounted in good positions with firm supports; riflemen were not placed where they could play a large part in the battle (those who did fire merely raised their flintlocks above the entrenchment and fired into the masses); a smoke-filled field and drifting fog left little room for marksmanship; and, most convincingly, the heaviest losses were not those nearest the American line but, rather, those caught in the deadly cross fire from the big guns.[15]

The significance of this analysis becomes obvious when one realizes that the vast majority of men who manned the artillery posts on Line Jackson were *not* Kentucky or Tennessee militia. Regular army soldiers, naval personnel, French Creoles, and Baratarian pirates operated the heavy guns, and if the lion's share of the American victory goes to artillery fire, then these men deserve their just rewards. This is not to say that Adair's Kentuckians and Carroll's Tennesseans should be relegated to secondary roles—the main British thrust of January 8 came directly at Carroll's position—but it cannot be said with certainty that rifle and musket fire alone stemmed the British advance. Artillery fire—devastating and overwhelming—conquered Wellington's finest. Yet it was important to westerners, in particular, that the militia be credited with the providential victory at Chalmette. In a broadside issued in April 1815 in Nashville by William Carroll, the Tennessee general acknowledged the international ramifications of the militia's victory at New Orleans: "Europe will be astonished at the success of the American arms at New Orleans.—They will pay every homage of respect to the American character." As historian Daniel Walker Howe has acutely pointed out, cannon represented technology—products of industry—and, consequently, were not favored by rural people who did not see their heroes as professional servicemen, ethnic city dwellers, or pirates. Overall, the performance of the militia throughout the war was not outstanding, yet the western states prided themselves on the idea of freemen acting in concert with their fellow freemen to defend their homes from any incursion or invasion. In February 1815 the Senate Committee on Military Affairs reported on a resolution tendering thanks to General Jackson and his men for their victory at New Orleans and a gold medal for Jackson. The House objected to the wording of the resolution, saying it was "defective," as it did not glorify the militia enough. George M. Troup of Georgia insisted it should applaud "the yeomen of the country marching to the defence [sic] of the city of New Orleans, leaving their wives, and children, and firesides, at a moment's warning."[16]

Nevertheless, in Jackson's adopted state of Tennessee, the militia came under scrutiny from former militia officers who experienced how undisciplined militiamen could be as a fighting unit. Major Lewis Dillahunty of the West Tennessee Militia submitted a petition in September 1815 to the Tennessee General Assembly suggesting changes be made to the state militia's regulations. "The War lately terminated has proven that the present organization & discipline of the militia of Tennessee is full of imperfections," Dillahunty stated. He added a quote from William Duane's 1810 *Military Dictionary*, a work he felt should be mandatory reading for all militia members: "An Army without discipline & subordination is but a mob more dangerous to itself, than to its Enemy." Actually, in Duane's original text, the word *subordination* is not mentioned. The fact that Dillahunty included it reflects the *in*subordination demonstrated by the militia during the war. The Tennessee legislature took no action on Dillahunty's petition, perhaps an indication of the impact the New Orleans victory had on the merits of the militia. "The War of 1812, with its initial setbacks, and its continued humiliations and frustrations, might have forced the young nation to clarify its military policy," according to historian Marcus Cunliffe. "Instead, Andrew Jackson's sensational victory at the Battle of New Orleans in January 1815 set the seal on everything that patriots liked to believe about themselves." Yet the days of the militia as an effective fighting force would dramatically wane. In America's next major conflict—the Mexican War of 1846–48—the militia comprised only 12 percent of the total forces, as opposed to 88 percent in the War of 1812.[17]

The War of 1812 represented a coming of age for most Americans, particularly those who directly participated in it. If the Revolutionary War constituted America's birth moment, then the War of 1812 symbolized the nation's leap into adolescence, if not manhood. "If our first struggle was a war of our infancy, this last war was that of our youth," observed James Madison in 1818. Many of the young men who fought in the war literally came of age during the conflict. Andrew Jackson Edmondson entered the war at age nineteen to serve in the Natchez Expedition and returned from the campaign at New Orleans in his twenty-second year, having served in all of Tennessee's operations during the war. In a poignant confession, Edmondson concluded his account of the war by noting: "I always thought until I went into the army, [that] my father had a poor opinion of my ever doing much but staying around my mother as her spoiled pet, which I was, but after my first Campaign he never complained of me in that way." Edmondson went into the war as an overindulged teen and came out an adult. The United States, an adolescent nation striving to live up to the accomplishments of its parents—the Founding Fathers—came through the test-by-fire experiment in a way that most people felt worthy enough (as they envisaged it) to carry the torch lit by their freedom-loving ancestors.[18]

What had Tennessee gained from the War of 1812 besides the grudging gratitude of a nation relieved that the fighting had finally come to an end? The themes that mattered most to Tennesseans at the onset of the conflict—more land, less foreign intrigue, and Indian removal—could now be brought into play. Eager to transform more "savage" wildernesses, Tennesseans looked southward to the broad tracts acquired through the 1814 Treaty of Fort Jackson. John Coffee, longing to trade in his sword for a surveyor's compass, sought to wrangle an appointment as surveyor as early as May 1814—even before the signing of the treaty at Fort Jackson—by contacting his friend George Washington Campbell (then secretary of the treasury) and offering his services. Noting the lands acquired from the Creeks "will be extensive and valuable," Coffee had no compunction about securing for himself an inside track on what would be a speculator's paradise. Although three commissioners had already been appointed to run the boundaries of the treaty, Coffee, through the influence of Andrew Jackson, managed to secure a provisional appointment as commissioner in late 1815. Coffee struck out for Fort Strother in January 1816 to rendezvous with the other three commissioners, but their delay caused the impatient Coffee to begin running his own line later that month, without informing the others of his actions. As he began to survey in a northwesterly direction toward Fort Deposit, the Cherokees protested, insisting parts of the area lay under Cherokee ownership. The land in question—a fifty-mile-wide stretch across northern Alabama south of the Big Bend of the Tennessee River—supposedly belonged to the Creeks, who had only loaned it to the Cherokees, a claim verified at the Treaty of Fort

Jackson. In reality, an 1806 treaty between the United States and the Cherokees *did* recognize the Cherokees as the proper possessors of the land. This
land, as Coffee and Jackson surely knew, contained some of the best cotton
acreage in the South, and they were not going to let it slip through their fin-
gers even after the federal government formally recognized Cherokee ownership in a March 1816 agreement.[19]

The 1816 treaty between the Cherokees and Secretary of War William
Crawford sparked an outrage from Tennesseans who believed the land was
theirs by right of conquest, if not by treaty. In a June 1816 letter to his old
comrade in arms, Major William Russell of Franklin County, John Coffee
expressed his frustration over "designing men" who imposed their will on
President Madison to take away "our hard earned Country" and relinquish it
to the Cherokees. "You who have contributed so bountifully, and who have
made so [many] noble sacrifices, to the acquirement of this Country," Coffee told the Creek War veteran, "know too well its value, to submit to its surrender." In Davidson County, a committee that included William Carroll
sent a remonstrance to President Madison demanding to know "upon what
principle of justice was this land ceded to the Cherokees?" The committee's
protest provided several arguments for reversing the agreement with the
Cherokees: first, the land had no real use for the Cherokees; second, it was
an area designated to have a "great highway" pass through to connect Tennessee with Mobile and New Orleans; and, third, white settlements there
would provide "a perpetual barrier to the communication of the northern
and southern tribes of Indians" and lead to security for travelers "without
the risk of being murdered at every wigwam by some drunken savage." To
make matters more pressing, thousands of impatient emigrants, including
Tennesseans, had already begun to settle in the disputed lands. Surely, Coffee insisted, the US government would not have the audacity to remove these
settlers (ten thousand of them by 1816). Major General Andrew Jackson, as
military commander of the district, found himself in the uncomfortable position of having to remove the squatters if so ordered. When those orders came,
Jackson refused, predicting the militia would never carry out such instructions; in fact, bloodshed might arise and vengeance be taken on the Cherokees. Former Tennessee congressman John Rhea picked up the torch on July
1, 1816, and wrote a long missive to President Madison verifying the anger
of the Tennesseans over the surrender of the lands to the Cherokees. Hoping to get the 1816 agreement revised, Rhea put forth his case by reminding
Madison that "the blood of Tennessee was poured out in subduing the hostile Creeks, and Citizens of Tennessee are not content that lands ceded by
the Creeks in consequence of that war are given to the Cherokees." Secre-

tary Crawford finally receded and agreed to hold treaties with the Cherokees, Choctaws, and Chickasaws—the latter two also having put in a claim
on the disputed lands. The subsequent treaty of September 1816, overseen by
Jackson and Coffee, witnessed the relinquishment of the tribal claims, including the potentially valuable cotton acreage.[20]

The running of the Creek treaty line proved to be a daunting task, the
Cherokee claims notwithstanding. The survey commissioners, William Barnett, Benjamin Hawkins, and Tennessee's John Sevier, faced embittered
Creeks, provision shortages, and sickness—Sevier would die in September
1815 with Hawkins following him in June 1816—in their attempts to mark
the boundaries. Barnett, writing to the secretary of war from Fort Decatur
in October 1815, related the apparent strain between the US troops and the
Creeks, which resulted in the murder of a few Creeks (one of the victims, a
pregnant Creek woman of a high-ranking Indian family, was killed by a sergeant). Barnett blamed the tension on the divisiveness within the Creek Nation and the failure of the government to reinstate the annuities promised to
the Creeks. No matter what the reasons, Andrew Jackson meant for the map-
ping to go on and sternly warned the Creeks in September 1815 that the slight-
est resistance would bring "instant destruction on the heads of the opposers."
The actual survey of the lands acquired by the treaty proceeded at a snail's
pace, due, in part, to the lack of proper equipment and the difficult terrain
involved. One of the surveyors, John Strother, even blamed Creek evil spirits
for the delay. Citing a Creek superstition that malevolent spirits dwelled "in
a deep hole in the ten islands," he insisted Fort Strother had a curse on it, as
there was always difficulty in getting supplies there. "Surely the place must
be inchanted [sic]," he informed Andrew Jackson in June 1815, "I have been
doomed to see & experience little else but troubles & heartakes [sic]."[21]

William Crawford, now secretary of the treasury since March 1817, became
impatient and organized the passage of a special congressional act creating
a surveyor for the northern Mississippi Territory. Chosen for this plum job
was John Coffee, who immediately hired a large number of surveyors to speed
up the charting of the ceded land. By mid-1817, Tennesseans were making
preparations to buy up the Alabama lands. Jacob McGavock, writing from
Nashville in August of that year, described to his father the excitement generated by the upcoming sales of land: "The people of this Country are making
great calculations and preparing extensively to purchase lands in the Country
lately acquired of the Cherokee and Creek Indians by treaty. The Surveyors
are now employed in running off and Sectioning the Country preparatory
to selling the same—the sale of which is generally supposed will take place
the latter part of this or the early next year . . . lands in that Country are and

will be very valuable (the climate and soil being well adapted to the growth of cotton)." At the center of all this activity stood John Coffee, ready to capitalize on the speculation boon about to occur. From his land office, Coffee began the process of entering detailed notes on the quality of the surveyed land and making arrangements with land-office clerks to get a kickback on any land or money they received for purchasing, locating, or giving information about land—all common practices of the day. Friends and relatives asked for, and usually received, special advice from Coffee, including Andrew Jackson (two of his nephews became surveyors for Coffee). Coffee formed his own land company, dividing shares among Jackson and other Tennesseans, as well as a group of wealthy Philadelphia speculators. When sales of the Alabama land began in 1818, Coffee entered eighty-three tracts in his own name, comprising 16,000 acres. He moved his family to Alabama and eventually became that state's most wealthy land speculator and planter. Others from Tennessee, many of them who fought with Jackson, removed to the lands they helped conquer. Nor was the "Alabama Fever" confined to Tennesseans. "The *Alabama Feaver* [*sic*] rages here with great violence," complained one North Carolinian in 1817, "and has *carried off* vast numbers of our citizens."[22]

The post–War of 1812 period saw a vast migration of slaveholders to the west, as well as to the south. Antebellum slaveholders were constantly migrating to the West for better economic opportunities, as westward migration was inextricably linked to upward mobility and material success. The Missouri Territory became the main target of emigration, eyed by many slaveowning Tennesseans, Kentuckians, and Virginians. Between the end of the War of 1812 and 1820, Missouri's population grew from 25,000 to 65,000. As early as 1811 Tennesseans extolled the benefits to be derived from the lands in "Upper Louisiana," as Missouri was then known. "It is I assure you, the finest [land] I ever saw," exclaimed one excited Nashville resident in 1811. "Come out, we'll go there & git as rich as we please." Several years later, another Tennessean sang the praises of the beauty and agricultural advantages of Missouri, with "grass as high as a man's head." "From the great influx of emigration," he forecasted, "the time cannot be afar off when it will be more thickly populated than any part of Tennessee." By the late 1820s, Tennesseans began leaving the state in great numbers. "The rage now seems [to be] for Indiana, Illinois and Missouri," grumbled East Tennessee merchant David Deaderick in 1829. Yet there were still enough new residents coming into Tennessee to keep its status as a "western" state. In fact, Tennessee and its sister states (Kentucky, Indiana, Illinois, and Missouri) experienced the most significant increase of total population in the United States during the decade 1810–20, going from 13.3 percent of the US population to 19.2 percent by 1820.[23]

The Cherokees represented one group of people that many Tennesseans *did* want to see leave the state. The ongoing pressure to force the Cherokees from Tennessee escalated after the war, despite the fact that the Cherokee had sacrificed its men to aid the American cause. Cherokee warriors who served under Jackson in the Creek War had not yet been paid in early 1815, with payments amounting to nearly $55,500. Furthermore, the US government still owed the Cherokees their annuities from 1813 through 1815, and the damage done by Tennessee militia marching through the Cherokee nation had reached an estimated $22,000. The imbroglio revolving around the disputed lands of the Treaty of Fort Jackson did little to smooth out the animosity brewing between the Cherokees and the Anglo-Americans. Tensions increased as land-hungry whites drifted over into Cherokee-held territory on the borders of Tennessee and the Carolinas. Indian agent Return Meigs began sending flyers to the white intruders by mid-1816, warning them they would be forcibly removed unless they vacated at once.[24]

The other Indian nations of the Old Southwest fared little better than the Cherokees. The Chickasaws, whose claim on the lands in Tennessee ranged from the Tennessee River to the Mississippi River, began to see the writing on the wall in 1816 when federal surveyors planned a road to run through the Chickasaw Nation from Reynoldsburg (in Humphreys County) to intersect with the Natchez Trace just south of Chickasaw Old Town (in present-day Lee County, Mississippi). State and federal officials followed up this initial foray into Chickasaw territory with a series of concessional treaties designed to extinguish all remaining tribal land claims in Tennessee—a feat accomplished in 1818 by the Jackson Purchase Treaty. The Choctaws, despite their loyalty and service to the Americans in the War of 1812, dealt with similar tactics, as government officials threatened, bribed, and coerced the tribe into a succession of treaties (1816, 1820, and 1825), eventually leading to their ultimate removal west of the Mississippi with the 1830 Treaty of Dancing Rabbit Creek.[25]

As to be expected, the Creek Indians suffered the most in the postwar period. Writing from Fort Jackson in June 1815, Major General Edmund Gaines painted a desperate picture of the remnants of the Creek Nation: starving families, fields laid to waste, no seeds to plant, no livestock, and no arms/ammunition to hunt for food. Gaines had to order rations of flour and meat just to sustain 2,500 refugee Creeks at the various posts. Coupled with these famine-like conditions and the wholesale destruction of crops and stocks, the allied Creeks still had yet to be compensated for their losses and expenditures. Notwithstanding their having fought for the Americans, the "friendly" Creeks had not received any federal annuities since 1811. When the Creeks tried to halt the running of the boundary line in Alabama, in what they deemed an unfair treaty, national sentiment naturally went against them. A Washington newspaper published a communication titled "Creek Indians Troublesome," based on a report dated May 29, 1815, coming out of Augusta, Georgia. The report condemned the Creeks for interfering with the surveying, referring to them as "these wretches, who after being supported by our government, when they otherwise must have inevitably starved, are pouring out the full cup of their ingratitude on the peaceful citizens of our country."[26]

After the War of 1812, renegade Creeks continued sporadic depredations on lands ceded to the whites, usually consisting of theft and the killing of livestock. These incidents increased Alabama's sense of insecurity, leading to fears that the Indians would again resort to mass violence. As a result, the state increasingly demanded the removal of the Creeks as the only reasonable solution to the situation. One lone voice, that of Nathaniel Claiborne (brother to W. C. C. Claiborne), spoke of the injustice involved with removing the Creeks from their homelands: "What! remove them beyond the Mississippi to become extinct in the wars that follow between them and their neighbors, and the tribes of savages by whom they will be environed! No, let them occupy the land of their fathers, but let them do it in peace." Claiborne devised a plan whereby alternate tracts of land would be carved out of the Creek Nation, with the larger tracts occupied by the Americans, while the Creeks held the smaller ones. Unfortunately, Claiborne's voice in the wilderness was drowned out by the incessant demand on the frontier for Indian land and, hence, Indian removal. In 1836, 17,000 Creeks were forcibly removed from their lands, after enduring years of fraud and intimidation, not to mention watching helplessly as 100,000 Americans poured into Alabama between 1815 and 1820. "Seldom in human history has so large a territory been settled so rapidly," one historian has noted. Between the years 1810–20, Alabama's population increased twelvefold to 128,000, while Mississippi's doubled to 75,000.[27]

With the Creeks soundly defeated and the other southeastern Indian tribes lining up for eventual removal, the War of 1812 concluded with a sense of security for Tennesseans regarding any future Indian incursions and/or alliances with foreign powers. "The Indian war-whoop is heard no more," proclaimed Tennessee minister Charles Coffin in an 1815 sermon. "The slumbers of the night are not now disturbed by the hideous yell of surprise and massacre. . . . The barbarous alliance of civilized and savage enemies on our extensive inland borders no longer threatens us." Although Tennesseans might have felt less endangered by Indians in the postwar period, they still clung to the traditional stereotypes that portrayed the "savages" as repugnant obstacles to peace and order on the frontier (the concept of the "noble savage" had yet to make an impact on the southern frontier). One of the impasses, as it had been in the past, revolved around the notion that, as a race, *all* Indians were the same. An 1818 article in the prestigious Philadelphia *Analectic Magazine* declared: "There is so little variety among the Indian tribes of North America, in any of the essential qualities which distinguish nations, that however they may differ in language, dress, or apparently in institutions, they may all be considered as one people." John Coffee, serving as one of the negotiators at the 1816 conference with the Choctaws, displayed an utter lack of appreciation for Indian customs and culture when he witnessed a Choctaw tribal dance and jotted in his diary, "it is a poor thing indeed—nothing I ever saw was so insipid."[28]

Many Creek Indians, encouraged by the British that Article 9 of the Treaty of Ghent (which insured the return of possessions held by the Indian tribes prior to the war) might restore their lands and privileges, joined the Seminoles in Florida, where they continued to threaten white settlers moving onto vacated lands. Organized under the leadership of the ever-present Colonel Edward Nicholls, the Creeks hoped the Madison administration would invalidate the Treaty of Fort Jackson. In fact, the government ordered General Andrew Jackson to begin to return the lands to the Creeks in June 1815, but Jackson adamantly refused, and the government felt loath to enforce an edict on the nation's most popular hero. Hostilities renewed in 1817 when the Seminoles refused to leave lands ceded by the Treaty of Fort Jackson. General Edmund P. Gaines, followed by Jackson, led an army into Florida comprised of Tennessee volunteers and allied Creeks. The Americans soon took over the Indian towns, executing two British subjects as spies in the process. In May 1818, Jackson moved against Pensacola, placing it under civil and military control, and then declared the war over. Despite staunch protests from British and Spanish officials, Jackson escaped official censure for his actions.[29]

Of course, Jackson could only achieve such political clout through the immense popularity of his victory at New Orleans in January 1815. The Hero of New Orleans rode into the White House in 1828 (after narrowly losing the 1824 election) on the coattails of his continuing popularity over the outcome of the War of 1812. The fact that the victory over the British occurred in New Orleans must have added more significance for westerners obsessed with the security of the Crescent City. The magnitude of the British defeat would have been hailed as an awe-inspiring event at any location, but the fact that it happened in New Orleans—a city Tennesseans revered as their economic lifeline, sacredly inscribed in the state constitution—surely amplified the "savior" status that Andrew Jackson had acquired. Furthermore, Jackson achieved most of his fame by relying on state support, rather than the federal government—a condition that harkened back to the glory days of the Frontier Fathers.

As Jackson's esteem grew in the public eye, the significance of January 8 continued to grow in America's public memory. Upon Jackson's death in 1845, George Bancroft, the most popular historian of his day, referred to January 8, 1815, as "that eventful morning when the day at Bunker Hill had its fulfillment in the glorious battle of New Orleans, and American independence stood before the world in the majesty of triumphant power!" Once more, the link to the American Revolution and the "second war for American independence" stood firm, although fractures began appearing by the 1830s. During a heated debate in Congress in 1834 over a commissioned painting of Jackson in New Orleans, Virginia congressman Henry A. Wise declared: "I would be content to confine the subjects to date prior to 1783." Wise directed his indignation more toward Jackson than the War of 1812, but by then the two had become synonymous.[30]

Of the thousands of Tennesseans who participated in the War of 1812, most faded into relative obscurity, leaving no way of knowing to what degree the war directly influenced their lives. Historian Michael Bellesiles, in his examination of the War of 1812, suggested there was no clear meaning to the service of the soldiers or any clear idea of why they were fighting, thus their experiences seemed mundane. "The American Revolution transformed its participants; the War of 1812 depressed most of those who played a part," Bellesiles insisted. But Bellesiles's unfair analysis overlooks the fact that war is war, whether on a grand scale or not. The experience and sting of battle or merely sharing the tedium with a thousand other soldiers *has* to make some impression on the individual. Were the Tennesseans who fought in the War of 1812 fighting *for* something—if so, what was it? As this book has attempted to point out, the motivations for any individual going to war vary greatly. And, in the end, taking part in the war seemed to be more important than the reasons for fighting it. When John Gordon, a veteran of the Creek War, died in 1819, the *Nashville Gazette* idealized his service in the war, without taking into any consideration *why* he participated: "The deceased was a man of considerable enterprise, great integrity and undaunted bravery. His services during the frequent and bloody Indian wars which depredated this state while a frontier, gained for him great popularity, and confidence among the then settlers. His conduct in the last war with the Creeks, secured to him the applause of every officer engaged in it." Gordon's life was memorialized by the attributes most valued on the frontier: energy, honesty, and daring. It is not known if Gordon ever expressed *why* he enlisted in the Creek War—perhaps it was just expected of him.[31]

Without a doubt, the inspired conclusion of the War of 1812 prompted many Americans to think their nation's status on the world stage had increased dramatically. Furthermore, it answered the question posed at the commencement of hostilities of whether the United States could hold its own in a contest with powers from the Old World. "We have solved our great question whether our government, formed as it is, was able to support under the shock of war," proclaimed one US congressman. "Such a character as we have now through Europe and even our enemy will be worth ten fold what the war has cost us." The experiment had been conducted with America surviving the great test of war. By supposedly subduing "the boasted mistress of the ocean," the United States had established "a lofty National Character," as a Charleston newspaper decried in February 1815. The identity crisis of the War-of-1812 generation had been solved—at least for the time being.[32]

On the eve of the war, Andrew Jackson instructed the men of the Second Division of militia on the reasons for their country's preparation for the conflict with England: "We are going to fight for the reestablishment of our national charector [*sic*], misunderstood and vilified at home and abroad; for the protection of our maritime citizens, impressed on board British ships of war and compelled to fight the battles of our enemies against ourselves; to vindicate our right to a free trade, and open a market for the productions of our soil." Jackson succinctly summed up the grievances of the United States at the onset of the War of 1812: impressment, trade restrictions, and the degradation of national character.

What Jackson did not expound on were the underlying issues of the war, specifically, territorial expansion and Indian removal. In congratulating Jackson on his Creek War victories, Kentucky politician Matthew Lyon, in a June 1814 letter, espoused these themes with this straightforward expression: "This Nation is destined to civilize & Govern this Continent. . . . This must be the work of time conducted by a wise & Energetic American government taking advantage of propitious circumstances." The War of 1812 offered the "propitious circumstances" sought by many Americans bent on expanding America's geographical destiny through the expulsion of British and Spanish influence.[33]

The War of 1812 also afforded the opportunity to set the wheels in motion to "solve" the Indian problem. The outcome of the Creek conflict, in particular, set the tone for future treaty negotiations. No longer would the Indians of the Old Southwest possess any large degree of bargaining power. As a result, all future dealings with the southeastern tribes pointed toward their ultimate removal from their homelands. Along with this process came a mixed bag of emotions from Anglo-Americans no longer threatened by Indian incursions. A Virginia periodical of 1819 exemplified the pity and guilt whites began to exhibit as the specter of extinction began to envelope the future of the Indians of the Old Southwest. "Whoever is acquainted in any manner with the history of the Indians, and divests his mind of prejudice, will pity their melancholy fate," the article proclaimed. "Surely there was no just cause to persecute and exterminate them." The government stepped up efforts to "civilize" the unfortunate Indians, but even these attempts, for the most part, failed in transforming the Indians into whites. Federal funding built schools staffed by missionary-society teachers bent on educating the Indians on the basis that Indians had to become "white." "Their whole character," US commissioner of Indian affairs Thomas L. McKenny said in 1819, "inside and out; language, and morals, must be changed." In time, white guilt became disguised through the claim that the preservation of Indians depended on their removal. Most of the people in Tennessee, however, held no guilt and would have disagreed with governmental attempts to change what, in their minds, could never be changed. One such Tennessean, expressing his opinion of the Creeks and Cherokees he encountered while growing up in Alabama and East Tennessee in the post–War of 1812 period, declared that an Indian "seems as a rule to have no desire to be anything but a savage and even prides in it."[34]

The bias Tennesseans shared against Indians came from the legacy of vicious border warfare transferred from one generation to the next. Andrew Jackson's forays during the Creek War merely echoed the western ideology of the early 1790s when "defending" the frontier implied ridding the region of Indians. Men on the frontier fought in order to protect their communities, property, and families, but they were also motivated by racial animosity toward Indians, coupled with the hopes of opening up a new supply of western lands by carrying offensive operations into Indian territory. The stories of Indian cruelty, heard around the firesides or read about in the newspapers and periodicals of the day, remained implanted in the public memory for much of the nineteenth century and into the twentieth. In 1918, Samuel G. Heiskell, a Knoxville attorney turned historian, published a three-volume tome, *Andrew Jackson and Early Tennessee History*, in which he lauded the achievements of Tennessee's early settlers by noting "white civilization was in daily and deadly combat with the red man's savagery, and both could not occupy the soil at the same time." Heiskell's comment not only reminded his readers of the "savagery" inherent in the American Indian, but also touched on the element of race, by noting "white civilization" had to come out on top—a scenario apropos to the ever-growing racial tensions in the postbellum South.[35]

Indian removal and the extension of slavery worked hand in hand for Tennessee in the period following the War of 1812. Logically, the absence of Indian owners equated to an influx of white, slaveholding proprietors—a condition southern Anglo-Americans aspired to achieve. However, one cannot dismiss another underlying motive for territorial expansion: security. Tennessee had dealt with "foreign" intrigue on its borders for decades—the British from the north and the Spanish from the south. In both cases, the perceived nefarious dealings with the southeastern tribes had led to depredations extending through the War of 1812. Indeed, Indian conspiracies were at the heart of the war's declaration, at least from the western point of view. In addition, Tennesseans claimed Indian territory by rule of natural right. When the unoccupied Indian lands in Tennessee lured emigrants and speculators into the state, the extinguishment of Cherokee and Chickasaw lands became of paramount importance in the halls of the state legislature. In March 1810, Tennessee's congressional delegation issued a message to President James Madison informing him of the resolutions the Tennessee General Assembly passed about Indian claims: a more direct route to the Mobile region (and, hence, the Atlantic states) was necessary for the state's suffering commerce, and the Indians' right of possession to the land could not equal Tennessee's undeniable right of economic self-preservation: "We cannot for One moment conceive, that the claim by which those Indians hold those lands . . . can or ought to preclude our fellow Citizens, from the free exercise of those *paramount rights*, which God and nature has given them—and which they are not only absolutely essential to enable them, to pass unmolested to the Ocean." For Tennesseans in the period of the War of 1812, "manifest destiny" (as the belief in the apparent and inexorable right for American expansion came to be known) served as a basic tenet of their economic and political principles.[36]

The pattern of regional discrimination so apparent in the 1790s confirmed itself in the War of 1812 when the northwestern regions received the full attention of the officials in Washington. Military campaigns on the southern frontier were largely a matter of local affairs, with Andrew Jackson filling the vacuum the lack of federal support created. Thus, the War of 1812 helped to shape the character of Tennessee in its nascent development. As a frontier state, rife with internal conflicts of interests, Tennessee, like much of the nation it was part of, sought an ordered structure and identity to build on—a definition of who it was. War, as a common danger, usually causes motives of self-interest to pull in the same direction and invigorates a unified, patriotic spirit. Yet the War of 1812 never really cemented the tensions existing between the two rival sections of Tennessee; in fact, the war actually illustrated the strain that would continue to pull at the sociopolitical threads of statehood. Still, the principal legacy of the state's participation in the war—that of the "Volunteers"—provided a chimera for future Tennesseans to cherish. To be sure, there is substance to this claim, as thousands came forth to make the same patriotic sacrifice their fathers had made in the American Revolution (or in the contested backcountry). The shadows of the towering figures from the revolution enveloped Tennesseans of the early republic with a mission to carry the torch, as it were, of their fathers' exploits. Yet emulating the deeds of the former generation would never be enough to forge a separate identity. Andrew Jackson, the undisputed hero of the War of 1812, became known as a second George Washington, but it was clear to most people that the irascible, ill-tempered Jackson was *not* the austere, cool-headed persona of a Washington. Nevertheless, in his own way, Jackson better represented the new American coming out of the West: audacious, overly aggressive, and proud to a fault. Jackson emitted the unbridled passions of a country on the move, certain that the uncertainties ahead could be overcome by the God-inspired convictions of rightfulness and destiny.

The forging of Tennessee's identity came at a cost that others often had to pay. Displaced Indians and shackled slaves lay stranded in the wake of Tennessee's progressive thrust—the former viewed as collateral damage, the latter seen as economic necessities. In the end, both would come to haunt the distinctiveness of the state, as it made its way from a frontier status to a "southern" entity. The War of 1812 provided Tennessee with much to be proud of and much to account for—a dual legacy that molded the history of the state and that still keeps shaping its character.

Notes

Abbreviations for Notes

AC   Annals of Congress
ASPIA   American State Papers, Indian Affairs
HNOC   Historic New Orleans Collection
LC   Library of Congress (Washington, DC)
LHQ   Louisiana Historical Quarterly
MDAH   Mississippi Department of Archives and History (Jackson)
NARA   National Archives and Records Administration (Washington, DC)
THS   Tennessee Historical Society (Nashville)
TSLA   Tennessee State Library and Archives (Nashville)

Introduction

1. (Nashville) *Republican Banner*, June 1, 1846.

2. Up to the mid-twentieth century, most historians assumed the title "Volunteer State" originated during the Mexican War, but Tennessee State Historian Robert White's research in the 1950s indicated the term probably came from the War of 1812. He based this on the numerous references—"the volunteers from Tennessee," "the volunteers and militia of the State of Tennessee," and "the Tennessee Volunteers"—found in the periodicals and correspondence of the War of 1812. He assumed the nickname "Volunteer State," used by newspapers during the Mexican War, came into vogue from these 1812 references. See White, *Messages of the Governors of Tennessee, 1845–1857*, 126n102; and Record Group 29, State Historian 1955–1970, TSLA, Box 23, Folder 10. In conjunction with White's research, I have found several references made to Tennessee as the "Volunteer State" before the Mexican War. See, for instance, the *Republican Banner*, July 28, 1843, and August 2, 1843. There is even a mention of Tennessee being called the "Volunteer State" in the October 15, 1836, issue of the *Nashville Republican*. This leads to the conclusion that the recognition of Tennessee's volunteer spirit, begun in the War of 1812, subsequently carried over into the next several conflicts that preceded the Mexican War, that is, the First and Second Seminole Wars and the Cherokee Removal.

3. Hickey, *The War of 1812: A Forgotten Conflict*.

4. Rossiter, *The American Quest, 1790–1860*, 261. Horwitz, "Remember the Raisin," 29.

5. Statistics taken from Thornton, *American Indian Holocaust and Survival*, 104; Clodfelter, *Warfare and Armed Conflicts*, 275; and Waselkov, *A Conquering Spirit*, 171.

6. George, *Memorandum of the Creek Indian War*, 3–5.

7. Somkin, *Unquiet Eagle*, 4.

8. Much of this paragraph is a distillation of my unpublished master's thesis, "Frontier Fathers and Martial Sons: Indian Hating in the Backcountry Prior to the War of 1812," Middle Tennessee State University, 2003.

9. Randal McGavock to Hugh McGavock, April 16, 1807, in Gower and Allen, *Pen and Sword: The Life and Journals of Randal W. McGavock*, 20–21.

10. (Nashville) *Tennessee Gazette and Metro District Advertiser*, July 17, 1805.

11. *Nashville Whig*, July 12, 1814.

12. Waselkov, *A Conquering Spirit*, 163.

Chapter 1

1. David Campbell to Thomas Jefferson, November 5, 1809, in Looney, *Papers of Thomas Jefferson: Retirement Series*, 1: 653. For land descriptions, see Finger, *Tennessee Frontiers*, 1–4. Note that the word *country* in the eighteenth and early nineteenth centuries indicated a region, locality, or state, in addition to a nation-state.

2. Bergeron, Ash, and Keith, *Tennesseans and Their History*, 70. (Baltimore) *Niles' Weekly Register*, June 10, 1815. Record Group 60, Legislative Materials, Reports, Receipts, Rejected Bills, etc., 1796–1865, TSLA, Box 10, Folder 2. Ray, *Middle Tennessee, 1775–1825*, 14, 60.

3. Smith, *Short Description of the Tennessee Government*, 15. James Winchester to William Blount, November 9, 1794, cited in Durham, *James Winchester*, 30–33. Hall's reminiscences are taken from "Narrative of General Hall," 1: 332–34; and 2: 14–15. The *Knoxville Gazette* cited in Abernethy, *From Frontier to Plantation in Tennessee*, 130n62. From the period 1790–96, Tennessee was known as the Territory South of the River Ohio, more commonly referred to as the Southwest Territory.

4. Goodpasture, "Indian Wars and Warriors of the Old Southwest, 1730–1807," 206–7. For the cost of Indian wars, see Holton, *Unruly Americans*, 268. For Cherokee annuities, see Prucha, *Sword of the Republic*, 46.

5. Downes, "Indian Affairs in the Southwest Territory, 1790–1796," 240–68. Hoig, *Cherokees and Their Chiefs*, 79–88. Smith, "Pioneers, Patriots, and Politicians: The Tennessee Militia System, 1772–1857" (PhD diss., University of Tennessee, 2003), 110–25. Finger, *Tennessee Frontiers*, 146–47.

6. Cited in Carter, *Territorial Papers of the United States*, 4: 366.

7. John Sevier to George Washington Sevier, May 31, 1812, cited in Sevier and Madden, *Sevier Family History*, 188–89. Hobohoilthle to James Madison, September 29, 1809, in Stagg, *Papers of James Madison: Presidential Series*, 4: 605–7. O'Brien, *In Bitterness and Tears*, 5.

8. Alfred Moore to James McHenry, June 30, 1799, cited in Steiner, *Life and Correspondence of James McHenry*, 446, 449. John Sevier to Daniel Smith, July 6, 1800,

Gov. John Sevier Papers, 1796–1801, TSLA, Box 1, Folder 8. Hoig, *Cherokees and Their Chiefs*, 92–99.

9. Willie Blount to John Gray Blount, March 18, 1811, in Morgan, *John Gray Blount Papers*, 4: 144–45. Lyman Copeland Draper Manuscript Collection, Wisconsin Historical Society (Madison), 5U192. Peeler, "The Policies of Willie Blount as Governor of Tennessee, 1809–1815," 312–14.

10. Durham, *Daniel Smith*, 107. Smith, *Short Description of the Tennessee Government*, 16. Holmes, "William C. C. Claiborne Predicts the Future of Tennessee," 184. The 1796 Tennessee constitution quoted in McClure, *State Constitution Making*, 42.

11. Holmes, *Gayoso*, 230. *Address of James Lyon. Wilson's Knoxville Gazette*, July 20, 1808.

12. Hamilton quoted in Colburn, *Fame and the Founding Fathers*, 267. For the early importance of West Florida, see Chambers, *West Florida and Its Relation to the Historical Cartography of the United States*, 25.

13. White, *Messages of the Governors of Tennessee, 1796–1821*, 98–99. RG 60, Legislative Materials, TSLA, Box 9, Folder 10. (Nashville) *Impartial Review and Cumberland Repository*, August 20, 1807. *Address of James Lyon. Wilson's Knoxville Gazette*, March 10, 1810, and August 25, 1810. *Carthage Gazette*, March 22, 1811.

14. Quotes in this paragraph are taken from ASPIA (Washington: Gales and Seaton, 1832), 1: 843, 856.

15. Ranck, "Andrew Jackson and the Burr Conspiracy," 17–28. For an overall account of the Burr Conspiracy, see Stewart, *American Emperor*. Nancy Isenberg, in her biography of Burr, claims that while Burr was certainly guilty of filibustering, he never conspired to overthrow Jefferson's administration. She portrays Burr as a victim of character assassination rather than as a conspirator. See Isenberg, *Fallen Founder*, chapter eight.

16. *Impartial Review and Cumberland Repository*, October 4, 1806, January 3, 1807, and July 11, 1807.

17. Cayton, "'When Shall We Cease to Have Judases?': The Blount Conspiracy and the Limits of the 'Extended Republic,'" 156–89. It is noteworthy to mention that some of Tennessee's Frontier Fathers, such as James Robertson and James Winchester, served as land agents for Blount. See Abernethy, *From Frontier to Plantation*, 119, 129.

18. Davis, *Jeffersonian America*, 80. "The Senate Debate on the Breckinridge Bill for the Government of Louisiana, 1804," 344. Smith, *Short Description of the Tennessee Government*, 3–4.

19. Folmsbee, *Sectionalism and Internal Improvements in Tennessee, 1796–1845*, 49–50. Morrow, "A Brief History of Theater in Nashville, 1807–1970," 178. Moore, "The First Century of Library History in Tennessee, 1813–1913," 3. *Nashville Whig*, April 28, 1813, May 3, 1814, and September 27, 1814. (Nashville) *Clarion, and Tennessee State Gazette*, October 18, 1814, and November 3, 1812. Abernethy, *From Frontier to Plantation*, 277. Thomas, *Old Days in Nashville*, 13. The Nashville *Clarion* used three different titles during the period of the War of 1812—all with variations of the word *Clarion*. For purposes of simplification, this book will cite *Clarion* for all subsequent references to this newspaper.

20. *Nashville Whig*, June 21, 1814. *Clarion*, July 7, 1812. Lovett, *The African-American History of Nashville*, 3–13. Thomas, *Old Days in Nashville*, 13. Goodstein, "Black History on the Nashville Frontier, 1780–1810," 17. Smith, *Civic Ideals*, 171, 179. RG 60, Legislative Materials, TSLA, Box 6, Folder 38. Ray, *Middle Tennessee 1775–1825*, 73–74, 144–45. Henry, "Slave Laws of Tennessee," 200. Also, see Apperson, "African Americans on the Tennessee Frontier," 2–19.

21. Kaplan, "To Live in Hearts We Leave Behind Is Not to Die," 3. Phillip Thomas to John Coffee, January 19, 1815, Dyas Collection, John Coffee Papers, THS, Box 12, Folder 8. For "blackman Bob," see Papers of Andrew Jackson, LC, microfilm edition, 5th series, reel 66. Boom, "John Coffee, Citizen Soldier," 235.

22. Quote in "The Reminiscences of General Bernard Pratte, Jr.," 96.

23. Ross, *Life and Times of Elder Rueben Ross*, 201. Clark, *Clark's Miscellany*, 114. Reynolds, *My Own Times*, 125.

24. Penick, *New Madrid Earthquakes*, 11–13. (Lexington) *Kentucky Gazette*, May 12, 1812. Ross, "The New Madrid Earthquake," 88–89.

25. *Carthage Gazette*, December 21, 1814. Ross, *Life and Times of Elder Reuben Ross*, 203. Nathan Vaught Memoir, 1871, TSLA, 9–10.

26. Narrative of the Birth and Life of Jesse Cox, TSLA, 4. William Alexander to John Owen, April 20, 1812, David Campbell Papers, TSLA. For a more detailed account of religious implications of the earthquakes, see Kanon, "'Scared from Their Sins for a Season': The Religious Ramifications of the New Madrid Earthquakes, 1811–1812," 21–38.

27. An account of Tippecanoe can be found in Smelser, "Tecumseh, Harrison, and the War of 1812," 25–44.

28. The best biography of Tecumseh remains Sugden, *Tecumseh: A Life*. For the background to unified Native American resistance, see Dowd, *A Spirited Resistance*. An analysis of the Creek spiritual movement can be found in Joel Martin's *Sacred Revolt*. For Creeks fighting with Tecumseh's forces, see Sugden, *Tecumseh's Last Stand*, 244n24.

29. Cady, "Western Opinion and the War of 1812," 453–54. "Diary of Jose Bernardo Gutierrez de Lara, 1811–1812," 69. Willie Blount Letter, 1811, MS-0737, Special Collections Library, University of Tennessee. *Carthage Gazette*, December 14, 1811. *Clarion*, January 7, 1812. John Sevier to George Washington Sevier, May 31, 1812, in Sevier and Madden, *Sevier Family History*, 189.

30. Andrew Jackson to William Henry Harrison, November 28, 1811, in Moser and Macpherson, *Papers of Andrew Jackson*, vol. 2, *1804–1813*, 270 (hereafter cited as Moser and Macpherson, *Papers of Andrew Jackson*, vol. 2.). Cady, "Western Opinion and the War of 1812," 454n75. William Henry Harrison to John Scott, December 12, 1811, reprinted in the *Clarion*, December 24, 1811. (Philadelphia) *Aurora General Advertiser*, November 29, 1811, and December 5, 1811.

31. Burt, *United States, Great Britain, and British North America*. Horsman, "British Indian Policy in the Northwest, 1807–1812," 51–66. Horsman, "British-Colonial Attitudes and Policies toward the Indian in the American Colonies" 81–106.

32. John Rhea Letter, 1813 (CR), Filson Historical Society (Louisville, Kentucky). Kreider, *Papers of James Madison: Presidential Series*, 6: 86. Owens, *Mr. Jefferson's Hammer*, 225–26. AC, 12th Cong., 2nd sess., 1362–63.

33. For a good summation of the embargoes, consult Heaton, "Non-Importation, 1806–1812," 178–98.

34. The quote at the beginning of the paragraph is by Mead, *Special Providence*, 17. For agricultural prices dropping, see Nelson, *Liberty and Property*, 136–37. For the effects of the embargo on Tennessee's economy, see Ray, *Middle Tennessee, 1775–1825*, 102–7. The 1808 petition is from the John Sevier Papers, 1803–1809, Second Series of Administrations, TSLA, Box 1, Folder 11.

35. (Nashville) *Impartial Review and Cumberland Repository*, July 12, 1806. James Winchester to John R. Eaton, August 8, 1809, in Hamilton, *Letters of John Rust Eaton*, 52. *Carthage Gazette*, March 13, 1809. William Dickson to James Madison, September 11, 1809, James Madison Papers, LC, 1st series, reel 11.

36. David Erskine to Edward Channing, July 17, 1807, quoted in White, *A Nation on Trial*, 41. Walker, "Martial Sons: Tennessee Enthusiasm for the War of 1812," 22–23. Clark, *Clark's Miscellany*, 27–28. *Impartial Review and Cumberland Repository*, July 30, 1807. LaFeber, "Jefferson and an American Foreign Policy," 383–84. For an overall examination of the *Chesapeake* incident, see Tucker, *Injured Honor*.

37. *Impartial Review and Cumberland Repository*, July 30, 1807 (emphasis is original). AC, 13th Cong., 2nd sess., 1779. McLeod, *Scriptural View of the Character, Causes, and Ends of the Present War*, 220.

38. The literature on the causation of the War of 1812 is extensive, but some of the more important works include: Goodman, "The Origins of the War of 1812: A Survey of Changing Interpretations," 171–86; Horsman, *Causes of the War of 1812*; Taylor, *The War of 1812*; Brown, *Republic in Peril: 1812*; Hatzenbuehler and Ivie, *Congress Declares War*; and Buel, *America on the Brink*. For a more recent interpretation, based on the international implications of the war, see Bickham, *The Weight of Vengeance*.

39. North, *Economic Growth of the United States, 1790–1860*, 53–56, 221, 231. The quote at the beginning of the paragraph is from McDougall, *Promised Land*, 35.

40. Williams, *The French Assault on American Shipping, 1793–1813*. James Bayard to Andrew Bayard, August 6, 1814, in "Letters Relating to the Negotiations at Ghent," 113. James Monroe to John Taylor, June 13, 1812, and Monroe to Joel Barlow, February 24, 1812, in Lucier, *Political Writings of James Monroe*, 437–38.

41. January 1812 speech in the US House by New Hampshire representative John A. Harper, cited in Merk, *Manifest Destiny*, 13. Errington and Rawlyk, "Creating a British-American Political Community in Upper Canada" 187–200. Other statistics taken from Bourne, *Britain and the Balance of Power in North America, 1815–1908*, 58.

42. Stagg, "James Madison and the Coercion of Great Britain: Canada, the West Indies, and the War of 1812," 3–34; and Stagg, "The Coming of the War of 1812: The View from the Presidency," 228–29. Also, see Stuart, "Special Interests and National Authority in Foreign Policy: American-British Provincial Links during the Embargo and the War of 1812," 311–28. James Monroe to John Taylor, June 13, 1812, in Lucier, *Political Writings of James Monroe*, 439.

43. AC, 13th Cong., 2nd sess., 1780. (Charleston, SC) *City Gazette* citied in Wolfe, *Jeffersonian Democracy in South Carolina*, 256. John Long to Joseph McMinn, December 8, 1813, "1813 Letter," 253.

44. *Carthage Gazette*, February 6, 1809. *Journal of the House of Representatives, at the Second Session of the Ninth General Assembly of the State of Tennessee . . . One Thousand Eight Hundred and Twelve*, 16. Andrew Jackson to John Armstrong, April 8, 1813, in Bassett, *Correspondence of Andrew Jackson*, 1: 303. Thomas Hart Benton to William P. Anderson, November 22, 1813, John Coffee Papers, THS, Box 17, Folder 9.

45. Wyatt-Brown, *Shaping of Southern Culture*, chap. 2. *Nashville Whig*, December 2, 1812. Andrew Jackson to Rachel Jackson, December 14, 1813, in Moser and Macpherson, *Papers of Andrew Jackson*, vol. 2, 487.

46. Worcester, "War and Popular Delusion," 378. Rowland, *Andrew Jackson's Campaign against the British*, 49.

47. Kanon, "'James Madison, Felix Grundy, and the Devil': A Western War Hawk in Congress," 449–50. Winn, "The War Hawks' Call to Arms: Appeals for a Second War with Great Britain," 402–12. Hatzenbuehler and Ivie, *Congress Declares War*, esp. chaps. 3 and 8. Felix Grundy to Andrew Jackson, December 24, 1811, in Moser and Macpherson, *Papers of Andrew Jackson*, vol. 2, 271, 276. Henry Clay to Caesar A. Rodney, August 17, 1811, in Hopkins, *Papers of Henry Clay*, 1: 574. Jonathan Russell to James Monroe, March 1812, quoted in Varg, *Foreign Policies of the Founding Fathers*, 286–87.

48. Kanon, "'James Madison, Felix Grundy, and the Devil': A Western War Hawk in Congress," 448, 452–55, 468. For a biography of Grundy, see Heller, *Democracy's Lawyer*.

49. Richardson, *Messages and Papers of the Presidents, 1789–1897*, 1: 504. George Washington Campbell to Willie Blount, June 18, 1812; and Willie Blount to James Monroe, July 4, 1812, both reprinted in *Wilson's Knoxville Gazette*, July 13, 1812. Felix Grundy, "Citizens of West Tennessee," June 19, 1812, in the July 7, 1812, issue of the *Clarion*. John Rhea to Peter Parsons, September 20, 1814, Rhea Family Papers, THS, Box 1, Folder 6.

Chapter 2

1. *Clarion*, July 7, 1812. Hamer, *Tennessee: A History, 1673–1932*, 221. Walker, "Martial Sons: Tennessee Enthusiasm for the War of 1812," 36. *Wilson's Knoxville Gazette*, July 6, 1812.

2. Moses Fisk to John Fisk, November 14, 1812, Moses Fisk Papers, TSLA, Folder 6. *Clarion*, April 28, 1812.

3. For a review of the congressional acts regarding the army in 1812, consult Upton, *Military Policy of the United States*, 92–96.

4. Jackson's divisional orders of July 31, 1812, and September 8, 1812, both in Moser and Macpherson, *Papers of Andrew Jackson*, vol. 2, 317, 320–21.

5. *Nashville Whig*, December 30, 1812, and December 2, 1812. *Wilson's Knoxville Gazette*, October 19, 1812.

6. Coleman and Majeske, "British Immigrants in Rhode Island during the War of 1812," 66–75; and Baseler, *"Asylum for Mankind": America, 1607–1800*, 313–22.

7. *Wilson's Knoxville Gazette*, June 22, 1808. *Clarion*, October 27, 1812.

8. *Carthage Gazette*, July 8, 1812. *Nashville Whig*, September 2, 1812. *Wilson's Knoxville Gazette*, October 19, 1812.

9. Thomas Jefferson to Thomas Lehre, August 8, 1812, cited in Wolfe, *Jeffersonian Democracy in South Carolina*, 257n47. John Sevier to Isaac Shelby, January 17, 1810, THS Miscellaneous Files 1688–1951 (T-100), Box 14, S-28. John Anderson to Willie Blount, July 20, 1812, RG 131, Tennessee Military Elections, TSLA, Box 6, Folder 19.

10. James Madison to Albert Gallatin, August 8, 1812, in Stagg, *Papers of James Madison: Presidential Series*, 5: 129. Barbuto, "1812: The United States Builds a Regular Army," 71–77. Denson, *A Compendium, of Useful Information*, 226. Martin and Lender, *A Respectable Army*, 6–9. Kahn, *A Republic of Men*, 110–12. Laver, "Refuge of Manhood: Masculinity and the Militia Experience in Kentucky," 2–12. Military Papers, Commissions, 1813–49, TSLA.

11. Skeen, *Citizen Soldiers*, 6–16. Callan, *Military Laws of the United States*, 95, 109, 198, 215.

12. Smith, "Pioneers, Patriots, and Politicians," 106–8, 138–40. Laver, "Rethinking the Social Role of the Militia: Community Building in Antebellum Kentucky," 810. *Journal of the Senate, at the Second Session of the Ninth General Assembly of the State of Tennessee, Begun and Held at Nashville . . . One Thousand Eight Hundred and Twelve*, 71.

13. Smith, "Pioneers, Patriots, and Politicians," 53–54, 58, 137–38, 143. *Acts Passed at the First Session of the Seventh General Assembly of the State of Tennessee Began and Held at Kingston . . . One Thousand Eight Hundred and Seven*, 158. *Wilson's Knoxville Gazette*, September 27, 1813.

14. *State of Tennessee vs. Palemon Winchester*, Sumner County Loose Records, Lawsuit #9330, reel A-5112, TSLA. The text from the 1803 act is taken from *Acts Passed at the First Session of the Fifth General Assembly of the State of Tennessee . . . One Thousand Eight Hundred and Three*, 20.

15. For an overall look at the resistance of New England regarding the federal use of state militia, see Stuart, *Civil-Military Relations during the War of 1812*, 89–91; and Upton, *Military Policy of the United States*, 96–98.

16. Willie Blount to Andrew Jackson, November 11, 1812, in Moser and Macpherson, *Papers of Andrew Jackson*, vol. 2, 338–39. "To the Tennessee Volunteers," November 14, 1812, in ibid., 341. James Hervey Maury Memoir, 1864, TSLA, 14. *Clarion*, December 15, 1812. Jackson's comment about "Columbia's true sons" is from his letter of March 15, 1813, to James Madison, in Bassett, *Correspondence of Andrew Jackson*, 1: 293.

17. Peeler, "The Policies of Willie Blount as Governor of Tennessee, 1809–1815," 320–22. "To the Tennessee Volunteers," December 31, 1812, in Moser and Macpherson, *Papers of Andrew Jackson*, vol. 2, 348–49 (emphasis is original). *Clarion*, December 29, 1812, and January 5, 1813.

18. James Wilkinson to Andrew Jackson, January 6, 1813, in Moser and Macpherson, *Papers of Andrew Jackson*, vol. 2, 353. According to journals kept by a young ensign named Andrew Jackson Edmondson (1793–1872), Jackson's army camped on the grounds of David McGavock's plantation, dubbing it Camp Extortion, until the end of December 1812. At that time the infantry moved to McGavock's ferry while Coffee's cavalry went a few miles south of town to form an encampment called Camp Good Exchange. On January 7, 1813, the infantry marched to Jonathan Robertson's, boarding the boats on the following evening. See Edmondson, *Journal When a Volunteer under General Andrew Jackson in 1812–1813*, 3–4 (hereafter cited as *Edmondson Journal*). Also, see "'The Departure from Nashville': A Journal of the Trip down the Mississippi," in Bassett, *Correspondence of Andrew Jackson*, 1: 256–71. The anonymous writer of the journal may have been Robert Searcy, an aide to Jackson. The poem is reprinted in its entirely from the *Nashville Whig*, February 17, 1813.

19. Rachel Jackson to Andrew Jackson, February 8, 1813, in Moser and Macpherson, *Papers of Andrew Jackson*, vol. 2, 361.

20. *Edmondson Journal*, 3. Lerner Blackman was a Methodist preacher who accompanied the flotilla as a regimental chaplain.

21. John Coffee to Mary Coffee, January 2, 1813, January 28, 1813, February 4, 1813, and February 21, 1813, in DeWitt, "Letters of General John Coffee," 267, 269–71. Also, an undated letter from John Coffee to William B. Lewis, published in the *Nashville Whig*, February 17, 1813.

22. *Edmondson Journal*, 6–7. Haynes, "Territorial Mississippi, 1798–1817," 300. Andrew Jackson to William Berkeley Lewis, February 21, 1813, and March 4, 1813; Jackson to James Wilkinson, February 16, 1813, and February 20, 1813, all in Moser and Macpherson, *Papers of Andrew Jackson*, vol. 2, 365–68; also John Armstrong to Andrew Jackson, February 6, 1813, in ibid., 361. For more on the reputation of Natchez, see Beard, "Natchez Under-the-Hill," 29–48.

23. John Coffee to Mary Coffee, February 28, 1813, in DeWitt, "Letters of General John Coffee," 271–72. *Nashville Whig*, March 3, 1813, and March 17, 1813. *Edmondson Journal*, 9 (punctuation and grammar slightly altered).

24. James Wilkinson to John Armstrong, March 9, 1813, cited in Skeen, *John Armstrong*, 157. Andrew Jackson to John Armstrong, March 15, 1813, in Moser and Macpherson, *Papers of Andrew Jackson*, vol. 2, 384. Jackson to Felix Grundy, March 15, 1813, ibid., 382. Jackson to Rachel Jackson, March 15, 1813, ibid., 387. Jackson to Willie Blount, March 15, 1813, Bassett, *Correspondence of Andrew Jackson*, 1: 295.

25. *Edmondson Journal*, 13–16. *Clarion*, April 27, 1813. Andrew Jackson to John Armstrong, April 24, 1813, Moser and Macpherson, *Papers of Andrew Jackson*, vol. 2, 404. Jackson to James Madison, March 15, 1813, Bassett, *Correspondence of Andrew Jackson*, 1: 293 (emphasis added). Most popular histories state the march back from Natchez as being the occasion for Jackson earning the nickname of "Old Hickory," but I have not been able to substantiate this claim with any certainty or documentary proof.

26. John Williams to James Madison, December 3, 1812, in Stagg, *Papers of James Madison: Presidential Series*, 5: 477–78 (emphasis is original). Smith, "Preventing the

'Eggs of Insurrection' from Hatching: The U.S. Navy and Control of the Mississippi River, 1806–1815," 87.

27. There are a number of secondary sources that ably cover the so-called Patriot War of 1812. At the top of the list are Cusick, *The Other War of 1812*; and Patrick, *Florida Fiasco*. Another key work is Kruse, "A Secret Agent in East Florida: General George Mathews and the Patriot War," 193–217. The Monroe quote is from Cusick, *The Other War of 1812*, 73.

28. (Milledgeville) *Georgia Journal*, June 2, 1812, cited in Stagg, *Mr. Madison's War*, 188. Stagg, *Papers of James Madison: Presidential Series*, 5: 478n1.

29. Frey, *Water from the Rock*, 174, 179–80. Porter, "Negroes and the East Florida Annexation Plot, 1811–1813," 9–29.

30. Unidentified "gentleman in East Tennessee" to a Nashville resident, November 16, 1812, reprinted in *Nashville Whig*, December 2, 1812. John Williams, "Fellow Citizens of East Tennessee," broadside published November 20, 1812 (Knoxville?: Wilson?, 1812).

31. John Williams provided details of the campaign in a March 25, 1813, letter to Governor Willie Blount, published in the July 20, 1813, issue of the *Nashville Whig*. Another primary source for the expedition is the "Diary Journal and Memoirs of Richard G. Waterhouse," in Layman, *Richard Green Waterhouse (1775–1827)*, 209–24. Subsequent details of the campaign are taken from these sources.

32. A February 24, 1813, letter from William Cocke to James Madison verifies the number of Seminole houses burned and places the total of captured cattle and horses at about 500 head. Cocke also enumerates 2,000 deerskins taken, along with 1,500 bushels of corn. See William Cocke to James Madison, February 24, 1813, in Kreider, *Papers of James Madison: Presidential Series*, 6: 64. A March 24, 1813 letter from Willie Blount to W. G. Blount, reprinted in the March 30, 1813, issue of the *Clarion*, indicates the East Tennessee Volunteers also captured about 300 scalps "taken off white persons of all ages."

33. Ray Clarke to Ethan Clarke, March 3, 1813 (Document RCL001), Hargrett Rare Book and Manuscript Library, University of Georgia (Athens). William Cocke to James Madison, February 24, 1813, in Kreider, *Papers of James Madison: Presidential Series*, 6: 64.

34. AC, 12th Cong., 2nd sess., 127–33. Stagg, *Papers of James Madison: Presidential Series*, 5: 577–79. George Washington Campbell to James Monroe, October 16, 1813, George Washington Campbell Correspondence 1793–1833, TSLA, Folder 23.

35. John Williams to James Madison, December 3, 1812, in Stagg, *Papers of James Madison: Presidential Series*, 5: 477. AC, 12th Cong., 2nd sess., 124. Murdoch, *The Georgia-Florida Frontier*, 4–6. For the annexation of Cuba, see W. C. C. Claiborne to Paul Hamilton, January 3, 1812, in Rowland, *Official Letter Books of W. C. C. Claiborne, 1801–1816*, 6: 27–28.

36. Brannan, *Official Letters of the Military and Naval Officers of the United States*, 31, 41.

37. Antal, *A Wampum Denied*, 99–100. Henry Clay to James Monroe, September 21, 1812, in Hopkins, *Papers of Henry Clay*, 1: 728. Thomas Jefferson to James Madison,

November 6, 1812, in Smith, *The Republic of Letters*, 1707. (Baltimore) *Niles' Weekly Register*, September 19, 1812. James Monroe to Thomas Jefferson, August 31, 1812, in Lucier, *Political Writings of James Monroe*, 444. *Nashville Whig*, September 16, 1812.

38. Durham, *James Winchester*, 117–20, 128–31. Skeen, *Citizen Soldiers*, 48, 58–59. For an analysis of the rivalry between Winchester and Harrison, see Skaggs, "The Making of a Major General: William Henry Harrison and the Politics of Command, 1812–13," esp. 39–47. Darnell, *A Journal*, 14. Thomas Eastland to James Winchester, October 22, 1812, James Winchester Papers, TSLA, Box 1, Folder 5. Antal, *A Wampum Denied*, 133–34.

39. Durham, *James Winchester*, 134–51. John Stites to Alexander A. Meek, January 25, 1813, in "Selections from the Gano Papers, III," 33.

40. John Coffee to Mary Coffee, March 8, 1813, in DeWitt, "Letters of General John Coffee," 273. By successfully resisting the Americans, the Canadians established their own legacy of liberation. See Taylor, *The Civil War of 1812*.

Chapter 3

1. *Clarion*, September 14, 1813. The term *Red Sticks* derives from the Creek sticks or clubs, painted red—the symbolic color of war.

2. Gallay, *The Indian Slave Trade*, 17–18, 139–40. Unser, *Indians, Settlers, and Slaves*, 99. Frank, *Creeks and Southerners*, chap. 1.

3. See, for instance, Braund, *Deerskins and Duffels*; Saunt, *A New Order of Things*; Ethridge, *Creek Country*; and Hahn, *The Invention of the Creek Nation*.

4. Hahn, "The Mother of Necessity: Carolina, the Creek Indians, and the Making of a New Order in the American Southeast, 1670–1763," 79–114. Piker, "Colonists and Creeks: Rethinking the Pre-Revolutionary Southern Backcountry," 503–40. Braund, *Deerskins and Duffels*, 121–27, 184–86. Wesson, *Households and Hegemony*; Unser, *Indians, Settlers, and Slaves*, 95. Saunt, "'Domestick . . . Quiet Being Broke': Gender Conflict among Creek Indians in the Eighteenth Century," 151–74. Ethridge, *Creek Country*. Saunt, *New Order of Things*. Martin, "Cultural Hermeneutics on the Frontier," 273–74.

5. Braund, *Deerskins and Duffels*, 170–80. William Patton to Gayoso de Lemos, May 22, 1798, in Corbitt, "Papers Relating to the Georgia-Florida Frontier, 1784–1800, XVII," 380. For an examination of Hawkins's public life, see Pound, *Benjamin Hawkins*.

6. Bast, "Creek Indian Affairs, 1775–1778," 1–25. O'Donnell, *Southern Indians in the American Revolution*, 129–31. Stiggins, *Creek Indian History*, 78–79, 86–87. Cutler, *Topographical Description of the State of Ohio, Indiana Territory, and Louisiana*, 215. Barber, "Council Government and the Genesis of the Creek War," 163–74.

7. Edmunds, *Tecumseh and the Quest for Indian Leadership*, 28–29, 146–53. Martin, "Cultural Hermeneutics on the Frontier," 288–90. Peeler, "The Policies of Willie Blount as Governor of Tennessee, 1809–1815," 316. Moore, "Farm Communities and Economic Growth in the Lower Tennessee Valley," 87. There had been rumors in the spring of 1812 that Tecumseh had set up a village consisting of three hundred war-

riors on the Sandy River in West Tennessee. See *Clarion*, April 14, 1812, and May 19, 1812.

8. For background to Humphreys County, see Moore, "Farm Communities and Economic Growth in the Lower Tennessee Valley," 72, 77, 85–86. The Crawley incident first appeared in a newspaper known as the (Nashville) *Tennessee Herald* (date unknown) and was reprinted in many newspapers across the nation. The account can be found in the June 13, 1812, edition of the (Baltimore) *Niles' Weekly Register*. The report was based on an affidavit from a Williamson County resident, John Bennett, who was in the vicinity of the Duck River at the time. He got the story from those claiming to have obtained the details from Mrs. Manley, shortly before she died (*Clarion*, May 23, 1812, and *Wilson's Knoxville Gazette*, May 25, 1812). Other sources, who claim they spoke to Martha Crawley after she escaped her Creek captors, provided further—if not conflicting—details of the incident. For instance, some say the incident took place at the Crawley, not the Manley, home, and there were eleven attacking Indians, not five. See William Henry to John J. Henry, June 26, 1812, included in a letter from Willie Blount to William Eustis, July 26, 1812, in ASPIA, 1: 814. Also, see "Extract of a Letter to the Editor of the 'Enquirer' from West Tennessee, Dated July 13th," in *Raleigh Register, and North-Carolina Gazette*, September 4, 1812. Martha Crawley gave a deposition on August 11, 1812, detailing her abduction, captivity, and subsequent escape from the Creeks. The deposition can be found in Bassett, *Correspondence of Andrew Jackson*, 1: 225–26n1. Twenty years after the event, pieces of the puzzle were still being gathered; see, for instance, the Petition of Jesse Manly to Committee of Claims, April 9, 1834, House of Representatives Report 402, 23rd Cong., 1st sess., series 262. The account in the next paragraph is an amalgamation of all these sources.

9. Thomas Johnson to John Hutchinson, May 17, 1812, published in *Clarion*, May 23, 1812. Thomas Johnson to Andrew Jackson, May 27, 1812, in Moser and Macpherson, *Papers of Andrew Jackson*, vol. 2, 298–99. *Wilson's Knoxville Gazette*, June 15, 1812.

10. Andrew Jackson to Willie Blount, in Bassett, *Correspondence of Andrew Jackson*, 1: 226. Peeler, "The Policies of Willie Blount as Governor of Tennessee, 1809–1815," 317; Jackson to Blount, July 3, 1812, in Moser and Macpherson, *Papers of Andrew Jackson*, vol. 2, 307–8. John Pitchlynn to James Robertson, August 2, 1812, James Robertson Papers, 1784–1814, TSLA, Box 3, Folder 14. Record Group 60, Legislative Materials, Reports, Receipts, Rejected Bills, etc., 1796–1865, TSLA, Box 10, Folder 40.

11. *Niles' Weekly Register*, June 13, 1812. *Clarion*, June 30, 1812. For more examples on how the Crawley incident provided propaganda, see my article "The Kidnapping of Martha Crawley and Settler-Indian Relations Prior to the War of 1812," 3–23.

12. Andrew Jackson to Willie Blount, July 3, 1812, and July 8, 1812, in Moser and Macpherson, *Papers of Andrew Jackson*, vol. 2, 307–8, 312. Jackson to Blount, July 10, 1812, in Bassett, *Correspondence of Andrew Jackson*, 1: 230–32. Blount to Jackson, July 12, 1812, Papers of Andrew Jackson, LC, 1st series, reel 5.

13. Andrew Jackson to George Colbert, June 5, 1812, in Moser and Macpherson, *Papers of Andrew Jackson*, vol. 2, 302–3. (Philadelphia) *Aurora General Advertiser*, July 2, 1812.

14. *Clarion*, June 30, 1812, and September 1, 1812. Ferdinand L. Claiborne to James

Caller, June 23, 1812, James Caller Papers (SPR554), Alabama Department of Archives and History (Montgomery), Folder 9.

15. *Clarion*, September 19, 1812.

16. *Journal of the Senate, at the Second Session of the Ninth General Assembly of the State of Tennessee... One Thousand Eight Hundred and Twelve*, 72–73. RG 60, Legislative Materials, TSLA, Box 11, Folder 2. Willie Blount to William Eustis, October 14, 1812, in Peeler, "The Policies of Willie Blount as Governor of Tennessee, 1809–1815," 318.

17. Unser, "American Indians on the Cotton Frontier: Changing Economic Relations with Citizens and Slaves in the Mississippi," 297–98, 314–15. Martin, "Cultural Hermeneutics on the Frontier," 358–59. Davis, "'Remembering Fort Mims': Reinterpreting the Origins of the Creek Civil War," 611–36.

18. Benjamin Hawkins informed the Creek chiefs of the atrocity in a March 29, 1813, letter. He received the news from James Robertson in a communication dated March 5, 1813. Hawkins addressed the Creek chiefs through a March 25, 1813, letter to Alexander Cornells, assistant agent and interpreter of the Upper Creeks. Both of Hawkins's letters can be found in the ASPIA, 1: 839.

19. Big Warrior and William McIntosh to Benjamin Hawkins, April 26, 1813; Alexander Cornells to Hawkins, June 22, 1813; and Hawkins to Peter McQueen, July 6, 1813, all in ASPIA, 1: 841, 846, 848. For more on the religious aspects of the Creek War, see Martin, *Sacred Revolt*. Martin sees the Red Stick movement as a rejection of dependence on Europeans/Americans by returning to the sacred rituals, myths, and values of traditional Creek culture.

20. Letter from Johann Christian Burckhard, dated July 4, 1813, cited in Mauelshagen and Davis, *Partners in the Lord's Work*, 76. Robert William Pierce and John Pierce to Harry Toulmin, July 18, 1813, cited in Lackey and Guice, *Claims Filed by Citizens*, 9–11. *Carthage Gazette*, August 6, 1813. Harry Toulmin to James Madison, August 13, 1813, in Kreider, *Papers of James Madison: Presidential Series*, 6: 520–23. *Nashville Whig*, August 18, 1813. Waselkov, *A Conquering Spirit*, 102–6. Also, see Lengel, "The Road to Fort Mims: Judge Harry Toulmin's Observations on the Creek War, 1811–1813," 16–36.

21. For rumors of a joint British/Spanish attack, see Rowland, *Andrew Jackson's Campaign against the British*, 67n2. "A Prelude to the Creek War of 1813–1814 in a Letter of John Innerarity to James Innerarity," 249–60. For details of the Battle of Burnt Corn, consult Halbert and Ball, *The Creek War of 1813 and 1814*, 125–42; and Waselkov, *A Conquering Spirit*, 98–102.

22. John Armstrong to Willie Blount, July 13, 1813; Blount to Armstrong, July 30, 1813; James P. Leary to James Madison, August 11, 1813; Madison to Daniel Parker, August 18, 1813; Parker to Blount, August 20, 1813; James Monroe to Madison, August 31, 1813, all in Kreider, *Papers of James Madison: Presidential Series*, 6: 539, 539n2, 547n3, 580. Brigadier General Thomas Flourney of the Seventh Military District (Louisiana, Tennessee, and Mississippi Territory) was passed over because, technically, Andrew Jackson (as Major General of the Tennessee Militia) outranked him. The choice of Major General Thomas Pinckney of the Sixth District (Georgia and

the Carolinas) outraged Flourney, who asked to be relieved of his command. See Skeen, *John Armstrong*, 173, 176.

23. Waselkov and Wood, "The Creek War of 1813–1814: Effects on Creek Society and Settlement Pattern," 8–14. Stiggins, *Creek Indian History*, 75, 107–14. Waselkov, *A Conquering Spirit*, 116–35, 142–44. Claiborne, *Supplement to the Mississippi Republican, 25 March 1814*. Watkins, "The Mississippi Panic of 1813," 483–91. Isaac Conger Diary, 1813, TSLA. *Nashville Whig*, September 7, 1813. Peter Perkins to Willie Blount, September 23, 1813, reprinted in ibid., September 29, 1813. After the assault on Fort Mims, the Red Sticks never made another concerted major attack on white settlements; instead, they conducted guerrilla-type raids in the Tensaw region. See Waselkov, *A Conquering Spirit*, 160–62. Waselkov also points out that fears of a slave uprising erupted throughout the territory in the wake of the Mims massacre, with many Anglo-Americans believing slaves would escape to aid the Red Sticks. See Waselkov, *A Conquering Spirit*, 147–49.

24. My account of the meeting and subsequent actions is based on two sources: the September 19, 1813, issue of the *Nashville Whig* and a September 12, 1844, letter from William Martin (one of the participants) to Lyman Draper, as found in the Lyman Copeland Draper Manuscript Collection, Wisconsin Historical Society (Madison) (hereafter cited as Draper Papers), 3XX31.

25. *Acts Passed at the First Session of the Tenth General Assembly of the State of Tennessee . . . One Thousand Eight Hundred and Thirteen*, 3–4. Record Group 60, Legislative Materials, TSLA, Box 23, Folder 1. Skeen, *John Armstrong*, 156–57. J. C. Isacks to "the citizens of Franklin and Warren counties," November 10, 1813, reprinted in *Nashville Whig*, November 9, 1813. Brigade Orders of September 26, 1813, Brig. Gen. Isaac Roberts, Creek War Papers, TSLA. Andrew Jackson to Willie Blount, January 2, 1814, in Moser et al., *Papers of Andrew Jackson*, vol. 3, *1814–1815*, 5 (hereafter Moser et al., *Papers of Andrew Jackson*, vol. 3). Harrison quoted in Jortner, *The Gods of Prophetstown*, 183.

26. Skeen, *Citizen Soldiers*, 65–70. Harry Toulmin to David Holmes, August 27, 1813, in Doster, "Letters Relating to the Tragedy of Fort Mims: August–September, 1813," 280.

27. (Washington, DC) *Daily National Intelligencer*, October 12, 1813. *Clarion*, November 2, 1813. George Washington Campbell to James Monroe, November 12, 1813, James Monroe Papers (microfilm edition), LC, 1st series, reel 5.

28. Thomas Flourney to James Madison, October 6, 1813, in Kreider, *Papers of James Madison: Presidential Series*, 6: 676–78. Hall, "The Red Stick War: Creek Indian Affairs during the War of 1812," 282. *Nashville Whig*, September 21, 1813. Andrew Jackson to John Coffee, September 29, 1813, in Moser and Macpherson, *Papers of Andrew Jackson*, vol. 2, 431–32. The genesis of the Benton/Jackson feud began when Jackson acted as a second for his young friend, William Carroll, who fought a duel in mid-June 1813 with Thomas Benton's brother, Jesse. The duel resulted in minor injuries: Carroll was shot in his left thumb, while Benton received a wound in his buttocks. Thomas Hart Benton, incensed that Jackson would involve himself in the proceedings, began a war of words against Jackson. According to a circular written by

Thomas Benton on September 10, 1813, the feud escalated into the September 4 incident when Jackson and some of his friends came to the inn where Thomas and Jesse Benton were staying. Jackson approached Thomas with a drawn pistol and Jesse fired at Jackson when the latter got within eight or ten feet of Thomas. Four other pistols were fired in quick succession—one by Jackson at Benton, two by Benton at Jackson, and one by John Coffee at Thomas Benton—but Jackson was the only one hit. Then daggers were drawn. Coffee and Alexander Donelson came at Thomas, giving him five slight wounds. Captain Eli Hammond and Stokley Hays went after Jesse, who tried to stave off his attackers with his bare hands while Hays tried to stab him and Hammond beat him on the head. Jesse managed to get his pistol out to shoot Hays but the gun misfired. See THS Miscellaneous Files 1688–1951, Box 1, B-107. For the Benton/Carroll duel, see Jacob McGavock to James McGavock, June 14, 1813, in Gower and Allen, *Pen and Sword: The Life and Journals of Randal W. McGavock*, 23.

29. Pension File of Mary Patrick (WC-34953), Record Group 15, Records of Veterans Administration, NARA. Journal of Governor Richard K. Call, Florida Historical Society Library (Cocoa), 17. Memoirs of James Norman Smith, 1789–1860, 4 vols., University of Texas Library (Austin), 2:15–16. Crockett, *A Narrative of the Life of David Crockett*, 72–73. William Woods to James Madison, August 10, 1812, in Stagg, *Papers of James Madison: Presidential Series*, 5: 137–39.

30. John Coffee to Andrew Jackson, October 22, 1813, in Moser and Macpherson, *Papers of Andrew Jackson*, vol. 2, 438. John Coffee to Mary Coffee, October 24, 1813, and October 25, 1813, in DeWitt, "Letters of General John Coffee," 275–76. For rumors of Creek attacks, see John Reid Journal, 1802–13, TSLA.

31. John Cocke Letter, MS-731, Special Collections Library, University of Tennessee (Knoxville). Andrew Jackson to John Cocke, September 28, 1813, cited in *Library of Congress Acquisitions*, 7–8. *Nashville Whig*, October 13, 1813.

32. Information taken from McCown, "The 'J. Hartsell Memora': The Journal of a Tennessee Captain in the War of 1812," 118–46 (hereafter cited as "J. Hartsell Memora").

33. *Edmondson Journal*, 27. "Sketch of William Trousdale as Told By Himself," in William Trousdale Papers 1828–1940, THS, Box 3, Folder 6, p. 1.

34. Andrew Jackson to David Holmes, October 17, 1813, in Rowland, *Andrew Jackson's Campaign against the British*, 128. "Order Book of General John Coffee—Creek War 1813–14," typescript copy, Coffee Vertical File, TSLA.

35. "Order Book of General John Coffee—Creek War 1813–14," typescript copy, Coffee Vertical File, TSLA; and Jackson's address to his troops, October 24, 1813, in Bassett, *Correspondence of Andrew Jackson*, 1: 315–17.

36. Andrew Jackson to residents of Madison County, October 23, 1813, in Bassett, *Correspondence of Andrew Jackson*, 1: 335–36. John Reid to William B. Lewis, October 24, 1813, THS Miscellaneous Files, Box 9, L-48 1/2. Also, see Jackson to Thomas Flourney, October 24, 1813, in Moser and Macpherson, *Papers of Andrew Jackson*, vol. 2, 441.

37. Andrew Jackson to Willie Blount, October 28, 1813, in Moser and Macpherson, *Papers of Andrew Jackson*, vol. 2, 442–43. Andrew Jackson to John Coffee, November 2, 1813, Papers of Andrew Jackson, LC, 1st series, reel 7.

38. Alexander Donelson Jr. to John Donelson, November 5, 1813, THS Miscellaneous Files, Box 4, D-72. Claiborne, *Notes on the War in the South*, 30. Crockett, *Narrative of the Life of David Crockett*, 88–89. Casualty figures taken from a November 12, 1813, letter from John Coffee to Mary Coffee, cited in DeWitt, "Letters of General John Coffee," 277; and Andrew Jackson to James White, November 4, 1813, John Cocke Papers, 1774–1851, TSLA. According to a November 4, 1813, letter from Andrew Jackson to Leroy Pope, forty of the eighty prisoners Coffee's men took were sent to Huntsville. See Bassett, *Correspondence of Andrew Jackson*, 1: 341.

39. John Reid Journal, TSLA. Crockett, *Narrative of the Life of David Crockett*, 89–90. Journal of Richard K. Call, 23. *Edmondson Journal*, 21. Burke, *David Crockett*, 83.

40. *Nashville Whig*, November 9, 1813 (emphasis is original). *Wilson's Knoxville Gazette*, November 15, 1813. "J. Hartsell Memora," 11: 101. Andrew Jackson to Willie Blount, November 4, 1813, in Bassett, *Correspondence of Andrew Jackson*, 1: 341.

41. Andrew Jackson to Willie Blount, November 15, 1813, in Bassett, *Correspondence of Andrew Jackson*, 1: 348. William Priestly, "A Short Sketch of the Creek War," TSLA. Journal of Richard K. Call, 20. *Nashville Whig*, November 24, 1813. A "6-pound" cannon was an indication it shot cannonballs weighing 6 pounds. Thus a 32-pound cannon, for instance, shot balls weighing 32 pounds.

42. Andrew Jackson to Willie Blount, November 15, 1813, in Bassett, *Correspondence of Andrew Jackson*, 1: 348–49.

43. Ibid., 349. Journal of Richard K. Call, 24. Priestly, "A Short Sketch of the Creek War." *Edmondson Journal*, 22–23. Samuel Bains to Christina Bains, November 12, 1813, Samuel Bains Letters, Manuscript Division, Western Kentucky University (Bowling Green). An illustration of the order of battle at Talladega can be found in the December 14, 1813, issue of the *Clarion*.

44. Genealogical Data, McEwen Family, TSLA, Box 33. Andrew Jackson to Willie Blount, November 15, 1813, in Bassett, *Correspondence of Andrew Jackson*, 1: 349–50. Jackson to Thomas Pinckney, February 17, 1814, in ibid., 465. In 1845, William Martin challenged Jackson's official account of the Battle of Talladega, calling it "much exaggerated." Martin claimed there were about 650 Creeks (not 1,080), and although the official count of the Indian dead was 299, it was the opinion of Martin and others at the time that not more than 150 were killed. He estimated the Tennessee forces at 2,000, with 800 of these mounted. See William Martin to Lyman Draper, September 5, 1845, Draper Papers, 3XX43. John Coffee, in line with Jackson, placed the Creek force at 1,000, while the Tennesseans were double that number. See his November 12, 1813, letter to his wife in DeWitt, "Letters of General John Coffee," 277–78.

45. John Coffee to John Donelson, November 12, 1813, THS Miscellaneous Files, Box 3, C-115. L. D. Hays to Robert Hays, November 11, 1813, Papers of Andrew Jackson, LC, 6th series, reel 71. John McKee to Andrew Jackson, January 6, 1814, ibid., 1st series, reel 8.

46. L. D. Hays to Robert Hays, November 11, 1813, Papers of Andrew Jackson, LC, 6th series, reel 71. *Nashville Whig*, November 9, 1813. "J. Hartsell Memora," 12: 126. *Clarion*, November 23, 1813. *Edmondson's Journal*, 24. William Martin and H. L.

Douglass, November 14, 1813, in Bassett, *Correspondence of Andrew Jackson*, 1: 346–47. Andrew Jackson Edmondson related that he never had to resort to eating raw hides, as there were usually beechnuts and acorns to eat. Although some men did eat hides, Edmondson felt they did it just so they could talk about it afterward. See *Edmondson Journal*, 24.

47. James White to John Cocke, November 7, 1813, John Cocke Papers, TSLA. Cocke to White, November 6, 1813, in Bassett, *Correspondence of Andrew Jackson*, 1: 342n2.

48. Gatschet, "Towns and Villages of the Creek Confederacy in the XVIII and XIX Centuries," 397. Robert Grierson to Andrew Jackson, November 13, 1813, in Moser and Macpherson, *Papers of Andrew Jackson*, vol. 2, 451–52. Jackson to Grierson, November 17, 1813, in ibid., 456–57. Jackson to John Cocke, November 18, 1813, in ibid., 457–58.

49. James White to John Cocke, November 24, 1813, reprinted in *Nashville Whig*, December 21, 1813. *Clarion*, December 21, 1813.

50. Gideon Morgan to Return J. Meigs, November 23, 1813, Gideon Morgan Papers, 1813–1826, TSLA.

51. Kanon, "'Glories in the Field': John Cocke vs. Andrew Jackson during the War of 1812," 53–54n8.

52. Brannon, "Journal of James A. Tait for the Year 1813," 234–35. *Nashville Whig*, November 9, 1813. Also, see Waselkov, *A Conquering Spirit*, 168–70.

Chapter 4

1. Andrew Jackson to John Cocke, December 6, 1813, in Moser and Macpherson, *Papers of Andrew Jackson*, vol. 2, 469. Willie Blount to Andrew Jackson, December 7, 1813, John Cocke Papers, TSLA.

2. Andrew Jackson to Willie Blount, November 14, 1813, in Moser and Macpherson, *Papers of Andrew Jackson*, vol. 2, 454. A similar situation in East Tennessee is reflected in a letter from Thomas Brown of Kingston, Tennessee, to George Washington Campbell, dated December 25, 1813, suggesting a draft be initiated in East Tennessee "for I think the volunteering is mostly over here for awhile." George Washington Campbell Correspondence, 1793–1833, TSLA, Folder 4.

3. Andrew Jackson to William Martin, December 4, 1813, in Bassett, *Correspondence of Andrew Jackson*, 1: 370–73; also, see "To Platoon Officers of Volunteers," December 8, 1813, in ibid., 376–77. Samuel Bains to Christina Bains, December 17, 1813, Samuel Bains Letters, Manuscripts Division, Western Kentucky University (Bowling Green); also, same to same, November 25, 1813, "Samuel Bains Letter," 406.

4. Andrew Jackson to Rachel Jackson, December 9, 1813, in Moser and Macpherson, *Papers of Andrew Jackson*, vol. 2, 478; also, same to same, December 14, 1813, in ibid., 486. Jackson to Abel Willis, February 2, 1814, Papers of Andrew Jackson, LC, 1st series, reel 61. Bassett, *Correspondence of Andrew Jackson*, 1: 382–83n1. Andrew Jackson to Rachel Jackson, December 29, 1813, in Moser and Macpherson, *Papers of Andrew Jackson*, vol. 2, 515.

5. Andrew Jackson to John Coffee, December 9, 1813, in Bassett, *Correspondence*

of Andrew Jackson, 1: 378; and same to same, in ibid., 391. Peter Perkins to Andrew Jackson, December 16, 1813, in ibid., 395.

6. Andrew Jackson to John Coffee, December 12, 1813, in ibid., 387; and same to same, December 13, 1813, in ibid., 390.

7. "J. Hartsell Memora," 12: 126–27, 131.

8. Andrew Jackson to Rachel Jackson, December 19, 1813, in Bassett, *Correspondence of Andrew Jackson*, 1: 400. John Coffee to John Donelson, December 22, 1813, THS Miscellaneous Files, Box 3, C-116.

9. Willie Blount to Andrew Jackson, December 7, 1813, ibid., Box 2, B-164. Blount to John Armstrong, December 10, 1813, ibid., Box 2, B-165. Armstrong to Blount, January 3, 1814, ibid., Box 1, A-33. Willie Blount to Andrew Jackson, December 15, 1813, and Jackson to William Hall, December 23, 1813, ibid., Box 2, B-166.

10. Akers, "The Unexpected Challenge: The Creek War of 1813–1814," 167–77. Neal Smith to James Smylie, January 8, 1814, published in *Alabama Historical Reporter* 1 (July 1880): 2–3. Halbert and Ball, *The Creek War of 1813 and 1814*, 246–58. Kanon, "Battle of Econochaca," 1: 212.

11. Andrew Jackson to Willie Blount, December 29, 1813, in Bassett, *Correspondence of Andrew Jackson*, 1: 416–20.

12. Abernathy, *A Memento*, 4–5. "J. Hartsell Memora," 12: 135–36. Andrew Jackson to William B. Lewis, February 21, 1814, "Letters and Papers of Andrew Jackson, Part I," 157.

13. *Nashville Whig*, December 14, 1813. William Carroll to Andrew Jackson, December 15, 1813, Papers of Andrew Jackson, LC, 1st series, reel 7. William Carroll to Andrew Jackson, December 29, 1813, ibid., 1st series, reel 8. John Coffee to Andrew Jackson, December 20, 1813, in Bassett, *Correspondence of Andrew Jackson*, 1: 401. John Coffee to Mary Coffee, January 8, 1814, in DeWitt, "Letters of General John Coffee," 280.

14. Andrew Jackson to John Coffee, December 27, 1813, in Bassett, *Correspondence of Andrew Jackson*, 1: 412–13. Coffee to Jackson, December 28, 1813, and same to same, December 29, 1813, Papers of Andrew Jackson, LC, 1st series, reel 8. John Coffee to Mary Coffee, January 8, 1814, in DeWitt, "Letters of General John Coffee," 280. *Nashville Whig*, February 22, 1814.

15. William Hawes to Andrew Jackson, January 7, 1814, Papers of Andrew Jackson, LC, 1st series, reel 8. Andrew Jackson to Thomas Pinckney, February 26, 1814, ibid., 3rd series, reel 62. Jackson address to troops, January 13, 1814, ibid., 3rd series, reel 62.

16. Journal of Richard K. Call, 61–62. The following account of the battle at Emuckfau is based chiefly on Call's journal (61–65); Andrew Jackson's official report to Thomas Pinckney, dated January 29, 1814, in Bassett, *Correspondence of Andrew Jackson*, 1: 448–51; and a January 29, 1814, letter from Ephraim Foster to his father, R. C. Foster, in Ephraim Hubbard Foster Papers, 1814–20, TSLA.

17. Details of the battle at Enitachopco are derived from Jackson's official report of January 29, 1814, to Thomas Pinckney, in Bassett, *Correspondence of Andrew Jackson*, 1: 451–53; Jackson's January 28, 1814, letter to his wife, Rachel, in Moser et al., *Papers of Andrew Jackson*, vol. 3, 19–20; Journal of Richard K. Call, 66–69; Priestly, "A

Short Sketch of the Creek War," TSLA; John Reid's February 14, 1813, letter to his father, in Papers of John Reid, 1802–16, LC; Ephraim Foster to R. C. Foster, January 29, 1814, Ephraim Hubbard Foster Papers, TSLA; and Narrative of Jesse Cox, TSLA, 5.

18. John Coffee to John Donelson, January 28, 1814, THS Miscellaneous Files, Box 4, D-73. Coffee to Mary Coffee, January 30, 1814, in DeWitt, "Letters of General John Coffee," 280–81. Andrew Jackson to Rachel Jackson, January 28, 1814, in Moser et al., *Papers of Andrew Jackson*, vol. 3, 19; and Rachel to Andrew, February 10, 1814, in ibid., 28.

19. Andrew Jackson to Rachel Jackson, January 28, 1814, in Moser et al., *Papers of Andrew Jackson*, vol. 3, 19–20. For details of the court-martial, see *Nashville Whig*, February 23, 1814, and the *Clarion*, March 15, 1814.

20. Elting, *Amateurs, to Arms*, 170n17. Andrew Jackson to Rachel Jackson, January 28, 1814, in Moser et al., *Papers of Andrew Jackson*, vol. 3, 19–20. Andrew Jackson to William Carroll, February 17, 1814, in ibid., 31.

21. Andrew Jackson to Thomas Pinckney, February 16, 1814, Papers of Andrew Jackson, LC, 3rd series, reel 62. Andrew Jackson to Rachel Jackson, March 4, 1814, in Craven, "Letters of Andrew Jackson," 116. William Cocke to Andrew Jackson, January 28, 1814, Cromwell Tidwell Collection, 1794–1976, THS, Box 12, Folder 16. George Doherty to Andrew Jackson, March 6, 1814, Papers of Andrew Jackson, LC, 1st series, reel 9. Also, see James Baxter to Andrew Jackson, February 22, 1814, in Bassett, *Correspondence of Andrew Jackson*, 1: 474n2.

22. *Clarion*, February 15, 1814, and March 1, 1814. Andrew Jackson to William B. Lewis, February 21, 1814, in "Letters and Papers of Andrew Jackson, Part I," 157. Also, see Jackson to Thomas Pinckney, February 17, 1814, in Bassett, *Correspondence of Andrew Jackson*, 1: 466.

23. Andrew Jackson to J. A. Smith, October 4, 1815, Papers of Andrew Jackson, LC, 3rd series, reel 62. Jackson to Robert Steele, March 22, 1814, ibid., 1st series, reel 9. Jackson to Leroy Pope and John Brahan, March 22, 1814, in Bassett, *Correspondence of Andrew Jackson*, 1: 484–86. Thomas Pinckney to Andrew Jackson, February 17, 1814, in ibid., 466–67.

24. Thomas Johnson to Richard Napier, February 5, 1814, and same to same, February 7, 1814, Papers of Andrew Jackson, LC, 1st series, reel 8. William Carroll to Andrew Jackson, February 16, 1814, ibid., 1st series, reel 9 (emphasis is original). Jackson to Robert Steele, May 22, 1814, ibid., 1st series, reel 9.

25. Andrew Jackson to John Cocke, December 28, 1813, in Moser and Macpherson, *Papers of Andrew Jackson*, vol. 2, 511. Return J. Meigs to John Armstrong, May 5, 1814, in Papers of Andrew Jackson, LC, 1st series, reel 10. Malone, "Cherokee-White Relations on the Southern Frontier in the Early Nineteenth Century," 9–10, 10n16. For more on the Cherokee participation in the Creek War, see Abram, "Cherokees in the Creek War: A Band of Brothers," 122–45. Ironically, some of the Cherokee leaders that fought *with* the Tennesseans in the Creek War, such as Major Ridge, were the same Cherokees who fought against Tennessee settlers in the early Indian wars.

26. Gideon Morgan to Andrew Jackson, February 27, 1814, in Papers of Andrew

Jackson, LC, 1st series, reel 9. John Ross to Return J. Meigs, March 2, 1814, in Moulton, *Papers of Chief John Ross*, 1: 19. Casualty Report, April 1814, in ibid., 20–21.

27. "General Orders, Case of John Woods," March 12, 1814, in Bassett, *Correspondence of Andrew Jackson*, 1: 479. Andrew Jackson to Thomas Pinckney, March 14, 1814, in ibid., 481.

28. Alexander McCulloch to Frances McCulloch, March 17, 1814, Ben and Henry Eustace McCulloch Family Papers, 1798–1961, Center for American History, University of Texas at Austin (hereafter cited as McCulloch Family Papers). Abernathy, *A Memento*, 5. Andrew Jackson to Robert Steele, Papers of Andrew Jackson, LC, 1st series, reel 9.

29. Jackson's orders of March 22 and 24, 1814, and Johnson's report of March 23, 1814, all in Papers of Andrew Jackson, LC, 1st series, reel 9.

30. Jackson's General Orders, March 23, 1814, in Bassett, *Correspondence of Andrew Jackson*, 1: 486–88. "Order Book of General John Coffee—Creek War 1813–14," typescript copy, Coffee Vertical File, TSLA.

31. Andrew Jackson to Willie Blount, March 31, 1814, in Bassett, *Correspondence of Andrew Jackson*, 1: 490. Jackson to Thomas Pinckney, March 28, 1814, ibid., 489. Jackson to James Baxter, April 1, 1814, Papers of Andrew Jackson, LC, 1st series, reel 9. For a detailed description of the Creek breastworks, see Waselkov, "A Reinterpretation of the Creek Indian Barricade at Horseshoe Bend," 94–107.

32. My account of the battle comes from a variety of primary sources: Jackson's official report to Governor Willie Blount, dated March 31, 1814, as found in Bassett, *Correspondence of Andrew Jackson*, 1: 489–92; John Coffee's report of April 1, 1814, in Moser et al., *Papers of Andrew Jackson*, vol. 3, 56; John Coffee's April 1, 1814, letter to his wife, located in DeWitt, "Letters of General John Coffee," 282–83; Coffee's April 1, 1814, letter to John Donelson, THS Miscellaneous Files, Box 3, C-118; John Reid's April 1, 1814, letter to his wife, in the Papers of John Reid; Alexander McCulloch's letter to his wife, dated April 1, 1814, in McCulloch Family Papers; Day and Ullom, *Autobiography of Sam Houston*, 11–14; various recollections from the Lyman Copeland Draper Manuscript Collection, Wisconsin Historical Society (Madison), 30S324–326, 10YY56–57, and 10YY101; War of 1812 Pension Files, RG 15, Records of Veteran's Administration, NARA, Old War WF #12736, Old War IF #317, Old War IF #20884, and Old War IF #149; and other various accounts, including letters from William Carroll, Gideon Morgan, and John Reid, as published in the Nashville *Clarion*, April 12, 1814. For more details of the battle than are provided in this chapter, see Kanon, "'A Slow, Laborious Slaughter': The Battle of Horseshoe Bend," 3–15.

33. For the Creek punishment of theft, see Mauelshagen and Davis, *Partners in the Lord's Work*, 70. Jackson, in his report to Governor Blount, indicates he ordered "officers of great responsibility" to conduct a body count, but does not mention the method. Halbert and Ball claim an aged man from Neshoba County, Mississippi, was the source of the story for their book on the Creek War. See Halbert and Ball, *Creek War of 1813 and 1814*, 277.

34. When Jackson ran for the office of president in 1828, opponents dredged up incidents such as this and the execution of John Woods to portray Jackson in an unfavorable light. See, for example, "A Review of the Battle of the Horseshoe." This 1828

pamphlet claims Jackson had the sixteen Creeks shot, but it is likely Jackson did not actually participate in the action that morning and was not sure himself what happened. For Wright's story, see (Memphis) *Weekly Public Ledger*, September 11, 1883.

35. The remains of Lemuel Montgomery's body were removed to a cemetery located in Dudleyville, Alabama, in 1839 and returned to Horseshoe Bend in 1972. See Montgomery Vertical File, TSLA. Benjamin Cloud, Widow's File 12736, RG15, Veterans Administration, NARA.

36. John Coffee to Mary Coffee, April 1, 1814, April 2, 1814, and April 6, 1814, in DeWitt, "Letters of General John Coffee," 283–84. Also, see Daniel Bradford to William H. Harrison, April 5, 1814, William H. Harrison Papers, LC, 1st series, reel 2. Gregory Waselkov is correct in pointing out that the Battle of Horseshoe Bend did not end the Creek War but, rather, ended the fighting in the Creek Nation. Following the debacle at Tohopeka, approximately 1,700 Creek refugees made their way into West Florida, where they hoped to be resupplied with food and ammunition. The Thirty-Ninth US Infantry, along with Colonel George Nixon's Mississippi Territory volunteers, searched the Escambia River for Red Sticks in July 1814. At the same time, Colonel Joseph Carson's Mississippi dragoons attacked a Red Stick settlement near Pensacola called Coneta, where they killed all the Indians they could find. See Waselkov, "Fort Jackson and the Aftermath," 162–63, 167.

37. "John Rhea, of Tennessee, to His Constituents," 5. Isaac Shelby to William Henry Harrison, in Clanin, *Papers of William Henry Harrison, 1800–1815*, microfilm edition, reel #10, frames 104–5. (St. Louis) *Missouri Gazette*, May 28, 1814, in Jones, *William Clark and the Shaping of the West*, 218.

38. Waselkov and Wood, "The Creek of 1813–1814: Effects on Creek Society and Settlement Pattern," 10. Andrew Jackson to Rachel Jackson, July 16, 1814, and August 10, 1814, in Moser et al., *Papers of Andrew Jackson*, vol. 3, 89, 114.

39. John Coffee to John Donelson, April 25, 1814, THS Miscellaneous Files, Box 3, C-121. *Clarion*, June 14, 1814, June 28, 1814, and July 12, 1814.

40. George Strother Gaines to James Gaines, June 11, 1814, in Owen, "Letters from George Strother Gaines Relating to Events in South Alabama, 1805–1814," 189–90. *Nashville Whig*, May 17, 1814, May 24, 1814, and May 31, 1814 (Jackson's remarks taken from the May 17 issue).

41. George Strother Gaines to James Gaines, February 8, 1814, in Owen, "Letters from George Strother Gaines Relating to Events in South Alabama, 1805–1814," 189. *Clarion*, May 3, 1814. John Coffee to William B. Lewis, April 18, 1814, in Bassett, *Correspondence of Andrew Jackson*, 2: 4n5. For original terms of the treaty, see Thomas Pinckney to Benjamin Hawkins, April 23, 1814, in ASPIA, 1: 857–58.

42. Andrew Jackson to Thomas Pinckney, May 18, 1814, in Bassett, *Correspondence of Andrew Jackson*, 2: 2–3. Andrew Jackson to James Monroe and Jackson to John Williams, both May 26, 1814, James Monroe Papers, LC, 1st series, reel 5.

43. Andrew Jackson to John Armstrong, June 13, 1814, in Bassett, *Correspondence of Andrew Jackson*, 2: 7–8.

44. Proceedings of treaty taken from Moser et al., *Papers of Andrew Jackson*, vol. 3, 106–11. Creek leaders quoted in Dowd, *A Spirited Resistance*, 189–90. Andrew Jackson to John Coffee, August 10, 1814, in Moser et al., *Papers of Andrew Jackson*, vol.

3, 112–13; and Jackson to Rachel Jackson, August 23, 1814, in Moser et al., *Papers of Andrew Jackson*, vol. 3, 117. *Clarion*, August 23, 1814.

45. John Strother to Jackson, June 23, 1815, in Moser et al., *Papers of Andrew Jackson*, vol. 3, 363–64; and Jackson to Creek chiefs, September 4, 1815, in ibid., 382–83.

Chapter 5

1. Entry from diary of James Rhea, June 27, 1814, Rhea Family Papers, THS, Box 1, Folder 9. *Clarion*, September 13, 1814. Andrew Jackson to David Holmes, September 30, 1814, in Bassett, *Correspondence of Andrew Jackson*, 2: 64.

2. Mahon, "British Strategy and Southern Indians: War of 1812," 285–90. Owsley, *Struggle for the Gulf Borderlands*, 100–102.

3. James Wilkinson to William Eustis, March 28, 1812, and Eustis to Wilkinson, April 15, 1812, both in Wilkinson, *Memoirs of My Own Times*, 1: 476, 496. Brooks, *Diplomacy and the Borderlands*, 21–22. Whitaker, *Mississippi Question*, 27.

4. Nasatir, *Spanish War Vessels on the Mississippi*, 1–8. Whitaker, *Mississippi Question*, 27–31, 176–82, 257–59. White, "A View of Spanish West Florida: Selected Letters of Governor Juan Vicente Folch," 138–47. Corbitt, "The Administrative System in the Floridas, 1781–1821," 113–23. Gibson, *The Black Legend*. Weber, *The Spanish Frontier in North America*, 336. Andrew Jackson to William C. C. Claiborne, November 12, 1806, in Bassett, *Correspondence of Andrew Jackson*, 1: 153.

5. Poitrineau, "Demography and the Political Destiny of Florida during the Second Spanish Period," 441–43. "John Adair to James Madison, Secretary of State," 17. McMichael, *Atlantic Loyalties*. Nasatir, *Borderlands in Retreat*, 37. Owsley and Smith, *Filibusters and Expansionists*, 7–12. Skipworth's inaugural address taken from the December 29 issue of (Washington, DC) *National Intelligencer*, cited in Cox, "The American Intervention in West Florida," 307.

6. David Holmes to Willie Blount, July 8, 1813, cited in Jenkins, "Alabama Forts, 1700–1838," 173–74. Andrew Jackson to John Coffee, October 20, 1814, in Moser et al., *Papers of Andrew Jackson*, vol. 3, 169. Faye, "British and Spanish Fortifications of Pensacola, 1786–1821," 287. Murdoch, "A British Report on West Florida and Louisiana, November, 1812," 45. "Pensacola in 1810," 44–48. Papers of Andrew Jackson, LC, 5th series, vol. 5, p. 957, reel 67. Sugden, "The Southern Indians in the War of 1812: The Closing Phase," 286, 291. Bassett, *Major Howell Tatum's Journal*, 88.

7. Willie Blount to John Sevier, January 5, 1814, Lyman Copeland Draper Manuscript Collection, Wisconsin Historical Society (Madison), 11DD162. Andrew Jackson to William B. Lewis, January 29, 1814, "Rare Letters of Great Democrats," *Nashville Banner Magazine* (September 6, 1936), 15. (Baltimore) *Niles' Weekly Register*, July 23, 1814. William C. C. Claiborne to James Monroe, October 24, 1814, cited in Adams, "New Orleans and the War of 1812, Part III," 697–98.

8. John Armstrong to Andrew Jackson, July 18, 1814, in Moser et al., *Papers of Andrew Jackson*, vol. 3, 90. Jackson did not receive this letter until January 17, 1815. The letter may have been detained to free the government of any responsibility should Jackson decide to operate on his own. Based on the normal flow of correspondence, Jackson should have received Armstrong's letter by the middle of August 1814. Arm-

strong later blamed Madison for the delay, but Madison denied it. Others implicated Monroe as the culprit. For a look at the possibility of Madison or Monroe holding up this letter, see ibid., 90n2. James Monroe to Andrew Jackson, October 21, 1814, in ibid., 171.

9. Andrew Jackson to John Armstrong, August 25, 1814, and August 27, 1814, in Moser et al., *Papers of Andrew Jackson*, vol. 3: 122–23. For exaggerated rumors, see Jackson to John Reid, August 27, 1814, and Jackson to Armstrong, September 5, 1814, both in ibid., 124–25, 126–27. Andrew Jackson to James Monroe, October 26, 1814, in ibid., 173. Jackson to Monroe, October 31, 1814, in Bassett, *Correspondence of Andrew Jackson*, 2: 85.

10. Owsley, *Struggle for the Gulf Borderlands*, 103–5. The name "Nicholls" is often spelled as "Nichols."

11. Cassell, "Slaves of the Chesapeake Bay Area and the War of 1812," 144–55. Millet, "Britain's 1814 Occupation of Pensacola and America's Response: An Episode of the War of 1812 in the Southeastern Borderlands," 229–55. Vincent Gray to James Monroe, August 13, 1814, cited in Coker, "How General Jackson Learned of the British Plans," 91.

12. Owsley, *Struggle for the Gulf Borderlands*, 109–12. Although Nicholls was too ill to participate in the land attack, he was aboard one of the attacking British vessels and was wounded in action, losing an eye.

13. Andrew Jackson to Mateo Gonzalez Manrique, September 9, 1814, in Moser et al., *Papers of Andrew Jackson*, vol. 3, 129–31. Basset, *Major Howell Tatum's Journal*, 69. "Brigadier General John Coffee's Order Book, 10 September 1814–15 March 1815," in William C. Cook Collection, War of 1812 in the South, Williams Research Center, HNOC, Folder 126 (hereafter cited as William C. Cook Collection, HNOC). George W. Martin to James G. Martin, October 29, 1814, Dyas Collection, John Coffee Papers, 1770–1917, THS, Box 17, Folder 3. Reid and Eaton, *Life of Andrew Jackson*, 225.

14. George H. Downs to Henry Douglas Downs, October 19, 1814, and November 2, 1814 (Z2122.000), Downs and Allied Families, MDAH, Box 1. "Personal Recollections of M. W. Trimble of Jefferson County, Mississippi," in the July 25, 1909, issue of the (Memphis) *Commercial Appeal*. Reid and Eaton, *Life of Andrew Jackson*, 226–27. John Innerarity to James Innerarity, November 10, 1814, in "Letters of John Innerarity," 127.

15. James McCutchen Diary, 1814–15, McCutchen Family Papers, TSLA, Box 2, Folder 5. This paragraph and the next several ones, containing accounts of the battle, are taken from Andrew Jackson to James Monroe, November 14, 1814, in Bassett, *Correspondence of Andrew Jackson*, 2: 96–99; John Coffee to Andrew Jackson, November 8, 1814, in Papers of Andrew Jackson, LC, 1st series, reel 14. Andrew Jackson to Benjamin Hawkins, November 15, 1814, in Papers of Andrew Jackson, LC, 3rd series, reel 62; "Journal of Richard K. Call"; Doherty, *Richard Keith Call*, 9; "Sketch of William Trousdale as Told by Himself," William Trousdale Papers, 1828–1940, THS, Box 3, Folder 6; *Edmondson Journal*, 28; Andrew Jackson to Mateo Gonzalez Manrique, November 6, 1814, and Manrique to Jackson, November 6, 1814, both in Moser et al., *Papers of Andrew Jackson*, vol. 3, 179–80; and especially Bassett, *Major*

Howell Tatum's Journal, 71–82. For a British viewpoint, consult Fisher, "The Surrender of Pensacola as Told by the British," 326–29.

16. John Innerarity to James Innerarity, November 10, 1814, "Letters of John Innerarity," 129. John Coffee to Mary Coffee, November 15, 1814, in DeWitt, "Letters of General John Coffee," 287–88. Bassett, *Major Howell Tatum's Journal*, 84. Andrew Jackson to William Crawford, December 7, 1815, Sir Emil Hurja Collection, 1793–1953, THS, Box 6, Folder 16. Jackson to Mateo Gonzalez Manrique, November 16, 1814, in Moser et al., *Papers of Andrew Jackson*, vol. 3, 189–90.

17. Andrew Jackson to James Monroe, November 14, in Bassett, *Correspondence of Andrew Jackson*, 2: 98–99. Monroe to Jackson, December 7, 1814, in Moser et al., *Papers of Andrew Jackson*, vol. 3, 200–201. Willie Blount to Moses Fisk, February 1, 1815, Moses Fisk Papers, TSLA, Folder 4.

18. Coker, "How General Jackson Learned of the British Plans," 84–95. Stagg, *Mr. Madison's War*, 489–90.

19. Rucker, "In the Shadow of Jackson: Uriah Blue's Expedition into West Florida," 325–38. Jackson's General Orders of November 16, 1814, in Bassett, *Correspondence of Andrew Jackson*, 2: 100–101. Bassett, *Major Howell Tatum's Journal*, 86. Also, see "Creek War: Report of M. C. Rogers," 180.

20. Edward Palfrey to John Palfrey, December 23, 1814, in Gatell, "Boston Boy in 'Mr. Madison's War': Letters by John Palfrey and His Sons, Henry and Edward," 155. Estaville, "The Louisiana French Language in the Nineteenth Century," 110. Hatcher, *Edward Livingston*, 190–91. John Cravath May Windship to William Plumer Jr., April 2, 1814, in Brown, "Letters from Louisiana, 1813–1814," 575. Toast quoted in Waldstreicher, *In the Midst of Perpetual Fetes*, 260. Keller, *The Nation's Advocate*, 142.

21. Berquin-Duvallon, *Travels in Louisiana and the Floridas, in the Year, 1802*, 46–71. Perrin du Lac, *Travels through the Two Louisianas, and among the Savage Nations of the Missouri . . . in 1801, 1802, and 1803*, 90. Mary Ann Hunter to Mrs. C. Y. McAllister, July 30, 1815, in McDermott, *The Western Journals of Dr. George Hunter, 1796–1805*, 17. Jackson anecdote from Hamilton, *Reminiscences of James A. Hamilton*, 69. For a more accurate view of Creole society, see Hanger, *Bounded Lives, Bounded Places*, esp. chap. 2.

22. Phelps, *Louisiana*, 226. Dargo, *Jefferson's Louisiana*, 112. James Brown to Henry Clay, March 12, 1805, in Padgett, "Letters of James Brown to Henry Clay, 1804–1835," 924. Waldstreicher, *In the Midst of Perpetual Fetes*, 280. Hunt, *Life of Edward Livingston*, 118–19.

23. Statistics taken from table 1.3 as found in Hanger, *Bounded Lives, Bounded Places*, 22. For background to the free black militia in New Orleans, see ibid., chap. 4; Hanger, "A Privilege and Honor to Serve: The Free Black Militia of Spanish New Orleans," 391–432. For more on the free black militia in New Orleans under American rule, see Bell, *Revolution, Romanticism, and the Afro-Creole Protest Tradition in Louisiana*, 29–36.

24. Hunt, *Haiti's Influence on Antebellum America*. Rothman, *Slave Country*, 85.

25. Malone, *Sweet Chariot*, 21. Rothman, *Slave Country*, 83. Saxon, *Laffite the Pirate*, 63.

26. Alexander Cochrane to Robert Melville, September 3, 1814, in Crawford, *The Naval War of 1812*, 3: 270. Greene, *Historic Resource Study—Chalmette Unit*, 14. "Observations Relative to New Orleans," February 19, 1813, Edward Alexander Parsons Collection, Center for American History, University of Texas at Austin, Box 3E480, Folder 40.

27. Both quotes taken from Kastor, "'Motives of Peculiar Urgency': Local Diplomacy in Louisiana, 1803–1821," 843–44 (emphasis is original). Tylden, "Journal on British Expedition from Portsmouth, England, to New Orleans, and Return" (copied from the original by John Cahill in 1879), Manuscripts and Archives Division, New York Public Library, 30. C. J. Forbes to James Cobb, January 28, 1815, in "Unpublished Letter Relative to the Battle of New Orleans," 77.

28. Mahon, "British Strategy and Southern Indians: War of 1812," 297. Dickson, "Journal of Operations in Louisiana," 13.

29. Rothman, *Slave Country*, 140–42. Captain Edward A. E. Wylly to the Duke of Wellington, March 4, 1815, in Pakenham, *Pakenham Letters, 1800 to 1815*, 255. Dickson, "Journal of Operations in Louisiana," 18–19. Smith, *A British Eyewitness at the Battle of New Orleans*, 61. Alexander Cochrane to Earl Bathurst, July 14, 1814, in Crawford, *Naval War of 1812*, 3: 131. Kanon, "Other Battle of New Orleans," 43.

30. Albert Gallatin to James Monroe, August 20, 1814, quoted in Dungan, *Gallatin*, 111. Zagarri, *Revolutionary Backlash*, 100. Rachel Johnson to William Johnson, January 6, 1815, William Johnson Papers, MDAH, Box 1, Folder 2. Talcott and Bowers Letter, Louisiana and Lower Mississippi Valley Collections, Louisiana State University Libraries (Baton Rouge).

31. William MacRea to Andrew Jackson, September 9, 1814, in Bassett, *Correspondence of Andrew Jackson*, 2: 46–47. Captain John Shaw to Paul Hamilton, August 23, 1812, in Dudley, *The Naval War of 1812*, 1: 400–401. Nolte, *Fifty Years in Both Hemispheres*, 188.

32. William C. C. Claiborne to Andrew Jackson, August 24, 1814, in Bassett, *Correspondence of Andrew Jackson*, 2: 29–30. John Smith to Andrew Jackson, August 30, 1814, in Papers of Andrew Jackson, LC, 1st series, reel 11. Andrew Jackson to William C. C. Claiborne, August 30, 1814, in Moser et al., *Papers of Andrew Jackson*, vol. 3, 126. Bassett, *Major Howell Tatum's Journal*, 102–3.

33. Greene, *Historic Resource Study—Chalmette Unit*, 21–22. Mahon, "The United States Army in the Gulf Coast Region," 89. Andrew Jackson to Robert Butler, August 27, 1814, in Bassett, *Correspondence of Andrew Jackson*, 2: 31–33; also, see Jackson to Willie Blount, August 27, 1814, in ibid., 33–34. James Monroe to Andrew Jackson, September 27, 1814, in Lucier, *Political Writings of James Monroe*, 469.

34. *Clarion*, November 1, 1814. *Nashville Whig*, November 8, 1814.

35. William Priestly, "Gen. Carroll's Expedition to New Orleans," TSLA; Company Book of Captain Lewis Dillahunty (private collection). "Diary of Dr. William P. Lawrence, 1814–1815," Lawrence Family Papers 1780–1944, TSLA, Box 1, Folder 18. Amos Kirkpatrick Diary in William Alexander Provine Papers, 1552–1935, THS, Box 18, Folder 1. White, "The Journal of Capt. Thomas Joyes from Louisville to the Battle of New Orleans," 19–39, esp. 24–25. Greene, *Historic Resource Study—Chalmette Unit*, 99–100.

36. Kanon, "Other Battle of New Orleans," 44–45. Nolte, *Fifty Years in Both Hemispheres*, 203–4.

37. Hunt, "Office Seeking during Jefferson's Administration," 285–87. Hatcher, *Edward Livingston*, 209. Remini, "Andrew Jackson's Account of the Battle of New Orleans," 37.

38. Kastor, "Local Diplomacy in Louisiana," 45. Bell, *Revolution, Romanticism, and the Afro-Creole Protest Tradition in Louisiana*, 51–56. "To the Free Colored Inhabitants of Louisiana," September 21, 1814, in Bassett, *Correspondence of Andrew Jackson*, 2: 58. Andrew Jackson to William C. C. Claiborne, October 31, 1814, in ibid., 88. Roumillat, "The French St. Domingue Refugees from Cuba and the Battle of New Orleans." For more on Jackson's use of free blacks at New Orleans, see Smith, "Sons of Freedom," 215–21.

39. The best source for Jean Laffite and his operations is Davis, *Pirates Laffite*, 174. For another look at the smuggling operations of the Baratarians, see De Grummond, *Renato Beluche*.

40. Parsons, "Jean Laffite in the War of 1812: A Narrative Based on the Original Documents," 209–16. Sugden, "Jean Laffite and the British Offer of 1814," 159–67. Davis, *Pirates Laffite*, 165–80. Saxon, *Laffite the Pirate*, 129–39.

41. Greene, *Historic Resource Study—Chalmette Unit*, 25–26. Pickles, *New Orleans 1815*, 18–20. Smith, *The Politics of the Jeffersonian Gunboat Program*, 122. Smith points out that Jones and other American prisoners fed faulty intelligence to the British about the locations and strengths of the American forces, providing Jackson with time.

42. Davis, *Pirates Laffite*, 206–10, 214–16. Pickles, *New Orleans 1815*, 21. De Grummond, *Renato Beluche*, 116–17. Andrew Jackson to James Monroe, December 29, 1814, in Moser et al., *Papers of Andrew Jackson*, vol. 3, 224. Bell, *Revolution, Romanticism, and the Afro-Creole Protest Tradition*, 56–57. There is no official documentation as to the whereabouts of Jean Laffite between December 23, 1814, and January 8, 1815.

43. Bassett, *Correspondence of Andrew Jackson*, 2: 85n2, 113n2. Maass, "Brownsville's Steamboat *Enterprise* and Pittsburgh's Supply of General Jackson's Army," 22–29. Edward Livingston to Nicholas Girod, December 29, 1814, in Moser et al., *Papers of Andrew Jackson*, vol. 3, 225. William Carroll to Andrew Jackson, December 14, 1814, in Papers of Andrew Jackson, LC, 1st series, reel 14. Andrew Jackson to John Coffee, December 11, 1814, in Bassett, *Correspondence of Andrew Jackson*, 2: 112–13. "Brigadier General John Coffee's Order Book, 10 September 1814–15 March 1815," William C. Cook Collection, HNOC, Folder 126.

44. Remini, *The Battle of New Orleans*, 60–66. Tylden, "Journal on British Expedition," 46. Edward Codrington to Jane Codrington, December 23, 1814, and December 27, 1814, in Bourchier, *Memoir of the Life of Admiral Sir Edward Codrington*, 241, 244.

45. Letter of Colonel Frederick Stovin to his mother, December 5, 1814, William C. Cook Collection, HNOC, Folder 86. (Baltimore) *Niles' Weekly Register*, February 18, 1815. Chevalier Anne Louis de Tousard to John Clement Stocker, January 20, 1815, in Wilkinson, "Assaults on New Orleans," 52. Mahon, "British Command Decisions Relative to the Battle of New Orleans," 63–66. Henderson, "Vice-Admiral Sir

Alexander Cochrane and the Southern Campaign to New Orleans," 24–38. "Letter of the Duke of Wellington (May 22, 1815) on the Battle of New Orleans," 8.

46. Edward Wylly to the Duke of Wellington, March 4, 1815, in Pakenham, *Pakenham Letters, 1800 to 1815*, 256. De Grummond, "Platter of Glory," 325–27. Adams, "New Orleans and the War of 1812, Part IV," 181. Gleig, *A Narrative of the Campaigns of the British Army at Washington and New Orleans*, 321. Andrew Jackson to David Holmes and William C. C. Claiborne, October 31, 1814, in Bassett, *Correspondence of Andrew Jackson*, 2: 86–87. Pickles, *New Orleans 1815*, 32, 37. David Weller to Samuel Weller, January 6, 1815, Samuel Weller Miscellaneous Papers, Filson Historical Society (Frankfort, KY). Kanon, "Other Battle of New Orleans," 54–55.

47. Jackson's proclamation in Bassett, *Correspondence of Andrew Jackson*, 2: 58. Lewis Livingston to Janet Montgomery, December 16, 1814, cited in Hunt, *Life of Edward Livingston*, 198. Chevalier Anne Louis de Tousard to John Clement Stocker, January 6, 1815, in Wilkinson, "Assaults on New Orleans," 46, 49. Remini, "Andrew Jackson's Account of the Battle of New Orleans," 33. James H. Gordon to David B. Morgan, January 2, 1815, Edward Alexander Parsons Collection, University of Texas, Box 3E479, Folder 9.

Chapter 6

1. James McCutchen Diary 1814–1815, McCutchen Family Papers, TSLA, Box 2. Folder 5. Journal of Richard K. Call, 107. Remini, "Andrew Jackson's Account of the Battle of New Orleans," 31.

2. Bassett, *Major Howell Tatum's Journal*, 107. William Carroll to Willie Blount, February 21, 1815, Andrew Hynes Papers, 1814–1951, Manuscripts Collection 32, Louisiana Research Collection, Howard-Tilton Memorial Library, Tulane University (New Orleans), Folder 14. Rowland, *Andrew Jackson's Campaign against the British*, 305.

3. Journal of Richard K. Call, 97, 99. *Edmondson Journal*, 30. King, *Memoirs of Eliza Williams (Chotard) Gould*, 13. "Account of M. W. Trimble," in Lowry and McGardle, *A History of Mississippi*, 226.

4. "Sketch of William Trousdale as Told by Himself," in William Trousdale Papers 1828–1940, THS, Box 2, Folder 6. "The Battle of New Orleans," 645. Lebreton, "The Man Who Won the Battle of New Orleans," 28. Rankin, *The Journal of Major C. R. Forrest*, 31. Mahon, "British Command Decisions Relative to the Battle of New Orleans," 72–73, 73n50. Remini, "Andrew Jackson's Account of the Battle of New Orleans," 26–31. *A Brief Sketch of the Life and Military Services of Arthur P. Hayne*, 7. Benjamin Story Diary (typescript copy), Louisiana Research Collection, Tulane University (New Orleans), 1.

5. "Account of M. W. Trimble," in Lowry and McGardle, *A History of Mississippi*, 226. Bourchier, *Memoir of the Life of Admiral Sir Edward Codrington*, 243. Gleig, *A Narrative of the Campaigns of the British Army at Washington and New Orleans*, 283–85. "General Jackson's Military Pretensions," 85.

6. Journal of Richard K. Call, 101. John Coffee to Pierre Denis de la Ronde, July

20, 1816, Edward Alexander Parsons Collection, Center for American History, University of Texas at Austin, Box 3E478, Folder 12. John Coffee to Mary Coffee, January 20, 1815, in DeWitt, "Letters of General John Coffee," 290. "Account of M. W. Trimble," in Lowry and McGardle, *A History of Mississippi*, 227.

7. Gleig, *Narrative of the Campaigns of the British Army at Washington and New Orleans*, 286–87. Journal of Richard K. Call, 104. Report of Colonel Robert Dyer, January 2, 1815, LC, 6th series, reel 71. *Edmondson Journal*, 31–32. "Biographical Sketch of the Late Lieutenant Colonel James Lauderdale, of Tennessee," 383–84. "Account of M. W. Trimble," in Lowry and McGardle, *A History of Mississippi*, 227–28.

8. *Edmondson Journal*, 32–33. "General Jackson's Military Pretensions," 85. Also, see William B. Fort to Abraham Fort, February 24, 1815, William C. Cook Collection, HNOC, Folder 120.

9. Report of Major General John Keane, December 26, 1814, reprinted in *European Magazine and London Review* 67 (March 1815): 256. Rachel Johnson to William Johnson, January 6, 1815, William Johnson Papers, MDAH, Box 1, Folder 2; *Edmondson Journal*, 34. Remini, "Andrew Jackson's Account of the Battle of New Orleans," 30. James Moore King Letter, 1815, James Moore King Collection, Albert Gore Research Center, Middle Tennessee State University (Murfreesboro), Series I, Box 1.

10. Gleig, *Narrative of the Campaigns of the British Army at Washington and New Orleans*, 292–93; Surtees, *Twenty-Five Years in the Rifle Brigade*, 354. John Coffee to Mary Coffee, January 20, 1815, in DeWitt, "Letters of General John Coffee," 290. *Edmondson Journal*, 34–35. Greene, *Historic Resource Study—Chalmette Unit*, 39. Amos Kirkpatrick Diary in William Alexander Provine Papers, THS, Box 18, Folder 1. Nolte, *Fifty Years in Both Hemispheres*, 212, 219–20.

11. "Account of M. W. Trimble," in Lowry and McGardle, *A History of Mississippi*, 228. Gleig, *Narrative of the Campaigns of the British Army at Washington and New Orleans*, 293–97. Ritchie, "Louisiana Campaign," 38.

12. Greene, *Historic Resource Study—Chalmette Unit*, 39. Walker, *Jackson and New Orleans*, 222. *Edmondson Journal*, 35–37. Lossing, "Defense of New Orleans," 180. Latour, *Historical Memoir*, 105.

13. John Coffee to Mary Coffee, January 30, 1815, in DeWitt, "Letters of General John Coffee," 292. "Contemporary Account of the Battle of New Orleans," 14. General John Lambert to Earl Bathurst, January 10, 1815, in *European Magazine and London Review* 67 (March 1815): 255. "General Court Martial Held at the Royal Barracks, Dublin, for the Trial of Brevet Lieutenant-Colonel Hon. Thomas Mullins," 55, 59. Davis, *Pirates Laffite*, 215–16.

14. *Edmondson Journal*, 35. Greene, *Historic Resource Study—Chalmette Unit*, 90–92. Surtees, *Twenty-Five Years in the Rifle Brigade*, 363. David B. Morgan to James H. Gordon, January 2, 1815, Edward Alexander Parsons Collection, University of Texas, Box 3E482, Folder 9. E. Clement Letter, 1815, TSLA. Rothman, *Slave Country*, 149–51.

15. Latour, *Historical Memoir*, 92–93. Brown, *Amphibious Campaign for West Florida*

and Louisiana, 109, 118. Gleig, *Narrative of the Campaigns of the British Army at Washington and New Orleans*, 306–7. Surtees, *Twenty-Five Years in the Rifle Brigade*, 356.

16. Greene, *Historical Resource Study—Chalmette Unit*, 40. Dickson, "Journal of Operations in Louisiana," 10–17. Edward Livingston to David B. Morgan, December 25, 1814, Edward Alexander Parsons Collection, University of Texas, Box 3E480, Folder 29. Dickson, "Journal of Operations in Louisiana," 20–23. Surtees, *Twenty-Five Years in the Rifle Brigade*, 359–61. Rankin, *Journal of Major C. R. Forrest*, 34–35. Gleig, *Narrative of the Campaigns of the British Army at Washington and New Orleans*, 308–11.

17. Brown, *Amphibious Campaign for West Florida and Louisiana*, 114–16. William Carroll to Willie Blount, April 1815, Butler Family Papers, 1778–1975, Williams Research Center, HNOC, Folder 1032. Bassett, *Major Howell Tatum's Journal*, 116–17.

18. Ritchie, "Louisiana Campaign," 44–56. Rankin, *Journal of Major C. R. Forrest*, 35. David Weller to Samuel Weller, January 6, 1815, Samuel Weller Miscellaneous Papers, Filson Historical Society (Frankfort, KY). Edward Palfrey to John Palfrey, December 30, 1814, in Gatell, "Boston Boy in 'Mr. Madison's War': Letters by John Palfrey and His Sons, Henry and Edward," 156. Andrew Hynes to "a friend in Nashville," January 6, 1815, reprinted in the *Nashville Whig*, January 17, 1815 (emphasis is original). Surtees, *Twenty-Five Years in the Rifle Brigade*, 366.

19. Gleig, *Narrative of the Campaigns of the British Army at Washington and New Orleans*, 313–19. Dickson, "Journal of Operations in Louisiana," 35. Rankin, *Journal of Major C. R. Forrest*, 36–37. F. A. Browder to James H. Bradford, January 6, 1815, Department of Archives and Manuscripts, Louisiana State University, quoted in Greene, *Historic Resource Study—Chalmette Unit*, 98–99. Smith, *Autobiography of Lieutenant-General Sir Harry Smith*, 1: 230–31.

20. *Nashville Whig*, January 17, 1815. C. J. Forbes to James Cobb, January 28, 1815, in "Unpublished Letter Relative to the Battle of New Orleans," 79. Statement of Dr. William P. Lawrence, February 29, 1851, Lawrence Family Papers 1780–1944, TSLA, Box 1, Folder 16. Chevalier Anne Louis de Tousard to John Clement Stocker, January 6, 1815, in Wilkinson, "The Assaults on New Orleans," 49. Lossing, "Defense of New Orleans," 178–79. Nolte, *Fifty Years in Both Hemispheres*, 217. Levi Lee Diary, TSLA (grammar and punctuation altered). Dickson, "Journal of Operations in Louisiana," 37. Edward A. E. Wylly to the Duke of Wellington, March 4, 1815, in Pakenham, *Pakenham Letters, 1800 to 1815*, 256. Also, see William Carroll to James Winchester, January 3, 1815, James Winchester Papers, 1787–1953, THS, Box 1, Folder 4.

21. James McCutchen Diary. Dickson, "Journal of Operations in Louisiana," 35–37. Pakenham, *Pakenham Letters, 1800 to 1815*, 256. Bassett, *Major Howell Tatum's Journal*, 120–21. *Edmondson Journal*, 35. General Order of January 1, 1815, Papers of Andrew Jackson, LC, 6th series, reel 71.

22. Smith, *The Memoir of Royal Navy Admiral Robert Aitchison*, 62. For British retreat, see Rankin, *Journal of Major C. R. Forrest*, 37–38.

23. Brown, *Amphibious Campaign for West Florida and Louisiana*, 128–31.

24. Isaac L. Baker to Stephen F. Austin, January 5, 1815, in Barker, "The Austin Papers," 2: 246. Brown, *Amphibious Campaign for West Florida and Louisiana*, 132–33. Greene, *Historical Resource Study—Chalmette Unit*, 60–61, 105–7.

25. Brown, *Amphibious Campaign for West Florida and Louisiana*, 140–42. Dixon, *The Battle on the West Bank*, 5–8.

26. Dickson, "Journal of Operations in Louisiana," 57–63. Smith, *Autobiography of Lieutenant-General Sir Harry Smith*, 1: 230–31, 235–36, 247. "General Court Martial Held at the Royal Barracks, Dublin, for the Trial of Brevet Lieutenant-Colonel Hon. Thomas Mullins," 82. McConnell, *Negro Troops of Antebellum Louisiana*, 74, 85. E. Clement Letter, 1815, TSLA. "Contemporary Account of the Battle of New Orleans," 11. *Liberty* (Missouri) *Weekly Tribune* (August 26, 1870).

27. Cooke, *Narrative of Events*, 227–28, 231. "General Court Martial Held at the Royal Barracks, Dublin, for the Trial of Brevet Lieutenant-Colonel Hon. Thomas Mullins," 45, 55–56, 59, 85. Ritchie, "Louisiana Campaign," 70. John Coffee to John Donelson, January 25, 1815, THS Miscellaneous Files 1688–1951, Box 3, C-120. De Grummond, "Platter of Glory," 346. Gleig, *Narrative of the Campaigns of the British Army at Washington and New Orleans*, 324–27. R. S., "Battle of New Orleans, 8th January, 1815," 356. *Nashville Whig*, January 24, 1815.

28. John Fort to unnamed brother, January 28, 1815, Edward Alexander Parsons Collection, University of Texas, Box 3E479, Folder 4. "A Massachusetts Volunteer at the Battle of New Orleans," 31. "Contemporary Account of the Battle of New Orleans," 11–12.

29. *Nashville Whig*, January 24, 1815. Ritchie, "Louisiana Campaign," 74. Bassett, *Major Howell Tatum's Journal*, 125, 127. De Grummond, "Platter of Glory," 344. John A. Fort to unnamed brother, January 28, 1815, Edward Alexander Parsons Collection, University of Texas, Box 3E479, Folder 4. Gabriel Willis to William Willis, January 12, 1815, Willis Family Papers, Louisiana State University Libraries.

30. Greene, *Historic Research Study—Chalmette Unit*, 93–95. R. S., "Battle of New Orleans," 355–56. Rowley and Hamilton, "A Missing Link in the History of American War Correspondents: James Morgan Bradford and *The Time Piece* of St. Francisville, Louisiana," 21. McManus, *American Courage, American Carnage*, 31–32. Levasseur, *Lafayette in America in 1824 and 1825*, 2: 98.

31. William Carroll to Andrew Jackson, March 4, 1815, Papers of Andrew Jackson, Supplement, Scholarly Resources, reel 4. Priestly, "Gen. Carroll's Expedition to New Orleans," TSLA. Latour, *Historical Memoir*, 110–11. *Edmondson Journal*, 37–38. Lossing, "Defense of New Orleans," 183. Andrew Jackson to Robert Hays, February 9, 1815, in Bassett, *Correspondence of Andrew Jackson*, 2: 162. Pakenham, *Pakenham Letters, 1800 to 1815*, 258.

32. Brown, *Amphibious Campaign for West Florida and Louisiana*, 151–56. For a firsthand account of the action on the West Bank, see White, "The Journal of Capt. Thomas Joyes from Louisville to the Battle of New Orleans," 29–32.

33. Smith, *Autobiography of Lieutenant-General Sir Harry Smith*, 1: 237–40. Remini, "Andrew Jackson's Account of the Battle of New Orleans," 36–37.

34. (Baltimore) *Niles' Weekly Register*, supplement to vol. 8 (1815), 166. "An Eye-Witness of the Battle of New Orleans," 160. De Grummond, "Platter of Glory," 346. William Carroll to Willie Blount, April 1815, Butler Family Papers, HNOC, Folder 1032. Archibald Young Letter, January 12, 1815, TSLA. "Contemporary Account of the Battle of New Orleans," 13–15. Tylden, "Journal on British Expedition

from Portsmouth, England, to New Orleans, and Return." R. S., "Battle of New Orleans," 357n.

35. Bassett, *Major Howell Tatum's Journal*, 127. McConnell, *Negro Troops of Antebellum Louisiana*, 87–88. Smith, *Autobiography of Lieutenant-General Sir Harry Smith*, 1: 241–42. Gleig, *Narrative of the Campaigns of the British Army at Washington and New Orleans*, 332. Adjutant General's report of January 16, 1815, published in *Niles' Weekly Register*, February 18, 1815.

36. "Contemporary Account of the Battle of New Orleans," 15. Smith, *Autobiography of Lieutenant-General Sir Harry Smith*, 1: 241. Andrew Jackson to James Monroe, February 17, 1815, in Papers of Andrew Jackson, LC, 3rd series, reel 62. De Grummond, "The Fair Honoring the Brave," 58. Andrew Hynes to Willie Blount, February 3, 1815, published in *Clarion*, February 21, 1815.

37. Duffy, *The Rudolph Matas History of Medicine in Louisiana*, 1: 477–83. *Niles' Weekly Register*, February 11, 1815. S. Simpson to Mary Simpson, January 9, 1815, in Kulick and Alonso, "An Eyewitness Account of the Battle of New Orleans," 124. Rachel Johnson to William Johnson, January 15, 1815, William Johnson Papers, MDAH.

38. Hunt, *Life of Edward Livingston*, 202. Remini, "Andrew Jackson's Account of the Battle of New Orleans," 38. Edward Codrington, to his wife, February 13, 1815, in Bourchier, *Memoir of the Life of Admiral Sir Edward Codrington*, 247. John Coffee to Mary Coffee, January 20, 1815, in DeWitt, "Letters of General John Coffee," 290–91. William Carroll to Willie Blount, April 1815, Butler Family Papers, HNOC, Folder 1032. *Niles' Weekly Register*, supplement to vol. 8 (1815), 166. Kulick and Alonso, "An Eyewitness Account of the Battle of New Orleans," 160.

39. Smith, *Memoir of Royal Navy Admiral Robert Aitchison*, 65. Bourchier, *Memoir of the Life of Admiral Sir Edward Codrington*, 245–46. Tylden, "Journal on British Expedition," 53–54, 66. James, *A Full and Correct Account of the Military Occurrences of the Late War between Great Britain and the United States of America*, 2: 379; R. S., "Battle of New Orleans," 356–57, 357n. Also, see Gleig, *Narrative of the Campaigns of the British Army at Washington and New Orleans*, 324–27.

40. Rankin, *Journal of Major C. R. Forrest*, 43–44. *Niles' Weekly Register*, supplement to vol. 8 (1815), 166. Thomas B. Johnson to Dolley Madison, January 19, 1815, in Cutts, *Memoirs and Letters of Dolly Madison*, 125.

41. Cooke, *Narrative of Events*, 268–71. Archibald Young Letter, January 12, 1815, TSLA. "The Diary of a Private Soldier in the Campaign of New Orleans," 331. Remini, "Andrew Jackson's Account of the Battle of New Orleans," 38–39. Dickson, "Journal of Operations in Louisiana," 76–77. Surtees, *Twenty-Five Years in the Rifle Brigade*, 384. Frederick Stovin to his mother, January 24, 1815, William C. Cook Collection, HNOC, Folder 10.

42. De Grummond, "The Fair Honoring the Brave," 54–55. Remini, *The Battle of New Orleans*, 169–76. Walter H. Overton to James H. Gordon, January 17, 1815, message contained in January 18, 1815, communication from Gordon to David B. Morgan, Edward Alexander Parsons Collection, University of Texas, Box 3E479, Folder 9. Benjamin Story Diary, Tulane Collection, 3. Thomas B. Johnson to Dolley Madison, January 19, 1815, in Cutts, *Memoirs and Letters of Dolly Madison*, 126–27.

Chapter 7

1. Most of the details of the January 24 ceremonies are taken from Latour, *Historical Memoir*, 135, and partly from a February 2, 1815, letter from Lewis Livingston to Janet Montgomery, cited in Hunt, *Life of Edward Livingston*, 201–2.

2. King, *Memoirs of Eliza Williams (Chotard) Gould*, 16–17; Rachel Jackson to Robert Hays, March 5, 1815, in Moser et al., *Papers of Andrew Jackson*, vol. 3, 297. *Nashville Whig*, May 31, 1814.

3. Ensign John Sevier to his mother, January 10, 1815, and John Sevier to George Washington Sevier, February 5, 1815, both cited in Sevier and Madden, *Sevier Family History*, 208, 369. James Rhea to Andrew Agnew, February 25, 1815, Rhea Family Papers, THS, Box 1, Folder 4. Thad Mayhew to Thaddus Mayhew, January 26, 1815, in "A Massachusetts Volunteer at the Battle of New Orleans," 31. Letter of Willie Blount, February 24, 1815, in James Winchester Papers, 1787–1953, THS, Box 2, Folder 8.

4. "Report of the Committee of Inquiry," 224–80. Andrew Jackson to Louisiana General Assembly, December 31, 1814, in Moser et al., *Papers of Andrew Jackson*, vol. 3, 226–27. Kanon, "Other Battle of New Orleans," 47–49.

5. Andrew Jackson to John McLean, March 22, 1824, in Moser, Hoth, and Hoemann, *Papers of Andrew Jackson*, vol. 5, 379–80 (emphasis is original). Parton, *Life of Andrew Jackson*, 2: 143.

6. Warshauer, "The Battle of New Orleans Reconsidered: Andrew Jackson and Martial Law," 268–69. Samuel Harper to John Coffee, January 10, 1817, Dyas Collection, John Coffee Papers, 1770–1917, THS, Box 7, Folder 3. Greene, *Historic Resource Study—Chalmette Unit*, 188. Kanon, "Other Battle of New Orleans," 49.

7. Ord, "Memoranda Respecting Mobile," 131–32. Mahon, "British Strategy and Southern Indians: War of 1812," 299–301. Andrew Jackson to James Monroe, February 10, 1815, in Papers of Andrew Jackson, LC, 3rd series, reel 62.

8. Heidler and Heidler, "'Where All Behave Well': Fort Bowyer and the War on the Gulf, 1814–1815," 194–96. Owsley, *Struggle for the Gulf Borderlands*, 171–72. Smith, *The Autobiography of Lieutenant-General Sir Harry Smith*, 1: 248–50. Dickson, "Journal of Operations in Louisiana," 99. Also, see Ritchie, "Louisiana Campaign," 85–89.

9. This paragraph and the next two paragraphs are condensed from my "Other Battle of New Orleans" article, 49–53.

10. Duffy, *The Rudolph Matas History of Medicine in Louisiana*, 1: 477. Gillett, *The Army Medical Department, 1775–1818*, 184. "The Battle of New Orleans," 646. William White Letter, 1815, THS. Rev. George Foster to editor of the *Clarion*, February 3, 1815, reprinted in *Clarion*, February 21, 1815. Isaac Shelby letter of February 10, 1815, reprinted in *Niles' Weekly Register*, March 18, 1815. John Coffee to John Donelson, THS Miscellaneous Files 1688–1951, T-100, Box 3, C-121. James Moore King Letter, 1815, James Moore King Collection, Albert Gore Research Center, Middle Tennessee State University (Murfreesboro, TN), Series I, Box 1. Report of March 9, 1815, Andrew Jackson Papers, LC, 5th series, reel 68. Rachel Jackson to Robert Hays, March 5, 1815, in Moser et al., *Papers of Andrew Jackson*, vol. 3, 298. *Niles' Weekly Register*, April 29, 1815.

11. Amos Kirkpatrick Diary in William Alexander Provine Papers, 1552–1935, THS, Box 18, Folder 1. Company Book of Captain Lewis Dillahunty (private collection). Wait, *Travel Diary of William Richardson*, 15, 18. Jones, *A Complete History of Methodism*, 382.

12. Bounty Land Warrant Application, BLW-4130, Record Group 15, NARA. *Edmondson Journal*, 41. *Nashville Whig*, April 11, 1815, and April 18, 1815. Wait, *Travel Diary of William Richardson*, 15. Lemuel Donelson to John Coffee, March 16, 1815, John Coffee Papers, THS, Box 6, Folder 6.

13. Broadside "To the Natchez Volunteer Rifle Corps," dated April 4, 1815, LC, Rare Book and Special Collections Division. At http://hdl.loc.gov/loc.rbc/rbpe .08500500, accessed January 28, 2012. *Nashville Whig*, January 24, 1815 (emphasis is original), and May 16, 1815. *Edmondson Journal*, 42.

14. Coffin, *Sermon Delivered in Rogersville*, 16. William P. Duvall to Andrew Hynes, February 1815, Andrew Hynes Papers, 1814–1951, Manuscripts Collection 32, Louisiana Research Collection, Howard-Tilton Memorial Library, Tulane University (New Orleans), Folder 15. Darby, *Emigrant's Guide to the Western and Southwestern States and Territories*, 196. Lost amidst this jubilation is the fact that Jackson approved the death sentence of six Tennessee militiamen, who were executed in February 1815 at Mobile for mutinous conduct relating to a September 1814 incident. Jackson could have commuted the sentence, but refused to do so, adding to his "villainous" legacy. For details, see Parton, *Life of Andrew Jackson*, 2: 277–300.

15. Andrew Hynes to William R. Hynes, February 2, 1815, Andrew Hynes Papers, Tulane University, Folder 12. John Coffee to John Donelson, January 25, 1815, THS Miscellaneous Files, Box 3, C-120. Gabriel Winter to William Willis, January 12, 1815, Willis Family Papers, Louisiana State University Libraries. Ritchie, "Guns of New Orleans," 9–13. Greene, *Historic Resource Study—Chalmette Unit*, 132n37. McCully, "'Too Much Praise Cannot Be Bestowed': Andrew Jackson's Artillery at the Battle of New Orleans," 88–100.

16. "To the Tennessee Volunteer Company," Butler Family Papers, 1778–1975, Williams Research Center, HNOC, Folder 1031. Howe, *What Hath God Wrought*, 17–18. AC, 13th Cong., 3rd sess., 233–34, 1155.

17. Record Group 60, Legislative Petitions, 27-2-1815, TSLA. Cunliffe, *Soldiers and Civilians*, 52–53. For a look at how the War of 1812 transformed the American conception of professional armies, consult Budiansky, "The War of 1812 and the Rise of American Military Power," 36–66.

18. James Madison to Charles Ingersoll, January 4, 1818, in Smith, *The Republic of Letters*, 1762. *Edmondson Journal*, 42.

19. Rogin, *Fathers and Children*, 169–71. Chappell, "John Coffee: Surveyor and Land Agent," 188–90.

20. John Coffee to William Russell, June 15, 1816, John Coffee Papers, THS, Box 13, Folder 21. ASPIA, 2: 89–91. Hudson, *Creek Paths and Federal Roads*, 121–22. Rogin, *Fathers and Children*, 172–74. John Rhea to James Madison, July 1, 1816, in Padgett, "Letters from John Rhea to Thomas Jefferson and James Madison," 120, 122. Between 1815 and 1820, Jackson and his fellow commissioners managed to "per-

suade" the southeast tribes to sell what amounted to half of Mississippi and most of Alabama.

21. Sevier and Madden, *Sevier Family History*, 218. Miller, *The Taking of American Indian Lands*, 119. Roberts, "Thomas Freeman: Surveyor of the Old Southwest," 228–29. John Strother to Andrew Jackson, June 23, 1815, in Moser et al., *Papers of Andrew Jackson*, vol. 3, 364.

22. Jacob McGavock to Hugh McGavock, August 2, 1817, McGavock Family Letters, 1798–1850, TSLA. Rogin, *Fathers and Children*, 174–77. Natalie Inman, "Networks in Negotiation: The Role of Family and Kinship in Intercultural Diplomacy on the Trans-Appalachian Frontier, 1680–1840," 195n3. James Graham to Thomas Ruffin, 1817 letter quoted in Lowery, "The Great Migration to the Mississippi Territory, 1798–1819," 182 (emphasis is original). For the immigration of slaveholders to Alabama, Mississippi, and such after the War of 1812, see Miller, *South by Southwest*.

23. Jones, *William Clark and the Shaping of the West*, 234. William P. Anderson to William Preston, January 28, 1811, Preston Family Papers, Joyes Collection, 1780–1956, Filson Historical Society (Louisville, KY). Randall McGavock to John Overton, November 25, 1818, John Overton Papers, 1797–1833, THS, Box 1, Folder 7. Williams, "Journal of Events (1825–1873) of David Anderson Deaderick," 133. North, *The Economic Growth of the United States*, 257.

24. Return Meigs to James Monroe, March 4, 1815, June 20, 1815, and December 20, 1815, in Records of the Cherokee Indian Agency in Tennessee, 1801–35, NARA, reel 6.

25. Report of Thomas Johnson and Michael Dickson to William H. Crawford, May 15, 1816, in *American State Papers: Documents*, 2: 402. Saltz, "Chickasaws," 153. DeRosier, "Andrew Jackson and Negotiations for the Removal of the Choctaw Indians," 343–62.

26. Edmund Gaines to Andrew Jackson, June 8, 1815, in Moser et al., *Papers of Andrew Jackson*, vol. 3, 361. Hudson, *Creek Paths and Federal Roads*, 119. (Washington, DC) *Daily National Intelligencer*, June 13, 1815.

27. Claiborne, *Notes on the War in the South*, 45–46. Waselkov, *A Conquering Spirit*, 204–6. Prucha, *Sword of the Republic*, 258–61. Howe, *What Hath God Wrought*, 125–26. As historian James Merrell has reflected, "If Creeks were angry, they had reason to be." Merrell posits that historians keep portraying the Creeks in an unfair fashion, particularly in regard to Fort Mims which was really more of a battle in the Creek civil war; furthermore, historians are loath to admit that these actions took place in "Creek country" rather than "southern Alabama" or "southeastern Mississippi Territory." See Merrell, "Second Thoughts on Colonial Historians and American Indians," 496–506 (quote on p. 501).

28. Coffin, *Sermon Delivered in Rogersville*, 11. "Reflections on the Institutions of the Cherokee Indians from Observations Made during a Recent Visit to That Tribe: In a Letter from a Gentleman of Virginia, to Robert Walsh, Juan.–June 1st, 1817," 36. John Coffee's diary entry for October 19, 1816, John Coffee Papers, THS, Box 22, Folder 13.

29. Heidler and Heidler, "Fort Bowyer and the War on the Gulf, 1814–1815," 185. Prucha, *Sword of the Republic*, 129–34. Howe, *What Hath God Wrought*, 75. In addition to the issues of territorial expansion, runaway slaves, and Indian depredations, the causes of the First Seminole War included a strong Anglophobia and fear of British intrigue on the Gulf Coast. For this, see Belko, "Epilogue to the War of 1812: The Monroe Administration, American Anglophobia, and the First Seminole War" 54–102.

30. Bancroft, *Literary and Historical Miscellanies*, 458. Wise cited in Kammen, *A Season of Youth*, 15.

31. Bellesiles, "Experiencing the War of 1812," 205, 210, 229. *Nashville Gazette*, June 23, 1819, quoted in Leach, "John Gordon of John Gordon's Ferry," 343.

32. Israel Pickens to General Lenoir, February 13, 1815, Pickens Family Papers, 1799–1855, Alabama Department of Archives and History (Montgomery), Box 1, Folder 4. (Charleston, SC) *Southern Patriot*, February 21, 1815, cited in Wolfe, *Jeffersonian Democracy in South Carolina*, 283–84.

33. "To the 2nd Division," in Moser and Macpherson, *Papers of Andrew Jackson*, vol. 2, 291 (emphasis is original). Matthew Lyon to Andrew Jackson, June 2, 1814, in Moser et al., *Papers of Andrew Jackson*, vol. 3, 78.

34. *Columbian Telescope and Literary Compiler* 1 (August 28, 1819), 45. McKenny quoted in Feller, *The Jacksonian Promise*, 144. Hsiung, *The Memoir of Dr. Abraham Jobe, 1817–1906*, 17.

35. Griffin, *American Leviathan*, 185. Knouff, "'An Arduous Service': The Pennsylvania Backcountry Soldiers," 56–70. Heiskell, *Andrew Jackson and Early Tennessee History*, 1: 18.

36. Joseph Anderson, Jenkins Whiteside, John Rhea, Robert Weakley, and Pleasant Miller to James Madison, March 1810, in Stagg, *The Papers of James Madison: Presidential Series*, 4: 612–14 (quote on 613) (emphasis is original).

Bibliography

Manuscripts and Primary Source Documents

Alabama Department of Archives and History (Montgomery)
Caller, James. Papers.
Pickens Family Papers, 1799–1855.

Filson Historical Society (Louisville, Kentucky)
Preston Family Papers. Joyes Collection, 1780–1956.
Rhea, John. Letter, 1813.
Weller, Samuel. Miscellaneous Papers.

Florida Historical Society Library (Cocoa)
Call, Governor Richard K. Journal.

Library of Congress (Washington, DC)
Harrison, William H. Papers (microfilm edition).
Jackson, Andrew. Papers (microfilm edition).
Madison, James. Papers (microfilm edition).
Monroe, James. Papers (microfilm edition).
Reid, John. Papers, 1802–16.
"To the Natchez Volunteer Rifle Corps" (broadside dated April 4, 1815).

Louisiana State University Libraries (Baton Rouge)
Louisiana and Lower Mississippi Valley Collections.
Willis Family Papers.

Middle Tennessee State University, Albert Gore Research Center (Murfreesboro)
James Moore King Collection.

Mississippi Department of Archives and History (Jackson)
Downs and Allied Families.
Johnson, William. Papers.

National Archives and Records Division (Washington, DC)
Record Group 15. Records of Veterans Administration.
Records of the Cherokee Agency in Tennessee, 1801–35.

New York Public Library, Manuscripts and Archives Division
Tylden, John Maxwell. "Journal on British Expedition from Portsmouth, England, to New Orleans, and Return. October 27, 1814–May 10, 1815."

Private Collection
Company Book of Captain Lewis Dillahunty.

Tennessee Historical Society (Nashville)
Coffee, John. Papers. Dyas Collection.
Sir Emil Hurja Collection, 1793–1953.
Overton, John. Papers, 1797–1833.
Provine, William Alexander. Papers.
Rhea Family Papers.
Tennessee Historical Society Miscellaneous Files.
Cromwell Tidwell Collection, 1794–1976.
Trousdale, William. Papers, 1828–1940.
White, William. Letter, 1815.
Winchester, James. Papers, 1787–1953.

Tennessee State Library and Archives (Nashville)
Campbell, David. Papers.
Campbell, George Washington. Correspondence, 1793–1833.
Clement, E. Letter, 1815.
Cocke, John. Papers, 1774–1851.
Coffee Vertical File.
Conger, Isaac. Diary.
Narrative of the Birth and Life of Jesse Cox.
Fisk, Moses. Papers.
Foster, Ephraim Hubbard. Papers, 1814–20.
Lawrence Family Papers, 1780–1944.
Lee, Levi. Diary.
Maury, James Hervey. Memoir, 1864.
McCutchen Family Papers.
McEwen Family. Genealogical Data.
McGavock Family Letters, 1798–1850.
Military Papers. Commissions, 1813–49.
Montgomery Vertical File.
Morgan, Gideon. Papers, 1813–26.
Priestly, William. "A Short Sketch of the Creek War." "Gen. Carroll's Expedition to New Orleans."
Reid, John. Journal.
Roberts, Brigadier General Isaac. Creek War Papers.
Robertson, James. Papers, 1784–1814.
Sevier, John. Papers, 1803–09, Second Series.
Sumner County Loose Records.
Vaught, Nathan. Memoir, 1871.

Tulane University, Howard-Tilton Memorial Library (New Orleans)
Hynes, Andrew. Papers.

University of Georgia, Hargett Rare Book and Manuscript Library (Athens)
Ray Clarke to Ethan Clarke, 3 March 1813. (Document RCL001).

University of Tennessee, Special Collections Library (Knoxville)
Blount, Willie. Letter, 1811, MS-0737.
Cocke, John. Letter, MS-731.

University of Texas, Center for American History (Austin)
Ben and Henry Eustace McCulloch Family Papers.
Edward Alexander Parsons Collection.
Smith, James Norman. Memoirs, 1789–1860.

Western Kentucky University, Manuscript Division (Bowling Green)
Bains, Samuel. Letters.

Williams Research Center of the Historic New Orleans Collection
Butler Family Papers, 1778–1975.
William C. Cook Collection. War of 1812 in the South.

Wisconsin Historical Society (Madison)
Lyman Copeland Draper Manuscript Collection (microfilm edition).

Published Primary Sources

"1813 Letter." *Register of the Kentucky Historical Society* 47 (July 1949): 253–54.
Acts Passed at the First Session of the Fifth General Assembly of the State of Tennessee, Began and Held at Knoxville, on Monday the Nineteenth Day of September, One Thousand Eight Hundred and Three. Knoxville: George Roulstone, 1803.
Acts Passed at the First Session of the Seventh General Assembly of the State of Tennessee Began and Held at Kingston, on Monday the Twenty-First Day of September, One Thousand Eight Hundred and Seven. Knoxville: William Moore, 1808.
Acts Passed at the First Session of the Tenth General Assembly of the State of Tennessee, Begun and Held at Nashville, on Monday the Twenty-First Day of September, One Thousand Eight Hundred and Thirteen. Nashville: T. G. Bradford, 1813.
Address of James Lyon, to the Electors of the Congressional District, Composed of the Thirteen Counties on the Waters of the Cumberland River, in Tennessee. Nashville?: Eastin?, 1807.
American State Papers: Documents. 2 vols. Washington, DC: Gales and Seaton, 1834.
American State Papers: Indian Affairs. 2 vols. Washington, DC: Gales and Seaton, 1832.
Annals of Congress. US Congress. Washington, DC: Gales and Seaton, 1834–56.
Barker, Eugene C., ed. "The Austin Papers." *Annual Report of the American Historical Association for the Year 1919.* 2 vols. Washington, DC: US Government Printing Office, 1924.

Bassett, John Spencer, ed. *The Correspondence of Andrew Jackson*. 7 vols. Washington, DC: Carnegie Institution of Washington, 1926–35.

———. *Major Howell Tatum's Journal to General Jackson*. Northampton, MA: Department of History of Smith College, 1921–22.

Brannan, John, comp. *Official Letters of the Military and Naval Officers of the United States, during the War with Great Britain in the Years 1812, 13, 14 & 15. With Some Additional Letters and Documents Elucidating the History of that Period*. Washington, DC: Way and Gideon, 1823; reprint, New York: Arno Press, 1971.

Brannon, Peter A., ed. "Journal of James A. Tait for the Year 1813." *Georgia Historical Quarterly* 8 (September 1924): 229–39.

Brown, Everett S., ed. "Letters from Louisiana, 1813–1814." *Mississippi Valley Historical Review* 11 (March 1925): 570–79.

Carter, Clarence Edwin, ed. *The Territorial Papers of the United States*. Vol. 4, *The Territory South of the River Ohio, 1790–1796*. Washington, DC: US Printing Office, 1936.

Claiborne, Ferdinand L. *Supplement to the Mississippi Republican, 25 March 1814*. Natchez, MS: n.p., 1814.

Clanin, Douglas E., ed. *The Papers of William Henry Harrison, 1800–1815*. Indianapolis: Indiana Historical Society, 1999 (microfilm edition).

Coffin, Charles. *A Sermon Delivered in Rogersville, April 13, 1815. The Day Appointed by the President of the United States as a Day of National Thanks-Giving for the Restoration of Peace*. Rogersville, TN: Carey and Early, 1815.

"A Contemporary Account of the Battle of New Orleans by a Soldier in the Ranks." *Louisiana Historical Quarterly* 9 (January 1926): 11–15.

Corbitt, D. C., ed. and trans. "Papers Relating to the Georgia-Florida Frontier, 1784–1800, XVII." *Georgia Historical Quarterly* 24 (December 1940): 374–81.

Craven, Avery O. "Letters of Andrew Jackson." *Huntington Library Bulletin* 1 (February 1933): 109–34.

"Creek War: Report of M. C. Rogers." *American Historical Magazine* 8 (April 1903): 180.

Cutts, Lucia B., ed. *Memoirs and Letters of Dolly Madison, Wife of James Madison, President of the United States*. Boston: Houghton Mifflin, 1886; reprint, Port Washington, NY: Kennikat Press, 1971.

Davis, Richard Beale, ed. *Jeffersonian America: Notes on the United States of America Collected in the Years 1805–6–7 and 11–12 by Sir Augustus John Foster*. San Marino, CA: Huntington Library, 1954.

DeWitt, John H., ed. "Letters of General John Coffee to His Wife, 1813–1815." *Tennessee Historical Magazine* 2 (December 1916): 264–95.

"Diary of a Private Soldier in the Campaign of New Orleans." *Macmillan's Magazine* 77 (March 1898): 321–33.

"Diary of Jose Bernardo Gutierrez de Lara, 1811–1812." *American Historical Review* 34 (October 1928): 55–77.

Dickson, Alexander. "Journal of Operations in Louisiana, 1814–1815." *Louisiana Historical Quarterly* 44 (July–October 1961): 1–110.

Doster, James F., ed. "Letters Relating to the Tragedy of Fort Mims: August–September, 1813." *Alabama Review* 14 (October 1961): 269–85.

Edmondson, Andrew Jackson. *Journal When a Volunteer under General Andrew Jackson in 1812–1813.* N.p.: n.p., n.d.

Gatell, Frank Otto, ed. "Boston Boy in 'Mr. Madison's War': Letters by John Palfrey and His Sons, Henry and Edward." *Louisiana Historical Quarterly* 44 (July–October 1961): 148–59.

"General Court Martial Held at the Royal Barracks, Dublin, for the Trial of Brevet Lieutenant-Colonel Hon. Thomas Mullins." *Louisiana Historical Quarterly* 9 (January 1926): 33–112.

"General John Lambert to Earl Bathurst, 10 January 1815." *European Magazine and London Review* 67 (March 1815): 254–56.

Hamilton, J. G. de Roulhac, ed. *Letters of John Rust Eaton.* Raleigh, NC: Commercial Printing, 1910.

Hopkins, James F., ed. *The Papers of Henry Clay.* Vol. 1, *The Rising Statesman, 1797–1814.* Lexington: University Press of Kentucky, 1959.

"John Adair to James Madison, Secretary of State." *Gulf States Historical Magazine* 1 (July 1902): 16–18.

John Rhea, of Tennessee, to His Constituents. Washington, DC: n.p., 1815.

Journal of the House of Representatives, at the Second Session of the Ninth General Assembly of the State of Tennessee, Begun and Held at Nashville, on Monday, the Seventh Day of September, One Thousand Eight Hundred and Twelve. Nashville: T. G. Bradford, 1813.

Journal of the Senate, at the Second Session of the Ninth General Assembly of the State of Tennessee. Begun and Held at Nashville, on Monday, the Seventh Day of September, One Thousand Eight Hundred and Twelve. Nashville: T. G. Bradford, 1813.

Kreider, Angela, ed., *The Papers of James Madison: Presidential Series.* Vol. 6, *8 February–24 October 1813.* Charlottesville: University of Virginia Press, 2008.

"Letters and Papers of Andrew Jackson, Part I." *Bulletin of the New York Public Library* 4 (January–December 1900): 154–62.

"Letter of the Duke of Wellington (May 22, 1815) on the Battle of New Orleans." *Louisiana Historical Quarterly* 9 (January 1926): 5–10.

"Letters of John Innerarity: The Seizure of Pensacola by Andrew Jackson, November 7, 1814." *Florida Historical Quarterly* 9 (January 1931): 127–34.

"Letters Relating to the Negotiations at Ghent." *American Historical Review* 20 (October 1914): 108–29.

Library of Congress Acquisitions: Manuscript Division. Washington, DC: Library of Congress, 1991.

Looney, J. Jefferson, ed. *The Papers of Thomas Jefferson: Retirement Series.* Vo. 1, *4 March to 15 November 1809.* Princeton, NJ: Princeton University Press, 2004.

Lucier, James P., ed. *The Political Writings of James Monroe.* Washington, DC: Regnery, 2001.

Mauelshagen, Carl, and Gerald H. Davis, eds. *Partners in the Lord's Work: The Diary of Two Moravian Missionaries in the Creek Indian Country, 1807–1813.* Atlanta: Georgia State College, School of Arts and Sciences Research Paper #21, 1969.

McCown, Mary Hardin, ed. "The 'J. Hartsell Memora': The Journal of a Tennessee Captain in the War of 1812." *East Tennessee Historical Society's Publications* 11 (1939): 93–115; and 12 (1940): 118–46.

McDermott, John Francis, ed. *The Western Journals of Dr. George Hunter, 1796–1805.* Philadelphia: American Philosophical Society, 1963.

Morgan, David T., ed. *The John Gray Blount Papers.* Vol. 4, *1803–1833.* Raleigh: North Carolina Department of Cultural Resources, Division of Archives and History, 1982.

Moser, Harold D., David R. Hoth, Sharon Macpherson, and John H. Reinbold, eds. *The Papers of Andrew Jackson.* Vol. 3, *1814–1815.* Knoxville: University of Tennessee Press, 1991.

Moser, Harold D., and Sharon Macpherson, eds. *The Papers of Andrew Jackson.* Vol. 2, *1804–1813.* Knoxville: University of Tennessee Press, 1984.

Moulton, Gary E., ed. *The Papers of Chief John Ross.* Vol. 1, *1807–1839.* Norman: University of Oklahoma Press, 1985.

"Neal Smith to James Smylie, 8 January 1814." *Alabama Historical Reporter* 1 (July 1880): 2–3.

Ord, Robert W. "Memoranda Respecting Mobile." *Louisiana Historical Quarterly* 44 (July–October 1961): 131–34.

Owen, Thomas McAdory, ed. "Letters from George Strother Gaines Relating to Events in South Alabama, 1805–1814." *Transactions of the Alabama Historical Society* 3 (1898–99): 184–92.

Pakenham, Thomas, ed. *Pakenham Letters, 1800 to 1815.* London: John and Edward Bumpus, 1914.

Padgett, James A., ed. "Letters from John Rhea to Thomas Jefferson and James Madison." *East Tennessee Historical Society's Publications* 10 (1938): 114–27.

———. "Letters of James Brown to Henry Clay, 1804–1835." *Louisiana Historical Quarterly* 24 (October 1941): 921–1177.

Rankin, Hugh F., ed. *The Battle of New Orleans: A British View; The Journal of Major C. R. Forrest.* New Orleans: Hauser Press, 1961.

"Rare Letters of Great Democrats." *Nashville Banner Magazine* (September 6, 1936): 13, 15.

"Reflections on the Institutions of the Cherokee Indians from Observations Made during a Recent Visit to That Tribe: In a Letter from a Gentleman of Virginia, to Robert Walsh, Jan.–June 1st, 1817." *Analectic Magazine* 12 (July 1818): 36–56.

Remini, Robert V., ed. "Andrew Jackson's Account of the Battle of New Orleans." *Tennessee Historical Quarterly* 26 (Spring 1967): 23–42.

"Report of Major General John Keane, 26 December 1814." *European Magazine and London Review* 67 (March 1815): 256–57.

"Report of the Committee of Inquiry." *Louisiana Historical Quarterly* 9 (April 1926): 224–80.

A Review of the Battle of the Horseshoe, and of the Facts Relating to the Killing of Sixteen Indians on the Morning after the Battle, by the Orders of Gen. Andrew Jackson. N.p.: n.p., 1828.

Richardson, James B., ed. *Messages and Papers of the Presidents, 1789–1897.* 10 vols. Washington, DC: US Government Printing Office, 1896.

Rowland, Dunbar, ed. *Official Letter Books of W. C. C. Claiborne, 1801–1816.* 6 vols. Jackson, MS: State Department of Archives and History, 1917.

"Samuel Bains Letter." *Alabama Historical Quarterly* 19 (Fall/Winter 1957): 405–6.

"Selections from the Gano Papers, III." *Quarterly Publication of the Historical and Philosophical Society of Ohio* 16 (April–June 1921): 25–50.

Smith, Gene A., ed. *A British Eyewitness at the Battle of New Orleans: The Memoir of Royal Navy Admiral Robert Aitchison, 1808–1827*. New Orleans: Historic New Orleans Collection, 2004.

Smith, James Morton, ed. *The Republic of Letters: The Correspondence between Thomas Jefferson and James Madison, 1776–1826*. Vol. 3, *1804–1826*. New York: Norton, 1995.

Stagg, J. C. A., ed. *The Papers of James Madison—Presidential Series*. Vol. 4, *5 November 1811–9 July 1812*. Charlottesville: University of Virginia Press, 1999.

———. *The Papers of James Madison—Presidential Series*. Vol. 5, *10 July 1812–17 February 1813*. Charlottesville: University of Virginia Press, 2004.

"Unpublished Letter Relative to the Battle of New Orleans." *Publications of the Louisiana Historical Society* 9 (1917): 76–80.

Wait, William Bell, ed. *Travel Diary of William Richardson from Boston to New Orleans by Land, 1815*. New York: Valve Pilot, 1938.

White, Ky W., ed. "The Journal of Capt. Thomas Joyes from Louisville to the Battle of New Orleans." *Ohio Valley History* 8 (Fall 2009): 19–39.

White, Robert H., ed. *Messages of the Governors of Tennessee, 1796–1821*. Nashville: Tennessee Historical Commission, 1952.

———. *Messages of the Governors of Tennessee, 1845–1857*. Nashville: Tennessee Historical Commission, 1957.

Williams, John. "Fellow Citizens of Tennessee." Knoxville?: Wilson?, 1812.

Williams, Samuel C. "Journal of Events (1825–1873) of David Anderson Deaderick." *East Tennessee Historical Society's Publications* 8 (1936): 121–37.

Newspapers

Aurora General Advertiser, Philadelphia.
Carthage Gazette, Carthage, Tennessee.
Clarion, and Tennessee State Gazette, Nashville.
Commercial Appeal, Memphis.
Daily National Intelligencer, Washington, DC.
Impartial Review and Cumberland Repository, Nashville.
Kentucky Gazette, Lexington.
Liberty (Missouri) *Weekly Tribune*.
Nashville Republican.
Nashville Whig.
Niles' Weekly Register, Baltimore.
Raleigh Register, and North-Carolina Gazette.
Republican Banner, Nashville.
Tennessee Gazette and Metro District Advertiser, Nashville.
Weekly Public Ledger, Memphis.
Wilson's Knoxville Gazette.

Secondary Sources: Books, Articles, and Essays

Abernathy, Charles Clayton. *A Memento*. Nashville: n.p., 1960.

Abernethy, Thomas Perkins. *From Frontier to Plantation in Tennessee: A Study in Frontier Democracy*. Memphis, TN: Memphis State College Press, 1955.

Abram, Susan M. "Cherokees in the Creek War: A Band of Brothers." In *Tohopeka: Rethinking the Creek War and the War of 1812*, edited by Kathryn E. Holland Braund, 122–45. Tuscaloosa: University of Alabama Press.

Adams, Reed Mc. B. "New Orleans and the War of 1812, Part III." *Louisiana Historical Quarterly* 16 (October 1933): 681–703.

———. "New Orleans and the War of 1812, Part IV." *Louisiana Historical Quarterly* 17 (January 1934): 169–82.

Antal, Sandy. *A Wampum Denied: Proctor's War of 1812*. Ottawa, ON: Carleton University Press, 1997.

Apperson, George M. "African Americans on the Tennessee Frontier." *Tennessee Historical Quarterly* 59 (Spring 2000): 2–19.

Bancroft, George. *Literary and Historical Miscellanies*. New York: Harper and Brothers, 1855.

Barber, Douglas. "Council Government and the Genesis of the Creek War." *Alabama Review* 38 (July 1985): 163–74.

Barbuto, Richard V. "1812: The United States Builds a Regular Army." *Journal of the War of 1812* 15 (Summer 2012): 71–77.

Baseler, Marilyn. *"Asylum for Mankind": America, 1607–1800*. Ithaca, NY: Cornell University Press.

Bast, Homer. "Creek Indian Affairs, 1775–1778." *Georgia Historical Quarterly* 33 (March 1949): 1–25.

"The Battle of New Orleans." *DeBow's Review* 16 (June 1854): 641–46.

Beard, Michael F. "Natchez Under-the-Hill: Reform and Retribution in Early Natchez." *Gulf Coast Historical Review* 4 (Fall 1988): 29–48.

Belko, William S. "Epilogue to the War of 1812: The Monroe Administration, American Anglophobia, and the First Seminole War." In *America's Hundred Years' War: U.S. Expansion to the Gulf Coast and the Fate of the Seminole, 1763–1858*, edited by William S. Belko, 54–102. Gainesville: University Press of Florida, 2010.

Bell, Caryn Cosse. *Revolution, Romanticism, and the Afro-Creole Protest Tradition in Louisiana, 1718–1868*. Baton Rouge: Louisiana State University Press, 1997.

Bellesiles, Michael A. "Experiencing the War of 1812." In *Britain and America Go to War: The Impact of War and Warfare in Anglo-America, 1754–1815*, edited by Julie Flavell and Stephan Conway, 205–40. Gainesville: University Press of Florida, 2004.

Bergeron, Paul H., Stephen V. Ash, and Jeanette Keith. *Tennesseans and Their History*. Knoxville: University of Tennessee Press, 1999.

Berquin-Duvallon, Pierre-Louis. *Travels in Louisiana and the Floridas, in the Year, 1802, Giving a Correct Picture of Those Countries*. Translated by John Davis. New York: I. Riley, 1806.

Bickham, Troy. *The Weight of Vengeance: The United States, the British Empire, and the War of 1812*. New York: Oxford University Press, 2012.

"Biographical Sketch of the Late Lieutenant Colonel James Lauderdale, of Tennessee." *Analectic Magazine* 5 (May 1815): 378–84.

Boom, Aaron. "John Coffee, Citizen Soldier." *Tennessee Historical Quarterly* 22 (September 1963): 223–37.

Bourchier, Jane, ed. *Memoir of the Life of Admiral Sir Edward Codrington with Selections from His Public and Private Correspondence*. 2nd ed. London: Longmans, Green, 1875.

Bourne, Kenneth. *Britain and the Balance of Power in North America, 1815–1908*. Berkeley: University of California Press, 1967.

Braund, Kathryn E. Holland. *Deerskins and Duffels: The Creek Indian Trade with Anglo-America, 1685–1815*. Lincoln: University of Nebraska Press, 1993.

A Brief Sketch of the Life and Military Service of Arthur P. Hayne, of Charleston, South Carolina. Philadelphia: T. K. and P. G. Collins, 1837.

Brooks, Philip Coolidge. *Diplomacy and the Borderlands: The Adams-Onís Treaty of 1819*. Berkeley: University of California Press, 1939; reprint, New York: Octagon Books, 1970.

Brown, Roger H. *The Republic in Peril: 1812*. New York: Norton, 1964.

Brown, Wilburt S. *The Amphibious Campaign for West Florida and Louisiana, 1814–1815: A Critical Review of Strategy and Tactics at New Orleans*. Tuscaloosa: University of Alabama Press, 1969.

Budiansky, Stephen. "The War of 1812 and the Rise of American Military Power." In *What So Proudly We Hailed: Essays on the Contemporary Meaning of the War of 1812*, edited by Pietro S. Nivola and Peter J. Kastor, 36–66. Washington, DC: Brookings Institution Press, 2012.

Buel, Jr., Richard. *America on the Brink: How the Political Struggle over the War of 1812 Almost Destroyed the Young Republic*. New York: Palgrave Macmillan, 2005.

Burke, James Wakefield. *David Crockett: The Man Behind the Myth*. Austin, TX: Eakin Press, 1984.

Burt, A. L. *The United States, Great Britain, and British North America from the Revolution to the Establishment of Peace after the War of 1812*. New York: Russell and Russell, 1961.

Cady, John F. "Western Opinion and the War of 1812." *Ohio Archaeological and Historical Quarterly* 33 (October 1924): 427–76.

Callan, John F. *The Military Laws of the United States, Relating to the Army, Volunteers, Militia, and to Bounty Lands and Pensions, from the Foundation of the Government to the Year 1863*. Philadelphia: George W. Childs, 1863.

Cassell, Frank A. "Slaves of the Chesapeake Bay Area and the War of 1812." *Journal of Negro History* 57 (April 1972): 144–55.

Cayton, Andrew R. L. "'When Shall We Cease to Have Judases?': The Blount Conspiracy and the Limits of the 'Extended Republic.'" In *Launching the "Extended Republic": The Federalist Era*, edited by Ronald Hoffman and Peter J. Albert, 156–89. Charlottesville: University of Virginia Press, 1996.

Chambers, Henry E. *West Florida and Its Relation to the Historical Cartography of the United States*. Baltimore: Johns Hopkins Press, 1898.

Chappell, Gordon T. "John Coffee: Surveyor and Land Agent." *Alabama Review* 14 (July 1961): 180–95.

Claiborne, Nathaniel Herbert. *Notes on the War in the South, with Biographical Sketches of the Lives of Montgomery, Jackson, Sevier, the Late Gov. Claiborne, and Others*. Richmond, VA: William Ramsey, 1819.

Clark, Isaac. *Clark's Miscellany, in Prose and Verse*. Nashville: T. G. Bradford, 1812.

Clodfelter, Michael. *Warfare and Armed Conflicts: A Statistical Reference to Casualty and Other Figures, 1500–2000*. 2nd. ed. Jefferson, NC: McFarland, 2002.

Coker, William S. "How General Jackson Learned of the British Plans *before* the Battle of New Orleans." *Gulf South Historical Review* 3 (Fall 1987): 84–95.

Colburn, Trevor, ed. *Fame and the Founding Fathers: Essays by Douglas Adair*. New York: Norton, 1974.

Coleman, Peter J., and Penelope K. Majeske. "British Immigrants in Rhode Island during the War of 1812." *Rhode Island History* 34 (August 1975): 66–75.

Cooke, John Henry. *A Narrative of Events in the South of France, and the Attack on New Orleans, in 1814 and 1815*. London: T. & W. Boone, 1835.

Corbitt, Duvon Clough. "The Administrative System in the Floridas, 1781–1821." In *The Spanish Presence in Louisiana, 1763–1803*, edited by Gilbert C. Din, 113–23. Lafayette: Center for Louisiana Studies, 1996.

Cox, Isaac Joslin. "The American Intervention in West Florida." *American Historical Review* 17 (January 1912): 290–311.

Crawford, Michael J., ed. *The Naval War of 1812: A Documentary History*. Vol. 3, *1814–1815: Chesapeake Bay, Northern Lakes, and Pacific Ocean*. Washington, DC: Naval Historical Center, Department of the Navy, 2002.

Crockett, David. *A Narrative of the Life of David Crockett, of the State of Tennessee*. Philadelphia: E. L. Carey and A. Hart, 1834; reprint, Knoxville: University of Tennessee Press, 1973.

Cunliffe, Marcus. *Soldiers and Civilians: The Martial Spirit in America, 1775–1865*. Boston: Little, Brown, 1968.

Cusick, James C. *The Other War of 1812: The Patriot War and the American Invasion of Spanish East Florida*. Gainesville: University Press of Florida, 2003.

Cutler, Jervis. *A Topographical Description of the State of Ohio, Indiana Territory, and Louisiana*. Boston: Charles Williams, 1812; reprint, New York: Arno Press, 1971.

Darby, William. *The Immigrant's Guide to the Western and Southwestern States and Territories*. New York: Kirk and Mercein, 1818.

Dargo, George. *Jefferson's Louisiana: Politics and the Clash of Legal Traditions*. Cambridge, MA: Harvard University Press, 1975.

Darnell, Elias. *A Journal, Containing an Accurate and Interesting Account of the Hardships, Sufferings, Battles, Defeat, and Captivity of Those Heroic Kentucky Volunteers and Regulars, Commanded by General Winchester, in the Year 1812 . . . 1813*. Paris, KY: Joel R. Lyle, 1813.

Davis, Karl. "'Remembering Fort Mims': Reinterpreting the Origins of the Creek Civil War." *Journal of the Early Republic* 22 (Winter 2002): 611–36.

Davis, William C. *The Pirates Laffite: The Treacherous World of the Corsairs of the Gulf.* Orlando, FL: Harcourt, 2005.

Day, Donald, and Harry Herbert Ullom, eds. *The Autobiography of Sam Houston.* Norman: University of Oklahoma Press, 1954.

De Grummond, Jane Lucas. "The Fair Honoring the Brave." *Louisiana History* 3 (Winter 1962): 54–58.

———. *Renato Beluche: Smuggler, Privateer, and Patriot, 1780–1860.* Baton Rouge: Louisiana State University Press, 1983.

De Grummond, Jane Lucas, ed. "Platter of Glory." *Louisiana History* 3 (Autumn 1962): 316–59.

Denson, Jesse. *A Compendium, of Useful Information.* Nashville: Printed for the author, 1813.

DeRosier, Arthur H., Jr. "Andrew Jackson and Negotiations for the Removal of the Choctaw Indians." *Historian* 29 (May 1967): 343–62.

Dixon, Richard Remy. *The Battle on the West Bank.* New Orleans: The Battle of New Orleans, 150th Anniversary Committee of Louisiana, 1965.

Doherty, Herbert J., Jr. *Richard Keith Call: Southern Unionist.* Gainesville: University Press of Florida, 1961.

Dowd, Gregory Evans. *A Spirited Resistance: The North American Indian Struggle for Unity, 1745–1815.* Baltimore: Johns Hopkins University Press, 1992.

Downes, Randolph C. "Indian Affairs in the Southwest Territory, 1790–1796." *Tennessee Historical Magazine* 2nd ser. 3 (January 1937): 240–68.

Dudley, William S., ed. *The Naval War of 1812: A Documentary History.* Vol. 1, *1812.* Washington, DC: Naval Historical Center, Department of the Navy, 1985.

Duffy, John, ed. *The Rudolph Matas History of Medicine in Louisiana.* Vol. 1. Baton Rouge: Louisiana State University Press, 1958.

Dungan, Nicholas. *Gallatin: America's Swiss Founding Father.* New York: New York University Press, 2010.

Durham, Walter T. *Daniel Smith: Frontier Statesman.* Gallatin, TN: Sumner County Library Board, 1976.

———. *James Winchester: Tennessee Pioneer.* Gallatin, TN: Sumner County Library Board, 1979.

Edmunds, R. David. *Tecumseh and the Quest for Indian Leadership.* Boston: Little, Brown, 1984.

Elting, John R. *Amateurs, to Arms! A Military History of the War of 1812.* Chapel Hill, NC: Algonquin Books of Chapel Hill, 1991.

Errington, Jane, and George A. Rawlyk. "Creating a British-American Political Community in Upper Canada." In *Loyalists and Community in North America,* edited by Robert M. Calhoun, Timothy M. Barnes, and George A. Rawlyk, 187–200. Westport, CT: Greenwood Press, 1994.

Estaville, Lawrence E. "The Louisiana French Language in the Nineteenth Century." *Southeastern Geographer* 30 (November 1990): 105–20.

Ethridge, Robbie. *Creek Country: The Creek Indians and Their World.* Chapel Hill: University of North Carolina Press, 2003.

"An Eye-Witness of the Battle of New Orleans." *Boston Public Library Quarterly* 9 (July 1957): 159–61.

Faye, Stanley. "British and Spanish Fortifications of Pensacola, 1786–1821." *Florida Historical Quarterly* 20 (October 1941): 277–92.

Feller, Daniel. *The Jacksonian Promise: America, 1815–1840.* Baltimore: Johns Hopkins University Press, 1995.

Finger, John R. *Tennessee Frontiers: Three Regions in Transition.* Bloomington: Indiana University Press, 2001.

Fisher, Ruth Anna. "The Surrender of Pensacola as Told by the British." *American Historical Review* 54 (January 1949): 326–29.

Folmsbee, Stanley John. *Sectionalism and Internal Improvements in Tennessee, 1796–1845.* Knoxville: East Tennessee Historical Society, 1939.

Frank, Andrew K. *Creeks and Southerners: Biculturalism on the Early American Frontier.* Lincoln: University of Nebraska Press, 2005.

Frey, Sylvia R. *Water from the Rock: Black Resistance in a Revolutionary Age.* Princeton, NJ: Princeton University Press, 1991.

Gallay, Alan. *The Indian Slave Trade: The Rise of the English Empire in the American South, 1670–1717.* New Haven, CT: Yale University Press, 2002.

Gatschet, Albert S. "Towns and Villages of the Creek Confederacy in the XVIII and XIX Centuries." *Publications of the Alabama Historical Society* 1 (1901): 386–415.

"General Jackson's Military Pretensions." *Truth's Advocate and Monthly Anti-Jackson Expositor* 1 (March 1828): 81–94.

Gibson, Charles, ed. *The Black Legend: Anti-Spanish Attitudes in the Old World and the New.* New York: Alfred A. Knopf, 1971.

George, Noah Jackson. *A Memorandum of the Creek Indian War.* Meredith, NH: R. Lanthrop, 1815.

Gillett, Mary C. *The Army Medical Department, 1775–1818.* Washington, DC: Center of Military History: United States Army, 1990.

Gleig, George G. *A Narrative of the Campaigns of the British Army at Washington and New Orleans, under Generals Ross, Pakenham, and Lambert, in the Years 1814 and 1815; with Some Account of the Countries Visited.* London: John Murray, 1821.

Goodman, Warren H. "The Origins of the War of 1812: A Survey of Changing Interpretations." *Mississippi Valley Historical Review* 28 (September 1941): 171–86.

Goodpasture, Albert V. "Indian Wars and Warriors of the Old Southwest, 1730–1807." *Tennessee Historical Magazine* 4 (September 1918): 161–210.

Goodstein, Anita S. "Black History on the Nashville Frontier, 1780–1810." *Tennessee Historical Quarterly* 38 (Winter 1979): 401–20.

Gower, Hershel, and Jack Allen, eds. *Pen and Sword: The Life and Journals of Randal W. McGavock.* Nashville: Tennessee Historic Commission, 1950.

Greene, Jerome A. *Historic Resource Study—Chalmette Unit, Jean Laffite National Historical Park.* Washington, DC: US Department of Interior/National Park Service, 1985.

Griffin, Patrick. *American Leviathan: Empire, Nation, and Revolutionary Frontier.* New York: Hill and Wang, 2007.

Hahn, Steven C. *The Invention of the Creek Nation, 1670–1763*. Lincoln: University of Nebraska Press, 2004.

———. "The Mother of Necessity: Carolina, the Creek Indians, and the Making of a New Order in the American Southeast, 1670–1763." In *The Transformation of Southeastern Indians, 1540–1760*, edited by Robbie Ethridge and Charles Hudson, 79–114. Jackson: University Press of Mississippi, 2002.

Halbert, Henry Sale, and Timothy Horton Ball. *The Creek War of 1813 and 1814*. Chicago: Donohue and Henneberry, 1895.

Hall, Arthur H. "The Red Stick War: Creek Indian Affairs during the War of 1812." *Chronicles of Oklahoma* 12 (September 1934): 264–93.

Hamer, Philip, ed. *Tennessee: A History, 1673–1932*. Vol. 1. New York: American Historical Society, 1933.

Hamilton, James A. *Reminiscences of James A. Hamilton or Men and Events at Home and Abroad during Three Quarters of a Century*. New York: Charles Scribner, 1869.

Hanger, Kimberly S. *Bounded Lives, Bounded Places: Free Black Society in Colonial New Orleans, 1769–1808*. Durham, NC: Duke University Press, 1997.

———. "A Privilege and Honor to Serve: The Free Black Militia of Spanish New Orleans." In *The Spanish Presence in Louisiana, 1763–1803*, edited by Gilbert C. Din, 391–432. Lafayette: Center for Louisiana Studies, University of Southwestern Louisiana, 1996.

Hatcher, William B. *Edward Livingston: Jeffersonian Republican and Jacksonian Democrat*. Baton Rouge: Louisiana State University Press, 1940.

Hatzenbuehler, Ronald, and Robert L. Ivie. *Congress Declares War: Rhetoric, Leadership, and Partisanship in the Early Republic*. Kent, OH: Kent State University Press, 1983.

Haynes, Robert V. "Territorial Mississippi, 1798–1817." *Journal of Mississippi History* 64 (Winter 2002): 283–305.

Heaton, Herbert. "Non-Importation, 1806–1812." *Journal of Economic History* 1 (November 1941): 178–98.

Heidler, David S., and Jeanne T. Heidler. "'Where All Behave Well': Fort Bowyer and the War on the Gulf, 1814–1815." In *Tohopeka: Rethinking the Creek War and the War of 1812*, edited by Kathryn E. Holland Braund, 182–99. Tuscaloosa: University of Alabama Press, 2012.

Heiskell, Samuel Gordon. *Andrew Jackson and Early Tennessee History*. 3 vols. Nashville: Ambrose Printing, 1918.

Heller, J. Roderick. *Democracy's Lawyer: Felix Grundy of the Old Southwest*. Baton Rouge: Louisiana State University Press, 2010.

Henderson, William Abbott. "Vice-Admiral Sir Alexander Cochrane and the Southern Campaign to New Orleans." *Southern Historian* 8 (Spring 1987): 24–38.

Henry, H. M. "The Slave Laws of Tennessee." *Tennessee Historical Magazine* 2 (September 1916): 175–203

Hickey, Donald R. *The War of 1812: A Forgotten Conflict*. Urbana: University of Illinois Press, 1989.

Holmes, Jack D. *Gayoso: The Life of a Spanish Governor in the Mississippi Valley, 1789–1799*. Baton Rouge: Louisiana State University Press, 1965.

Holmes, Jack D., ed. "William C. C. Claiborne Predicts the Future of Tennessee." *Tennessee Historical Quarterly* 24 (Summer 1965): 181–84.

Hoig, Stan. *The Cherokees and Their Chiefs: In the Wake of Empire*. Fayetteville: University of Arkansas Press, 1989.

Holton, Woody. *Unruly Americans and the Origins of the Constitution*. New York: Hill and Wang, 2007.

Horsman, Reginald. "British-Colonial Attitudes and Policies toward the Indian in the American Colonies." In *Attitudes of Colonial Powers toward the American Indian*, edited by Howard Peckham and Charles Gibson, 81–106. Salt Lake City: University of Utah Press, 1969.

———. "British Indian Policy in the Northwest, 1807–1812." *Mississippi Valley Historical Review* 45 (June 1958): 51–66.

———. *The Causes of the War of 1812*. Philadelphia: University of Pennsylvania Press, 1962.

Horwitz, Tony. "Remember the Raisin." *Smithsonian* 43 (June 2012): 28–35.

Hoskins, Katherine B. *Anderson County*. Memphis, TN: Memphis State University Press, 1979.

Howe, Daniel Walker. *What Hath God Wrought: The Transformation of America, 1815–1848*. New York: Oxford University Press, 2007.

Hsiung, David C. *A Mountaineer in Motion: The Memoir of Dr. Abraham Jobe, 1817–1906*. Knoxville: University of Tennessee Press, 2009.

Hudson, Angela Pulley. *Creek Paths and Federal Roads: Indians, Settlers, and Slaves and the Making of the American South*. Chapel Hill: University of North Carolina Press, 2010.

Hunt, Alfred N. *Haiti's Influence on Antebellum America: Slumbering Volcano in the Caribbean*. Baton Rouge: Louisiana State University Press, 1988.

Hunt, Charles Havens. *Life of Edward Livingston*. New York: D. Appleton, 1864.

Hunt, Gaillard. "Office Seeking during Jefferson's Administration." *American Historical Review* 3 (January 1898): 270–91.

Isenberg, Nancy. *Fallen Founder: The Life of Aaron Burr*. New York: Viking Penguin, 2007.

James, William. *A Full and Correct Account of the Military Occurrences of the Late War between Great Britain and the United States of America; with an Appendix, and Plates*. 2 vols. London: Published by the author, 1818.

Jenkins, William H. "Alabama Forts, 1700–1838." *Alabama Review* 12 (July 1959): 163–79.

Jones, John G. *A Complete History of Methodism as Connected with the Mississippi Conference of the Methodist Episcopal Church, South*. Vol. 1. Nashville: Publishing House of the M. E. Church, South, 1908.

Jones, Landon Y. *William Clark and the Shaping of the West*. New York: Hill and Wang, 2004.

Jortner, Adam. *The Gods of Prophetstown: The Battle of Tippecanoe and the Holy War for the American Frontier*. New York: Oxford University Press, 2012.

Kahn, Mark E. *A Republic of Men: The American Founders, Gendered Language, and Patriarchal Politics*. New York: New York University Press, 1998.

Kammen, Michael. *A Season of Youth: The American Revolution and the Historical Imagination.* New York: Alfred A. Knopf, 1978.

Kanon, Tom. "Battle of Econochaca." In *The Encyclopedia of the War of 1812: A Political, Social, and Military History.* 3 vols., ed. Spencer C. Tucker, 1: 212. Santa Barbara, CA: ABC-CLIO, 2012.

———. "'Glories in the Field': John Cocke vs. Andrew Jackson during the War of 1812." *Journal of East Tennessee History* 71 (1999): 47–65.

———. "'James Madison, Felix Grundy, and the Devil': A Western War Hawk in Congress." *Filson History Quarterly* 75 (Fall 2001): 433–68.

———. "The Kidnapping of Martha Crawley and Settler-Indian Relations Prior to the War of 1812." *Tennessee Historical Quarterly* 64 (Spring 2005): 3–23.

———. "The Other Battle of New Orleans: Andrew Jackson and the Louisianans." *Gulf South Historical Review* 17 (Spring 2002): 40–61.

———. "'Scared from Their Sins for a Season': The Religious Ramifications of the New Madrid Earthquakes, 1811–1812." *Ohio Valley History* 5 (Summer 2005): 21–38.

———. "'A Slow, Laborious Slaughter': The Battle of Horseshoe Bend." *Tennessee Historical Quarterly* 58 (Spring 1999): 3–15.

Kaplan, Carol. "To Live in Hearts We Leave Behind Is Not to Die." *Monuments and Milestones* 5 (Fall/Winter 2009): 3.

Kastor, Peter J. "'Motives of Peculiar Urgency': Local Diplomacy in Louisiana, 1803–1821." *William and Mary Quarterly* 3rd ser. 58 (October 2001): 819–48.

Keller, William F. *The Nation's Advocate: Henry Marie Brackenridge and Young America.* Pittsburgh: University of Pittsburgh Press, 1956.

King, George Harrison Sanford. *The Memoirs of Eliza Williams (Chotard) Gould: Wife of William P. Gould of Tuscaloosa, Ala., Daughter of John Marie Chotard da Place and His Wife Sarah (Williams) Willis Chotard.* Fredericksburg, VA: Published by the author, 1953.

Knouff, Gregory T. "'An Arduous Service': The Pennsylvania Backcountry Soldiers." *Pennsylvania History* 61 (January 1994): 45–74.

Kruse, Paul. "A Secret Agent in East Florida: General George Mathews and the Patriot War." *Journal of Southern History* 18 (May 1952): 193–217.

Kulick, William K., and Leroy Alonso. "An Eyewitness Account of the Battle of New Orleans." *Manuscripts* 51 (Spring 1999): 121–25.

Lackey, Richard S., and John D. W. Guice, comps. *Claims Filed by Citizens of the Alabama and Tombigbee River Settlements in the Mississippi Territory for Depredations by the Creek Indians during the War of 1812.* New Orleans: Polyanthos, 1977.

LaFeber, Walter. "Jefferson and an American Foreign Policy." In *Jeffersonian Legacies,* edited by Peter S. Onuf, 370–91. Charlottesville: University of Virginia Press, 1993.

Latour, Arsene Lacarriere. *Historical Memoir of the War in West Florida and Louisiana in 1814–15, with an Atlas.* Edited by Gene A. Smith. Gainesville: University Press of Florida, 1999.

Laver, Harry S. "Refuge of Manhood: Masculinity and the Militia Experience in Kentucky." In *Southern Manhood: Perspectives on Masculinity in the Old South,* edited by Craig Thompson Friend and Lorri Glover, 1–21. Athens: University of Georgia Press, 2004.

———. "Rethinking the Social Role of the Militia: Community Building in Antebellum Kentucky." *Journal of Southern History* 68 (November 2002): 777–816.

Layman, Elizabeth Waterhouse, comp. *Richard Green Waterhouse (1775–1827): Tennessee Pioneer.* Wolfe City, TX: Henington Publishing, 1996.

Leach, Douglas Edward. "John Gordon of John Gordon's Ferry." *Tennessee Historical Quarterly* 18 (December 1959): 322–44.

Lebreton, Dagmar Renshaw. "The Man Who Won the Battle of New Orleans." *Louisiana Historical Quarterly* 38 (July 1955): 20–34.

Lengel, Leland L. "The Road to Fort Mims: Judge Harry Toulmin's Observations on the Creek War, 1811–1813. *Alabama Review* 29 (January 1976): 16–36.

Levasseur, Auguste. *Lafayette in America in 1824 and 1825; or, Journal of a Voyage to the United States.* 2 vols. Philadelphia: Carey and Lea, 1829.

Lossing, Benson J. "Defense of New Orleans." *Harper's New Monthly Magazine* 30 (January 1865): 168–86.

Lovett, Bobby L. *The African-American History of Nashville, Tennessee, 1780–1930.* Fayetteville: University of Arkansas Press, 1999.

Lowery, Charles D. "The Great Migration to the Mississippi Territory, 1798–1819." *Journal of Mississippi History* 30 (August 1968): 178–92.

Lowry, Robert, and William H. McGardle. *A History of Mississippi, from the Earliest Settlement Made by the French, under Iberville, to the Death of Jefferson Davis.* Jackson, MS: R. H. Henry, 1891.

Maass, Alfred A. "Brownsville's Steamboat *Enterprise* and Pittsburgh's Supply of General Jackson's Army." *Pittsburgh History* 77 (Spring 1994): 22–29.

Mahon, John K. "British Command Decisions Relative to the Battle of New Orleans." *Louisiana History* 6 (Winter 1965): 53–76.

———. "British Strategy and Southern Indians: War of 1812." *Florida Historical Quarterly* 44 (April 1966): 285–302.

———. "The United States Army in the Gulf Coast Region." In *The Military Presence on the Gulf Coast,* edited by William S. Coker, 82–96. Pensacola, FL: Gulf Coast History and Humanities Conference, 1978.

Malone, Ann Patton. *Sweet Chariot: Slave Family and Household Structure in Nineteenth-Century Louisiana.* Chapel Hill: University of North Carolina Press, 1992.

Malone, Henry T. "Cherokee-White Relations on the Southern Frontier in the Early Nineteenth Century." *North Carolina Historical Review* 34 (January 1957): 1–14.

Martin, James Kirby, and Mark Edward Lender. *A Respectable Army: The Military Origins of the Republic, 1763–1789.* Arlington Heights, IL: Harlan Davidson, 1982.

Martin, Joel W. *Sacred Revolt: The Muskogees' Struggle for a New World.* Boston: Beacon Press, 1991.

"A Massachusetts Volunteer at the Battle of New Orleans." *Louisiana Historical Quarterly* 9 (January 1926): 30–31.

McClure, Wallace. *State Constitution Making with Especial Reference to Tennessee.* Nashville: Marshall and Bruce, 1916.

McConnell, Roland C. *Negro Troops of Antebellum Louisiana: A History of the Battalion of Free Men of Color.* Baton Rouge: Louisiana State University Press, 1968.

McCully, Robert. "'Too Much Praise Cannot Be Bestowed': Andrew Jackson's Artillery at the Battle of New Orleans." *Military Collector and Historian* 62 (Summer 2010): 88–100.

McDougall, Walter A. *Promised Land, Crusader State: The American Encounter with the World since 1776.* Boston: Houghton Mifflin, 1997.

McLeod, Alexander. *A Scriptural View of the Character, Causes, and Ends of the Present War.* 2nd ed. New York: Eastburn, Kirk; Whiting and Watson; and Smith and Forman, 1815.

McManus, John. *American Courage, American Carnage: The 7th Infantry Regiment's Combat Experience, 1812 through World War II.* New York: Tom Doherty Associates, 2009.

McMichael, Andrew. *Atlantic Loyalties: Americans in Spanish West Florida, 1785–1810.* Athens: University of Georgia Press, 2008.

Mead, Walter Russell. *Special Providence: American Foreign Policy and How It Changed the World.* New York: Alfred A. Knopf, 2001.

Merk, Frederick. *Manifest Destiny and Mission in American History: A Reinterpretation.* New York: Alfred A. Knopf, 1963.

Merrell, James H. "Second Thoughts on Colonial Historians and American Indians." *William and Mary Quarterly,* 3rd ser., 69 (July 2012): 451–512.

Miller, David W. *The Taking of American Indian Lands: A History of Territorial Cessions and Forced Relocations, 1607–1840.* Jefferson, NC: McFarland, 2011.

Miller, James David. *South by Southwest: Planter Emigration and Identity in the Slave South.* Charlottesville: University of Virginia Press, 2002.

Millet, Nathaniel. "Britain's 1814 Occupation of Pensacola and America's Response: An Episode of the War of 1812 in the Southeastern Borderlands." *Florida Historical Quarterly* 84 (Fall 2005): 229–55.

Moore, Mary Daniel. "The First Century of Library History in Tennessee, 1813–1913." *East Tennessee Historical Society's Publications* 16 (1944): 3–21.

Morrow, Sara Sprott. "A Brief History of Theater in Nashville, 1807–1970." *Tennessee Historical Quarterly* 30 (Spring 1971): 178–89.

Murdoch, Richard K. "A British Report on West Florida and Louisiana, November, 1812." *Florida Historical Quarterly* 43 (July 1964): 36–51.

———. *The Georgia-Florida Frontier: Spanish Reaction to French Intrigue and American Designs.* Berkeley: University of California Press, 1951.

"Narrative of General Hall." *South-Western Monthly* 1 (June 1852): 331–36; and 2 (July 1852): 11–16.

Nasatir, Abraham P. *Borderlands in Retreat: From Spanish Louisiana to the Far Southwest.* Albuquerque: University of New Mexico Press, 2008.

———. *Spanish War Vessels on the Mississippi, 1792–1796.* New Haven, CT: Yale University Press, 1968.

Nelson, John R., Jr. *Liberty and Property: Political Economy and Policymaking in the New Nation, 1789–1812.* Baltimore: Johns Hopkins University Press, 1987.

Nolte, Vincent. *Fifty Years in Both Hemispheres; or, Reminiscences of the Life of a For-mer Merchant.* New York: Redfield, 1854.

North, Douglass C. *The Economic Growth of the United States, 1790–1860.* Englewood Cliffs, NJ: Prentice-Hall, 1961.

O'Brien, Sean Michael. *In Bitterness and Tears: Andrew Jackson's Destruction of the Creeks and Seminoles.* Westport, CT: Praeger, 2003.

O'Donnell, James H., III. *Southern Indians in the American Revolution.* Knoxville: University of Tennessee Press, 1973.

Owens, Robert M. *Mr. Jefferson's Hammer: William Henry Harrison and the Origins of American Indian Policy.* Norman: University of Oklahoma Press, 2007.

Owsley, Frank Lawrence, Jr. *Struggle for the Gulf Borderlands: The Creek War and the Battle of New Orleans.* Gainesville: University Press of Florida, 1981.

Owsley, Frank Lawrence, Jr., and Gene A. Smith. *Filibusters and Expansionists: Jef-fersonian Manifest Destiny, 1800–1821.* Tuscaloosa: University of Alabama Press, 1997.

Parsons, Edward Alexander. "Jean Laffite in the War of 1812: A Narrative Based on the Original Documents." *Proceedings of the American Antiquarian Society* 50 (1940): 205–24.

Parton, James. *Life of Andrew Jackson.* 3 vols. New York: Mason Brothers, 1861.

Patrick, Rembert W. *Florida Fiasco: Rampart Rebels on the Georgia-Florida Border, 1810–1815.* Athens: University of Georgia Press, 1954.

Peeler, Elizabeth H. "The Policies of Willie Blount as Governor of Tennessee, 1809–1815." *Tennessee Historical Quarterly* 1 (December 1942): 309–27.

Penick, James L. *The New Madrid Earthquakes.* Columbia: University of Missouri Press, 1981.

"Pensacola in 1810." *Florida Historical Quarterly* 32 (July 1953): 44–48.

Perrin du Lac, François Marie. *Travels through the Two Louisianas, and among the Savage Nations of the Missouri; also, in the United States, along the Ohio, and the Ad-jacent Provinces, in 1801, 1802, and 1803.* London: Richard Phillips, 1807.

Phelps, Albert. *Louisiana: A Record of Expansion.* Boston: Houghton Mifflin, 1905.

Pickles, Tim. *New Orleans 1815: Andrew Jackson Crushes the British.* London: Reed International, 1993.

Piker, Joshua. "Colonists and Creeks: Rethinking the Pre-Revolutionary Southern Backcountry." *Journal of Southern History* 70 (August 2004): 503–40.

Poitrineau, Abel. "Demography and the Political Destiny of Florida during the Second Spanish Period." *Florida Historical Quarterly* 66 (April 1988): 420–43.

Porter, Kenneth Wiggins. "Negroes and the East Florida Annexation Plot, 1811–1813." *Journal of Negro History* 30 (January 1945): 9–29.

Pound, Merritt B. *Benjamin Hawkins: Indian Agent.* Athens: University of Georgia Press, 1951.

"A Prelude to the Creek War of 1813–1814 in a Letter of John Innerarity to James In-nerarity." *Florida Historical Quarterly* 18 (April 1940): 247–66.

Prucha, Francis Paul. *The Sword of the Republic: The United States Army on the Fron-tier, 1783–1846.* New York: Macmillan, 1969.

Ranck, James B. "Andrew Jackson and the Burr Conspiracy." *Tennessee Historical Magazine* 2nd ser. 1 (October 1930): 17–28.

Ray, Kristopher. *Middle Tennessee, 1775–1825: Progress and Popular Democracy on the Southwestern Frontier.* Knoxville: University of Tennessee Press, 2007.

Reid, John, and John Henry Eaton. *The Life of Andrew Jackson.* Edited by Frank Lawrence Owsley Jr. Tuscaloosa: University of Alabama Press, 1974.

Remini, Robert V. *The Battle of New Orleans: Andrew Jackson and America's First Military Victory.* New York: Viking, 1999.

"The Reminiscences of General Bernard Pratte, Jr." *Bulletin of the Missouri Historical Society* 6 (October 1949): 59–71.

Reynolds, John. *My Own Times, Embracing Also, the History of My Life.* Belleville, IL: B. H. Perryman and H. L. Davison, 1855.

Ritchie, Carson I. A. "The Guns of New Orleans." *History Teacher* 2 (May 1969): 9–13.

———. "The Louisiana Campaign." *Louisiana Historical Quarterly* 44 (January–April 1961): 13–103.

Roberts, Frances C. "Thomas Freeman: Surveyor of the Old Southwest." *Alabama Review* 40 (July 1987): 216–30.

Rogin, Michael. *Fathers and Children: Andrew Jackson and the Subjugation of the American Indian.* New York: Alfred A. Knopf, 1975.

Ross, James. *Life and Times of Elder Rueben Ross.* Philadelphia: Grant, Faires, and Rodgers, 1882.

Ross, Margaret. "The New Madrid Earthquake." *Arkansas Historical Quarterly* 27 (Summer 1968): 83–104.

Rossiter, Clinton. *The American Quest, 1790–1860: An Emerging Nation in Search of Identity, Unity, and Modernity.* New York: Harcourt Brace Jovanovich, 1971.

Rothman, Adam. *Slave Country: American Expansion and the Origins of the Deep South.* Cambridge, MA: Harvard University Press, 2005.

Roumillat, Shelene C. "The French St. Domingue Refugees from Cuba and the Battle of New Orleans." Paper presented at the 49th Annual Meeting of the Louisiana Historical Association, March 2007 (Alexandria).

Rowland, Eron. *Andrew Jackson's Campaign against the British, or the Mississippi Territory in the War of 1812.* New York: Macmillan, 1926.

Rowley, Karen M., and John Maxwell Hamilton. "A Missing Link in the History of American War Correspondents: James Morgan Bradford and *The Time Piece* of St. Francisville, Louisiana." *American Journalism* 22 (Fall 2005): 7–26.

Rucker, Brian R. "In the Shadow of Jackson: Uriah Blue's Expedition into West Florida." *Florida Historical Quarterly* 73 (January 1995): 325–38.

R. S. [Robert Simpson?]. "Battle of New Orleans, 8th January, 1815." *Blackwood's Edinburgh Magazine* 24 (September 1828): 354–57.

Saltz, Ronald N. "Chickasaws." In *Tennessee Encyclopedia of History and Culture,* edited by Carroll Van West, 153. Nashville: Tennessee Historical Society, 1998.

Saunt, Claudio. "'Domestick . . . Quiet Being Broke': Gender Conflict among Creek Indians in the Eighteenth Century." In *Contact Points: American Frontiers from the Mohawk Valley to the Mississippi, 1750–1830,* edited by Andrew R. L. Cayton and Fredrika J. Tuete, 151–74. Chapel Hill: University of North Carolina Press, 1998.

———. *A New Order of Things: Property, Power, and the Transformation of the Creek Indians, 1733–1816.* Cambridge: Cambridge University Press, 1999.

Saxon, Lyle. *Laffite the Pirate.* Gretna, LA: Pelican, 1989.

"The Senate Debate on the Breckinridge Bill for the Government of Louisiana, 1804." *American Historical Review* 22 (January 1917): 340–64.

Sevier, Cora Bales, and Nancy S. Madden. *Sevier Family History with the Collected Letters of Gen. John Sevier, First Governor of Tennessee.* Washington, DC: Published by the authors, 1961.

Skaggs, David Curtis. "The Making of a Major General: William Henry Harrison and the Politics of Command, 1812–13." *Ohio Valley History* 10 (Spring 2010): 32–52.

Skeen, C. Edward. *Citizen Soldiers in the War of 1812.* Lexington: University Press of Kentucky, 1999.

———. *John Armstrong, Jr., 1758–1843: A Biography.* Syracuse, NY: Syracuse University Press, 1981.

Smelser, Marshall. "Tecumseh, Harrison, and the War of 1812." *Indiana Magazine of History* 65 (March 1969): 25–44.

Smith, Daniel. *A Short Description of the Tennessee Government, or the Territory of the United States South of the River Ohio, to Accompany and Explain a Map of that Country.* Philadelphia: Mathew Carey, 1793.

Smith, Gene Allen. *"For the Purposes of Defense": The Politics of the Jeffersonian Gunboat Program.* Newark: University of Delaware Press, 1995.

———. "Preventing the 'Eggs of Insurrection' from Hatching: The U.S. Navy and Control of the Mississippi River, 1806–1815." *Northern Mariner* 18 (July–October 2008): 79–91.

———. "'Sons of Freedom': African Americans Fighting the War of 1812." *Tennessee Hisotrical Quarterly* 71 (Fall 2012): 206–27.

Smith, Gene Allen, ed. *A British Eyewitness at the Battle of New Orleans: The Memoir of Royal Navy Admiral Robert Aitchison, 1808–1827.* New Orleans: Historic New Orleans Collection, 2004.

Smith, G. C. Moore, ed. *The Autobiography of Lieutenant-General Sir Harry Smith.* 2 vols. London: John Murray, 1902.

Smith, Rogers M. *Civic Ideals: Conflicting Visions of Citizenship in U.S. History.* New Haven, CT: Yale University Press, 1997.

Somkin, Fred. *Unquiet Eagle: Memory and Desire in the Idea of American Freedom.* Ithaca, NY: Cornell University Press, 1967.

Stagg, J. C. A. "The Coming of the War of 1812: The View from the Presidency." *Quarterly Journal of the Library of Congress* 37 (Spring 1980): 223–41.

———. "James Madison and the Coercion of Great Britain: Canada, the West Indies, and the War of 1812." *William and Mary Quarterly* 3rd ser. 38 (January 1981): 3–34.

———. *Mr. Madison's War: Politics, Diplomacy, and Warfare in the Early American Republic.* Princeton, NJ: Princeton University Press, 1983.

Steiner, Bernard C. *The Life and Correspondence of James McHenry, Secretary of War under Washington and Adams*. Cleveland: Burrows Brothers, 1907.

Stewart, David O. *American Emperor: Aaron Burr's Challenge of Jefferson's America*. New York: Simon and Schuster, 2011.

Stiggins, George. *Creek Indian History: A Historical Narrative of the Genealogy, Traditions, and Downfall of the Ispocoga or Creek Indian Tribe of Indians*. Edited by Virginia Pounds Brown. Birmingham, AL: Birmingham Public Library Press, 1989.

Stuart, Reginald C. *Civil-Military Relations during the War of 1812*. Santa Barbara, CA: ABC-CLIO, 2009.

———. "Special Interests and National Authority in Foreign Policy: American-British Provincial Links during the Embargo and the War of 1812." *Diplomatic History* 8 (Fall 1984): 311–28.

Sugden, John. "Jean Laffite and the British Offer of 1814." *Louisiana History* 20 (Spring 1979): 159–67.

———. "The Southern Indians in the War of 1812: The Closing Phase." *Florida Historical Society* 60 (January 1982): 273–312.

———. *Tecumseh: A Life*. New York: Henry Holt, 1997.

———. *Tecumseh's Last Stand*. Norman: University of Oklahoma Press, 1985.

Surtees, William. *Twenty-Five Years in the Rifle Brigade*. Edinburgh: William Blackwood, 1833.

Taylor, Alan. *The Civil War of 1812: American Citizens, British Subjects, Irish Rebels, and Indian Allies*. New York: Alfred A. Knopf, 2010.

Taylor, George Rogers. *The War of 1812: Past Justifications and Present Interpretations*. Boston: D. C. Heath, 1963.

Thomas, Jane H. *Old Days in Nashville, Tenn.: Reminiscences*. Nashville: Publishing House Methodist Episcopal Church, South, 1897; reprint, Nashville: Charles Elder Bookseller and Publisher, 1969.

Thornton, Russell. *American Indian Holocaust and Survival: A Population History since 1492*. Norman: University of Oklahoma Press, 1987.

Tucker, Spencer. *Injured Honor: The Chesapeake-Leopold Affair*. Annapolis, MD: Naval Institute Press, 2006.

Unser, Daniel H., Jr. "American Indians on the Cotton Frontier: Changing Economic Relations with Citizens and Slaves in the Mississippi." *Journal of American History* 72 (September 1985): 297–317.

———. *Indians, Settlers, and Slaves in a Frontier Exchange Economy: The Lower Mississippi Valley before 1783*. Chapel Hill: University of North Carolina Press, 1992.

Upton, Emory. *The Military Policy of the United States*. 4th ed. Washington, DC: US Government Printing Office, 1917.

Varg, Paul A. *Foreign Policies of the Founding Fathers*. Lansing: Michigan State University Press, 1963.

Waldstreicher, David. *In the Midst of Perpetual Fetes: The Making of American Nationalism, 1776–1820*. Chapel Hill: University of North Carolina Press, 1997.

Walker, Alexander. *Jackson and New Orleans: An Authentic Narrative of the Memo-*

rable Achievements of the American Army, under Andrew Jackson, before New Orleans, in the Winter of 1814, '15. New York: J. C. Derby, 1856.

Walker, William A., Jr. "Martial Sons: Tennessee Enthusiasm for the War of 1812." *Tennessee Historical Quarterly* 20 (March 1961): 20–37.

Warshauer, Matthew. "The Battle of New Orleans Reconsidered: Andrew Jackson and Martial Law." *Louisiana History* 39 (Summer 1998): 261–91.

Waselkov, Gregory A. *A Conquering Spirit: Fort Mims and the Redstick War of 1813–1814*. Tuscaloosa: University of Alabama Press, 2006.

———. "Fort Jackson and the Aftermath." In *Tohopeka: Rethinking the Creek War and the War of 1812*, edited by Kathryn E. Holland Braund, 138–69. Tuscaloosa: University of Alabama Press.

———. "A Reinterpretation of the Creek Indian Barricade at Horseshoe Bend." *Journal of Alabama Archaeology* 32 (December 1986): 94–107.

Waselkov, Gregory A., and Brian M. Wood. "The Creek War of 1813–1814: Effects on Creek Society and Settlement Pattern." *Journal of Alabama Archaeology* 32 (June 1986): 1–24.

Watkins, John A. "The Mississippi Panic of 1813." *Publications of the Mississippi Historical Society* 4 (1901): 483–91.

Weber, David J. *The Spanish Frontier in North America*. New Haven, CT: Yale University Press, 1992.

Wesson, Cameron B. *Households and Hegemony: Early Creek Prestige Goods, Symbolic Capital, and Social Power*. Lincoln: University of Nebraska Press, 2008.

Whitaker, Arthur Preston. *The Mississippi Question, 1795–1803: A Study in Trade, Politics, and Diplomacy*. New York: Appleton-Century, 1934.

White, David H. "A View of Spanish West Florida: Selected Letters of Governor Juan Vincente Folch." *Florida Historical Quarterly* 56 (October 1977): 138–47.

White, Patrick C. *A Nation on Trial: America and the War of 1812*. New York: John Wiley and Sons, 1965.

Wilkinson, James. *Memoirs of My Own Times*. 3 vols. Philadelphia: Abraham Small, 1816.

Wilkinson, Norman B., ed. "The Assaults on New Orleans, 1814–1815." *Louisiana History* 3 (Winter 1962): 43–53.

Williams, Greg H. *The French Assault on American Shipping, 1793–1813: A History and Comprehensive Record of Merchant Marine Losses*. Jefferson, NC: McFarland, 2009.

Winn, Larry James. "The War Hawks' Call to Arms: Appeals for a Second War with Great Britain." *Southern Speech Communication Journal* 37 (Summer 1972): 402–12.

Wolfe, John Harold. *Jeffersonian Democracy in South Carolina*. Chapel Hill: University of North Carolina Press, 1940.

Worcester, Noah. "War and Popular Delusion." In *The Annals of America*. Vol. 4, *1797–1820: Domestic Expansion and Foreign Entanglements*, 375–382. Chicago: Encyclopedia Britannica, 1968.

Wyatt-Brown, Bertram. *The Shaping of Southern Culture: Honor, Grace, and War, 1760s–1890s*. Chapel Hill: University of North Carolina Press, 2001.

Zagarri, Rosemarie. *Revolutionary Backlash: Women and Politics in the Early American Republic*. Philadelphia: University of Pennsylvania Press, 2007.

Theses and Dissertations

Akers, Frank H. "The Unexpected Challenge: The Creek War of 1813–1814." PhD diss., Duke University, 1975.

Inman, Natalie. "Networks in Negotiation: The Role of Family and Kinship in Intercultural Diplomacy on the Trans-Appalachian Frontier, 1680–1840." PhD diss., Vanderbilt University, 2010.

Kanon, Tom. "Frontier Fathers and Martial Sons: Indian Hating in the Backcountry Prior to the War of 1812." Master's thesis, Middle Tennessee State University, 2003.

Martin, Joel Wayne. "Cultural Hermeneutics on the Frontier: Colonialism and the Muscogulge Millenarian Revolt of 1813." PhD diss., Duke University, 1988.

Moore, Wayne C. "Farm Communities and Economic Growth in the Lower Tennessee Valley: Humphreys County, Tennessee, 1785–1980." PhD diss., University of Rochester, 1990.

Smith, Trevor Augustine. "Pioneers, Patriots, and Politicians: The Tennessee Militia System, 1772–1857." PhD diss., University of Tennessee, 2003.

Index